Václav Havel

OPEN LETTERS

VÁCLAV HAVEL was born in Czechoslovakia in 1936. Among his plays are *The Garden Party, The Memorandum, Largo Desolato, Temptation,* and three one-act plays, *Audience, Private View,* and *Protest.* He is a founding spokesman of Charter 77 and the author of many influential essays on totalitarianism and dissent. In 1979, he was sentenced to four and a half years in prison for his involvement in the Czech human rights movement; out of this came his book of letters to his wife, *Letters to Olga* (1988). In November 1989 he helped found the Civic Forum, the first legal opposition movement in Czechoslovakia in forty years, and the following month he became his country's president.

OPEN LETTERS

OPEN LETTERS

Selected Writings
1965–1990

by

Václav Havel

Selected and Edited by Paul Wilson

Vintage Books
A Division of Random House, Inc.
New York

FIRST VINTAGE BOOKS EDITION, JUNE 1992

Preface and translations copyright © 1985, 1988, 1991 by Paul Wilson
"On the Theme of an Opposition," "Letter to Alexander Dubček,"
"Farce, Reformability, and the Future of the World,"
copyright © 1991 by A.G. Brain

Czech originals copyright by Václav Havel

All rights reserved under International and
Pan-American Copyright Conventions. Published in the United States
by Vintage Books, a division of Random House, Inc., New York.
Originally published in hardcover by Alfred A. Knopf, Inc.,
New York, in 1991 and simultaneously in Great Britain by
Faber & Faber, Limited, London.

Grateful acknowledgment is made to the following for permission
to publish these previous English translations:
"Thinking About František K.," "Testing Ground," and "A Word
About Words," copyright © 1988, 1989, 1990 by A.G. Brain.
"Six Asides About Culture" and "Anatomy of a Reticence,"
copyright © 1985 by Erazim Kohák.
"Politics and Conscience," copyright © 1985 by
Erazim Kohák and Roger Scruton.
" 'I Take the Side of Truth': An Interview with Antoine Spire"
and "Meeting Gorbachev," copyright © 1983, 1988
by George Theiner.

Library of Congress Cataloging-in-Publication Data
Havel, Václav.
Open letters: selected writings, 1965-1990 by Václav Havel;
selected and edited by Paul Wilson.
p.   cm.
Translated from the Czech.
Includes index.
ISBN 0-679-73811-8 (pbk.)
1. Czechoslovakia—Politics and government—1968-1989.
2. Czechoslovakia—Politics and government—1989-   3. World
politics—1945-   4. Ethics. 5. Life. 6. Communism. I. Wilson,
Paul. II. Title.
DB2241. H38A5   1992
909.82—dc20   91-50721
CIP

Author photograph © Miloš Fikejz

Manufactured in the United States of America
10 9 8 7 6 5

Contents

Contents

Preface

*I am unwilling to believe that this whole civilization is
no more than a blind alley of history and a fatal error of
the human spirit. More probably it represents a necessary
phase that man and humanity must go through, one that
man—if he survives—will ultimately, and on some higher
level (unthinkable of course without the present phase),
transcend.* —Václav Havel, "Thriller"

T HE IDEA of putting together a selection of Václav
Havel's nondramatic writing seemed at first like a simple
enough proposition. The purpose was, and remains, for this
to be a companion volume to *Letters to Olga, Disturbing the
Peace,* and his plays. *Open Letters* will round out the picture
these other works give us of Václav Havel as dramatist, writer,
thinker, and future statesman.

The problem, however, was that many of Havel's major essays and articles had already been translated and published,
and some, like "The Power of the Powerless"—Havel's most
penetrating analysis of the totalitarian system and how people resist it—had been widely reprinted. It still made sense to
bring these essays together in a single volume, but the risk
was that such a volume might not have given readers who had
been following Havel's work much that was new.

Thinking about this problem, I realized that the distinction
between major and minor works in what I was trying to do
was misleading. Havel's lesser-known pieces—his speeches,
letters, newspaper articles, his *samizdat* reports meant mainly
for friends, the profiles of people he admired, the conversations and interviews—provide us with the humus of his thinking and give us glimpses of the man that are sometimes

missing from his more substantial works. Therefore, they belong in a book that intends to present the reader with Havel the man, not just Havel the dissident thinker.

The twenty-five items assembled here cover Václav Havel's nondramatic writing from 1965—when he was a young playwright with the Theatre on the Balustrade in Prague—to his New Year's Address to Czechoslovakia on January 1, 1990, shortly after he had become the country's president. The chronological arrangement (with the exception of the first item, "Second Wind") comes naturally out of the book's purpose. Havel is, in the best sense of the word, an occasional writer; he responds, in his writing, to events, experiences, insights, arguments, states of mind. When his pieces are assembled in the order in which he wrote them, they become a chronicle both of his intellectual life, and, implicitly, of his times as well.

Many of Havel's essays were, in fact, agents of history. I don't know whether his private letter to Alexander Dubček in 1969 influenced the agonizing decision Dubček had to make at the time, but I remember clearly the deep transformation in the mood in Prague brought about by "Dear Dr. Husák," Havel's widely circulated open letter to the Czechoslovak president in 1975. This essay raised the hope that Husák's regime would one day end, made that end seem inevitable, and thus brought it closer. But the best testimony to the power of Havel's prose comes from the Polish politician and former Solidarity activist Zbygniew Bujak. In the late 1970s, when Bujak was a young activist trying to organize resistance to the communist bosses in the Ursus factory near Warsaw, he became discouraged at the lack of response and began to doubt the meaning of what he was doing. Then he came across a copy of "The Power of the Powerless," by Havel. "Its ideas," he told me, "strengthened us and persuaded us that what we were doing would not evaporate without a trace, that this was the source of our power, and that one day this power would manifest itself. . . .When I look at the victories of Solidarity and of Charter 77, I see in them an astonishing fulfillment of the prophecies contained in Havel's essay."

FOR READERS as yet unfamiliar with Havel's other work, it may be worth reviewing, briefly, the phases of his life encompassed in this volume. In the earliest stage, up to the Soviet-led invasion of Czechoslovakia in August 1968 and its immediate aftermath, Havel was known mainly as a playwright, and only occasionally an essayist. When he became active in public life, in the mid-1960s, he spoke chiefly as a member of the editorial board of *Tvář* magazine and a member of the Union of Czechoslovak Writers. His chief target was not so much communism as it was the ideology of reform communism, that "peculiar dialectical dance of truth and lies" which suggested that with certain minor adjustments, the beast that Marx conceived, Lenin unleashed, and Stalin goaded into a fury could be tamed and domesticated. In an early speech to the Writers' Union ("On Evasive Thinking") Havel talks, with remarkable prescience, about the destruction and tragedy that result when language and ideology turn away from reality, when thought becomes disengaged from the world, when writers avoid problems by putting them in false contexts. Later, his quarrel with the reformers becomes more specific. "On the Theme of an Opposition," written during the Prague Spring of 1968, is his most openly political clash with that viewpoint.

In the 1970s, along with many of his old reform communist adversaries, Havel became an outcast and later an active dissenter. As a dramatist without a stage, he continued to write plays (some of his best, in fact, come from this period), but his impact as a playwright was now almost exclusively abroad. Inside Czechoslovakia his influence now came through his power as an essayist. He dissected aspects of the new repression, examining its effect on culture and everyday life ("Dear Dr. Husák"), on the way laws were applied ("The Trial," "Article 202," and "Article 303"), and on the growth of an "antipolitical politics" in which dissidents of all hues harnessed the power of truth ("The Power of the Powerless"). He was a founding member and spokesman of the human rights "initiative" Charter 77 and the Committee to Defend the Unjustly Prosecuted, and he published his own *samizdat* series of books called *Edice Expedice*. These activities, as well as his essays, landed him in prison in 1979 where, in a remarkable series of letters to his wife Olga, he was compelled by circumstances and the prison censor to dig deeply into his own personality and beliefs and explore their broader, more philosophical implications.

The essays Havel wrote on his return from prison in 1983 reflect this deeper view of things. In "Politics and Conscience," for instance, he returns to his old themes, but in a broader context this time, arguing that the problems the world faces are rooted in "the irrational momentum of anonymous, impersonal and inhuman power," and that while the crisis is deepest and most acute in communist countries, it is a worldwide phenomenon. In the meantime, Havel had become an international cause célèbre, which meant that he spent a good deal of his time talking to journalists, intellectuals, and activists from the West. This gave him the opportunity to reflect, as he does in "Anatomy of a Reticence," upon why there were such deep misunderstandings between people on either side of the Iron Curtain, when they should find themselves natural allies. Finally, when Mikhail Gorbachev, about whom Havel was initially skeptical, becomes head of the Soviet Union, a period begins in which Havel can see the end of communism, or at least its gradual transformation into something more tolerable. All his writing from the mid-eighties on is strongly colored by this conviction. In one of the last pieces in this book, "A Word About Words," he returns to an early theme: the destructive power of language, this time to examine the words that have contained the hopes and the horrors of this century. By now he has the experience of the dissident movement behind him, and he writes as someone who knows, at first hand, about "the mysterious power of words in human history."

· · ·

I HAVE excluded far more of Havel's prose than I have included. The most painful omissions were two of Havel's
youthful essays, "The Anatomy of a Gag" and "On Dialectical
Metaphysics," because they were too long and too abstract,
and two of his later essays on theatre, because Havel had said
much the same things elsewhere, more forcefully. I have included none of Havel's introductions to *samizdat* books or
anthologies, and only one of his many profiles of friends and
colleagues ("Thinking About František K.," which is more
than just a reminiscence). Havel drafted countless declara-
tions, protests, and brief public speeches, most of which are
too occasional and too slight to use. Nor have I included any
of the several statements he made in his own defense in court,
mostly because the texts we have are not necessarily from
Havel's own hand, but rather based on clandestinely pro-
cured transcriptions. As he became better known, Havel was
asked for, and granted, many interviews. Some of these provide excellent surveys of his thought, but precisely for that
reason they are repetitive; thus, with two exceptions, they too
were excluded. Finally, in the year and a half before the "revolution" of 1989, Havel was a regular contributor to the underground (now legal) newspaper *Lidové noviny*. As interesting
as these articles are historically, I felt they were too closely
tied to specific events.

If there is one class of items I regret not being able to
include, it is Havel's polemical articles. Havel never shied
away from a good debate, not even when he ran the risk of
alienating a colleague or disturbing the solidarity of the Charter 77 community. One important exchange was with Milan
Kundera in late 1968 over the meaning of the popular resistance to the Soviet invasion—and more broadly, over how the
Czechs and Slovaks view their own history. Another, in the
late 1970s, was a debate with Ludvík Vaculík and Petr Pithart
over the kinds of activities that were worth risking jail sentences for. In both cases, I felt it would have been unfair to
publish Havel's side of the polemic without also including the
texts he was responding to.

As I WRITE this preface, more than a year has elapsed since the miraculous and sudden collapse of communism in Central Europe. The euphoric hopes of a year ago seem dampened, though not extinguished, by the stark economic difficulties faced by the new democracies, by the resurgence of old, hard-line habits of rule in the Soviet Union, and by the war in the Middle East and its aftermath. It is a tribute to the vitality and depth of Václav Havel's writing that, though these essays were written in a different world and a different time, they still illuminate the present. For did not Havel warn that the damage to individuals and societies left behind by totalitarianism would be worse than even its victims could imagine, and take a long time to repair? Did he not point out that the root cause of war does not lie in the weaponry that each side deploys against the other, but in the political realities of a divided world, and that the greatest danger—one that should be clearly foreseeable—comes from willful indifference to regimes that humiliate and oppress and silence their own citizens in the name of some expediency, or grand, utopian scheme? And does he not remind us, both in his words and by his example, that the starting point for change must be the human conscience at work in the "hidden sphere" of society, and that not to believe in its power, despite all the forces arrayed against it, is at the very least a matter of bad faith?

PAUL WILSON
Toronto, March 1991

Acknowledgments

DURING my work on this book, I have come to owe a great deal, as always, to many people. My editors at Alfred A. Knopf and Faber & Faber, Bobbie Bristol and Frank Pike, were solidly behind this project from the beginning, and gave me invaluable advice, support, and encouragement. Their help was a sine qua non. I am also grateful to my colleagues at *The Idler* magazine, David Warren, Gerald Owen, Alexander Szemberg, and Miroslav Scholz, not only for their advice in matters of editing and translation, always freely given, but for their patience and understanding during my absences from work. David Schmalz and the staff of the Hartley House hotel in Walkerton, Ontario, helped to make my week-long retreat there pleasant and productive. I'm also thankful to Gordon Skilling and Josef Škvorecký for providing helpful advice and obscure bits of information unavailable in any reference book.

I owe a special debt of gratitude to Dr. Vilém Prečan, head of the Documentation Center for the Promotion of Independent Czechoslovak Literature in Scheinfeld, Germany. Dr. Prečan assembled and edited two volumes of Václav Havel's nondramatic writings: *Václav Havel on Human Identity*, which covers 1969–79, and *Václav Havel: Different Destinations*, covering the period 1983–89. Much of the new material in this book was translated from those volumes, and I drew liberally on his excellent bibliographical material in the assembly of my own notes and comments. I'm also grateful to the help rendered in communicating with President Havel by his private secretary, Vladimír Hanzel.

I owe more than I can say to my wife, Helena, and my son, Jake, for tolerating my absences and helping me in all kinds of ways when I needed it.

Acknowledgments

Particular thanks, and perhaps my apologies for minor editorial changes, are due to the other translators for permission to use their work in this book: A. G. Brain (a pseudonym which, I can now reveal because it is no longer necessary, conceals the team of Alice and Gerry Turner, who have done heroic work over the past decade translating documents, essays, and books from the Czechoslovak dissident underground); Erazim Kohák, a philosopher and writer in his own right who has likewise labored long and selflessly in the field; Roger Scruton, editor of the *Salisbury Review,* which first published "Politics and Conscience" and many other important documents by Czech dissident writers.

And last, though certainly not least, to George Theiner. George died in 1988, but were he still alive, he would certainly have been involved in this project. Both as a translator of many Czech writers, and as the editor of *Index on Censorship,* he made a great contribution to the cause of political liberty and freedom of expression, not just in Czechoslovakia, but all over the world. I think it is fitting that this volume of essays be dedicated to his memory.

—P. W.

OPEN LETTERS

Second Wind

"Second Wind" is excerpted from the untitled "Author's Afterword" to *Václav Havel: Hry 1970–1976 (Plays 1970–1976)*, published in Czech by 68 Publishers in Toronto (1977). Although it is the only piece in the book out of chronological sequence, it is the first substantial autobiographical work published by Havel, and as such provides a natural introduction to this selection of his writing. This is its first appearance in English. Translated by Paul Wilson.

WHEN A writer is twenty, something we might call his initial experience of the world usually begins to ripen within him, and becomes a source he will draw on for a long time to come. It is about this age, after a lot of initial groping, that he comes to a more serious understanding of himself, looks about the world with his own eyes, and discovers his own way of bearing witness to it, and to himself. Then it takes roughly ten years for him to investigate, think through, and exhaust this initial experience of the world from all angles. It is an important ten years: a time of getting under way, of heroic self-discovery, a time of relative bravery and relative optimism.

I do not belong to that fortunate class of authors who write constantly, quickly, easily, and always well, whose imaginations never tire and who—unhampered by doubts or inhibitions—are by nature open to the world. Whatever they touch, it is always exactly right. That I do not belong in such company, of course, bothers me, and sometimes even upsets me: I am ambitious and I'm angry with myself for having so few ideas, for finding it so difficult to write, for having so little faith in myself, and for thinking so much about everything that I often feel crippled by it.

3

And yet I must admit that in my writing too, there was something like that first "heroic" period when—self-confident, uninhibited, without a lot of overblown ambition—I was simply mapping out my initial experience of the world. Of course, I didn't see it that way at the time and I'm well aware today that it was only relatively true: even then, after all, I rewrote everything a hundred times, I groped in the dark and succumbed to despair. Still, with the passing of time, it seems to me that everything was easier then, and my first plays were— on their own level—in many ways more masterful than much of what I wrote later.

This relatively confident start of mine, of course, was influenced—and I've only really become fully aware of this today—by a fortunate interplay of several quite accidental circumstances.

Thanks to the apparent disadvantage of coming from a bourgeois background and growing up in a communist state, I had the opportunity, right from the start, of seeing the world "from below," that is, as it really is. This helped me to escape certain eventual illusions and mystifications. Of course I don't think that, had I grown up in a different state with the same background, I would necessarily have become a capitalist, any more than, had I grown up in the same state with a different background, I would necessarily have become a party functionary. In either case, I would probably still have become a writer. But I'm well aware that because in both those cases I would have been, in some ways, externally better off, internally I'd have been far worse off, because I'd have been denied that initial experience of the world "from below," which probably gave me more than I was willing to admit at the time. If I displayed—as they used to write about me—a certain sensitivity for the absurd dimensions of the world, then it was not just because of my temperament, but also because of my experience: as we know, the absurd and comic dimensions of the world are always best seen from below.

I was twenty in 1956. It was the time of the famous revelations, the first widespread collapse of illusions, and the first efforts to reconstruct them again in a more or less "renewed" or "reformist" shape. Historically, it was a fascinating period; for the first time in our part of the world the merry-go-round of hope and disappointment, of half-baked remedies and their half-baked liquidation, of renewed ideals and their renewed betrayal, began to turn. For the first time, that peculiar dialectical dance of truth and lies began its whirl in society and in people's minds, of truth alienated by lies and the phony manipulation of hopes that we know so intimately today and which is brought home to us in such an original way by one of the basic themes of modern art: the theme of human identity and existential schizophrenia.

Naturally, I don't know how I'd have written if I'd turned twenty earlier, in 1950, for instance, but I feel that the chronological coincidence of my first serious attempt at self-definition with that particular historical moment was for me—as a writer—most fortunate. Equipped with my view "from below," the experience of Franz Kafka and the French theatre of the absurd, and somewhat obsessed with a tendency to elaborate on things rationally to the point of absurdity, I found in those remarkable social conditions (hitherto unprecedented and therefore undescribed) a wonderful horizon for my writing. I am not claiming that in my first plays there was nothing more going on, or that my only concern was describing the dialectical mechanisms behind those pseudo-reforms and the irresistible decay of the system that was trying to bring them about, but I can scarcely imagine having written them without the inspiration provided by that particular background.

There are several reasons, some deep and some accidental, why I began to write plays in the late fifties after several years of trying to write poetry, but none are important in this connection. What is important is that it is far harder to store a play away in your desk drawer than it is poetry or prose. Once written, a play is only half done, and it is never complete and itself until it has been performed in a theatre. Theatre is an art form so social that, more than any other art form, it depends on having a public existence, and that means it is at the mercy of cultural conditions. (Whereas one can imagine a movie shot for audiences in the future, theatre either exists in the present or not at all.)

The fortunate way in which my own "bioliterary" time meshed with historical time gave me another tremendous advantage: my early beginnings as a playwright coincided with the 1960s, a remarkable and relatively favorable era in which my plays, despite being so different from what had been permitted until then, could actually reach the stage, something that would have been impossible both before and after that. I don't suppose I need emphasize how important this was for my writing. It was not just the formal fact that my plays were permitted; there was something deeper and more essential here: that society was capable of accepting them, that they resonated with the general state of mind, that the intellectual and social climate of the time, open to new self-knowledge and hungry for it, not only tolerated them, but—if I may say so—actually wanted them. And of course every such act of social self-awareness—that is, every genuine and profound acceptance of a new work, identification with it, and the integration of it into the spiritual reality of the time—immediately and inevitably opens the way for even more radical acts. With each new work, the possibilities of the repressive system were weakened; the more we were able to do, the more we did, and the more we did, the more we were able to do. It was a state of accelerated metabolism between art and its time, and it is always inspiring and productive for phenomena as social as theatre. (Of course many of my generation active in other areas were blessed with the same fortunate coincidence of the times with their first artistic efforts: the whole "new wave" of Czech film, for instance.)

The final circumstance that had a positive influence on the first stage of my writing was the fact that in 1960—again as a result of many fortunate coincidences—I found myself working in the Theatre on the Balustrade in Prague. Here was a theatre with a specific artistic profile. Its ambition was not to become a part of the country's cultural industry, as one of the institutions that helped to keep the world of appearances running smoothly; it was to be something essentially different: a place where that unsettling process of social self-awareness could occur. In other words, it was precisely the kind of theatre I believe in and which inspires me. I was not only an author who occasionally came up with a new play, I was able to take part in the everyday running of the theatre in all kinds of ways: I could help influence its profile, be a part of its organism, test my work in it from day to day, and— last but certainly not least—enjoy the dramaturgical assistance of Jan Grossman. At the Balustrade, there was something happening—and throughout the sixties, this created extraordinarily favorable conditions for my writing: I knew why I was writing, and who I was writing for. [. . .]

Sooner or later, however, a writer (or at least a writer of my type) finds himself at a crossroads: he has exhausted his initial experience of the world and the ways of expressing it and he must decide how to proceed from there. He can, of course, seek ever more brilliant ways of saying the things he has already said; that is, he can essentially repeat himself. Or he can rest in the position he achieved in his first burst of creativity, subordinate everything he learned to the interests of consolidating that position, and thus assure himself a place on Parnassus.

But he has a third option: he can abandon everything proven, step beyond his initial experience of the world, with which he is by now all too familiar, liberate himself from what binds him to his own tradition, to public expectation and to his own established position, and try for a new and more mature self-definition, one that corresponds to his present and authentic experience of the world. In short, he can find his "second wind." Anyone who chooses this route—the only one (if one wishes to go on writing) that genuinely makes sense—will not, as a rule, have an easy time of it. At this stage in his life, a writer is no longer a blank sheet of paper, and some things are hard to part with. His original élan, self-confidence, and spontaneous openness have gone, but genuine maturity is not yet in sight; he must, in fact, start over again, but in essentially more difficult conditions.

I found myself at this crossroads in the late 1960s, and I'm afraid I'm still looking for my second wind. In my case, the search is harder not just because of what I am, but also because the very factors that favored me in the past are now working against me.

First of all, when I arrived at this point, my external situation had also changed for the worse. I lost the possibility not only of working in the Theatre on the Balustrade, but of having anything to do with Czech theatre whatsoever. And as an author, I was one of the ones most completely prohibited. True, they couldn't stop my plays from being produced abroad, but that wasn't much use to me; I had become too accustomed to writing from a particular social situation, for a particular theatre, and a particular audience; in other words, I'd become too used to that special interaction between the time and my writing to be able to write just for the sake of writing, for "the world in general," and then send the play somewhere without knowing how, by whom, why, or for whom it would be produced. I had learned to understand a play as something that could fly into the world only from a specific home that alone could breathe specific meaning into the play; it was not something you tossed experimentally into the air in the hopes that it would land somewhere, catch on, and only then gain some kind of meaning. And if my older plays were performed in so many countries, it wasn't because I'd planned them to be "world-class," but because the charge of energy given to them by their maternal environment was obviously capable of being discharged elsewhere. So, for a long time, the search for that second wind meant trying to overcome a feeling of emptiness and futility.

Even more serious, however, was the fact that I was standing at this inner crossroads at a time of deep change in the surrounding world. August 1968 did not just mean the routine replacement of a more liberal regime with a more conservative one; it was not just the usual freeze after a thaw. It was something more: it was the end of an era; the disintegration of a spiritual and social climate; a profound mental dislocation. The seriousness of the events that caused this transformation and the profound experiences that came with it seemed to alter our prospects completely. It was not just that the carnival-like elation of 1968 had come to an end; the whole world crumbled, a world in which we had all learned to live well and move with some ease, a world that had, as it were, weaned us—the peaceful, somewhat comic, somewhat dis-jointed, and very Biedermeier world of the 1960s. For a while, the nerves of society were still strung as taut as piano wire, but the tension could not last, and out of the rubble of the old world a sinister new world grew, one that was intrinsically different, merciless, gloomily serious, Asiatic, hard. The fun was definitely over, and things began to get tough.

In my earlier plays, I had said enough about the seesaw of liberators and liquidators that one might have thought I'd be prepared for this new reversal. And yet I was not: everything was suddenly too different, too serious, too dramatic and tragic, and I was experiencing it all too much as a participator to be able to deal with it in my traditional manner—with irony, a wry grin, or a cool piece of analysis. Suddenly, my position as a distant, amused observer "from below" seemed inadequate, a relic of the past, and yes, even somewhat eva-sive. The new world into which we entered began to touch each one of us too insistently, and it had a far different ex-istential dimension than the one we were used to. After all, not only did it arrive bathed in the glow of a human torch, but Jan Palach's act of self-immolation was immediately un-derstood by the whole of society. No, this had nothing what-soever in common with the sixties. Certainly, once again people's spines were bent, and lying, cheating, and betrayal became common; once again, the theme of human identity and existential schizophrenia was everywhere—but now, it all seemed to take place on a completely different level: the time of oral juggling was over and it became increasingly obvious that human existence itself was at stake. Suddenly, instead of laughing, one felt like shouting.

December 1976

On Evasive Thinking

"On Evasive Thinking" was originally written as a speech, delivered in Prague on June 9, 1965, at a Union of Czechoslovak Writers' conference to mark the twentieth anniversary of Czechoslovakia's liberation at the end of the Second World War. An excerpt was reprinted in *Literární noviny (The Literary News)*, no. 25, June 19, 1965. The speech was reprinted in full under the present title in *Sešity pro mladou literaturu (Notebooks for Young Literature)*, a Prague literary magazine, in June 1968. This is its first appearance in English. The translation, by Paul Wilson, is based on the full text as it appeared in *Sešity*.

SOME time ago, as we know, a stone window ledge came loose and fell from a building on Vodičkova Street, killing a woman. Not long afterwards, an article appeared in *Literární noviny* commenting on the event, or rather on the spontaneous wave of outrage that followed. The author began by assuring us that window ledges ought not to fall, that it was entirely proper for the public to criticize such things, and how wonderful it was that we could openly criticize such things today. He then went on to talk about the enormous progress we'd made as a whole, and to illustrate this he mentioned that whereas before young girls used to wear duffel coats, today they dress in the latest Parisian fashions. This rather graphic example of the achievements of our time ultimately led him to ask whether there wasn't, after all, just a little too much criticism, and he appealed to us not to limit ourselves to what he called local matters, but to focus on themes that were more worthy of the dignity of the human mission and more appropriate to the humanistic notion of man. He concluded with a challenge to literature, too, to free itself from all petty, local, municipal matters and to begin, at last, to deal with mankind and our prospects for the future.

Fortunately, the public opinion to which this author had appealed ignored his advice and last week, when a second window ledge fell, on Spálená Street, and killed someone else, an even greater wave of outraged protest followed. As it had done many times before, the public again showed more intelligence and humanity than the writer, for it had understood that the so-called prospects of mankind are nothing but an empty platitude if they distract us from our particular worry about who might be killed by a third window ledge, and what will happen should it fall on a group of nursery-school children out for a walk.

If the author of the article were a cold cynic, fully aware of the amoral implications of his conclusions, his piece would have been no more than a harmless oddity meriting scant attention. But—and this is what is tragic about the whole affair—it was written with the purest of intentions, in the sincere belief that it was contributing, albeit tactically, to a good cause.

Here is a clear example of how any intention can become its exact opposite if it is carried forward in the conventionalized, pseudo-ideological thinking that has become so dangerously domesticated in all areas of our social life. This way of thinking, in my opinion, is causing immense damage. The essence of it is that certain established dialectical patterns are deformed and fetishized and thus become an immobile system of intellectual and phraseological schemata which, when applied to different kinds of reality, seem at first to have achieved, admirably, a heightened ideological view of that reality, whereas in fact they have, without our noticing it, separated thought from its immediate contact with reality and thus crippled its capacity to intervene in that reality effectively.

This happens chiefly through a ritualization of language. From being a means of signifying reality, and of enabling us to come to an understanding of it, language seems to have become an end in itself. In this process, language—and, because it is related to it, thought as well—may appear to have increased in importance (the duty to name things having been superseded by the duty to qualify things ideologically), but in fact language is thus degraded: the imputation to language of functions that are not proper to it has made it impossible for language to fulfill the function it was meant to fulfill. And thus, ultimately, language is deprived of its most essential importance.

Notice, for example, how often the words we use these days are more important than what we are talking about. The word—as such—has ceased to be a sign for a category, and has gained a kind of occult power to transform one reality into another. Arguments are not carried on through ideas, but through concepts. We need only to use the magic word "disproportion," and something unforgivably half-baked is suddenly not only excused but may even be raised to the level of an historical necessity. Sadism need only be cloaked in the grandiose notion of an "offense against socialist legality" and suddenly it ceases to appear to us in such an evil light. It's enough to call a fallen window ledge a "local matter," and criticism of the way buildings are maintained as "municipal criticism," and we immediately feel that nothing so terrible has happened. It's enough for a good old fireman, a quite ordinary man whose job it is to put out fires, to be called an "incendiary engineer," and immediately we not only think of him as having some higher function, we also begin to be somewhat afraid of him. And finally, when you need to save money by leaving the upkeep of buildings not to a superintendent, but to a voluntary brigade of doctors, lawyers, and office clerks working on weekends, you need only to call it "socialist maintenance by the tenants" and a doctor chipping away at a rotting window ledge on his building is warmed by the feeling that in doing so, he is helping to fulfill some higher phase in the development of socialism.

Such verbal mysticism, of course, is a rather simple and transparent trick. What is more dangerous is the manipulation of certain established relational schemata.

A typical example is how reality can be liquidated with the help of a false "contextualization": the praiseworthy attempt to see things in their wider context becomes so formalized that instead of applying that technique in particular, unique ways, appropriate to a given reality, it becomes a single and widely used model of thinking with a special capacity to dissolve—in the vagueness of all the possible wider contexts—everything particular in that reality. Thus what looks like an attempt to see something in a complex way in fact results in a complex form of blindness. For if we can't see individual, specific things, we can't see anything at all. And the more we know only what is apparent about reality, the less we know about reality in fact.

This mechanism can clearly be seen at work in the article I was talking about: the falling window ledges and criticism of the condition of the facades are set so masterfully in the context of the world that we end up with the powerful feeling that if window ledges were not falling off our buildings in Prague we would have long ago been involved in World War Three, so there is something healthy in the fact that they are falling.

If it was taken for granted that aboriginal, social man somehow managed to throw himself together a shelter that would not fall on his head, then it must be taken equally for granted that a modern socialist society should be able to provide people safe passage through the streets. This is where the whole thing begins and ends, and all the other "ifs, ands, and buts" are just attempts to muddy the water, cloud over the matter, and change the subject. Factories, housing estates, and power dams are no doubt wonderful things, and we must even appreciate the fact that girls no longer wear duffel coats, but this has nothing to do with window ledges. When we talk about window ledges, we should talk about window ledges and not bring the prospects of mankind into it. And if we do, then only in the sense that in the given context, people have only two possible prospects: either the window ledges fall on them or they don't. And in any case, who knows whether the preventative maintenance of facades in Prague was not neglected precisely because someone, somewhere, was waxing eloquent about the prospects for mankind instead of paying attention to where particular men and women live.

Everything is related to everything else, of course. But still, I fear that Engels would want to retract that idea if he knew what use it would eventually be put to—that is, allowing everyone to talk about something other than what he ought to be talking about.

The application of this false contextualization in the *causal* field is usually accompanied by its application in the *historical* field: delight in the fact that today—as opposed to recent times—one can bravely and publicly criticize falling window ledges derives from a comparison that, while based on history, is so pointless that it inevitably leads to the quite ahistorical and absurd impression that such criticisms are not something every society takes completely for granted, but rather an admirable and original achievement of the present stage of socialism. But what kind of socialism is it that takes something so obviously normal for an achievement?

Another characteristic mechanism of this dematerialized way of thinking is something that, for my own purposes, I have called "dialectical metaphysics." By that I mean the type of fetishized dialectics that—by freezing into formal phraseological schemata—degenerates (dialectically) into the pure metaphysics of vacuous verbal balancing acts, expressed in constructions such as "on the one hand—but on the other hand," "in a certain sense yes, but in another sense no," "we must not, on the one hand, overestimate, nor, on the other hand, should we underestimate," "though some characteristics, in a certain situation, may—other characteristics, in another situation, may also . . . ," and so on and on.

When we lose touch with reality, we inevitably lose the capacity to influence reality effectively. And the weaker that capacity is, the greater our illusion that we have effectively influenced reality. Just think, for instance, of how confidently we make predictions about what will be, and with what re-markable precision we can interpret, explain, and classify what has already happened. Yet we never seem to notice how suspiciously often what happens—in fact—does not conform to what—according to our prognoses—was to have happened. We know with utter certainty what should happen and how it should happen, and when it turns out differently, we also know why it had to be different. The only thing that causes us trouble is knowing what will really happen. To know that assumes knowing how things really are now. But that is pre-cisely where the catch lies: between a detailed prediction of the future and a broad interpretation of the past, there is somehow no room for what is most important of all—a down-to-earth analysis of the present.

And so, in the end, the only thing that fails to conform to our wishes is reality. Not surprisingly: we don't have time for it. In any case, it's generally recognized today that it's better to plan less, but on the basis of genuine research, than to indulge in unbridled planning and then have to explain to people every two weeks why some basic commodity is un-available. It is probably less important that someone be will-ing or able to explain, in terms of a world view, why a window ledge fell into the street, than it is for him to know what measures to take to ensure that the Jirásek Bridge, for exam-ple, won't collapse in ten years. In any case, anyone who has the latter ability will not, on the whole, require the former.

If I were to give a name to the collection of thought mech-anisms I've been talking about, I would call it something like "evasive thinking." That is, a way of thinking that turns away from the core of the matter to something else—from a fallen window ledge to the prospects for mankind, from the word "laziness" to the word "disproportion," from the word "cow-ardice" to the word "tactics," or from the concrete fact of personal guilt to the abstract category called "the atmosphere of the cult of personality." If, for instance, one quite logically says that a power dam was built by people and not by "the atmosphere of enthusiasm for building," one must also admit that the false testimony and forged documents of the show trials were not created by the atmosphere of the cult of personality, but also by concrete people. To say anything else is pure evasion.

We live in a time of struggle between two ways of thinking: thinking evasively and thinking to the point. Between half-baked thinking and consistent thinking.

We live in a time when reality is in conflict with platitude, when a fact is in conflict with an *a priori* interpretation of it, when common sense is in conflict with a distorted rationality. It is a time of conflict between theory that plays fast and loose with practice, and theory that learns from practice; a conflict between two gnoseologies: the one that, from an *a priori* interpretation of the world, deduces how that reality should be seen, and the one that, from how reality is seen, deduces how that reality must be interpreted. In my opinion, how quickly our society evolves will depend on how quickly we can replace the first gnoseology—the metaphysical one—with the second, the dialectical one.

I would like to say a few words about how this conflict manifests itself in two areas that it is appropriate to talk about in this forum: first, in something I would call the literary climate; and second, in the work of the Union of Writers.

First, the literary climate. The main part of my work is connected with the Theatre on the Balustrade, where I'm a dramaturge, and for which I also write. This means I'm fortunate enough to find myself in a relatively quiet oasis where I think something important is going on and where, consequently, there isn't a lot of time to track the climate—literary, theatrical, or any other kind. This, I'm sure you will agree, is an advantage. Then, a few months ago, I was invited to join the editorial board of *Tvář*. The concept behind this magazine is not sophisticated; all it wants to do is call things by their proper names, to allow its authors to say what they really think without their having to resort to the ritual invocation of all those "buts," "to a certain extents," "even though on the other hands," and the like. It wants to print things it feels to be authentic, underived, consistent with what they wish to be. It wants to get along without compromise, without those compulsory duties, evasions, and concessions—regardless of which side they are intended to satisfy. In the area of criticism, it wants to do no more than treat things as they really are; that is, a poem as a poem, a novel as a novel, literature as literature, thus freeing them from all false contexts which, though they pretend to be the essence of the work, in fact obscure a concrete view of it. Whether *Tvář* is successful on its own terms can, of course, be disputed; but after all, the magazine has only taken its first five steps on this road.

I wasn't really prepared for how difficult it has been for the literary climate to come to terms with something as natural as the attempt to speak without using established phraseological evasions; for how this climate—still dominated by evasive thinking—has suddenly begun to cling to these evasions; for how hard it is to come to terms with someone actually enjoying the luxury of openness; and for the irritation, the sour looks, the snide remarks evoked by something so down to earth as a group of people attempting to be true to themselves, without having to cut a deal with the literary climate.

Of course, the matter often doesn't stop with sour looks; sometimes there is ill will. How else am I to explain the fact that, for example, ever since an article on Florian appeared in *Tvář*, one is always hearing from certain sources that *Tvář* is actually a Catholic magazine? If this were not a serious matter, we would have to laugh at the notion that were it to run a study on Masaryk, *Tvář* would have to be considered a Catholic-Protestant magazine, and if it then published a story by Kerouac, it would ultimately become a Catholic-Protestant-Buddhist magazine. That this kind of irritation is most often expressed by the literati is, I think, symptomatic: people who are not in daily touch with the backrooms of the literary world and are therefore unfamiliar with the nuances of its internal relations, forces, and categories will probably never understand what the fuss is all about.

There was a time when criticism was inseparable from power and it had an impact on power relations. This meant that, often, decent people did not criticize something they didn't like so as not to bring harm to other people, and cowards often criticized things they did like so as not to bring harm to themselves. This time is long past, yet many behave as though it has persisted, and they are still willing to characterize every attempt at open criticism as naked terrorism, and every clear opinion as the new face of dogmatism. Thus writers who have become used to praise because they are against dogmatism become, the moment they are subjected to criticism, convinced that they are the victims of a witch-hunt, character assassination, a terrorist plot, and born-again dogmatism. And although these are frequently people who have often been honored by the state and hold many functions, and although the one who criticizes them often has no other power than his ability to say what he thinks, they see in this critic someone who is practically the state prosecutor.

To be clear: every creative work runs the risk of being criticized, and I am not talking about these matters as a plea for special understanding. I speak about them because I don't see them merely as an expression of something as natural and normal as disagreement, but as far more: they are proof of how abnormal it is when a stabilized system of evasive thinking appears normal, whereas something that is genuinely normal seems like unforgivable arrogance.

The second area I would like to talk about has to do with the practices of the Union of Writers. But I can only do so against the background of certain ideas about its aim and purpose.

The main speech at this conference was entitled "The Tasks of Literature and the Work of the Czechoslovak Union of Writers," which may leave us with the impression that the job of the Union is to assign tasks to literature. In reality, it should be the other way around: literature should set the tasks for the Union of Writers. The point is that every good writer is the best judge of what his job is. The Union of Writers should merely provide the necessary backing so that writers and magazines can best fulfill the tasks they set for themselves. I'm of the opinion that the function of the Union of Writers, thus limited, is in no way inferior or less dignified. On the contrary, giving appropriate assistance to writers is always more difficult than telling them what to do.

My work in the theatre—and I'm thinking now of my work as a playwright—taught me one thing: a really good dramaturge (and there aren't many of them around) never forces a playwright to write the way he, the dramaturge, would write. He leads the playwright—but in the playwright's image, not his own—which means that by methods most proper to him, dramaturgically, he helps the playwright to be as true to himself and as authentic as possible, so that he will realize and develop that which makes him what he is.

I think the Union of Writers should have the qualities of a good dramaturge. It should never hand out directives on how to write, or impose any artistic program on literature. Precisely the contrary, it must help literature and authors to be true to themselves; help magazines to be what they want to be, which is the only way they will be good magazines. This doesn't mean laying out a program so vague it can accommodate everyone, but helping each writer to be himself to a maximum degree—unique, well defined, and clear on how to go about fulfilling his own program. The point is that if literature is to be genuine, it cannot be anything but concrete, unique, authentic and unevasive, sovereign and consistent. How else do Vladimír Holan and Bohumil Hrabal achieve what they do except by how consistently they are themselves, how directly they are obsessed by their methods, how indifferent they remain to the world of categories, intellectual evasions, the norms and interests of the time by which they will be measured?

In its own way, literature always was, is, and must be intolerant. And the clearer it is, the more intolerant it is—that is

part of its nature. We can have lunch every day in the Writers'
Club with anyone we want, or go fishing with anyone we want.
But the minute we begin turning a blind eye to what we don't
like in each other's writing, the minute we begin to back away
from our own inner norms, to accommodate ourselves to each
other, cut deals with each other over poetics, we will in fact
set ourselves against each other, because we will naturally begin to subtract from our own uniqueness and thus retreat
from ourselves—until one day we will disappear in a general
fog of mutual admiration.

The only one who must remain genuinely tolerant and
farsighted in this brew of mutual intolerance is the Union
of Writers. If one theatre rejects a playwright's play, he can
always submit it to another, or establish his own theatre. None
of us can found our own Union of Writers. But this means
that the Union must be all the better at being a dramaturge;
that is, it must be all the more tolerant of intolerant individuals. Not, of course, in order to make peace among them—
because if it tried to do that, it would be acting against their
uniqueness and thus against literature—but rather by doing everything to enable them to realize themselves fully
in all their differences, which means even in their mutual
intolerance.

I can well imagine how hard it must be for writers in the
Union leadership and in responsible positions in Union publishing ventures, given their intellectual and artistic backgrounds and their experience of society, not only to tolerate
but to support something that is, from start to finish, run by
people from an entirely different intellectual background and
with quite different experiences of society—people such as,
let's say, those around *Tvář*. Especially since *Tvář* is intolerant
of what they are doing, and defines itself, in a sense, in direct
counterposition to them. These writers naturally are and must
remain intolerant to that counterposition. As writers. But as
representatives of the Union of Writers, they must be—in this
and thousands of other cases as well—deeply tolerant, not
only in the passive sense of letting things be, but in the sense

of an active will to understanding. This split is not at all easy to make—I know a little about it from my own experience as both a writer and a dramaturge—but I don't think there is any other way to do it.

I don't think that the Union of Writers is not fulfilling its role as I have defined it. But I can't shake the feeling that it often does so in a very halfhearted, inconsistent, and feeble way, and that dangerously often our old friend evasion is lurking behind this halfheartedness. I'm not thinking now of *Tvář*, but of some other things. At random: in 1957 a group of writers, including Jiří Kolář, Josef Hiršal, Jan Grossman, Jan Vladislav, and Bohumil Hrabal, requested permission to publish a magazine under the aegis of the Union. This group was not united by a shared idea of what art was, but simply by a shared experience: all of them, for many years before, had been blacklisted. At the time, they received no response whatsoever to their request. About three months ago, they applied again. They haven't received an answer yet either, but it's more or less common knowledge that the Union executive discussed the matter and ultimately decided to support the publication of such a magazine, although the Union itself would not be the publisher.

What else is that but evasion? No doubt there would be all sorts of problems connected with such a publication. But in that case, shouldn't finding a solution to those problems be the priority? It's as though the dramaturgy department of a theatre were to reject a wonderful play because they couldn't be bothered with the problems involved in putting it on. Or were there some fears about the magazine's politics? I can't understand how the Union of Writers could recommend that those writers find another publisher, when the only logical thing to do would have been to persuade them not to pub-lish their magazine anywhere else but with the Union, just as a dramaturge tries to persuade a playwright not to give his play to any other theatre but his. This doesn't seem to be the way to help literature.

Or another example: every student of literature today

knows that the two best postwar Czech literary magazines were *Kritický měsíčník (The Critical Monthly)* and *Listy pro umění a filosofii (Papers on Arts and Philosophy)*. These magazines had nothing in common, and on many matters they opposed each other, with that healthy intolerance which marks everything that has a conception behind it. Later, both magazines were forced to stop publishing and their names became synonymous with everything that was bad. If we read old back issues today, we may find ourselves disagreeing with some things here or there, but we would search in vain to find anything to justify such drastic repression. On the contrary, not only could many of the articles in them easily appear today in *Plamen, Host do domu,* or even *Tvář,* but they would seem to us far more current than much of what these magazines print, and in any case, they would certainly be more relevant to our present situation than entire volumes of *Nový život.* And yet there has not yet been a single effort to clear the names of those two magazines. The prevailing opinion seems to be that the people who put them out were guilty of realizing certain things sooner than others. The only ones associated with them who today enjoy all the rights and perks of Union status are those who retreated from their former positions, only to come back gradually to them today. Those who never did anything worse than stand by their opinions—despite the disfavor—do not have these rights. Václav Černý and Jindřich Chalupecký—the respective editors-in-chief of *Kritický měsíčník* and *Listy pro umění a filosofii*—not only remain outside the Union's active interest, they have not even been accorded the minimum courtesy of an invitation to join. At the same time, Jindřich Chalupecký is on the praesidium of the Union of Visual Artists, and Václav Černý, since then, has published several important scholarly books. If the Union is not interested in matters of principle, I don't see why it isn't at least interested in matters of practical import: I cannot understand on what grounds it affords itself the luxury of voluntarily keeping the best people out.

Jan Grossman, who used to be co-editor of *Listy* with Chalupecký, was blacklisted for eight years because he once said things about literature which it would be practically a faux pas today *not* to say. I'm constantly hearing people criticizing him for writing so little about literature; they say his voice is sorely missed. But what has the Union done to get him back, except for what it did a while ago, acknowledging that he was fit to be considered a candidate? Grossman is not the type to toss something down on paper and send it off just any-where. He's a man with a conception, and he can realize it anywhere, but he must do so completely, not in a half-baked, evasive way. Today, he is head of the Theatre on the Balus-trade. The work of this body, and Grossman's work, is gen-erally recognized both at home and abroad. Grossman has fully realized himself in the theatre, and time and the conti-nuity of his work have confirmed that back then, it was he who was right, and not those who excluded him from litera-ture. Grossman's signature appeared on both the unanswered requests I have mentioned. It should be clear enough now where those who criticize Grossman for not taking sufficient interest in literature should turn for an answer.

[. . .]

I do not mention these examples of halfheartedness only to document evasive thinking in action, but primarily so that I can pose this question: Is it not finally time, after all those somersaults, executions, rehabilitations, enthusiastic declara-tions, and crestfallen retractions, those hysterical criticisms and self-criticisms that the writers' community has had to un-dergo in recent years, to clear the air, calmly, honorably, matter-of-factly, but at the same time consistently and with something like final authority? Would this not be our finest contribution to the twentieth anniversary of our liberation?

The point is, we must never forget that everything good and positive will, sooner or later, find its place, for such is the nature of historical necessity. Vladimír Holan waited for recognition, Hrabal waited, Josef Škvorecký waited. Jiří Kolář is still waiting, but he's not the only one. Richard Weiner is waiting, Kabeš's collection of Ladislav Klíma is waiting, the edited works of Jakub Deml are waiting. Holan lost nothing by waiting; the loser was Czech poetry. If Holan's books had come out when they should have, perhaps new Czech poetry today would be more original than it is, if for no other reason then simply because it would have had a chance to experience his work earlier. Shouldn't it be one of the primary tasks of the Union of Writers to fight for things, to fight for literature?

What I called the clearing of the air will not be done for writers by politicians; that is not their job. And literature would be against its own essence if it did not rely entirely on itself. I think that the Union of Writers makes sense only if it ceases to act as a broker between politics and literature, and starts defending the right of literature to be literature; that is, not a reinterpretation of something already known, but a special, autonomous form of knowledge. Only in this way can literature be as well, and in the best sense of the word, a political entity.

[. . .]

I don't suppose anyone wants window ledges to fall on people's heads. Earlier it was impossible to say that they had fallen even when they fell. Today this can be said, but it must be added that girls no longer wear duffel coats. This kind of phraseological ritual is first of all undignified—and, to ordinary people who have no reason to speak otherwise than plainly, ridiculous—and in the second place it holds the world back: it prevents whoever has it in his power to solve the problem of the Prague facades from understanding that he bears responsibility for something and that he can't lie his way out of that responsibility, either by conducting a victorious war against duffel coats, or by abstract talk about the prospects of mankind, or by pointing to the progress of industrialization in Slovakia.

June 1965

On the Theme
of an Opposition

"On the Theme of an Opposition" first appeared
in the April 4, 1968, edition of *Literární listy,* the
successor to *Literární noviny* and the most influential weekly at the time in Czechoslovakia. It was
Havel's contribution to the debate on the political
future of Czechoslovakia during the Prague Spring,
when an easing of censorship made such a public
discussion possible. In an interview with John
Keane, who used the wonderful pseudonym "Erica
Blair," in the *Times Literary Supplement* of January
23, 1987, Havel had this to say: "The article attracted
quite a lot of attention because, if I'm not wrong,
it was the first time that a demand for [a new democratic opposition party] was voiced publicly. For
a long time now, I've had serious reservations about
it. I've come to be rather skeptical about the very
principle of mass political parties. I suspect that
involvement in government inevitably leads to parties' bureaucratization, corruption, and loss of democracy. I'm not opposed to the solidarity and
cohesion of various interest groups of like-minded
people. It's just that I'm against anything that serves
to cloud personal responsibility, or rewards anyone
with privileges for devotion to a particular power-
oriented group.

"But something more important worries me
about that original article. I saw myself then as a
writer who was a witness to the times. . . . I had no
intention of becoming a politician, in the sense of
someone who goes about the practical business of

putting the world right. In my view, however, proposals to found political parties should come from
people who are genuinely disposed to found
them—and that wasn't true of me."

This article appears for the first time in English,
in a translation by A. G. Brain.

I T SHOULD not be surprising to find that some of the ideas
put forth so far in various official statements about the
possible forms of political opposition in Czechoslovakia
sound like trying to have one's cake and eat it too. In the past
few weeks, the more progressive and democratically minded
people in the Communist Party have scored a victory over
the conservatives, but this still does not mean they are capable
of taking the idea of an opposition seriously. In fact, in the
past, whenever they managed to establish themselves in positions of power, they never once attempted to go beyond the
principle of one-party rule. Since they are now prepared to
allow a public debate about this formerly taboo subject, however, it seems a good idea for everyone who has some thoughts
on the subject to join in on the discussion.

First of all: what is wrong with all of the suggestions put
forward so far?

We are frequently told that because we now have freedom
of speech (which is supposedly the basis of democracy), public opinion, assisted by the media, will carry out the natural
restraining function of an opposition. This notion is based
on the faith that government will draw the appropriate conclusions from public criticism. The trouble is, democracy is
not a matter of faith, but of guarantees. And although public
debate is a primary condition of democracy, the essence of
democracy—the real source of those guarantees—is something else: a public, legal contest for power. At the same
time, public opinion (as represented by the press, for instance) can act as an effective check on government, and

thereby improve its quality, only if it also has the power to influence government, and this can only be done if public opinion leads to a process of public choice—through elections, for example. Ultimately, power only really listens to power, and if government is to be improved, we must be able to threaten its existence, not merely its reputation. [. . .]

Another illusion is the assumption that an internal democratization of the ruling party, a willingness to tolerate an opposition inside the party, is a sufficient guarantee of democracy. This is an illusion not just because the only genuine democracy is one that applies equally to everyone; there is another reason. The bitter experience of all revolutions is that unless the group that takes absolute power into its own hands moves in time to restore external restraints to that power, sooner or later the internal, self-imposed limitations begin to degenerate as well. When they are not nourished by external restraints that act to improve the quality of the group as a whole, the internal restraints meant to improve the quality of its leadership also wither, and instead of constantly regenerating itself, the group becomes more and more rigid and alienated from reality.

The outcome of this process is familiar: when the situation becomes impossible to maintain, the first breakdown can cause an explosion, followed by a bloody period of palace revolutions, putsches, plots, absurd trials, counterrevolutions, and suicides. Having been overtly eliminated, the struggle for power continues to influence things in a far more insidious way, precisely because it is hidden. And now the absence of legal guarantees boomerangs on the group that failed to institute them, and it annihilates itself.

In other words, if the Communist Party does not take urgent steps to foster powerful external restraints on its power, there is no guarantee that it will not degenerate again in time. Without democracy throughout society, inner party democracy cannot be maintained for long. It is not the latter that guarantees the former; it is the former that guarantees the latter.

Another idea being mooted about is that independent in-

dividuals, working both in elected bodies and in other organizations, might function as an opposition. In my view, this
is a perfect way to undermine an opposition before it has a
chance to get started. In this conception, a well-organized,
disciplined political party, complete with an ideology, an organizational machine, with its own press, propaganda, and
programs for society as a whole, would face a handful of
private individuals with no political backing, no way of agreeing on strategy, no candidates, and no comprehensive, co-
ordinated, and broadly conceived political program. These
individuals would have no more than local community responsibilities and powers, and in the event of an election,
they would be at a tremendous disadvantage, since most voters choose not between individuals, but between parties and
programs. Likewise, within institutions, such individuals, lacking the political organization of the communists, would not
stand a chance. Thus, without permitting organized political
forces to compete against it, the ruling party cannot talk seriously about a struggle for power, or suppose that it is sub-
mitting its monopoly on power to any serious test of quality
control.

Another possible source of control or direct opposition being proposed is the existing social organizations and interest
groups. Yet despite any political influence some of these
might eventually acquire, they do not represent a real or fundamental solution. They are not associations based on the
political convictions of their members, nor are they geared
to sharing political power, and thus they are hardly suited to
act as a restraint on government. Moreover, they do not fulfill
a basic condition, which is that the restraining body should
be independent of the body to be restrained. Not only does
membership in these organizations not exclude membership
in the ruling party (or any other party), but their leading
executive positions are almost always occupied by party members, who are answerable to higher party authorities. Given
the fact of block voting based on party discipline, it is obvious
that even with the changes in manipulatory voting practices,

these organizations will hardly represent anything like a genuine opposition. [...]

The logical and most practical solution would be to establish an opposition in the manner most often proposed in official circles: by reactivating the existing noncommunist parties in the National Front coalition. Of course it is not impossible that within these parties, forces capable of leading such an opposition might emerge. But I don't have much faith in this solution. Over the past twenty years, these parties have never managed to do anything but slavishly endorse the ruling party's every action, and by now they are so compromised that the advantages of this proposal (that their party structures are already in place, that they have their own newspapers, and so on) cannot outweigh its biggest disadvantage: the difficulty of winning back lost credibility. Besides, this approach could easily be criticized as a "return to obsolete forms of bourgeois democracy," which is an argument occasionally made against the idea of an opposition from inside official circles. In this case, the critics would be right, for it would amount to no more than an attempt to resuscitate the mummified remains of the pre–February 1948 alignment of political forces, which was already a highly dubious arrangement.

THE FLAWS in all these concepts have the same source: none of them allows for genuine choice. The plain truth is that you can only talk seriously about democracy where the people have the opportunity—once in a while—to choose freely who is to govern them. And this assumes the existence of at least two commensurable alternatives, that is, two autonomous and mutually independent political forces enjoying equal rights and the equal opportunity to become the leading force in the country, should the people so decide.

As long as it is considered proper for the Communist Party to exist as a party, then the demand for a second political party as a dignified and autonomous partner in the struggle for power, and thus as a guarantee that this power will be restricted from without, is also proper. Therefore I see the only genuinely consequential and effective route to the ideal of democratic socialism (that is, until someone persuades me there is a better way) is a revitalized model of a two-party system, one that corresponds to a socialist social structure. And because they would obviously no longer be parties based on social classes, and therefore would not promote conflict-ing concepts of social and economic organization dictated by class interests, their relations could be based on an histori-cally new type of coalition. Each party would have full polit-ical autonomy in the exercise of mutual control, but at the same time, they would be bound by an agreement on the basic outlines of their common goal, which would be the hu-mane, socially just, and civilized self-realization of the nation on the way to democratic socialism. This could be anchored and developed in a kind of basic "national program" (which would also formulate, for example, the principles of our for-eign policy and so on) accepted by both parties (and eventu-ally by other social organizations) and binding on their activities. The degree and methods of fulfilling (or not fulfill-ing) this program, as well as its eventual modification, would be evaluated by people in general elections that would reflect the degree of their confidence in the two parties, both as a coalition and separately.

I'm not going to invent a "positive" program for some as yet nonexistent party and project it into the different spheres of social life, although as a writer, and therefore someone who works in the area of fiction and fantasy, I would find it amusing. You can't invent strategy without an army: political programs are not born at writers' desks, but only in the ev-eryday political activity of those who carry them out, from their constant reflection on the interests the movement should express, and their constant confrontation with social reality, public opinion, the analyses of experts, and so on. I shall limit myself, therefore, to one remark.

Mention is often made these days of the strong and specific Czechoslovak democratic and humanistic tradition. What is forgotten, however, is that there are many people today who genuinely espouse democratic and humanistic values, yet who are not involved in political life (within the Communist Party), whether for reasons of opinion, or because the practice of the Communist Party so far has been insufficiently democratic and humanistic. This suggests a potential intellectual and spiritual framework for a new party: it could be a democratic party drawing on this tradition of democracy and humanism. Of course this does not mean that the party would arrogate to itself the right to be the only legitimate representative of democracy, just as the Communist Party cannot arrogate to itself the claim to be the only genuine force of socialism. Democracy and socialism can only be categories that apply to all of society, and their development is everybody's business.

If, then, the two main partners in this coalition were the Communist Party and the democratic party, this would merely mean that their names would be symbolic guarantees of the two poles of this "coalitional" task: the creation of democratic socialism. I would see the positive point of departure for such a democratic party to be the concept of—to put it in rather emotional terms—the moral reawakening of the nation.

During the years of dictatorship, suprapersonal categories and general social ideals were emphasized in order to suppress the rights of people to an individual life. As we often hear today, this approach has brought our country to the brink of a moral crisis, which has become particularly acute as the central control of society by an impersonal party bureaucracy, with its all-encompassing, alienated phraseological rituals, gradually degenerates. Demoralization in the workplace is only a natural product of this degeneration in the economic sphere. The Communist Party is facing a long, complex struggle—within itself—against all the assumptions and consequences of this process.

The new party would be unencumbered by any of this, and could more quickly and radically place human individuality once more at the center of its concern, and make real individuals the measure of society and the system. Not in such a way as to choose an abstract idea of man as the starting point for a new phraseological ritual, but in a simple and practical manner: by taking an interest in concrete human lives, not distanced from their immediate and unconditional needs by ideological filters; by struggling for particular human rights, demands, and interests; by rehabilitating values that have, until recently, been considered "metaphysical," values like conscience, love of one's neighbor, compassion, trust, understanding, and so on; by redefining human dignity; by concern for the personality and moral continuity of leaders; and so on.

It seems to me that thanks to such demands, new possibilities have opened up here, not only for people of widely different ages, social backgrounds, and views of the world who have been unjustly cast to the margins of social involvement because of their concrete and radical humanism, but, to a significant degree, for the youngest generation as well. From what I know about their process of self-awareness (for example, from various conceptual speeches in the student movement, which, by the way, I consider one of the few social forces that is attempting to create a genuine political independence for itself), I suspect that for various reasons such a spiritual climate could be close to them. Of course it's certainly not a matter of "capturing" these young people for politics (the Communist Party failed to capture young people precisely because that was all it ever tried to do), but of making it possible for them to become subjects, rather than objects, of political activity; not of forcing upon them the will and ideas of others, but also of accepting their will and their ideas.

So much for the theme of a second party.

IN CONCLUSION, I would like to touch on a matter I regard as extremely important. I'm afraid it will never be possible to create a broader and more active political force among noncommunists—who form the majority of the nation—until noncommunist points of view are accorded a certain basic political and moral recognition, stemming from the acceptance of certain evident truths, and taking the form of clear practical measures aimed at redressing wrongs that no one so far has tried to right. Without such recognition, noncommunists will never feel any confidence in the purpose and possible success of their venture.

This is not surprising: it is truly hard to commit oneself politically in any major way without a minimal guarantee that communist error will not forever count for more than noncommunist truth. And the fact that many noncommunists saw communist error for what it was at a time when communists did not have the slightest idea they were wrong, needs to be acknowledged in retrospect, however unpleasant this may be. If this is not done, it means that communists are a special breed of superhumans who are—on principle—right even when they are wrong, while noncommunists are—on principle—wrong even when they are right. In such a situation, it would be imprudent for noncommunists to commit themselves to anything. If communists have a guaranteed right to be wrong on occasions, then noncommunists must have a guaranteed right to be right; everything is pointless otherwise.

What does this mean in practice? At the very least the comprehensive rehabilitation of all noncommunists who were made to suffer for years because they knew certain things before the communists got around to figuring them out (they still bear traces of the mark of Cain on their foreheads). It is particularly urgent now that some of those who were punished for doubting the virtues of a socialism that was prepared to sacrifice democracy and freedom in the interests of its own development are growing increasingly bitter over the fact that while the country's leadership is reaching the same conclusions, and therefore acknowledging that they were right, it has not shown the same sort of willingness to say so publicly and draw certain practical conclusions from it.

One small example: in 1949 and 1950, thousands of talented students were forced to abandon their university studies merely for disagreeing (or, in the view of their fanatical col-

leagues on the screening committees, being capable of disagreeing) with the policies of the Communist Party, or simply
because they were not communists. [...] Would it not be
appropriate if the people who conducted those purges (and
who may now be seen at public meetings and student rallies,
decrying the "dark ages" with Komsomol-like zeal and carrying on about freedom, democracy, and justice) were to make
a gesture that would be somewhat less attractive, but a more
substantial confirmation of their credentials as progressives,
namely, to stand up for the rights of their former "ideological
opponents" who, because of an irony of history, are still
forced to pay for having believed in those values twenty years
ago?

There are some things that cannot be redressed. But there
are many others that can. One could mention far more drastic injustices that affected just about all levels of society, from
farmers to small craftsmen, from university professors and
writers to village priests. (In this respect, the eighty thousand
or so political prisoners of the 1950s represent a most important segment of society, whose political potential has scarcely
been tapped: they come from every walk of life, and their
common fate was such a test of their moral fiber and cohesion that it would be unforgivable not to integrate them into
the political life of the country.)

There is another related matter that might appear not to
concern us: the question of those who left the country in the
wake of February 1948. These people continue to be regarded,
in the main, as enemies of our country and our people, even
though, again, most of them were guilty of nothing worse
than being persuaded that democracy must not be sacrificed
to the socialist system. Many of them emigrated solely because
they faced the threat of prison and persecution if they remained, or because they would have had no opportunity to
work here in their chosen field. In the case of those who left
illegally, it is disputable whether, in the light of the Declaration of Human Rights, their action can be considered a crime
when there are no legal provisions for emigrating. Until the

state shows magnanimity to these emigrants, the situation among us here will not be entirely normalized; after all, a democratic state takes pride in not having emigration as a debit on its international account.

To put it simply, I believe that it is now both untenable and unhistorical to go on viewing this country solely in terms of the February 1948 conflict—and that goes, of course, for both of the camps that clashed then. I am not saying this because I would fight to restore the status quo ante (even though we are now strenuously engaged in restoring many things taken for granted then) but, on the contrary, because such a restoration is now out of the question.

A consistent moral and political recognition of the non-communist position is unlikely to be a simple matter, and no one will be handed the rights that stem from such a recognition on a platter. It is up to the noncommunists themselves gradually to win those rights. It is also possible that different noncommunist forces will arise even in the absence of such recognition. My feeling, however, is that without it, opposition can only remain a halfhearted affair, hampered by reservations and mistrust. And since such an opposition would not be entirely authentic, it would not be entirely effective, either. Those who have had it drummed into them for the past twenty years that they are outsiders and second-class citizens are going to have difficulty entering the arena of public political life.

April 1968

Letter to Alexander Dubček

"Letter to Alexander Dubček" is a private letter dated August 9, 1969, almost a year after the Soviet Union led an invasion of Czechoslovakia. The preceding April, Dubček had resigned as First Secretary of the Communist Party and formally nominated Gustáv Husák to succeed him. In August, Dubček was still a member of the praesidium, but as the first anniversary of the Soviet invasion approached, he was under increasing pressure to repudiate the programs he had championed during the Prague Spring. In *Disturbing the Peace,* Havel said: "I know that [Dubček] got the letter; I don't know what he thought of it. He disappeared rather quietly and inconspicuously from political life; he didn't betray his own cause by renouncing it, but he didn't bring his political career to a very vivid end either." In fact, he was removed from the praesidium in September 1969, and expelled from the party the following January.

The letter's only appearance in Czech is as an addendum to *Václav Havel: Do různých stran (Different Destinations: Essays and Articles, 1983–1989),* edited by Vilém Prečan (Scheinfeld: 1989). This is its first appearance in English, in a slightly abridged version translated by A. G. Brain.

Dear Mr. Dubček,

I don't know whether you remember me: we talked once a year ago at a small gathering of writers and politicians. Nor do I know if you know me as a writer, nor even whether you will take this letter as I intend it, as a sincere expression of sincerely held convictions. After lengthy consideration, I decided to write to you because I believe that at this moment, it is the only way—within the limited scope available to me—that I can do something for a cause I regard as crucial to the whole country in which I live and in whose language I write. Besides, it has always been your practice to trust people (sometimes more than was appropriate), so I may, perhaps, hope that you won't take what I say with the prejudicial antagonism reserved these days for everything that doesn't endorse the official line.

One needn't be an experienced political observer (and I certainly am not) to realize that it is only a matter of weeks, perhaps days, before the highest party (and hence state) authorities give their assent to the Soviet intervention and endorse, without reservation, the Soviet interpretation of events in Czechoslovakia in 1968. Nor does it require much experience to see that the whole purpose of the official propaganda now is to prepare us, ideologically, for that final step, which will transform the post-intervention policies of the government into political, ideological, and moral capitulation. And with hopes now dwindling that pressure from different sections of the population, the intelligentsia, and certain forces within the leadership might avert that shameful step, the gaze of all Czechs and Slovaks (and the world public) is now on you and some of your companions, in anticipation of how you will act, now that the moment has come for you to take a stand.

From the human point of view it is probably unjust that so grave a decision should rest on the shoulders of a single man, and yet it is immensely important that you, here and now, behave the way a majority of us still hope you will behave. It may seem like an exaggeration, but regardless of how I look at it, or who I talk about it with, I realize that in some respects the hope of a meaningful future for us all now rests with the position you take. My awareness of this is also the immediate motivation for writing this letter, through which I appeal to you, with all the urgency I can muster, not to disappoint people's final hope, which is focused on you. At the same time, I claim no right to instruct you, nor do I intend to play the "conscience of the nation." My purpose is nothing more than to bring to your own private deliberations different viewpoints and arguments from those which no doubt surround you in abundance now, and to strengthen your inner certainties, which are probably being subjected to powerful external assaults and powerful inner doubts. My appeal to you, therefore, is not an expression of mistrust, but rather of confidence: without confidence in your judgment and honesty, I would probably never have decided to write such a letter.

For both our nations you are a symbol of all our hopes for a better, more decent, and freer life. For the world public, you are the symbol of Czechoslovakia's experiment in "socialism with a human face." People see you as an honorable, honest, and courageous man; they regard you as a politician devoted to a just cause. They like you for your sincere looks and friendly smile. They believe you to be incapable of betrayal. All these things are equally obvious to those who are trying to restore the old order under the protection of Soviet guns. That is why one of their probable aims at the present moment is to induce you not only to bow to their ideology, but also to endorse their policies. I don't know how true it is, but I have even heard that they intend to turn you into the chief prosecutor of your own policies. It would be the first time you have publicly endorsed the action aimed at destroying those policies.

You must avoid this at all costs. It has long ceased to be just a matter of your personal honor, pride, and dignity. There is far more at stake now. There is the honor and pride of all those who had faith in your policies and who—now silenced—cling to you as their last chance, in the hope that you will salvage from the Czechoslovak experiment—and you alone can do it—the only thing that can now be salvaged: self-respect.

The reasons why your opponents seek your support are transparent enough: they want to use your unsullied name as a cover for their squalid dealings, and through you, to lay a veneer of political foresight over something that has resulted solely from their own incompetence and impotence. At the same time, they want to publicly discredit and humiliate you, and deprive you of the thing that makes them hate you most, and which sets you apart from them: the people's confidence. Their desire to bring you to your knees will not be satisfied simply because you no longer have power; they need more: they need you to lose face. Moreover, their efforts are aimed at something even worse: a cold-blooded attempt to take away the people's last hope, and foster in them profound depression, indifference, and skepticism, which is precisely what they need to wield power. Their goal is clear: to wreak vengeance on you for everything that makes you superior to them; to erase you from the people's minds and use you to manipulate the nation. (And in all this, they are—among other things— ultimately preparing the ground for sending you to trial.)

I can readily imagine how your opponents will argue. First and foremost, they will probably exploit your communist faith, stressing the interest of the party, of the movement, and of socialism. They will appeal to party discipline. And they will demand all this from you in the name of a cause that is dearest to you and to which you have devoted your life. (How similar this is to the way self-accusatory confessions were wrung from disciplined communists, with the aim of confusing the public and making the eventual convictions easier to believe!) No doubt they will also seek to exploit your responsible attitude toward the interests of our nations and argue that if you don't do what is expected of you, you will provoke a further crisis, sabotage the consolidation process, and throw the country into disarray and even civil war; that you will provoke a further intervention, mass deportations, and possible annexation by the U.S.S.R.; that you will be risking the lives of millions of people who have no interest in your gesture and only want to go on working in peace. [. . .]

However hard it will be for you, you must not yield to these demagogic arguments. Remember the dilemma Edvard Beneš faced at the time of Munich. In those days it was not demagogy—there was a real danger that the nation would be exterminated. And at that time, it was you, the communists, who resisted the persuasive arguments for capitulation, and who rightly understood that a *de facto* defeat need not be a moral defeat; that a moral victory may later become a *de facto* victory, but a moral defeat, never.

If you resist and stick to your own truth, you may succeed in striking a blow against the policies of the present party leadership, but it will not be against your party as such. On the contrary, if you take a stand you will be rendering it a great service in the long run. You will give people back a little hope in that party, since you will have demonstrated that lies and dishonor are not necessarily an inseparable part of communism. You may help to discredit certain members of the present leadership, but you won't discredit communism and its ideals. In fact, the only hope you have of rehabilitating them is to show that communists can be principled and that they are capable of placing truth above the demands of party discipline and the wishes of party authorities. If, however, you recant, you can discredit communism more than anyone else: you would demonstrate once and for all that values like truth, honor, and freedom are meaningless illusions within your party and movement.

Naturally I know nothing of the atmosphere in the party leadership, nor about its imminent plans or its objective situation. Nevertheless, I have tried to think about the possible alternatives, as they appear to me—as an ordinary citizen.

The first option you have—the one, I assume, being pressed upon you—is to carry out a thorough self-criticism, acknowledge the failings and negligence of your leadership, entirely endorse the Soviet interpretation of events, admit that you failed to grasp the underlying significance and direction of those events, that you neglected your duty and thereby played into the hands of counterrevolutionary forces, culminating in your condemnation of the Soviet intervention. Then you would stress that in the course of time, you have come to realize the inevitability of that operation and recognized that we must, in fact, be grateful to the Soviet leadership for their "fraternal assistance" in sending tanks here to preserve our socialist accomplishments.

To go this route would be to deny, "in the interest of the party," yourself, the truth as you see it, your convictions, your work, and your ideals. You would belittle your own achievement and betray all the hopes associated with your name. You would humiliate yourself and deeply insult the majority of Czechs and Slovaks who know how things really were. You would deprive people of their last certainty, their last remaining ideal, the last trace of their belief in human honor, in the meaning of principled behavior, in a better future, and in the merit of any sacrifice for the community. It would plunge the country deep into moral misery and cause people to lose sight of higher values, leading to a proliferation of selfishness, conformity, careerism, and indifference toward the fate of others.

In this way, of course, you would greatly assist the present party leadership, but at the cost of dealing a terrible blow to the moral fiber of our nations that might take a whole generation to recover from. It would amount to the destruction of the last remnants of national pride, as well as the last remnants of belief in communism. You would probably be allowed to stay on—for a while, at least—in some state or party office (though with no real political influence), but our nations would condemn you as a traitor without precedence in Czech or Slovak politics (at least I cannot think of a single instance here in which someone who represented certain policies actively approved of a military intervention designed to quash those policies).

Another option open to you is to remain silent. You would not conduct a self-critique, nor would you argue against a resolution to endorse the occupation. You would simply bow to the decision and then take subsequent events as they came.

I don't think this is a realistic option, but suppose it were:

what would be its outcome? You would probably be dropped from public office more rapidly than in the first place, and condemned much sooner and more caustically as the main villain. In the eyes of the people, however, you wouldn't fare much better. Though it would be less shocking than an active endorsement of the occupation, your silence would gain you only universal opprobrium. You would neither help nor harm the party leadership to any degree, and your attempt to deceive yourself and slip unscathed, Svejk-like, through history would only lead, ultimately, to the same moral crisis as the first alternative.

The third option available to you—the one I would recommend and which I believe the majority of people are expecting of you—is the most difficult. It will mean resisting all the pressures on you and once again spelling out openly and truthfully your plans, your policy, and your understanding of the reform politics of the Prague Spring. You will have to stress clearly your belief that the democratization process did not threaten the existence of socialism, but on the contrary, held out the promise of regeneration. And you will also have to state your position on the Soviet intervention openly and truthfully: You have always regarded it as unjustified interference in the process of democratization; at the same time, your original shock at the military invasion, which you condemned as an act of great injustice, betrayal, and lawlessness, was later modified to an acceptance of the military presence as a reality, while simultaneously seeking a political solution that would enable the domestic situation and international relationships to be consolidated in the framework of that "reality" without retreating from your belief that the intervention was unjustifiable. In other words, it amounts to speaking the truth, keeping to it, and rejecting everything that stands that truth on its head.

What will happen if you act in this most demanding, but also most natural way?

Unless your statement succeeds in having these questions removed from the agenda—which is most unlikely—the occupation will be endorsed by the Central Committee, and soon afterwards you will be expelled from the Central Committee and most likely from the Communist Party as well, along with a few others who continue to support you, and you will be vilified at least as harshly as Dr. František Kriegel was recently. This will strike a hard blow at the party leadership and its policies, because you will prove them guilty of an unprincipled distortion of reality, which is inexcusable in terms of any political tactics. You will seriously hamper the consolidation process as currently conceived. Most probably you will provoke a fresh "crisis," since disturbances might break out and strikes could be called in your support. Eventually, however, calm of a sort will be restored and the disturbances put down, and in a few weeks everything will slide back into a state of affairs that we have no trouble imagining.

Your act, therefore, will have no positive effect on the immediate situation; on the contrary, it will probably be exploited to justify further repression. But that is all negligible when set beside the immeasurable moral significance of your act for the social and political destiny of our two nations. People would realize that it is always possible to preserve one's ideals and one's backbone; that one can stand up to lies; that there are values worth struggling for; that there are still trustworthy leaders; and that no political defeat justifies complete historical skepticism as long as the victims manage to bear their defeat with dignity. Your act would place before us an ethical mirror as powerful as that of Jan Palach's recent deed, though the impact of what you do will be of longer duration. For many citizens, your act would become a yardstick for their own behavior, a compass needle pointing to a more meaningful future. You would not be forgotten, even were you to live in isolation, and your very existence would be a mote in the eye of all careerists attempting to profit from the occupation. You would enhance the prestige of Czechoslovakia's struggle in the eyes of the world, and you would keep alive one of the more positive aspects of the communist movement. After some years (especially in the event of changes in the leadership of the Communist Party of the Soviet Union) you would undoubtedly be rehabilitated—quietly, no doubt, as tends to be the case in the Communist Party—because history cannot be halted and time must vindicate you in the end. And when the opportunity arose to attempt once more—more gradually, perhaps, but more consistently too—what was tried unsuccessfully in 1968, society might make productive use of this enormous moral and political potential which—because you stood firm—was kept alive and continued to have an influence. [...]

Yes, I realize it's easy for me to give advice when I'm not in your shoes and don't have your responsibility. But I think that as a playwright I can—if you'll allow me—get inside your skin, at least to a certain extent. I think I understand something of your way of thinking, your problems, your hardships, your attitudes, and your intellectual and political traditions, relations, prejudices, and feelings.

Nevertheless, the only course I can recommend to you is—unfortunately—the hardest and most dangerous one: the path of truth.

On the other hand, to be fair, I must say I am convinced that you must share some of the blame for your present situation. There is, unhappily, a degree of merciless historical justice in the fact that you are now required to make decisions in such difficult circumstances. I can't help recalling my own reaction to your return from Moscow last August. Though moved by the physical and psychological pressures you endured, and deeply aware of the complexity of the situation and never for a moment doubting the honesty of your intentions, I was still convinced from the beginning that by signing the Moscow Agreements, you were making a terrible mistake that you would end up paying for dearly sooner or later.

My prediction is, unhappily, now coming true. The Moscow Agreements were in fact no more than a postponement of the moment when it would be necessary to say yes or no to the intervention. Avoiding this question could lead to a provisional state of affairs, but it could never be the starting point for any long-term political solution. The schizophrenic tension created in the first few months after the intervention had to end sooner or later, either in a new clash or, more probably, in complete capitulation. I don't condemn postponement in itself: at the right place and the right time, it can be an effective political weapon. In this case, however—and here, I think, is the crux of your error—postponement put the Czechoslovak side at a terrible disadvantage. It could only work against you. Whereas some form of "no" at that time on your part (such as a request to consult the nation before signing) might well have brought some concrete political gain (things were working in your favor: the attempted putsch within the party had failed, there was no political support for the intervention, the Soviet leadership were embarrassed), putting off a clear answer could only mean deferring it to a time when conditions were increasingly unfavorable for you, so that now, any "no" from you can have only the long-term effects I've already mentioned.

It's understandable: the Moscow Agreements were in fact the instrument of your self-deception. Because they did not clearly and unambiguously say yes to the intervention, they provided you with the illusion of success, while at the same time they laid all the groundwork for the eventual necessity of saying "yes" unambiguously, starting with the annulment of the 14th Congress, and ending with negotiations to sign a treaty of occupation. The Moscow protocol bought time for the uninterrupted and quiet stabilization of all those regressive structures that were prepared under your protection, for the purpose of swallowing you up; none of these structures existed last August, nor could they have. The gradual psychological and organizational disintegration of the active units that you might have been able to rely on last August is one of the natural and deliberate consequences of those new structures—in your name and under your aegis—that are intended to deprive you of all the most important sources of your authority and power.

Please understand me: I am not saying this in order to recriminate against the past and be clever in retrospect. Nor is it my intention, in the light of experience that you did have at the time, to point out all the things you did wrong and could and should have done better. This is irrelevant now, and I refer to them only to make the point that the difficult circumstances surrounding your decision are not a natural disaster, but follow logically from your past political decisions, intentions, and illusions. (And of course I am deliberately not going into the matter of some serious errors in your pre-August policies which, out of naive faith in the common sense of the Soviet leadership, contained no realistic measures that might have drawn on the strength of the "popular" movement and averted the danger of military intervention, or at least made it more difficult.) The integrity of your reasoning and the honesty of your intentions do not, unfortunately, mitigate your share of the responsibility: it is results that count in politics, not good intentions.

[. . .]

And so it's really only now that the fatal moment has arrived when you must render a final account of your actions and reveal what really lay behind the movement you came to represent. Through the position you take now, you will either write off the entire Czechoslovak democratization process as an irresponsible mistake, or you will take the bold, risky, and difficult step of reaffirming its authenticity as an irrepressible source of inspiration that is worth your challenging the authority of your party, your movement, and your comrades. The question now is: Will all the miscalculations and failures of you and your companions be redeemed a thousandfold by your decision to stand by your convictions and put your future on the line? Or will your reluctance to stake your career and even your life on last year's experiment lead people to see it as no more than an enormous con game, which they naively fell for?

It may occur to you at this point that I am actually asking you to wash away the sins of all of us, to make the symbolic, redemptive sacrifice that our nations are themselves incapable—unsymbolically—of making. Perhaps you are thinking that those who expect this of you are only passing the buck and merely want to use you to ease their own consciences.

In many respects such thinking is justified, but it doesn't alter the fact that you must act in the way expected of you. A politician—and any social elite, for that matter—is not merely a "function" of society. Society is also, to a certain extent, a "function" of its politicians and its elites. These elites act on society and mobilize those forces within it that can be mobilized. Cowardly policies encourage cowardice in society; courageous policies stimulate people's courage. Our nations have a capacity for both cowardly and courageous behavior, for demonstrating holy zeal or selfish indifference. Czechs and Slovaks are capable of struggling heroically or shamelessly denouncing their neighbors. Which of these propensities prevails at a given moment, both in society and in individuals, largely depends on what situation the political elite has created, the choices it places before the people, the qualities it encourages in them: in short, it depends on what the elite's activities and examples stimulate. This is why politics makes great demands on the human and moral qualities of those who practice it. The more power politicians have, the greater the demands on them.

If the regime today is allowing chiefly for the development of selfishness, cowardice, and careerism, and if it bases its power to a considerable extent on precisely the existence of these qualities, then it is even more incumbent now on you, in particular, to demonstrate whether Czechoslovak politics, or rather the communist movement, can offer another model of behavior and mobilize in people and society other, better forces. In any case, one of the reasons you are in such difficulties today is because through your policies you made possible—with good intentions, of course—the systematic demobilization of all that strong and unprecedented support from large sectors of society that spontaneously formed precisely so that people could work—with you—for a common goal, regardless of the dangers involved. As one who believes in the leading role of the party and its democratic-centralist principle, you acted voluntarily in the spirit of those beliefs to deprive all of us ordinary citizens (most of whom are not party members) of a large part of our power to decide. Now you are in a situation in which the leading role you claimed for yourself and which you—with far more justice—actually held, makes you responsible for acting in our names in another sense as well: not in the exercise of power, but in opposition to it.

The task facing you is clear. If you believe that the attempt made under your leadership in 1968 to humanize and democratize socialism and bring it in line with conditions in the industrially and culturally advanced countries of Europe was a just and justifiable experiment, and in accordance with people's wishes, and that it was not prejudicial to their standard of living, and if you are convinced that the sudden invasion of Czechoslovakia by Soviet troops in 1968 was an unjust and unjustifiable interference in that experiment, then you must clearly say so. And you must say so regardless of the enormous difficulties you will cause the present Communist Party leadership, regardless of the consequences for you personally, and even regardless of the political situation you will thereby provoke. If you don't, you will have to say the opposite, and that would have far more destructive consequences.

[. . .]

It is not my intention to be a self-appointed spokesman of the people. But if anything is certain today, it is this: that most Czechs and Slovaks today think as I do. It's hardly possible to think otherwise. The matter is essentially simple. You, however, are at the center of extremely complex pressures, forces, and viewpoints. The point is to be able to find your way out of this dark and tangled wood into the light of what we might call "simple human reasoning." To think the way every ordinary, decent person thinks. There are moments when a politician can achieve real political success only by turning aside from the complex network of relativized political considerations, analyses, and calculations, and behaving simply as an honest person. The sudden assertion of human criteria within a dehumanizing framework of political manipulation can be like a flash of lightning illuminating a dark landscape. And truth is suddenly truth again, reason is reason, and honor honor.

Dear Mr. Dubček, in the coming days and weeks, I, along with thousands of my fellow citizens, will be thinking of you. I will be anxious, but will also expect great things of you.

Yours sincerely,
Václav Havel

August 1969

"Dear Dr. Husák"

"Dear Dr. Husák" (April 1975), addressed to Dr. Gustav Husák, who was then the general secretary of the Czechoslovak Communist Party, is Havel's first major public statement after being blacklisted in 1969. He describes the circumstances surrounding the writing of this letter in the interview with Jiří Lederer on page 84. The letter was first published in English, in this translation, in *Encounter* (September 1975). It has subsequently appeared in several anthologies of Czech writing, most recently in *Václav Havel or Living in Truth*, edited by Jan Vladislav (London: Faber & Faber, 1986). The translator is not identified.

Dear Dr. Husák,

In our offices and factories work goes on, discipline prevails. The efforts of our citizens are yielding visible results in a slowly rising standard of living: people build houses, buy cars, have children, amuse themselves, live their lives.

All this, of course, amounts to very little as a criterion for the success or failure of your policies. After every social upheaval, people invariably come back in the end to their daily labors, for the simple reason that they want to stay alive; they do so for their own sake, after all, not for the sake of this or that team of political leaders.

Not that going to work, doing the shopping, and living their own lives is all that people do. They do much more than that: they commit themselves to numerous output norms which they then fulfill and over-fulfill; they vote as one man and unanimously elect the candidates proposed to them; they are active in various political organizations; they attend meetings and demonstrations; they declare their support for everything they are supposed to. Nowhere can any sign of dissent be seen from anything that the government does.

These facts, of course, are not to be made light of. One must ask seriously, at this point, whether all this does not confirm your success in achieving the tasks your team set it-self—those of winning the public's support and consolidating the situation in the country.

The answer must depend on what we mean by consolidation.

Insofar as it is to be measured solely by statistical returns of various kinds, by official statements and police accounts of the public's political involvement, and so forth, then we can hardly feel any doubt that consolidation has been achieved.

But what if we take consolidation to mean something more, a genuine state of mind in society? Supposing we start to inquire about more durable, perhaps subtler and more im-ponderable, but nonetheless significant factors, such as what, by way of genuine personal, human experience lies hidden behind all the figures? Supposing we ask, for example, what has been done for the moral and spiritual revival of society, for the enhancement of the truly human dimensions of life, for the elevation of man to a higher degree of dignity, for his truly free and authentic assertion in this world? What do we find when we thus turn our attention from the mere outward manifestations to their inner causes and consequences, their connections and meanings, in a word, to that less obvious plane of reality where those manifestations might actually ac-quire a general human meeting? Can we, even then, consider our society "consolidated"?

I make so bold as to answer, No; to assert that, for all the outwardly persuasive facts, inwardly our society, far from be-ing a consolidated one, is, on the contrary, plunging ever deeper into a crisis more dangerous, in some respects, than any we can recall in our recent history.

I shall try to justify this assertion.

. . .

The basic question one must ask is this: Why are people in fact behaving in the way they do? Why do they do all these things that, taken together, form the impressive image of a totally united society giving total support to its government? For any unprejudiced observer, the answer is, I think, self-evident: They are driven to it by fear.

For fear of losing his job, the schoolteacher teaches things he does not believe; fearing for his future, the pupil repeats them after him; for fear of not being allowed to continue his studies, the young man joins the Youth League and participates in whatever of its activities are necessary; fear that, under the monstrous system of political credits, his son or daughter will not acquire the necessary total of points for enrollment at a school leads the father to take on all manner of responsibilities and "voluntarily" to do everything required. Fear of the consequences of refusal leads people to take part in elections, to vote for the proposed candidates, and to pretend that they regard such ceremonies as genuine elections; out of fear for their livelihood, position, or prospects, they go to meetings, vote for every resolution they have to, or at least keep silent: it is fear that carries them through humiliating acts of self-criticism and penance and the dishonest filling out of a mass of degrading questionnaires; fear that someone might inform against them prevents them from giving public, and often even private, expression to their true opinions. It is the fear of suffering financial reverses and the effort to better themselves and ingratiate themselves with the authorities that in most cases makes working men put their names to "work commitments"; indeed, the same motives often lie behind the establishment of Socialist Labor Brigades, in the clear realization that their chief function is to be mentioned in the appropriate reports to higher levels. Fear causes people to attend all those official celebrations, demonstrations, and marches. Fear of being prevented from continuing their work leads many scientists and artists to give allegiance to ideas they do not in fact accept, to write things they do not agree with or know to be false, to join official organizations or to take part in work of whose value they have the lowest opinion, or to distort and mutilate their own works. In the effort to save themselves, many even report others for doing to them what they themselves have been doing to the people they report.

The fear I am speaking of is not, of course, to be taken in the ordinary psychological sense as a definite, precise emotion. Most of those we see around us are not quaking like aspen leaves: they wear the faces of confident, self-satisfied citizens. We are concerned with fear in a deeper sense, an ethical sense if you will, namely, the more or less conscious participation in the collective awareness of a permanent and ubiquitous danger; anxiety about what is being, or might be, threatened; becoming gradually used to this threat as a substantive part of the actual world; the increasing degree to which, in an ever more skillful and matter-of-fact way, we go in for various kinds of external adaptation as the only effective method of self-defense.

Naturally, fear is not the only building block in the present social structure.

Nonetheless, it is the main, the fundamental material, without which not even that surface uniformity, discipline, and unanimity on which official documents base their assertions about the "consolidated" state of affairs in our country could be attained.

The question arises, of course: What are people actually afraid of? Trials? Torture? Loss of property? Deportations? Executions? Certainly not. The most brutal forms of pressure exerted by the authorities upon the public are, fortunately, past history—at least in our circumstances. Today, oppression takes more subtle and selective forms. And even if political trials do not take place today—everyone knows how the authorities manage to manipulate them—they only represent an extreme threat, while the main thrust has moved into the sphere of existential pressure. Which, of course, leaves the core of the matter largely unchanged.

Notoriously, it is not the absolute value of a threat which counts, so much as its relative value. It is not so much what someone objectively loses, as the subjective importance it has for him on the plane on which he lives, with its own scale of values. Thus, if a person today is afraid, say, of losing the chance of working in his own field, this may be a fear equally strong, and productive of the same reactions, as if—in another historical context—he had been threatened with the confiscation of his property. Indeed, the technique of existential pressure is, in a sense, more universal. For there is no one in our country who is not, in a broad sense, existentially vulnerable. Everyone has something to lose and so everyone has reason to be afraid. The range of things one can lose is broad, extending from the manifold privileges of the ruling caste and all the special opportunities afforded to the powerful—such as the enjoyment of undisturbed work, advancement and earning power, the ability to work in one's field, access to higher education—down to the mere possibility of living in that limited degree of legal certainty available to other citizens, instead of finding oneself amongst the special class to whom not even those laws which apply to the rest of the public apply, in other words, among the victims of Czechoslovak political apartheid. Yes, everyone has something to lose. The humblest workman's mate can be shifted to an even more lowly and worse-paid job. Even he can be cruelly punished for speaking his mind at a meeting or in the pub.

This system of existential pressure, embracing the whole of society and every individual in it, either as a specific everyday threat or as a general contingency, could not, of course, work effectively if it were not backed up—exactly like the former, more brutal forms of pressure—by its natural hinterland in the power structure, namely, by that force which renders it comprehensive, complex, and robust: the ubiquitous, omnipotent state police.

For this is the hideous spider whose invisible web runs right through the whole of society; this is the vanishing point where all the lines of fear ultimately intersect; this is the final and irrefutable proof that no citizen can hope to challenge the power of the state. And even if most of the people, most of the time, cannot see this web with their own eyes, nor touch its filaments, even the simplest citizen is well aware of its existence, assumes its silent presence at every moment in every place, and behaves accordingly—behaves, that is, so as to acquit themselves in those hidden eyes and ears. And he knows very well why he must. For the spider can intervene in someone's life without any need to have him in his jaws. There is no need at all actually to be interrogated, charged, brought to trial, or sentenced. For one's superiors are also ensnared in the same web; and at every level where one's fate is decided, there are people collaborating or forced to collaborate with the state police. Thus, the very fact that the state police can intervene in one's life at any time, without his having any chance of resisting, suffices to rob his life of some of its naturalness and authenticity and to turn it into a kind of endless dissimulation.

If it is fear which lies behind people's defensive attempts to preserve what they have, it becomes increasingly apparent that the chief impulses for their aggressive efforts to win what they do not yet possess are selfishness and careerism.

Seldom in recent times, it seems, has a social system offered scope so openly and so brazenly to people willing to support anything as long as it brings them some advantage; to unprincipled and spineless men, prepared to do anything in their craving for power and personal gain; to born lackeys, ready for any humiliation and willing at all times to sacrifice their neighbors' and their own honor for a chance to ingratiate themselves with those in power.

In view of this, it is not surprising that so many public and influential positions are occupied, more than ever before, by notorious careerists, opportunists, charlatans, and men of dubious record; in short, by typical collaborators, men, that is, with a special gift for persuading themselves at every turn that their dirty work is a way of rescuing something, or, at least, of preventing still worse men from stepping into their shoes. Nor is it surprising, in these circumstances, that corruption among public employees of all kinds, their willingness openly to accept bribes for anything and allow themselves shamelessly to be swayed by whatever considerations their private interests and greed dictate, is more widespread than can be recalled during the last decade.

The number of people who sincerely believe everything that the official propaganda says and who selflessly support the government's authority is smaller than it has ever been. But the number of hypocrites rises steadily: up to a point, every citizen is, in fact, forced to be one.

This dispiriting situation has, of course, its logical causes. Seldom in recent times has a regime cared so little for the real attitudes of outwardly loyal citizens or for the sincerity of their statements. It is enough to observe that no one, in the course of all those self-criticisms and acts of penance, really cares whether people mean what they say, or are only considering their own advantages. In fact, one can safely say that the second assumption is made more or less automatically, without anything immoral being seen in this. Indeed, the prospect of personal advantage is used as the main argument in obtaining such statements. For the most part no one tries to convince the penitent that he was in error or acted wrongly, but simply that he must repent in order to save himself. At the same time, the benefits he stands to gain are colorfully magnified, while the bitter taste, which will remain after the act of penance, is played down as an illusion.

And should some eccentric repent in all sincerity and show it, for example, by refusing the appropriate reward on principle, the regime would, in all probability, treat him with suspicion.

In a way, we are all being publicly bribed. If you accept this or that official position at work—not, of course, as a means of serving your colleagues, but of serving the management— you will be rewarded with such-and-such privileges. If you join the Youth League, you will be given the right and access to such-and-such forms of entertainment. If, as a creative artist, you take part in such-and-such official functions, you will be rewarded with such-and-such genuine creative opportunities. Think what you like in private; as long as you agree in public, refrain from making difficulties, suppress your interest in truth, and silence your conscience, the doors will be wide open to you.

If the principle of outward adaptation is made the keystone to success in society, what sort of human qualities will be encouraged and what sort of people, one may ask, will come to the fore?

Somewhere between the attitude of protecting oneself from the world out of fear, and an aggressive eagerness to conquer the world for one's own benefit, lies a range of feelings which it would be wrong to overlook, because they, too, play a significant role in forming the moral climate of today's "united society": feelings of indifference and everything that goes with them.

It is as though after the shocks of recent history, and the kind of system subsequently established in this country, people had lost all faith in the future, in the possibility of setting public affairs right, in the meaning of a struggle for truth and justice. They shrug off anything that goes beyond their everyday, routine concern for their own livelihood; they seek ways of escape; they succumb to apathy, to indifference toward suprapersonal values and their fellow men, to spiritual passivity and depression.

And everyone who still tries to resist by, for instance, refusing to adopt the principle of dissimulation as the key to survival, doubting the value of any self-fulfillment purchased at the cost of self-alienation—such a person appears to his ever more indifferent neighbors as an eccentric, a fool, a Don Quixote, and in the end is regarded inevitably with some aversion, like everyone who behaves differently from the rest and in a way which, moreover, threatens to hold up a critical mirror before their eyes. Or, again, those indifferent neighbors may expel such a person from their midst or shun him as required, for appearance' sake while sympathizing with him in secret or in private, hoping to still their conscience by clandestine approval of someone who acts as they themselves should, but cannot.

Paradoxically, though, this indifference has become an active social force. Is it not plain indifference, rather than fear, that brings many to the voting booth, to meetings, to membership in official organizations? Is not the political support enjoyed by the regime to a large degree simply a matter of routine, of habit, of automatism, of laziness behind which lies nothing but total resignation? Participation in political rituals in which no one believes is pointless, but it does ensure a quiet life—and would it be any less pointless *not* to participate? One would gain nothing, and lose the quiet life in the bargain.

Most people are loath to spend their days in ceaseless conflict with authority, especially when it can only end in the defeat of the isolated individual. So why not do what is required of you? It costs you nothing, and in time you cease to bother about it. It is not worth a moment's thought.

Despair leads to apathy, apathy to conformity, conformity to routine performance—which is then quoted as evidence of "mass political involvement." All this goes to make up the contemporary concept of "normal" behavior—a concept which is, in essence, deeply pessimistic.

The more completely one abandons any hope of general reform, any interest in suprapersonal goals and values, or any chance of exercising influence in an "outward" direction, the more his energy is diverted in the direction of least resistance, i.e., "inwards." People today are preoccupied far more with themselves, their families and their homes. It is there that they find rest, there that they can forget the world's folly and freely exercise their creative talents. They fill their homes with all kinds of appliances and pretty things, they try to improve their accommodations, they try to make life pleasant for themselves, building cottages, looking after their cars, taking more interest in food and clothing and domestic comfort. In short, they turn their main attention to the material aspects of their private lives.

Clearly, this social orientation produces favorable economic results. It encourages improvements in the neglected fields of consumer goods production and public services. It helps to raise the general living standard. Economically, it is a significant source of dynamic energy, capable, at least partially, of developing society's material wealth, which the inflexible, bureaucratized, and unproductive state sector of the economy could hardly ever hope to accomplish. (It is enough to compare state and private housing construction as to quantity and quality.)

The authorities welcome and support this spillover of energy into the private sphere.

But why? Because it stimulates economic growth? Certainly, that is one reason. But the whole spirit of current political propaganda and practice, quietly but systematically applauding this "inward" orientation as the very essence of human fulfillment on earth, shows only too clearly why the authorities really welcome this transfer of energy. They see it for what it really is in its psychological origins: an escape from the public sphere. Rightly divining that such surplus energy, if directed "outward," must sooner or later turn against them—that is, against the particular forms of power they obstinately cling to—they do not hesitate to represent as human life what is really a desperate substitute for living. In the interest of the smooth management of society, then, society's attention is deliberately diverted from itself, that is, from social concerns. By fixing a person's whole attention on his mere consumer interests, it is hoped to render him incapable of realizing the increasing extent to which he has been spiritually, politically, and morally violated. Reducing him to a simple vessel for the ideals of a primitive consumer society is intended to turn him into pliable material for complex manipulation. The danger that he might conceive a longing to fulfill some of the immense and unpredictable potential he has as a human being is to be nipped in the bud by imprisoning him within the wretched range of parts he can play as a consumer, subject to the limitations of a centrally directed market.

All the evidence suggests that the authorities are applying a method quite adequate for dealing with a creature whose only aim is self-preservation. Seeking the path of least resistance, they completely ignore the price that must be paid—the harsh assault on human integrity, the brutal castration of man's humanity.

Yet these same authorities obsessively justify themselves with their revolutionary ideology, in which the ideal of man's total liberation has a central place! But what, in fact, has happened to the concept of human personality and its many-sided, harmonious, and authentic growth? Of man liberated from the clutches of an alienating social machinery, from a mythical hierarchy of values, formalized freedoms, from the dictatorship of property, the fetish and the might of money? What has happened to the idea that people should live in full enjoyment of social and legal justice, have a creative share in economic and political power, be elevated in human dignity and become truly themselves? Instead of a free share in economic decision making, free participation in political life, and free intellectual advancement, all people are actually offered is a chance freely to choose which washing machine or refrigerator they want to buy.

In the foreground, then, stands the imposing facade of grand humanistic ideals—and behind it crouches the modest family house of a socialist bourgeois. On the one side, bombastic slogans about the unprecedented increase in every sort of freedom and the unique structural variety of life; on the other, unprecedented drabness and the squalor of life reduced to a hunt for consumer goods.

Somewhere at the top of the hierarchy of pressures by which man is maneuvered into becoming an obedient member of a consumer herd, there stands, as I have hinted, a concealed, omnipotent force: the state police. It is no coincidence, I suppose, that this body should so aptly illustrate the gulf that separates the ideological facade from everyday reality. Anyone who has had the bad luck to experience personally the "working style" of that institution must be highly amused at the official explanation of its purpose. Does anyone really believe that that slimy swarm of thousands of petty informers, professional narks, complex-ridden, sly, envious, malevolent *petits bourgeois*, and bureaucrats, that malodorous agglomeration of treachery, evasion, fraud, gossip, and intrigue "shows the imprint of the working man, guarding the people's government and its revolutionary achievements against its enemies' designs"? For who would be more hostile to a true workers' government—if everything were not upside down—than your *petit bourgeois*, always ready to oblige and sticking at nothing, soothing his arthritic self-esteem by informing on his fellow citizens, a creature clearly discernible behind the regular procedures of the secret police as the true spiritual author of their "working style"?

It would be hard to explain this whole grotesque contrast between theory and practice, except as a natural consequence of the real mission of the state police today, which is not to protect the free development of man from any assailants, but to protect the assailants from the threat which any real attempt at man's free development poses.

The contrast between the revolutionary teachings about the new man and the new morality, and the shoddy concept of life as consumer bliss, raises the question of why the authorities actually cling so tenaciously to their ideology. Clearly, only because their ideology, as a conventionalized system of ritual communications, assures them the appearance of legitimacy, continuity, and consistency, and acts as a screen of prestige for their pragmatic practice.

The actual aims of this practice do, of course, leave their traces on the official ideology at every point. From the bowels of that infinite mountain of ideological rhetoric by which the authorities ceaselessly try to sway people's minds, and which—as its communication value is nil—the public, for the most part, scarcely notices, there emerges one specific and meaningful message, one realistic piece of advice: "Avoid politics if you can; leave it to us! Just do what we tell you, don't try to have deep thoughts, and don't poke your nose into things that don't concern you! Shut up, do your work, look after yourself—and you'll be all right!"

This advice is heeded. That people need to make a living is, after all, the one point on which they can rather easily agree with their government. Why not make good use of it, then? Especially as you have no other choice anyway.

Where is the whole situation which I have tried to outline here ultimately leading?

What, in other words, is the effect on people of a system based on fear and apathy, a system that drives everyone into a foxhole of purely material existence and offers him hypocrisy as the main form of communication with society? To what level is a society reduced by a policy where the only aim is superficial order and general obedience, regardless of by what means and at what price they have been gained?

It needs little imagination to see that such a situation can only lead toward the gradual erosion of all moral standards, the breakdown of all criteria of decency, and the widespread destruction of confidence in the meaning of values such as truth, adherence to principles, sincerity, altruism, dignity, and honor. Amidst a demoralization "in depth," stemming from the loss of hope and the loss of the belief that life has a meaning, life must sink to a biological, vegetable level. It can but confront us once more with that tragic aspect of man's status in modern technological civilization marked by a declining awareness of the absolute, and which I propose to call a "crisis of human identity." For how can the collapse of man's identity be slowed down by a system that so harshly requires a man to be something other than he is?

Order has been established. At the price of a paralysis of the spirit, a deadening of the heart, and devastation of life.

Surface "consolidation" has been achieved. At the price of a spiritual and moral crisis in society.

Unfortunately, the worst feature of this crisis is that it keeps deepening. We only need to raise our sights a little above our limited daily perspective in order to realize with horror how hastily we are all abandoning positions which only yesterday we refused to desert. What social conscience only yesterday regarded as improper is today casually excused; tomorrow it will eventually be thought natural, and the day after be held up as a model of behavior. What yesterday we declared impossible, or at least averred we would never get accustomed to, today we accept, without astonishment, as a fact of life. And, conversely, things that a little while ago we took for granted we now treat as exceptional: and soon—who knows—we might think of them as unattainable chimeras.

The changes in our assessment of the "natural" and the "normal," the shifts in moral attitudes in our society over the past few years have been greater than they might appear at first glance. As our insensitivity has increased, so naturally has our ability to discern that insensitivity declined.

The malady has spread, as it were, from the fruit and the foliage to the trunk and roots. The most serious grounds for alarm, then, are the prospects which the present state of affairs opens up for the future.

The main route by which society is inwardly enlarged, enriched, and cultivated is that of coming to know itself in ever greater depth, range, and subtlety.

The main instrument of society's self-knowledge is its culture: culture as a specific field of human activity, influencing the general state of mind—albeit often very indirectly—and at the same time continually subject to its influence.

Where total control over society completely suppresses its differentiated inner development, the first thing to be suppressed regularly is its culture: not just "automatically," as a phenomenon intrinsically opposed to the "spirit" of manipulation, but as a matter of deliberate "programming" inspired by justified anxiety that society be alerted to the extent of its own subjugation through that culture which gives it its self-awareness. It is culture that enables a society to enlarge its liberty and to discover truth—so what appeal can it have for the authorities who are basically concerned with suppressing such values? They recognize only one kind of truth: the kind they need at the given moment. And only one kind of liberty: to proclaim that "truth."

A world where "truth" flourishes not in a dialectic climate of genuine knowledge but in a climate of power interests is a world of mental sterility, petrified dogmas, rigid and unchangeable creeds leading inevitably to creedless despotism. This is a world of prohibitions and limitations and of orders, a world where cultural policy means primarily the operations of the cultural police force.

Much has been said and written about the peculiar degree of devastation which our present-day culture has reached: about the hundreds of prohibited books and authors and the dozens of liquidated periodicals; about the carving up of publishers' projects and theatre repertoires and the cutting off of all contact with the intellectual community; about the plundering of exhibition halls; about the grotesque range of persecution and discrimination practiced in this field; about the breaking up of all the former artistic associations and countless scholarly institutes and their replacement by dummies run by little gangs of aggressive fanatics, notorious careerists, incorrigible cowards, and incompetent upstarts anxious to seize their opportunity in the general void. Rather than describe all these things again, I will offer some reflections on those deeper aspects of this state of affairs which are germane to the subject of my letter.

In the first place, however bad the present situation, it still does not mean that culture has ceased to exist altogether. Plays are put on, television programs go out every day, and even books get published. But this overt and legal cultural activity, taken as a whole, exhibits one basic feature: an overall externalization due to its being estranged in large measure from its proper substance through its total emasculation as an instrument of human, and, therefore of social, self-awareness. And whenever something of incontestably excellent value does appear—a superb dramatic performance, let us say, to stay in the sphere of art—then it appears, rather, as a phenomenon to be tolerated because of its subtlety and refinement, and hence, from an official point of view, its relative innocuousness as a contribution to social self-awareness. Yet even here, no sooner does that contribution begin to be at all keenly perceived than the authorities start instinctively to defend themselves: there are familiar instances where a good actor was banned, by and large, simply for being too good.

But that is not what concerns me at this point. What interests me is how this externalization works in fields where it is possible to describe the human experience of the world far more explicitly and where the function of promoting social self-awareness is, thus, far more manifestly fulfilled.

For example, suppose a literary work, a play perhaps, undeniably skillful, suggestive, ingenious, meaningful, is published (it does happen from time to time). Whatever the other qualities of the work may be, of one thing we may always be perfectly certain: whether through censorship or self-censorship, because of the writer's character or his self-deception, as a consequence of resignation or of calculation, it will never stray one inch beyond the taboos of a banal, conventional and, hence, basically fraudulent social consciousness that offers and accepts as genuine experience the mere appearance of experience—a concatenation of smooth, hackneyed, superficial trivia of experience; that is, pallid reflections of such aspects of experience as the social consciousness has long since adopted and domesticated. Despite, or rather, because of this fact, there will always be people who find such a work entertaining, exciting, and interesting, although it sheds no light, offers no flash of real knowledge in the sense that it reveals something unknown, expresses something unsaid, or provides new, spontaneous, and effective evidence of things hitherto only guessed at. In short, by imitating the real world, such a work in fact, falsifies the real world. As regards the actual forms this externalization takes, it is no accident that the vat most frequently tapped should be the one which, thanks to its proven harmlessness, enjoys the warmest approval of the authorities in our country, whether bourgeois or proletarian. I refer to the aesthetics of banality, safely housed within the four walls of genial *petit bourgeois* morality; the sentimental philosophy of kitchen-sink, country-bumpkin earthiness, and the provincial conception of the world based on the belief in its general goodness. I refer to the aesthetic doctrine whose keystone is the cult of right-thinking mediocrity, bedded in hoary national self-satisfaction, guided by the principle that everything must be slick, trivial, and predigested, and culminating in that false optimism which puts the basest interpretation on the dictum that "truth will prevail."

Of works designed to give literary expression to the government's political ideology, there is today—as you must be aware—an extreme scarcity, and those few are clearly, by professional standards, bad ones. This is not merely because there is no one to write them, but also, I am sure, paradoxical as it may appear, because they would not be particularly welcome. For, from the standpoint of actual contemporary attitudes (those of the consumer society, that is), even if such works were available, were professionally competent, and attracted somebody's interest, they would divert too much attention "outwards," rub salt into too many old wounds, provoke— through their general and radical political character—too much general and radical political reaction, thus stirring up too many pools that are meant to be left as stagnant as possible. Far more suitable to the real interests of the authorities today is what I have called the aesthetics of banality, which misses the truth much more inconspicuously, acceptably, and plausibly, and (since it is far more digestible for the conventional mind) is far more suited to the role accorded to culture in the consumer philosophy: not to excite people with the truth, but to reassure them with lies.

This kind of artistic output, of course, has always predominated. But in our country, there had always been some chinks at least through which works of art that could truthfully be said to convey a more genuine kind of human self-awareness reached the public. The road for such works was never particularly smooth. They met resistance not only from the authorities, but from the easygoing inertia of conventional attitudes as well. Yet until recently they had always managed in some mysterious way, by devious paths and seldom without delay, to get through to the individual and to society, and so to fulfill the role of culture as the agent of social self-awareness.

This is all that really matters. This is precisely what I take to be really important. And it is also precisely this that the present government—arguably for the first time since the age of our national revival—has managed to render almost completely impossible, so total is the present system of bureaucratic control of culture, so perfect the surveillance of every chink through which some major work might see the light of day, so greatly does that little band of men, who hold the keys to every door in their own pockets, fear the government and fear art.

You will, of course, appreciate that I am speaking at this moment not of the indexes, listing the names of all creative artists subject to a total or partial ban, but of a much worse list—of that "blank index" which includes, *a priori,* everything which might contain the spark of a slightly original thought, a perceptive insight, deeper sincerity, an unusual idea, or a suggestive form; I am speaking of that open warrant for the arrest of anything inwardly free and, therefore, in the deepest sense "cultural," I am speaking of the warrant against culture issued by your government.

Once more the question which I have been posing from the start arises. What does it all really mean? Where is it leading? What is it going to do to society?

Once more, I take a particular case. Most of the former cultural periodicals, as we know, have ceased to appear in our country. If any have survived, they have been so made to conform to official policy that they are hardly worth taking seriously.

What has been the effect of that?

At first glance, practically none. The wheels of society continue to go round even without all those literary, artistic, theatrical, philosophical, historical, and other magazines whose number, even while they existed, may never have filled the latent needs of society, but which nevertheless were around and played their part. How many people today still miss those publications? Only the few tens of thousands of people who subscribed to them—a very small fraction of society.

Yet this loss is infinitely deeper and more significant than might appear from the numbers involved. Its real implications are again, of course, hidden, and can hardly be assessed precisely.

The forcible liquidation of such a journal—a theoretical review concerned with the theatre, say—is not just an impoverishment of its particular readers. It is not even merely a severe blow to theatrical culture. It is simultaneously, and above all, the liquidation of a particular organ through which society becomes aware of itself and hence it is an interference, hard to describe in exact terms, in the complex system of circulation, exchange, and conversion of nutrients that maintain life in that many-layered organism which is society today. It is a blow against the natural dynamic of the processes going on within that organism; a disturbance of the balanced interplay of all its many functions, an interplay reflecting the level of complexity reached by society's anatomy. And just as the chronic deficiency of a vitamin (amounting in quantitative terms only to a negligible fraction of the human diet) can make a person ill, so, in the long run, the loss of a single periodical can cause the social organism far more damage than would appear at first sight. And what if the loss involves not just one periodical, but virtually all?

It is easy to show that the real importance of knowledge, thought, and creation is not limited, in the stratified world of a civilized society, to the significance these things have for the particular circle of people who are primarily, directly and, as it were, physically involved with them, either actively or passively. This is always a small group, especially in the sciences. Yet the knowledge in question, conveyed through however many intermediaries, may in the end profoundly affect the whole society, just as politics, including the nuclear threat, physically concerns each one of us, even though most of us have had no experience of the speculations in theoretical physics which led to the manufacture of the atom bomb. That the same holds for nonspecific knowledge is shown by many historic instances of an unprecedented cultural, political, and moral upsurge throughout society, where the original nucleus of crystallization, the catalyst, was an act of social self-awareness carried out, and indeed directly and "physically" perceived, only by a small and exclusive circle. Even subsequently, that act may have remained outside the apperception of society at large, yet it was still an indispensable condition of its upsurge. For we never know when some inconspicuous spark of knowledge, struck within range of the few brain cells, as it were, specially adapted for the organism's self-awareness, may suddenly light up the road for the whole of society, without society ever realizing, perhaps, how it came to see the road. But that is far from being the whole story. For even those other countless flashes of knowledge which never illuminate the path ahead for society as a whole have their deep social importance, if only through the mere fact that they happened; that they might have cast light; that in their very occurrence they fulfilled a certain range of society's potentialities—either its creative powers, or simply its liberties; they, too, help to make and maintain a climate of civilization without which none of the more illuminating flashes could ever occur.

In short, the space within which spiritual self-awareness operates is indivisible; the cutting of a single thread must injure the coherence of the whole network, and this itself showed the remarkable interdependence of all those fine processes in the social organism that I spoke of, the transcendent importance of each one of them, and hence the transcendent destructiveness wrought by its disruption.

I would not wish to reduce everything to this single and still relatively minor aspect of the problem. Still, does it not in itself confirm the deeply injurious influence on the general spiritual and moral state of society which the "warrant against culture" already has and will have in future, even though its immediate impact is only on a limited number of heads?

If not a single new Czech novel, of which one could safely say that it enlarges our experience of the world, has appeared in recent years in the bookshops, this will certainly have no public effect. Readers are not going to demonstrate in the streets and, in the end, you can always find something to read. But who will dare assess the real significance of this fact for Czech society? Who knows how the gap will affect the spiritual and moral climate of the years to come? How far will it weaken our ability to know ourselves? How deeply will such an absence of cultural self-knowledge brand those whose self-knowing begins only today or tomorrow? What mounds of mystification, slowly forming in the general cultural consciousness, will need to be chipped away? How far back will one need to go? Who can tell which people will still find the strength to light new fires of truth, when, how, and from what resources, once there has been such thorough wastage not only of the fuel, but of the very feeling that it can be done?

A few novels of the kind absent from the bookshops do nevertheless exist: they circulate in manuscript. In this respect, the situation is not yet hopeless: it follows from everything I have said that if such a novel, over the years, remained unknown to all but twenty people, the fact of its existence would still be important. It means something that there is such a book, that it could be written at all, that it is alive in at least one tiny area of the cultural consciousness. But what about the fields in which it is impossible to work, except through the so-called legal channels? How can one estimate the damage already done, and still to be done, by the strangling of every interesting development in the stage and cinema, whose role as social stimuli is so specific? How much greater still may be the long-term effect of the vacuum in the humanities and in the theory and practice of the social sciences? Who dares measure the consequences of the violent interruption of the long processes of self-knowledge in ontology, ethics, and historiography, dependent as they are on access to the normal circulation of information, ideas, discoveries, and values, the public crystallization of attitudes?

The overall question, then, is this: What profound intellectual and moral impotence will the nation suffer tomorrow, following the castration of its culture today?

I fear that the baneful effects on society will outlast by many years the particular political interests that gave rise to them. So much more guilty, in the eyes of history, are those who have sacrificed the country's spiritual future for the sake of their present power interests.

Just as the constant increase of entropy is the basic law of the universe, so it is the basic law of life to be ever more highly structured and to struggle against entropy.

Life rebels against all uniformity and leveling; its aim is not sameness, but variety, the restlessness of transcendence, the adventure of novelty and rebellion against the status quo. An essential condition for its enhancement is the secret constantly made manifest.

On the other hand, the essence of authority (whose aim is reduced to protecting its own permanence by forcibly imposing the uniformity of perpetual consent) consists basically in a distrust of all variety, uniqueness, and transcendence; in an aversion to everything unknown, impalpable, and currently obscure; in a proclivity for the uniform, the identical, and the inert; in deep affection for the status quo. In it, the mechanical spirit prevails over the vital. The order it strives for is no frank quest for ever higher forms of social self-organization, equivalent to its evolving complexity of structure, but, on the contrary, a decline toward that "state of maximum probability" representing the climax of entropy. Following the direction of entropy, it goes against the direction of life.

In a person's life, as we know, there is a moment when the

complexity of structure begins suddenly to decline and his path turns in the direction of entropy. This is the moment when he, too, succumbs to the general law of the universe: the moment of death.

Somewhere at the bottom of every political authority which has chosen the path to entropy (and would like to treat the individual as a computer into which any program can be fed with the assurance that he will carry it out), there lies hidden the death principle. There is an odor of death even in the notion of "order" which such an authority puts into practice and which sees every manifestation of genuine life, every exceptional deed, individual expression, thought, every unusual idea or wish, as a red light signaling confusion, chaos, and anarchy.

The entire political practice of the present regime, as I have tried to outline it here step by step, confirms that those concepts which were always crucial for its program—order, calm, consolidation, "guiding the nation out of its crisis," "halting disruption," "assuaging hot tempers" and so on—have finally acquired the same lethal meaning that they have for every regime committed to entropy.

True enough, order prevails: a bureaucratic order of gray monotony that stifles all individuality; of mechanical precision that suppresses everything of unique quality; of musty inertia that excludes the transcendent. What prevails is order without life.

True enough, the country is calm. Calm as a morgue or a grave, would you not say?

In a society which is really alive, something is always happening. The interplay of current activities and events, of overt and concealed movement, produces a constant succession of unique situations which provoke further and fresh movement. The mysterious, vital polarity of the continuous and the changing, the regular and the random, the foreseen and the unexpected, has its effect in the time dimension and is borne out in the flow of events. The more highly structured the life of a society, the more highly structured its time dimension, and the more prominent the element of uniqueness and unrepeatability within the time flow. This, in turn, of course, makes it easier to reflect its sequential character, to represent it, that is, as an irreversible stream of noninterchangeable situations, and so, in retrospect, to understand better whatever is governed by regular laws in society. The richer the life society lives, then, the better it perceives the dimension of social time, the dimension of history.

In other words, wherever there is room for social activity, room is created for a social memory as well. Any society that is alive is a society with a history.

If the element of continuity and causality is so vitally linked in history with the element of unrepeatability and unpredictability, we may well ask how true history—that inextinguishable source of "chaos," fountainhead of unrest, and slap in the face to law and order—can ever exist in a world ruled by an "entropic" regime.

The answer is plain: it cannot. And, indeed, it does not—on the surface, anyway. Under such a regime, the elimination of life in the proper sense brings social time to a halt, so that history disappears from its purview.

In our own country, too, one has the impression that for some time there has been no history. Slowly but surely, we are losing the sense of time. We begin to forget what happened when, what came earlier and what later, and the feeling that it really doesn't matter overwhelms us. As uniqueness disappears from the flow of events, so does continuity; everything merges into the single gray image of one and the same cycle and we say, "There is nothing happening." Here, too, a deadly order has been imposed: all activity is completely organized and so completely deadened. The deadening of the sense of unfolding time in society inevitably kills it in private life as well. No longer backed by social history or the history of the individual within it, private life declines to a prehistoric level where time derives its only rhythm from such events as birth, marriage, and death.

The loss of the sense of social time seems, in every way, to cast society back into the primeval state where, for thousands of years, humanity could get no further in measuring it than by the cosmic and climatic pattern of endlessly repeated annual seasons and the religious rites associated with them.

The gap left by the disquieting dimension of history has, naturally, to be filled. So the disorder of real history is replaced by the orderliness of pseudo-history, whose author is not the life of society, but an official planner. Instead of events, we are offered nonevents; we live from anniversary to anniversary, from celebration to celebration, from parade to parade, from a unanimous congress to unanimous elections and back again; from a Press Day to an Artillery Day, and vice versa. It is no coincidence that, thanks to this substitution for history, we are able to review everything that is happening in society, past and future, by simply glancing at the calendar. And the notoriously familiar character of the recurrent rituals makes such information quite as adequate as if we had been present at the events themselves.

What we have, then, is perfect order—but at the cost of reverting to prehistory. Even so, we must enter a caveat: whereas for our ancestors the repeated rituals always had a deep existential meaning, for us they are merely a routine performed for its own sake. The government keeps them going to maintain the impression that history is moving. The public goes through the motions to keep out of trouble.

An "entropic" regime has one means of increasing the general entropy within its own sphere of influence, namely, by tightening its own central control, rendering itself more monolithic, and enclosing society in a straitjacket of one-dimensional manipulation. But with every step it takes in this direction, it inevitably increases its own entropy too.

In an effort to immobilize the world, it immobilizes itself, undermining its own ability to cope with anything new or to resist the natural currents of life. The "entropic" regime is, thus, doomed to become the victim of its own lethal principle, and the most vulnerable victim at that, thanks to the absence of any impulse within its own structure that could, as it were, make it face up to itself. Life, by contrast, with its irrepressible urge to oppose entropy, is able all the more successfully and inventively to resist being violated, the faster the violating authority succumbs to its own sclerosis.

In trying to paralyze life, then, the authorities paralyze themselves and, in the long run, make themselves incapable of paralyzing life.

In other words, life may be subjected to a prolonged and thorough process of violation, enfeeblement, and anesthesia. Yet, in the end, it cannot be permanently halted. Albeit quietly, covertly, and slowly, it nevertheless goes on. Though it be estranged from itself a thousand times, it always manages in some way to recuperate; however violently ravished, it always survives, in the end, the power which ravished it. It cannot be otherwise, in view of the profoundly ambivalent nature of every "entropic" authority, which can only suppress life if there is life to suppress and so, in the last resort, depends for its own existence on life, whereas life in no way depends on it. The only force that can truly destroy life on our planet is the force which knows no compromise: the universal validity of the second law of thermodynamics.

If life cannot be destroyed for good, then neither can history be brought entirely to a halt. A secret streamlet trickles on beneath the heavy cover of inertia and pseudo-events, slowly and inconspicuously undercutting it. It may be a long process, but one day it must happen: the cover will no longer hold and will start to crack.

This is the moment when once more something visibly begins to happen, something truly new and unique, something unscheduled in the official calendar of "happenings," something that makes us no longer indifferent to what occurs and when—something truly historic, in the sense that history again demands to be heard.

. . . .

But how, in our particular circumstances, could it come about that history "demands to be heard"? What does such a prospect really imply?

I am neither historian nor prophet, yet there are some observations touching on the structure of these "moments" which one cannot avoid making.

Where there is, in some degree, open competition for power as the only real guarantee of public control over its exercise and, in the last resort, the only guarantee of free speech, the political authorities must willy-nilly participate in some kind of permanent and overt dialogue with the life of society. They are forced continually to wrestle with all kinds of questions which life puts to them. Where no such competition exists and freedom of speech is, therefore, of necessity sooner or later suppressed—as is the case with every "entropic" regime—the authorities, instead of adapting themselves to life, try to adapt life to themselves. Instead of coping openly and continually with real conflicts, demands, and issues, they simply draw a veil over them. Yet somewhere under this cover, these conflicts and demands continue, grow, and multiply, only to burst forth when the moment arrives when the cover can no longer hold them down. This is the moment when the dead weight of inertia crumbles and history steps out again into the arena.

And what happens after that?

The authorities are certainly still strong enough to prevent those vital conflicts from issuing in the shape of open discussion or open rivalry for power. But they have no longer the strength to resist this pressure altogether. So life vents itself where it can—in the secret corridors of power, where it can insist on secret discussion and finally on secret competition. For this, of course, the authorities are unprepared: any substantive dialogue with life is outside their range of competence. So they panic. Life sows confusion in their council chambers in the shape of personal quarrels, intrigues, pitfalls, and confrontations. It even infects, as it were, their own representatives: the death mask of impersonality that their officials wore to confirm their identity with the monolith of power is suddenly dropped, revealing live people competing for power in the most "human" way and struggling in self-defense, one against the other. This is the notorious moment for palace revolutions and putsches, for sudden and outwardly mystifying changes of portfolio and changes of key points in set speeches, the moment when real or construed conspiracies and secret centers are revealed, the moment when real or imaginary crimes are made known and ancient guilt unearthed, the moment for mutual dismissals from office, mutual denigration, and perhaps even arrests and trials. Whereas before every man in authority had spoken the same language, used the same clichés, applauded the successful fulfillment of the same targets, now suddenly the monolith of power breaks down into distinguishable persons, still speaking the same language, but using it to make personal attacks on one another. And we learn with astonishment that some of them—those, that is, who lost in the secret struggle for power—had never taken their targets seriously and never successfully fulfilled them— far from it—whereas others—the winners—had really meant what they said and are alone capable of achieving their aims.

The more rational the construction of the official calendar of nonevents over the years, the more irrational the effect of a sudden irruption of genuine history. All its long-suppressed elements of unrepeatability, uniqueness, and incalculability, all its long-denied mysteries, come rushing through the breach. Where for years we had been denied the slightest, most ordinary surprise, life is now one huge surprise—and it is well worth it. The whole disorderliness of history, concealed under artificial order for years, suddenly spurts out.

How well we know all this! How often we have witnessed it in our part of the world! The machine that worked for years to apparent perfection, faultlessly, without a hitch, falls apart overnight. The system that seemed likely to reign unchanged, world without end, since nothing could call its power in question amid all those unanimous votes and elections, is shattered without warning. And, to our amazement, we find that nothing was the way we had thought it was.

The moment when such a tornado whirls through the musty

edifice of petrified power structures is, of course, far from being just a source of amusement for all of us who are outside the ramparts of authority. For we, too, are always involved, albeit indirectly. Is it not the quiet perennial pressure of life, the ceaselessly resisted, but finally irresistible demands and interests of all society, its conflicts and its tensions, which ever and again spoke the foundations of power? No wonder society continually reawakens at such moments, attaches itself to them, receives them with great alertness, gets excited by them, and seeks to exploit them! In almost every case, such tremors provoke hopes or fears of one kind or another, create—or seem to create—scope for the realization of life's various impulses and ambitions, and accelerate all kinds of movements within society.

Yet, in almost every case, it is equally true that this situation, owing to the basically unnatural structure of the kind of confrontation with life which such shakeups of power bring about, carries with it many incalculable risks.

I shall try to illuminate further one such risk.

If every day someone takes orders in silence from an incompetent superior, if every day he solemnly performs ritual acts which he privately finds ridiculous, if he unhesitatingly gives answers to questionnaires which are contrary to his real opinions and is prepared to deny himself in public, if he sees no difficulty in feigning sympathy or even affection where, in fact, he feels only indifference or aversion, it still does not mean that he has entirely lost the use of one of the basic human senses, namely, the sense of dignity.

On the contrary: even if they never speak of it, people have a very acute appreciation of the price they have paid for outward peace and quiet: the permanent humiliation of their human dignity. The less direct resistance they put up to it—comforting themselves by driving it from their mind and deceiving themselves with the thought that it is of no account, or else simply gritting their teeth—the deeper the experience etches itself into their emotional memory. The man who can resist humiliation can quickly forget it; but the man who can long tolerate it must long remember it. In actual fact, then, nothing remains forgotten. All the fear one has endured, the dissimulation one has been forced into, all the painful and degrading buffoonery, and, worst of all, perhaps, the feeling of having displayed one's cowardice—all this settles and accumulates somewhere in the bottom of our social consciousness, quietly fermenting.

Clearly, this is no healthy situation. Left untreated, the abscesses suppurate; the pus cannot escape from the body, and the malady spreads throughout the organism. The natural human emotion is denied the process of objectivization and instead, caged up over long periods in the emotional memory, is gradually deformed into a sick cramp, into a toxic substance not unlike the carbon monoxide produced by incomplete combustion.

No wonder, then, that when the crust cracks and the lava of life rolls out, there appear not only well-considered attempts to rectify old wrongs, not only searchings for truth and for reforms matching life's needs, but also symptoms of bilious hatred, vengeful wrath, and a feverish desire for immediate compensation for all the degradation endured. (The impulsive and often wayward forms of this desire may also spring largely from a vague impression that the whole outbreak has come too late, at a time when it has lost its meaning, having no longer any immediate motive and so carrying no immediate risk, when it is actually just an ersatz for something that should have happened in quite a different context.)

No wonder, again, that the men in power, accustomed for years to absolute agreement, unanimous and unreserved support, and a total unity of total pretense, are so shocked by the upsurge of suppressed feelings at such a moment that they feel exposed to such an unheard-of threat and, in this mood (assuming themselves to be the sole guarantors of the world's survival), detect such an unprecedented threat to the rest of the world, too, that they do not hesitate to call upon millions of foreign soldiers to save both themselves and the world.

We experienced one such explosion not long ago. Those who had spent years humiliating and insulting people and were then so shocked when those people tried to raise their own voices, now label the whole episode an "outbreak of passions." And what, pray, were the passions that broke out? Those who know what protracted and thoroughgoing humiliations had preceded the explosion, and who understand the psycho-social mechanics of the subsequent reaction to them should be more surprised at the relatively calm, objective and, indeed, loyal form which the explosion took. Yet, as everyone knows, we had to pay a cruel price for that moment of truth.

The authorities in power today are profoundly different from those who ruled prior to that recent explosion. Not only because the latter were, so to speak, "originals" and their successors a mere formalized imitation, incapable of reflecting the extent to which the "originals" had meanwhile lost their mystique, but primarily for another reason.

For whereas the earlier version rested on a genuine and not inconsiderable social basis derived from the trustful support accorded, though in declining measure, by one part of the population, and on the equally genuine and considerable attractiveness (which also gradually evaporated) of the social benefits it originally promised, today's regime rests solely on the ruling minority's instinct for self-preservation and on the fear of the ruled majority.

In these circumstances, it is hard to foresee all the feasible scenarios for a future "moment of truth": to foresee how such a complex and undisguised degradation of the whole of society might one day demand restitution. And it is quite impossible to estimate the scope and depth of the tragic consequences which such a moment might inflict, perhaps must inflict, on our two nations.

In this context, it is amazing that a government which advertises itself as the most scientific on record is unable to grasp the elementary rules of its own operations or to learn from its own past.

. . .

I have made it clear that I have no fear of life in Czechoslo-vakia coming to a halt, or of history being suspended forever with the accession to power of the present leaders. Every sit-uation in history and every epoch have been succeeded by a fresh situation and a new epoch, and for better or worse, the new ones have always been quite remote from the expecta-tions of the organizers and rulers of the preceding period.

What I am afraid of is something else. The whole of this letter is concerned, in fact, with what I really fear—the point-lessly harsh and long-lasting consequences which the present violent abuses will have for our nations. I fear the price we are all bound to pay for the drastic suppression of history, the cruel and needless banishment of life into the under-ground of society and the depths of the human soul, the new compulsory deferment of every opportunity for society to live in anything like a natural way. And perhaps it is apparent from what I wrote a little way back that I am not only worried about our current payments in terms of everyday bitterness at the spoliation of society and human degradation, or about the heavy tax we shall have to pay in the long-lasting spiritual and moral decline of society. I am also concerned with the scarcely calculable surcharge which may be imposed on us when the moment next arrives for life and history to demand their due.

The degree of responsibility a political leader bears for the condition of his country must always vary and, obviously, can never be absolute. He never rules alone, and so some portion of responsibility rests on those who surround him. No coun-try exists in a vacuum, so its policies are in some way always influenced by those of other countries. Clearly the previous rulers always have much to answer for, since it was their pol-icies which predetermined the present situation. The public, too, has much to answer for, both individually, through the daily personal decisions of each responsible human being which went to create the total state of affairs, or collectively, as a socio-historic whole, limited by circumstances and in its turn limiting those circumstances.

Despite these qualifications, which naturally apply in our current situation as in any other, your responsibility as a political leader is still a great one. You help to determine the climate in which we all have to live and can therefore directly influence the final size of the bill our society will be paying for today's process of consolidation.

The Czechs and Slovaks, like any other nation, harbor within themselves simultaneously the most disparate potentialities. We have had, still have, and will continue to have our heroes, and, equally, our informers and traitors. We are capable of unleashing our imagination and creativity, of rising spiritually and morally to unexpected heights, of fighting for the truth and sacrificing ourselves for others.

But it lies in us equally to succumb to total apathy, to take no interest in anything but our bellies, and to spend our time tripping one another up. And though human souls are far from being mere pint pots that anything can be poured into (note the arrogant implications of that dreadful phrase so frequent in official speeches, when it is complained that "we"—that is, "the government"—find that such-and-such ideas are being instilled into people's heads), it depends, nevertheless, very much on the leaders which of these contrary tendencies that slumber in society will be mobilized, which set of potentialities will be given the chance of fulfillment, and which will be suppressed.

So far, it is the worst in us which is being systematically activated and enlarged—egotism, hypocrisy, indifference, cowardice, fear, resignation, and the desire to escape every personal responsibility, regardless of the general consequences.

Yet even today's national leadership has the opportunity to influence society by its policies in such a way as to encourage not the worse side of us, but the better.

So far, you and your government have chosen the easy way out for yourselves, and the most dangerous road for society: the path of inner decay for the sake of outward appearances; of deadening life for the sake of increasing uniformity; of deepening the spiritual and moral crisis of our society, and ceaselessly degrading human dignity, for the puny sake of protecting your own power.

Yet, even within the given limitations, you have the chance to do much toward at least a relative improvement of the situation. This might be a more strenuous and less gratifying way, whose benefits would not be immediately obvious and which would meet with resistance here and there. But in the light of our society's true interests and prospects, this way would be vastly the more meaningful one.

As a citizen of this country, I hereby request, openly and publicly, that you and the leading representatives of the present regime consider seriously the matters to which I have tried to draw your attention, that you assess in their light the degree of your historic responsibility, and act accordingly.

April 1975

"It Always Makes Sense to Tell the Truth"

An Interview with Jiří Lederer

" 'It Always Makes Sense to Tell the Truth': An Interview with Jiří Lederer" (April 29, 1975) was originally published in Czech as part of the *samizdat* volume *Jiří Lederer: Czech Conversations, 1975–76*, no. 177 in *Edice Petlice*. In his introduction to this interview, Lederer wrote: "In the spring of 1975, my family and I were visiting friends in the Krkonoše Mountains. As usual on such visits, I dropped in on Havel at Hrádeček near Trutnov. It was the second-to-last day of April, a beautiful sunny afternoon, the first real day of spring. Havel said he'd rather talk in the yard, but I always find spring weather too seductive and distracting. We settled into his living room, and we went on talking long into the night."

This is a slightly abridged version, and its first appearance in English. Translation by Paul Wilson.

What made you decide to write that open letter to Dr. Husák?

The main reason should be clear to some extent from the letter itself. I felt that if I said what I thought openly, I'd be contributing—perhaps—to the process of social self-awareness I talk about in the letter. I simply wrote it in the belief that it might have, let's say, a certain "socio-hygienic" significance. In general, I believe it always makes sense to tell the truth, in all circumstances.

The second reason is entirely personal: a need to somehow transcend my own predicament. For some time now I've been burdened by a feeling that I've been thrust into a predetermined, static situation, that someone, somewhere, has already described me and classified me, and that I've merely been accepting this passively and playing the role I've been handed without engaging my own imagination. I got tired of always wondering how to move in this situation, and I felt the need to stir things up, to confront others for a change and force them to deal with a situation that I myself had created.

When was the last time you made a public statement?

In the fall of 1969 I signed a petition called Ten Points. Since then I've not expressed myself in public, unless you count the occasional production of my plays abroad. And by the way, in the fall of 1970 I was to have gone to court, along with the other signatories, for signing that petition, but a day before the trial the case was adjourned and to this day it hasn't been resumed. So the charges still stand.

What were your expectations when you finished this letter? What did you think? How did you feel?

I was mainly interested in whether the text was good, that is, if it made sense, if it wasn't too abstract and boring, if it radiated a certain sense of exhortation, of urgency—otherwise I might as well have written it as an essay, not a letter. I wondered if it didn't just summarize things that were notoriously familiar to everyone, and if in some ways it didn't distort reality. In short, I wondered if I wasn't just spitting in the wind.

The second thing I worried about was the "administrative" side of things. I thought a long time about when I should send it, and how and to whom. Should I send it to the addressee first, and only then to the media, or to both at the same time? Mainly I worried about how to keep the secret police from finding out about it and somehow foiling my attempt to send it. For particular reasons, I didn't want to actually send the letter until a few days after it had been written and copied. During those few days, I was rather nervous and took a lot of complicated, secretive measures for security. One of the more piquant incidents from that period happened on the very eve of the day I'd planned to send it off. I ran into a certain high-ranking officer in the secret police who had often interrogated me and who, in the restaurant, made a lot of wisecracks about whether they were following me or not, and whether or not I was preparing to do something that might fall within their sphere of competence, and so on. When I sent my letter off the next morning at the post office without the slightest hitch, I breathed a huge sigh of relief.

What sort of consequences did you expect to follow?

Though it didn't seem possible at the time—and still doesn't—I was prepared to be arrested, because one should be ready for anything. This makes me all the more concerned about the worth and impact of my letter. I wouldn't mind sanctions if I knew that my letter had meaning, that I had not written and published it in vain, that it had given someone hope—even just a few people. On the other hand, if I had to pay for something that wasn't worthwhile, that didn't make sense, I'd only have succeeded in making myself look ridiculous.

You say you're ready for anything, even going to jail. Do you mean prepared intellectually, or do you mean something concrete?

I think I'm ready either way. Obviously I'll only know if I'm truly ready after having actually been there. Of course, I hope I'll be spared that final test of my readiness.

Have you made any specific preparation?

I've put together something I call my "emergency packet," containing cigarettes, a toothbrush, toothpaste, soap, some books, a T-shirt, paper, a laxative, and a few other small things—I can't remember everything. I keep this packet with me at all times, or more precisely, I take it with me whenever I leave the house.

In your letter to Husák, you write a lot about fear. Have you ever experienced the kind of overwhelming fear that rules your whole organism and all its physiological functions?

I can't recall ever having experienced that kind of "global" fear. I have known different kinds of fear, of course. As a driver I'm afraid of the police, especially when I've been drinking. I get the jitters easily, which means that I fear the kind of situations where it's entirely up to me whether I pass muster or not, for example, in various public appearances, tests, and so on. I have a rather irrational fear of the telephone—I loathe telephoning, in fact. I occasionally suffer a kind of "postal nervousness," that is, fear of the mail, without really knowing of any concrete evil the post might bring. I naturally experience what almost everyone does—that is, an occasional, general anxiety about life, a kind of worry about whether I can bear my life, and whether I will acquit myself well. One fear I don't have—and I don't know why this is—is political fear, or political-existential fear, or fear of the political police: I've never experienced such fears, and I'm glad I'm spared that.

[. . .]

Scarcely three weeks have gone by since you sent the letter off. Has anyone written you yet?

I've heard some good reports about the letter through various channels, but for understandable reasons people haven't written me directly. In fact, I asked my friends not to write me. I had to assume that my mail would now be opened and it made no sense to give the security forces such easy access to information. Only one person has written me directly so far—Dr. Prokop Drtina, a former Minister of Justice. It's a fine letter and I treasure it greatly. Of course, I got a letter from the addressee, too, or more precisely, from a Mrs. Sedláčková in the president's office, who returned my letter with the explanation that I had made it available to hostile press agencies and thus revealed my hostility to my country. I don't place much importance in the gesture because I know that whether Dr. Husák reads my letter or not will depend on many things, but certainly not on whether Mrs. Sedláčková returns it to me.

What about the local people here in Hrádeček? Neighbors and friends? Did they know about the letter? What did they say to you?

They knew about it very soon. Foreign radio broadcasts carried the news, and someone always hears it and passes it on. As far as their reactions are concerned, I can't say I've encountered a single expression of indignation or disagreement. But that may be because I don't meet the kind of people you'd expect not to agree with it.
[. . .]

Whatever possessed you to move to the country, 150 kilometers from Prague? Do you miss Prague?

Originally we bought this house for recreational purposes, the way people buy cottages so they'll have somewhere to go

on holidays or weekends. Gradually, however, we found ourselves spending more and more time here and less and less
time in Prague, until one day we realized, to our surprise,
that we were in fact living here. It seemed to happen by itself,
without being planned. Of course, thinking back on it, I realize there are lots of different reasons for this move. In the
first place, I think I finally left Prague the moment I realized
I had nothing to do there, that I could no longer work in my
profession, at work I'm qualified to do. Another factor may
have been the political apartheid. You run into this at every
step in Prague; you're always having to worry about whom
you'll be getting into trouble by visiting them, whom you can
invite to your place knowing they won't just come because if
they don't, you'll think they're afraid. You're always worrying
about silly problems like whom to admit you know and whom
not, where you can go and where you shouldn't so as not to
make someone nervous or cause them unpleasantness with
the police. These kinds of worries can't help but leave their
mark on you in one way or another.

Here, all that is gone. My friends come out here to see me,
and I needn't feel guilty for exposing them to some kind of
risk. Anyone undertaking the long journey has time enough
to think about where he's going and whether it's worth it to
him. Here in the country—away from the nearest house—I
feel far more normal than in the city, where life is always
putting me into awkward situations, which inevitably has an
effect on my nerves. And of course there are other reasons:
it's a lot quieter out here; life is less expensive; we have more
room; we're surrounded by nature—in short, we live better.
We don't miss Prague, and even if we did, we can go there
any time we feel like it, and just knowing that is enough.

*I understand you even went to work in a brewery in Trutnov for a
time. Why? Did you need the money? And what did you do there?*

I worked as a casual laborer. My reasons were financial—
we simply didn't have any money. Now we have some money

again, so I don't work there. I certainly didn't go there to "see life" or to prove to the world and myself that I don't mind rolling barrels around the brewery yard or getting up at four in the morning. I don't believe in playing at being a worker, and I've always thought that those "creative voluntary labor" things where writers would go to work in factories were ridiculous. I worked in the brewery for not quite a year, and got paid about seventeen hundred crowns a month. Of course the money wasn't the only thing I got from the work, far from it. But if it gave me something as a writer, it certainly wasn't getting to know a new environment—a visit to the brewery would have been enough for that—but because I experienced for myself what kind of situation the other brewery workers were in; I mean the situation of a man who works in the brewery because he has to, not because he wanted to "know life."

How did the workers accept you? And how did they react to your driving to work in a Mercedes?

I must say they accepted me wonderfully well. You know, I've done many things in my life, and I've even worked manually for a number of years, but I have always suffered, and still suffer, something that might be called awkwardness or shyness in the presence of the working class. This may just be my character, or it may be that vague feeling of guilt intellectuals sometimes have regarding workers. Or perhaps it's a holdover from my ancient experience as a "son of the manor," that is, the child of a bourgeois family who had certain privileges which he saw not as an advantage, but as a handicap. When I started working at the brewery, I understandably took those feelings of awkwardness and fear with me, and I was all the more delighted to discover that the other workers liked me and accepted me without the slightest reluctance. They even offered me help when I didn't really need it. I think I have a couple of good friends there now, and if I remember correctly, the only person who showed any antipathy to me was the director. As for the car, my fellow workers were curious about it mainly as a piece of machinery. And when there was something wrong with it, they were glad to repair it for me.

Do you have any stories from the brewery that are worth telling?

I do. We called it the "Watergate Affair." One day an amateur listening device was found in the brewery cellars where I worked. The brewmaster had installed it himself and the wires led to his flat. The man was trying to kill two birds with one stone: he wanted to know what the workers were saying about him, and at the same time, he wanted to ingratiate himself with the authorities by offering to keep an eye on me. But the whole thing was discovered—luckily in a way that couldn't be covered up—and the brewmaster had to leave in shame. Of course, once the matter had become a scandal, the state police tried to disassociate themselves from it by claiming the device had been installed without their knowledge. But the brewmaster couldn't claim that, and so all that remained of the affair in the end was that the working class had been offended by a manager no one dared defend. Afterwards, everyone—the district bureaucracy, the secret police, the director of the brewery, and the brewmaster—was afraid. And do you know who they were afraid of? Me! They were afraid I'd publish the story abroad, that I would take this shameful little scandal beyond the borders of the district and call down the wrath of their superiors upon them for behaving in such an amateurish way.

Of course I experienced many such paradoxical situations. Right after I started work, the director was instructed by the district party people—in writing, of all things—to keep an eye on me, because there was the risk that I would "inform the world press," as they wrote, about any eventual injustice. I was a casual laborer in the provinces and at the same time an "enemy of the country" of so-called central importance, and that was the source of many comic situations.

[. . .]

You've mentioned the political police several times. Now that you're here, at some distance from Prague, are things quieter on that front?

I've been interrogated many times in my life. It began long before 1968, and I have to admit—even though it may sound perverse—I've always found interrogations amusing. It's a strange and interesting experience. I have a lot of thoughts on the subject and sometime I'd like to write an essay on the "philosophy of interrogations." I've elected different tactics on different occasions. My longest interrogation was in 1969. A special team of investigators came to my house and spent three whole weeks with me. At that time, I elected the "explanatory tactic," which at the time seemed more productive than if I had refused to talk about anything at all. Today, on the contrary, I incline increasingly to the tactic of refusing to talk about anything at all.

What do you do all day long, now that you're not working in the brewery anymore?

What I should be doing is working hard on a play I've got started. But I'm not really writing very hard, and I rather enjoy looking for excuses not to write, such as doing some necessary odd jobs around the house. I'm not very happy with the state of my self-discipline. The brewery didn't help much, either, though at the time I thought it would have a positive effect on my work because it would teach me to be more economical with my time.

I have two ways of explaining my lack of discipline. In the first place, those several years when I haven't been pressured by any commissions or deadlines, with no one waiting urgently for me to finish a play, have probably demoralized me

more than I realize. I was used to writing for a specific theatre, where I also worked as a dramaturge, so I knew the
importance of deadlines. I wrote for a specific audience, under pressure from a specific spiritual and social moment in
time, and I knew what it was to write knowing that I could
miss that moment altogether. I had before me the prospect
of production; I looked forward to working with the director,
and I had an interest, not only as playwright but also as a
member of the theatre, in my play's being performed. All of
this naturally forced me to get down to work. But for several
years now I haven't had any of that; I write abstractly, in a
sense—for history, or for a foreign audience I don't know.
And this hasn't been good for me. When you know it doesn't
matter whether you finish a play today or a year from now,
and when you don't know whom you're writing it for anyway,
it's not easy to write.

The second reason why I'm trying to avoid writing is probably that the play I'm working on at the moment has very
specific complexities. I've been working on it for a long time
now, it's hard going, and I'm still at the beginning. Maybe I've
set myself a task I'm not up to and so I welcome any opportunity to get out of doing it. One friend told me he secretly
suspects that I wrote this letter to Dr. Husák mainly to avoid
having to write my play.

[. . .]

*You are a scientific type. I heard from the teachers at the Academy
of Performing Arts that when you wrote your dissertation play, you
apparently added a commentary in which you analyzed the play in
a way that fascinated some teachers and shocked others.*

It's probably true that I'm a rational type and have a tendency to theorize. I sometimes get the urge to write theoretical texts, and I do. But a play is a play; it should speak for
itself, and I would never write a commentary on it of my own
accord. If I have done so, it was always because something
external to the play led me to do it. In the case of *The Increased*

Difficulty of Concentration, which I submitted to the Drama department of the Academy as the "literary" part of my dissertation, I wrote a commentary because it was expected.

As for the plays themselves, regardless of their aesthetics or
style—and my rationalism is certainly reflected in their aesthetics and style—I certainly don't write them to illustrate a
theory, and their source of inspiration is definitely not abstract thought. Like most other plays, they come out of specific and mundane experience or ideas. It is only in working
on them that I breathe a particular meaning into the material—or rather, I don't do that consciously; such meanings appear automatically on their own, simply because it can't be any
other way. And I think that's normal. I'm convinced that someone like Beckett, an author whose plays are extraordinarily
rich in so-called philosophical meaning, writes no differently.
For instance, I wouldn't be surprised if his *Happy Days* started
with a real woman who had buried herself in the sand on a
beach somewhere. The author saw it, and in a moment of sudden enlightenment he understood that this mundane appa-
rition contained within itself the possibility of a parable and
a wealth of potential poetic meanings—and so he went to
work and wrote one of his most beautiful and profound plays.

What would you say about your own plays? What are they about?

All my plays so far have essentially been about a single
theme: the crisis of human identity. I keep coming back to it
in different ways and in different forms, but always in the
end—whether I want to or not—that theme somehow appears
in what I write.

Could you expand on this idea of human identity?

I believe that with the loss of God, man has lost a kind of
absolute and universal system of coordinates, to which he

could always relate anything, chiefly himself. His world and his personality gradually began to break up into separate, incoherent fragments corresponding to different, relative coodinates. And when this happened, man began to lose his inner identity, that is, his identity with himself. Along with it, of course, he lost a lot of other things, too, including a sense of his own continuity, a hierarchy of experience and values, and so on. It's as if we were playing for a number of different teams at once, each with different uniforms, and as though—and this is the main thing—we didn't know which one we ultimately belonged to, which of those teams was really ours.

What psychological effect does it have on a writer if his books can't appear on the domestic market?

It obviously differs from writer to writer. Some come to terms with it more easily than others. For some, it makes writing harder; others may even find that it frees them internally. If you know that no one will publish you anyway, you don't have to worry about what you assume to be the taste of editors and censors and so on. I frankly worry less about those who have already published and become known than I do about those who haven't yet published anything and who still can't today, not because their names are blacklisted—they couldn't possibly be, for the simple reason that they haven't made a name for themselves yet—but because what they write does not fit into the narrow framework of what, today, is possible and publishable. Established writers are banned today, true, but society continues to think of them as writers and take an interest in their work. Let's face it, such writers have it easier today, at least they find it easier to get published abroad, and they have easier access to the unofficial domestic market—I mean, in manuscript form. Ask someone if he wants the new Hrabal and he will naturally say yes, because everyone knows who Hrabal is and everyone is interested in his new work.

But try asking someone if he wants the new Vopička! He'll just give you a dumb look because he won't know who you're talking about.

I meant the question personally, though. What does this do to your psyche?

When I was associated with the Theatre on the Balustrade and my plays were produced there, I got used to being in living contact with theatre, with that "metabolism" or inter-change between author and audience. Naturally I miss that, but being banned has not affected me as much as it has many of my colleagues. One reason is that, as I've said, I don't have a new play ready any more often than roughly once every two years. Whereas some of my colleagues—some-one like Ludvík Vaculík, for instance—were used to having steady, uninterrupted contact with readers through the news-papers they wrote for. Another important factor is that not being published is really nothing new for me. When I was young, I wrote "for the drawer" for many years, because publishing my texts was out of the question. When I began to write plays, I didn't really think they would ever be pro-duced, and later, when this started to happen, I couldn't help feeling that it was all a bit of a fluke. And so when I look back, I realize that my period at the Balustrade, when I was being produced and got recognition and even made it into the textbooks and histories of theatre, was in fact very brief compared with the period that preceded and then followed it. If I'm known, then it's really only because of those five years, and that writing "for the drawer" is more natural and usual for me. Whereas writers who were used to having their things published officially from their student days on are probably much worse off than I am. To tell you the truth, I suffer far more from the impediments I find within myself, and which have to do with trying to find my "second wind."

Quite a few of the writers in Czechoslovakia who have meant some-thing in the three decades since the war have been members of the Communist Party. You never were. Why not?

I consider myself a socialist. I even think that I have taken something from Marxism. But I have never identified with the ideology of the communist movement, in other words, I have never been a communist—and therefore, naturally, I've never been in the Communist Party of Czechoslovakia. I have never accepted communist ideology, not even the re-form ideology, and this is probably because the world appears to me a thousand times more complex and mysterious than it does to communists. Their feeling that they have com-pletely understood the world—except perhaps for a couple of details which they will soon master—is alien to me. They may have understood some things correctly, but they have greatly exaggerated that understanding and moreover, they have gone against that understanding in practice and thus have become alienated from themselves. In any case, anyone who can look at this matter truly dialectically will see at once that this alienation was inevitable, and not just a tragic mistake or an oversight, as some reform communists would have it.

Have you ever felt handicapped by not belonging to the Communist Party?

I can't say that I have. If I longed to be the director of a brewery, for instance, or Minister of Communications, or a secretary in the Union of Writers, it would be a handicap. But I've never had such ambitions, though many suspect that I do and that in reality I am hungry for power. And the am-bitions I did have I could ultimately realize quite well without belonging to the Communist Party, though not without com-plications, of course.

How did your attitudes toward politics take shape? What traditions influenced you the most?

I grew up in the spirit of Masarykian humanism. The first books I found in our library at home and read were books from that tradition, and at first I must have been influenced by them, even though later the influence was transformed—as it almost always is—into a kind of overblown adolescent rebellion against it. Later I settled down and began, gradually, to form my own view of the world. I've always been very interested in politics, but I've never wanted to be a politician. I'm not introverted, but rather a *zoon politikon*, but I don't want to take part in active politics. I want to be a writer, and I want to work in the theatre. One day I'd like to realize an ancient dream of mine—to make a movie. And I want to be involved in politics only to a degree that is appropriate to the writer's estate—that is, as someone who comments on it rather than someone who actually does it. Or more precisely, as someone who does it only by commenting on it.

Since we're on the subject of politics, I'd like to ask you what you think the main feature of Czech politics is?

I'd rather not talk about Czech politics as a whole. I would only say, though, that there is one line in Czech politics that I consider very dangerous, and it keeps cropping up again and again in one form or another, regardless of the thousands of times it's been proven wrong. I'm talking about "degenerate realism," which is to say, not the realism of Havlíček or Masaryk, but the "realism" summed up in the old saying that a bird in the hand is worth two in the bush. It's a provincial political tradition. Instead of attempting what all proper politics aims at—which is transcending the limitations of the socio-historical state of society—"degenerate realism" not only tries to come to terms with those limitations, but it reinforces them as well. I'm talking about the "realism" of the Czech representatives in the Austrian Assembly, with their back-room deals and their humiliating concessions, the "realism" of the stifling party squabbles in the First Republic, the "realism" of Beneš's position on the Munich crisis, the "realism" of the sentimental, self-pityingly patriotic philosophy of the Second Republic, the "realism" of the Hácha conception of Bohemia as an oasis of peace and quiet in a stormy Europe, the "realism" of the slavish postwar orientation toward Stalin that both Beneš and Gottwald indulged in, and the "realism" of Husák's consolidation process. This line, of course, faithfully mirrors the long and involved evolution of Czech society, but—as I've already said—politics shouldn't just traipse along after society, offering its services and ultimately only confirming everything given in it; it should try, intelligently, to transcend the framework of what is given and somehow to squeeze out of society the best and the most promising qualities in it, rather than complacently relying on the worst.

[...]

To come back to literature for a moment, there is a huge gap between the part of Czech literature that you belong to and the official world of politics that decides which authors will be published and which will not. Are you willing to make some concessions to narrow that gap? And are such concessions even possible?

I occasionally get asked this question and I never know what to say. The thing is, I haven't a clue what is meant by it. Or what concessions I might make. Naturally I'm not going to write something I don't believe—neither in my plays nor in my prose: it's simply out of the question. What other concessions could I possibly offer? Should I give my plays to a theatre run by people I have serious doubts about? That's a somewhat absurd alternative, because as we know, such an offer will never be made. But even if it were made, it's hard to talk about this hypothetically, since everything would depend on the situation as a whole. In general, I am quite prepared to make such concessions, because I know that theatres are never run, in any situation, exclusively by the people dramatists would most like to see run them. But whether I would do such a thing under any circumstances, I just don't know. I could hardly imagine, for instance, agreeing to a production of my play in a situation where most of my colleagues are banned. That would seem immoral to me. In any case, even if there were to be a gradual lifting of those bans, I'll probably be one of the last in line.

[. . .]

Have you ever thought about emigrating as a way out of your present situation?

I would love to travel. I'd love to live for a long time in America, which I find immensely fascinating. But I would never want to be an émigré, and I've never seriously given any thought to that possibility.

[. . .]

Do you ever reminisce about 1968?

To tell you the truth, if I ever reminisce at all, then it's about the whole 1960s. That was an extraordinarily interesting, fertile, and inspiring period, not only here, but in the culture of the entire world. Personally, too, it was a relatively happy time: 1968 was, for me, just a natural climax of that whole period.

[. . .]

What gives you the most real satisfaction? Have you experienced something you might call happiness in the last few years?

I experience a lot of small, everyday pleasures. I feel happy when the weather is fine, when our roses aren't frostbitten, when my letter to Dr. Husák speaks to someone's soul, when I get a beautiful letter from Alfred Radok, when my friends come to see me and we have a good party, when I cook a meal that everyone likes, when we burn less fuel than we thought we would, when the carpenter made us a nice piece of furniture and charged us less than I expected, and so on. But I get the greatest pleasure—and unfortunately this is becoming rarer and rarer—when I finish writing something and feel that it's finished and that I accomplished what I set out to do.

Do you ever expect to see a premiere of one of your plays in a Prague theatre again?

That depends on how long I live. If I die tomorrow, or next year, then I won't. But if I'm here until I'm sixty, let's say, then I will certainly live to see it.

April 1975

The Trial

"The Trial" (October 1976): In September 1976, Havel managed to be one of the few nonparticipants allowed in to observe the trial in Prague of four musicians from the Czech underground music scene, including Ivan Jirous, artistic director of "The Plastic People of the Universe," a rock band that found itself at the center of a growing underground music scene. Havel describes the circumstances surrounding the trial in *Disturbing the Peace*. The fundamental shift in attitude described in this essay was shared by many other writers and intellectuals, and led to the creation of the human rights group called Charter 77. The essay was widely circulated inside Czechoslovakia. Its first appearance in English was in a book called *The Merry Ghetto*, which was included in The Plastic People's first record album, *Egon Bondy's Happy Hearts Club Banned*, published by Invisible Records in Paris (1978). The present translation, by Paul Wilson, is adapted from that version.

I T DOESN'T often happen and when it does it usually happens when least expected: somewhere, something slips out of joint and suddenly a particular event, because of an unforeseen interplay between its inner premises and more or less fortuitous external circumstances, crosses the threshold of its usual place in the everyday world, breaks through the shell of what it is supposed to be and what it seems, and reveals its innermost symbolic significance. And something originally quite ordinary suddenly casts a surprising light on the time and the world we live in, and dramatically highlights its fundamental questions.

On the surface of things, nothing special happened. The trial took place on schedule, lasted as long as it was supposed to, and turned out as intended: with the conviction of the defendants. Yet everything one saw here was clearly and compellingly more than that, so much so that even those who had the least reason to admit it could feel it. This sensation was in the air from the start, and it intensified relentlessly from hour to hour. The strangest thing of all was that nothing could be done about it. Once begun, the game had to be played out, only to reveal, ultimately, how terribly entangled those who started it had become in the web of their own prestige: rather than simply calling a halt and admitting their error, they let this disgraceful spectacle carry on to the end.

The players in this spectacle found themselves in a paradoxical situation. The more candidly they played their role, the more clearly they revealed its unpremeditated significance, and thus they gradually became co-creators of a drama utterly different from the one they thought they were playing in, or wanted to play in.

What was the public prosecutor originally supposed to have been in this trial? Undoubtedly a plausible spokesman and guardian of society's interests, convincingly demonstrating how offensive, vulgar, immoral, and antisocial the defendants' creative work was.

But what did this man become? The symbol of an inflated, narrow-minded power, persecuting everything that does not fit into its sterile notions of life, everything unusual, risky, self-taught, and unbribable, everything that is too artless and too complex, too accessible and too mysterious, everything in fact that is different from itself. He was a mouthpiece for the world of spiritual manipulation, opportunism, emotional sterility, banality, and moral prudery. In short, he represented the world of the "masters," those masters who for as long as we can remember—whether they spoke in religious, liberal, patriotic, or socialist platitudes—have always tried to turn artists into lackeys, and whom artists have always rebelled against, or at least ridiculed. At the same time this cramped, unimaginative, and humorless man stood cloaked in the garb that "masters" traditionally don when they try to deal with an unclassifiable creative phenomenon: the garb of histrionic disgust at moral degeneration and lack of respect for traditional values.

What did Ivan Jirous and his friends in the dock wish to be? Certainly not heroes who, like Dimitrov, would rise from the dock to become prosecutors and condemn the world that was trying to condemn them. I doubt they had any other aim in mind than persuading the court of their innocence and defending their right to compose and sing the songs they wanted. What did the author of the scenario want them to be? Repulsive, long-haired hooligans from the "underworld," as they were treated by the director of Czechoslovak Television, to be rejected in disgust by all serious people.

But what did they ultimately become? The unintentional personification of those forces in man that compel him to search for himself, to determine his own place in the world freely, and in his own way, not to make deals with his heart and not to cheat his conscience, to call things by their true names and to penetrate—as Pavel Zajíček said at the trial—to the "deeper level of being," and to do so at one's own risk, aware that at any time one may come up against the disfavor of the "masters," the incomprehension of the dull-witted, or their own limitations.

And what, finally, did the presiding judge try to be? My feeling is that at the outset, she simply wanted to be an objective arbiter, listening without prejudice to the arguments of the prosecution and the defense, the testimony of the witnesses and the defendants, and come to a just decision.

But what did the trial turn her into? The tragic symbol of a judiciary incapable of maintaining its independence and handing down the kind of verdicts that flow from the human, civil, and legal conscience of the judges; a judiciary fully aware of how it is manipulated by power, but incapable of defying that power and so, ultimately, accepting the pitiful role of a subordinated employee of the "masters."

And what was the whole trial meant to be? Obviously no more than an ordinary element in the practice of justice that traditionally converts human lives, actions, and crimes into a boring pile of documents, files, reports, and articles, a routine treatment of one of hundreds of similar crimes. This superficial similarity to ordinary criminal cases, by the way, was maintained for some time. A great deal of time was spent hearing dozens of written and oral eyewitness accounts that dealt at great length with questions such as whether, at a concert of "The Plastic People of the Universe" in Bojanovice or Postupice, the doors to the hall were open or closed.

Soon, however, this facade of judicial thoroughness and objectivity began to appear as a mere smokescreen to hide what the trial really was: an impassioned debate about the meaning of human existence, an urgent questioning of what one should expect from life, whether one should silently accept the world as it is presented to one and slip obediently into one's prearranged place in it, or whether one has the strength to exercise free choice in the matter; whether one should be "reasonable" and take one's place in the world, or whether one has the right to resist in the name of one's own human convictions.

For a long time, I sought, without much success, for the best way to characterize this process of "slipping out of joint."

Was it depressing? Of course it was: what other feelings could have been aroused when the most humanly authentic impression was made by those who sat in the dock, surrounded by policemen and even taken to the toilet in handcuffs? Or by the fact that the defense lawyers presented an excellent and exhaustive defense, the accused pleaded their innocence convincingly, and the case for the prosecution gradually fell into disarray, all in a situation where—as everyone must have known—the accused had already been found guilty long before? And anyway, the whole case was depressing simply because it had slipped out of joint. How could it have been otherwise, when this controversy over the meaning of human life took place here, in the district court for the Prague-West region, and when no one present could do the one thing that was appropriate in this situation: stand up and shout: "Enough of this comedy! Case dismissed!"?

Was it moving? Naturally. There were moments when a lump came to one's throat, such as when Svatopluk Karásek said quietly that if Jirous was found guilty, he wanted to be found guilty, too. From the legal point of view, this was obvious nonsense, but at that moment and in those circumstances, it was so humanly right that it told us more in a single second about the essence of the case than a whole pile of official documents.

At times it was tense, at times disturbing, at times agonizing (there were moments when one felt like shouting); very often, on the contrary, it flung one back into the world of sheer absurdity.

But none of this does justice to the experience. At a deeper level it was, oddly enough, not depressing at all. There was even something elevating about it. This was perhaps because of the very awareness that we were participants in a unique illumination of the world. But chiefly, I suppose, it was the exciting realization that there are still people among us who assume the existential responsibility for their own truth and are willing to pay a high price for it. (Whereas those who judge them can only depend on the collective backing of a colossal social power and would rather send someone to prison for no reason at all than risk even a minor blemish on their record.)

Somewhere deep down, however, I discerned yet another element in this experience, perhaps the most important of all. It was something that aroused me, a challenge that was all the more urgent for being unintentional. It was the challenge of example. Suddenly, much of the wariness and caution that marks my behavior seemed petty to me. I felt an increased revulsion toward all forms of guile, all attempts at painlessly worming one's way out of vital dilemmas. Suddenly, I discovered in myself more determination in one direction, and more independence in another. Suddenly, I felt disgusted with a whole world, in which—as I realized then—I still have one foot: the world of emergency exits.

As we have seen, if a certain event slips out of joint—and if it does so in the deeper sense that I have in mind here—then inevitably something slips out of joint in ourselves, too: a new view of the world gives us a new view of our own human potential, of what we are and might be. Abruptly jerked out of our "routine humanness," we stand once more face to face with the most important question of all: How do we settle accounts with ourselves?

I would probably not be writing about this challenging aspect of things at all were I not convinced that it is not simply a product of my tendency to dramatize (for which I am often taken to task, by the way). But it was not. The universality of this feeling was underlined as well by the fact that it seeped out of the hermetically sealed courtroom into the corridors and stairwells of the courthouse. Only the exalting awareness of an important, shared experience, and only the urgency of the challenge that everyone felt in it, could have explained the rapid genesis of that very special, improvised community that came into being here for the duration of the trial, and which was definitely something more than an accidental assembly of friends of the accused and people who were interested in the trial. For instance, a new and quite unusual etiquette appeared: no one bothered with introductions, getting acquainted, or feeling one another out. The usual conventions were dropped and the usual reticence disappeared, and this happened right before the eyes of several squads of those "others" (though they wore no uniforms, they were identifiable at once). Dozens of things were discussed that many of us, in other circumstances, might have been afraid to talk about even with one other person. It was a community of people who were not only more considerate, communicative, and trusting toward each other, they were in a strange way democratic. A distinguished, elderly gentleman, a former

member of the praesidium of the Communist Party of Czechoslovakia, spoke with long-haired youths he'd never seen in
his life before, and they spoke uninhibitedly with him, though
they had known him only from photographs. In this situation,
all reserve and inner reticence seemed to lose its point; in
this atmosphere, all the inevitable "buts" seemed ridiculous,
insignificant, and evasive. Everyone seemed to feel that at a
time when all the chips are down, there are only two things
one can do: gamble everything, or throw in the cards.

On the second day of the trial, when I left the courthouse
on Karmelitská Street and walked to the Malá Strana Café
(where we all went, us and the "others"), and I was still so full
of impressions that I could scarcely think of anything else, I
met a certain Czech film director of the middle generation.
When he asked me how I was, I replied, none too logically,
that I had just been at a trial of the Czech underground. He
asked whether it was about those drugs. I said that it had
nothing to do with drugs at all, and I tried, succinctly, to
explain the essence of things. When I had finished, he nod-
ded and then said, "Apart from that, what else are you up
to?"

Perhaps I'm doing him an injustice, but at that moment, I
was overwhelmed by an intense feeling that this dear man
belonged to a world that I no longer wish to have anything
to do with—and Mr. Public Prosecutor Kovařík, pay attention, because here comes a vulgar word—I mean the world of
cunning shits.

October 1976

Article 202

"Article 202" (January 1978) and the essay following it, "Article 203" (April 1978), reveal the kind of thinking that lay behind the creation of VONS, the Committee to Defend the Unjustly Prosecuted, for which Havel and others later went to prison. VONS monitored trials, wrote reports and updates that were sent to the authorities and circulated abroad, offered assistance to the families of prisoners, and tried to ensure that no case of unjust prosecution went unnoticed. VONS is now an official organization and still active in Czechoslovakia. In one recent (Fall 1990) report, it condemned the arrest of two communists for "slandering the President." Both these essays were circulated in *samizdat* inside Czechoslovakia. This is their first appearance in English. Translations by Paul Wilson.

I T WAS midnight on a Sunday, and two friends and I were looking for a place in Prague where we could have a glass of wine. Oddly enough, we found one that was not only open, and on Sunday, but it was open until one o'clock. The door was locked, which was not unusual, so we rang the bell. Nothing happened. After a short pause, we rang again. Again, nothing happened. After a longer pause this time, we knocked politely. Still nothing happened. Just as we were about to walk away, the door suddenly opened, not for us, of course, but because the headwaiter was letting one of his friends out. Seizing the opportunity, we asked him, politely, if there might not be room for us inside. Without even bothering to tell us that he was full, or that he didn't want any more customers, or that he was letting only his friends in, in fact, without so much as a reply or a shake of his head or even a glance, the headwaiter simply slammed the door in our faces.

So far, there is nothing unusual in this story: such things happen every night in Prague outside the doors of the few pubs and wine bars left for the use of ordinary citizens.

What is unusual is what happened next: I lost my temper. If I say it's unusual, that's because I'm not at all a short-tempered person, and I rarely have the kind of tantrums in which the world goes dark before my eyes and I'm capable of doing things I would never normally do; if they happen at all, then at the most only once every seven to ten years. When they do occur, such tantrums are never provoked by anything important, like being arrested, or insulted, or having my flat confiscated; the cause is always something petty. (Once, in the army, a Private Ulver tripped me as a joke, and I suddenly found myself pounding him.) In that sense, my tantrum in front of the wine bar was entirely consistent with my personal tradition.

I don't exclude the possibility that the petty things that so anger me may often be merely substitutes for the big things that don't seem to upset me. Perhaps somewhere in the basement of my calm soul a mysterious battery is slowly charging, and when the potential of this secretly accumulated exasperation reaches a certain level, the first petty irritation suddenly causes the entire charge to be released for what seem to be utterly inappropriate reasons. And Ulver, the innocent practical joker, is cruelly punished because I have had to spend two years building pontoon bridges and taking them down again.

So I lost my temper and began furiously kicking the door of the wine bar. (Oddly enough, there was no damage; the door was obviously made of thick glass.) Naturally, my behavior was absurd and reprehensible; I was behaving like a hooligan. My rational mind knew this, but at that moment, it was not in control.

The wine bar door was probably playing the same role that

Private Ulver had played years before. It was being kicked for all the disparagement, the contempt, the humiliation, the rudeness and lack of respect that are, more and more, the daily lot of anonymous man on his journey through life. It was kicked for all that time spent waiting in offices, standing in line at the store, for all the institutions that never answer polite letters, for all the ordinary policemen who can no longer talk to a citizen except as an officer to his batboy, for all that strange conspiracy of finks and informers and black marketeers who have managed to drive the once innocent gaiety out of Prague nightlife. It was probably even kicked for those fellows who kicked Ladislav Hejdánek, or twisted the arms of the Tomín children on the staircase of the apartment block where the Uhls live. It was kicked for all the contemptuous disdain of officials and the fearful timidity of those who are not, a disdain and a timidity that are slowly but surely invading every aspect of life and dehumanizing all manner of living relationships and environments. It was, in short, the outburst of a helpless man who has projected into this minor indignity all the large and complex indignities that surround his life.

None of this, of course, excuses my violent act. On the contrary, it was no way to deal with the whole situation; I was merely succumbing to it. But people are not superhuman and it's no surprise that they occasionally snap. Especially when something is always making them tense.

What followed is not at all surprising: the headwaiter (a mountain of a man) ran into the street, caught me by the collar and, with the help of a friend, dragged me into the wine bar, where both of them began to beat me, yelling at me as they did so that I was a filthy son-of-a-bitch and that they would call the police, who would kick my teeth in. Because my anger had long since been discharged, I behaved realistically, that is to say, like a coward: I did not defend myself. I have my realism to thank for the fact that they soon grew tired of hitting me, and threw me back out into the street. I had gotten off without serious harm being done. My rather rash protest against a minor humiliation (that the waiter had ignored our request) had no serious consequences only be-cause I had silently endured a greater humiliation (allowing myself be beaten).

But what would have happened had I acted like a man and defended myself?

1. In the first place, I would have paid the tax that is usually paid for such manliness: I would have lost an ear and several teeth, I would have had a broken nose and an arm, two black eyes, and blood on my overcoat.

2. A more serious consequence, however, would have been that as the one who started it all by kicking the door, I would probably have been charged and found guilty of disturbing the peace, according to Article 202 of the Criminal Code, which would mean that I'd probably have been given a sec-ond conditional sentence (that is, if I weren't sent straight to jail for the sum of both sentences, with the added advantage, for them, that this time, I wouldn't be a "political" prisoner).

3. An article would appear in the Prague *Evening News* about an incident in front of a wine bar involving the great human rights activist.

4. A lot of circumspect people would say it was my own fault for behaving like a hooligan.

None of that happened. But I realized that Article 202 is lurking out there every step of the way and that, moreover, it has established its own diplomatic mission inside each one of us. I also realized how this paragraph can entangle a temper-amental person in a vicious circle.

Observe the following:

1. Phase one: the spread of humiliation throughout society creates the conditions in which someone like that is bound to lose his temper one day and create a minor "disturbance."

2. As soon as that happens, he can be subjected, by those who have humiliated him, to a new and far deeper humilia-tion, and, if he is incapable of responding "realistically," as I

was, he will defend himself. Once he does so, however, he commits a far more serious "disturbance of the peace," perhaps even "assault on a peace officer."

3. Regardless of how he is punished, humiliation triumphs once more, this time the worst kind of all. If a truly temperamental person is involved, he will thus find himself well on the way to committing some kind of super-disturbance, the consequences of which don't bear thinking about.

Where does all this end?

Isn't the specter of this vicious circle one of the ways to induce in people the required "realism," including the surrender of one's own dignity and honor and the acceptance of what amounts to an official moral commandment: "Don't try to put out a fire that's not burning you"? (A friend of mine was once sentenced for disturbing the peace because he slapped a man who had insulted his girlfriend.)

Everyone knows that people shouldn't slap each other around whenever they feel like it, or kick the doors to wine bars with impunity. And yet there is something about this Article 202 that I find suspect. Not long ago, I talked about it with a lawyer, who told me it was an "import from the East" that has no legal precedent in this country. It is not a political law, but it is the child of a certain way of governing. And in any case, it has some things in common with political laws.

1. It is malleable: essentially anything can be called disturbing the peace if someone declares that it has offended him— a real paradise for informers.

2. The way the article is used depends more than is healthy on the political and spiritual climate. If Ivan Jirous had behaved ten times as eccentrically in 1963 (when he opened the first show of Jiří Laciný's work) as he did in 1977 (when he opened Laciný's most recent show), it would never have occurred to anyone to arrest him and charge him with disturbing the peace, as they have done now.

3. It may easily be, and often is, used for political repres-

sion. Do you need to clap some nonconformist band in jail?
Accuse them of disturbing the peace. Do you want to stop a
group of young people from meeting at someone's place? Just
lock the host up for disturbing the peace; you can always cook
up some evidence, and it's easy to find an "outraged" witness.
Do you want to make life miserable for a Charter 77 signatory? Just wait until he's had a little too much to drink and is
sick in an empty streetcar—and there's your disturbance of
the peace. (How many such "disturbers of the peace" could
be found in our present political establishment if they were
to apply this law in the same way to themselves? Or on the
contrary, what would have become of the artistic avant-garde
between the wars if Article 202 had existed then and the bourgeois government of the time had applied it politically in this
fashion?)

4. Accusations are made, or not, entirely according to the
whims of the authorities. If, for instance, the director of an
important Prague factory were to rant and rave on Wenceslas
Square and I were to be outraged to the point where I would
file a suit against him, the prosecutor's office would merely
laugh at it or—which is more probable—they would send my
suit straight to Martinovský, who would file it away in the
collection of documents he has against me. Whereas if I were
the one to rant and rave and the factory director were doing
the reporting, I would probably be found guilty of disturbing the peace.

5. It may easily be, and often is, used to settle personal
accounts. If Mr. A, who is an enemy of Mr. B, has a good
position, all he has to do is say he is outraged by Mr. B's
behavior, and Mr. B will find himself saddled with Article 202,
when all he may have done is complained about the boss, or
about "conditions," or used a crude word, or dressed differently, or have different habits, sing in the stairwell, or have a
dog that barks too loudly.

Everything indicates that Article 202 of our Criminal Code
was created as one of the countless instruments by which the

centralist authorities (originally Czarist, now obviously our own) keep their citizens under permanent control. People may not know very much about the article, but they cannot help but feel it in the air. It is a law that faithfully mirrors a power that is happiest when people don't socialize too much with each other (that is, unless the authorities organize and control it themselves), when they don't go out very often and, when they do go out, always behave quietly, inconspicuously, and with proper humility. It's a power that finds it convenient when people keep an eye on each other, watch each other, are afraid of each other, a power that sees society as an obedient herd whose duty is to be permanently grateful that it has what it has.

I would be interested to know how many people in prison now are there because of Article 202 and what they did to get there. None of them are considered political prisoners and nothing is really known about them. Specific facts about the application of this paragraph might tell us more about conditions in our country and the nature of social power than what we can learn from the known facts about how overtly political laws are applied. What do we know about how many minor expressions of civic discontent have been quickly and easily avenged by this law? About how many personal accounts, masked in a servile loyalty, have been settled? About how many powerless and defenseless people have had their lives ruined for doing something foolish that a powerful person can do with impunity as often as he wants? About how many of those in prison are victims of this application of arbitrary power? And not only that: can it be judged at all how this paragraph has contributed to the leveling, the uniformity, the blandness, and the deadening of life? How it has contributed to the flourishing of informing, to the boom in selfish conformity, to the apathy, the general timidity, and the decline in spontaneous joy of life? How it has become part of the atmosphere of the world in which we live?

I repeat that one should not kick at the door of a wine bar and that every society has the right to defend itself against hooligans and vandals who do that kind of thing. That is one matter.

But this omnipresent, elastic Article 202, which can be used against anyone at any time—especially in *their* hands—that is another matter.

Political trials are a lot of work and make a lot of noise. And people don't really believe in the outcome. Article 202 is much more workable: in the end, who wants to come to the defense of some violent hooligans?

At the same time, the possibilities are limitless: someday, perhaps, an inconspicuous sneer will be enough, a scarcely audible "hurrah," a moment of suspicious reverie, a different-colored tie.

It's definitely a law with a future.

You might call it the law of the future.

The law of 1984.

At the end of 1977, I was able to get away—barely, and at a rather depressing price—with kicking the door of a wine bar. Would I get away with it this year?

January 1978

Article 203

The earth is trembling,
What can it be?
Don't worry
It's just the nation at work ...

—Charlie Soukup

T HANKS to the fact that I was only, formally, a criminal prisoner that time and was therefore not isolated from the rest, I met during those six weeks of investigative custody, on various occasions (at the doctor's, taking a shower, in the exercise yard) roughly fifty other prisoners, and I was able to ask them what they were in for. It may seem unbelievable, but despite the fact that the Czechoslovak Criminal Code has three hundred articles, at least thirty of those fifty prisoners were being prosecuted under the same single article: parasitism, Article 203. I can't claim that my accidental encounters form a representative sampling of the people in investigative custody or of those serving their sentences. But since statistics of that kind are strictly secret, I can only draw on my own experience and assume that more than half the population in Czechoslovak prisons have been prosecuted and punished for parasitism.

Where, in a nation of traditional hard workers, did so many parasites come from?

Prisoners—at least as far as their own cases are concerned—don't usually lie. What I heard from all those "parasites" gave me this answer to my question: There are so many of them only because most of them are not parasites at all.

An old man washes dishes in a pub and at the same time—in a very dilatory fashion—he goes about getting an invalid pension for himself. The pubkeeper hires him "on the sly," that is, without a proper contract. They are discovered—and the result? The old man is charged with Article 203 and finds himself in custody.

A worker isn't allowed to do the work he's qualified for, the trade union won't back him up, he gets mad and stops going to work, and foolishly waits for them to come to him. Something like a private strike. A month later they do come to him—but with an indictment based on Article 203, so they can drag him off to prison.

But these are far from being the most drastic cases. Most "parasites" are people who have simply quit one job and, before they have managed to find another, are stopped and have their ID booklets checked by the police, who discover they haven't got a valid stamp from their employer, and so they are accused of parasitism and thrown in jail. I have spoken to people who were waiting for trial simply because they were out of work for a month, or even three weeks. They can be sent to prison for up to three years (more, if they are repeat offenders). These people, of course, do not correspond in the least to the popular image of a "parasite": they are not charming gigolos, kept men, or playboys, but ordinary workers, overworked fellows with large families, people who have obviously worked hard all their lives (and it's not surprising that these people find the inactivity of investigative custody hardest of all to take).

There are thousands of them. Yes, in a country that calls itself a workers' state, the prisons are full of workers.

The right to work is entrenched in the Czechoslovak Constitution. But the constitution says nothing about the duty to work. And yet the duty to work exists here—enshrined in Article 203. And this is not a hidden duty to work, but one that is quite blatant: the police, the investigators, and the public prosecutors talk about it openly: if you don't have a stamp from your employer in your ID booklet, you are considered to have broken the law.

Article 203 says: "Anyone who systematically evades honest work and allows himself to be supported by someone else, or gains his living in some other underhanded manner, shall be liable to imprisonment for up to three years."

At first glance, there is nothing terrible about this. But the way the law is applied is quite alarming:

1. The undefined notion of "systematic evasion" is simply never taken into account: practically anyone can be prosecuted for parasitism who remains without proper employment for a certain period; the length of that period is entirely up to the whim of the officials, or of current trends.

2. The vague notion of "honest work" is automatically interpreted to mean official employment. That people who have official employment may systematically evade honest work, or that it is possible to work honestly without such employment—such considerations, obviously, interest no one.

3. The other indication of parasitism, that is, gaining a living "in an underhanded manner," also remains undefined and therefore it too can be interpreted according to the whim of the moment; often, no effort is made to prove it at all. Guilty verdicts are frequently brought in if only the first condition is fulfilled: "evading honest work." That a person may live from savings, from lottery winnings, from unofficial literary activity (as in my case), from an inheritance, etc., and that it is ultimately his own business—none of this is taken into account. And if the investigator takes the trouble to look for something "underhanded," then any trifle at all may serve as proof. I have met people who were serving a sentence for "parasitism" only because they borrowed two hundred crowns from a friend and had the misfortune not to be employed and to have been arrested before they had a chance to return the money, or ask their friend to forgive the loan. Many—in separate conversations—assured me that it was enough for two people to testify that they had given the accused supper or had paid his tab in a pub to prove that his "living" had been gained in an "underhanded manner." One worker—who was even properly employed at the time—was charged according to Article 203

because a co-worker had invited him to the cafeteria and he had let her pay the bill, which was 175 crowns; they then had a falling out and she turned him in. In this case, all that was required, for a change, was the second indication of guilt (support by someone else)—clearly an absurd application—for them to lay a serious charge of parasitism on an employed worker and throw him into prison.

4. The application of Article 203 does not respect the main principle of any decent legal code since the time of ancient Rome, which is that guilt, and not innocence, must be proven. The investigators, the prosecutors, the judges, and even many of the defense attorneys take it for granted that they do not have to show that the accused supported himself in an "underhanded way," but that, on the contrary, it is up to the defendant to explain how he makes his living, in other words, to establish his own innocence. Unproved innocence is taken as a proof of guilt, so that if the defendant, for instance, cannot show that he is living from his savings, this is considered proof that he is a parasite. (The point here is not whether he can provide proof of innocence or not, but the illegitimacy of demanding that he provide that proof in the first place.)

A single vague and inconspicuous little sentence at the heart of Article 203 is thus, thanks to its vagueness, and thanks to its arbitrary and often illegitimate application, the key to extraordinarily tough and widespread measures taken against all persons who in any way go against the nonexistent law that every citizen must be permanently employed. (The little sentence that underwrites this practice is, at the same time, dubious even in the little it does say: I have serious doubts about the moral right of society to punish citizens for being supported by other citizens, that is, even when it is the free choice of both the parties involved. But that is another question: I am not trying to analyze the legal code here, merely to consider some of its practical applications.)

Where are we to seek the causes of this puzzling state of

affairs? Is there perhaps some hidden intention here (derived, for instance, from the requirements of the national economy)? Or is it merely an oversight, deriving from a misunderstanding of the lawgiver's intention? Is it simply a bad habit of certain departments of state power, or a mistaken attempt to stem the deepening demoralization of workers not by dealing with its causes, but by sanctioning its results?

All of these things may play a role. But in my opinion, the most essential cause of the whole phenomenon lies elsewhere: the notion that everyone must have constant, and if possible unchanging, employment, confirmed by a stamp in his or her ID booklet, is ultimately nothing more and nothing less than a product of a system in which people are mere cogs in the social machinery, cogs that have meaning only insofar as they blindly carry out the function assigned to them. Such a notion, however, assumes that the machine operator must be able to check on the cogs at all times, must have perfect control over how they work, and must not allow them the slightest deviation, autonomy, or private intention—nothing that would even faintly resemble freedom.

What we have here is the inevitable result of a system which by its very nature must know, at all times, where you are, what you are doing, whom you are influenced by, and how much you earn, just as it must know where you live, how you live, whom you live with, where you go and how you get there, what you read, the people you meet, what you think. [...]

The principle of the duty to work is an aspect of the absolute right the state exercises over people: it is the logical expression of state centralism, which has as its ideal the quasi-military organization of society; it is merely the natural expression of the necrophilic nature of bureaucratic power (as Fromm analyzed it).

If, however, the increasingly tough measures taken against every irregularity in employment come from a misguided understanding of life and the place of work in it (not as a way of liberating man, but as an instrument of his increasing enslavement) that is proper to the present political system, this means that most of the "parasites" who are locked up today are, in fact, indirect political prisoners.

I don't want to idealize them all and turn them into lambs of God. But I'm convinced that in an overwhelming number of cases, these people don't belong in prison. They are not dumb. Most of them are only unfortunate people, hard-luck cases, losers, people who aren't clever enough, or adaptable enough. Often they are victims of their own "incapacity for freedom," people who couldn't stand it any longer and tried, for a while, to disengage themselves from the galley-slave notion of labor; petty rebels against the vacuous order of the bureaucratic-consumer society; people who simply cannot spend their whole lives feudally chained to a single workbench and who are incapable of finding a smart way of camouflaging the transcendental breeze that still ruffles the surface of their souls. Many find themselves on the fringes of society and are branded as criminals only because they refused to fit into the anonymous life on the housing estates; they remain individuals whose colorful stories stand out so dangerously against the horizon of general grayness. The typical "parasite" in Ruzyně Prison, in short, strikes me as a sad product of an age that demands that people pay for their external happiness with the loss of their own identity. It is a sacrifice they make for a time which, in its very essence, denies and must deny to people one of their most important human rights: the right to movement, in the widest sense of that word. (It is not uninteresting to note that from the ethnic point of view, those most frequently punished for "parasitism" today have the strongest "ethno-genetic" tendency toward nomadism—the Gypsies.)

What at first seems paradoxical is in fact inevitable: ultimately the present system not only limits people as human beings, but also as consumers: for is not a certain spontaneous ebb and flow in the labor pool, a consequence of unplannable social situations and relationships (somewhat like the Brownian movement of molecules) a natural component of a healthy labor market, which acts as a dynamic stimulus to the economy? And is not the administrative manipulation of this sphere, drastically intensified by the present application of Article 203, just another brake on normal economic development?

I can't help but think that the spectacle of a worker who has paved streets all his life and then one day decides to stay home, and for that is sent to prison by a life-long bureaucrat, is one of the most devastating condemnations of the present bureaucratic power.

There aren't many of us, and yet we exist: intellectuals who, though we've all been pushed out of our positions and branded "has-beens," have lived—many of us for years—without steady employment. They haven't yet come looking for us with Article 203 in hand, despite the fact that they don't consider our work to be work at all (let alone "honest") and that they constantly and publicly refer to the living we make as "underhanded." True, it would be silly to expect us to be employed when no one will employ us. Still, they could demand it of us, and when we failed, it would be no problem to transform us from free "has-beens" into prisoners—parasites. Why haven't they done so yet? Why are we, of all people, better off than that old man who washed dishes without a regular contract and was too sluggish about getting his status as an invalid recognized?

Perhaps it's somewhat of an atavism: for they do, without realizing it, grant us a kind of right to be sluggish, because we are "born" intellectuals. (A worker—I mean a "born" worker—who became an unofficial poet today would quickly find himself in Ruzyně Prison.) The main reason, however, is something else: they know that we would defend ourselves.

What should our attitude be toward this special position of ours? To ask to have our "privileges" revoked would be not only ridiculous, but above all nonsense: we all know it is not a privilege at all, but simply a milder form of injustice. But we can't silently flatter ourselves that, thanks to this minor blessing, we are better off than that old man.

There is only one natural solution: we must defend him as well as ourselves.

For more than a year now, there has been a community in this country that, although it doesn't have the resources to fight for every unjustly imprisoned old man, can still do quite a bit for him. And in fact, it must do this, because part of its spiritual legacy is a revolt against the very principle of "divide and rule."

April 1978

The Power of the Powerless

To the memory of Jan Patočka

"The Power of the Powerless" (October 1978) was originally written ("quickly," Havel said later) as a discussion piece for a projected joint Polish-Czechoslovak volume of essays on the subject of freedom and power. All the participants were to receive Havel's essay, and then respond to it in writing. Twenty participants were chosen on both sides, but only the Czechoslovak side was completed. Meanwhile, in May 1979, some of the Czechoslovak contributors who were also members of VONS (the Committee to Defend the Unjustly Prosecuted), including Havel, were arrested, and it was decided to go ahead and "publish" the Czechoslovak contributions separately.

Havel's essay has had a profound impact on Eastern Europe. Here is what Zbygniew Bujak, a Solidarity activist, told me: "This essay reached us in the Ursus factory in 1979 at a point when we felt we were at the end of the road. Inspired by KOR [the Polish Workers' Defense Committee], we had been speaking on the shop floor, talking to people, participating in public meetings, trying to speak the truth about the factory, the country, and politics. There came a moment when people thought we were crazy. Why were we doing this? Why were we taking such risks? Not seeing any immediate and tangible results, we began to doubt the purposefulness of

125

what we were doing. Shouldn't we be coming up with other methods, other ways?

"Then came the essay by Havel. Reading it gave us the theoretical underpinnings for our activity. It maintained our spirits; we did not give up, and a year later—in August 1980—it became clear that the party apparatus and the factory management were afraid of us. We mattered. And the rank and file saw us as leaders of the movement. When I look at the victories of Solidarity, and of Charter 77, I see in them an astonishing fulfillment of the prophecies and knowledge contained in Havel's essay."

Translated by Paul Wilson, "The Power of the Powerless" has appeared several times in English, foremost in *The Power of the Powerless: Citizens Against the State in Central-Eastern Europe,* edited by John Keane, with an Introduction by Steven Lukes (London: Hutchinson, 1985). That volume includes a selection of nine other essays from the original Czech and Slovak collection.

I

dissent + non-conformity

A SPECTER is haunting Eastern Europe: the specter of what in the West is called "dissent." This specter has not appeared out of thin air. It is a natural and inevitable consequence of the present historical phase of the system it is haunting. It was born at a time when this system, for a thousand reasons, can no longer base itself on the unadulterated, brutal, and arbitrary application of power, eliminating all expressions of nonconformity. What is more, the system has become so ossified politically that there is practically no way for such nonconformity to be implemented within its official structures.

why it emerges

power alone fails

Who are these so-called dissidents? Where does their point of view come from, and what importance does it have? What is the significance of the "independent initiatives" in which "dissidents" collaborate, and what real chances do such initiatives have of success? Is it appropriate to refer to "dissidents" as an opposition? If so, what exactly is such an opposition within the framework of this system? What does it do? What role does it play in society? What are its hopes and on what are they based? Is it within the power of the "dissidents"—as a category of subcitizen outside the power establishment—to have any influence at all on society and the social system? Can they actually change anything?

I think that an examination of these questions—an examination of the potential of the "powerless"—can only begin with an examination of the nature of power in the circumstances in which these powerless people operate.

II

OUR SYSTEM is most frequently characterized as a dictatorship or, more precisely, as the dictatorship of a political bureaucracy over a society which has undergone economic and social leveling. I am afraid that the term "dictatorship," regardless of how intelligible it may otherwise be, tends to obscure rather than clarify the real nature of power in this system. We usually associate the term with the notion of a small group of people who take over the government of a given country by force; their power is wielded openly, using the direct instruments of power at their disposal, and they are easily distinguished socially from the majority over whom they rule. One of the essential aspects of this traditional or classical notion of dictatorship is the assumption that it is temporary, ephemeral, lacking historical roots. Its existence seems to be bound up with the lives of those who established it. It is usually local in extent and significance, and regardless of the ideology it utilizes to grant itself legitimacy, its power derives ultimately from the numbers and the armed might of its soldiers and police. The principal threat to its existence is felt to be the possibility that someone better equipped in this sense might appear and overthrow it.

Even this very superficial overview should make it clear that the system in which we live has very little in common with a classical dictatorship. In the first place, our system is not limited in a local, geographical sense; rather, it holds sway over a huge power bloc controlled by one of the two superpowers. And although it quite naturally exhibits a number of local and historical variations, the range of these variations is fundamentally circumscribed by a single, unifying framework throughout the power bloc. Not only is the dictatorship everywhere based on the same principles and structured in the same way (that is, in the way evolved by the ruling superpower), but each country has been completely penetrated by a network of manipulatory instruments controlled by the superpower center and totally subordinated to its interests. In the stalemated world of nuclear parity, of course, that circumstance endows the system with an unprecedented degree of external stability compared with classical dictatorships. Many local crises which, in an isolated state, would lead to a change in the system, can be resolved through direct intervention by the armed forces of the rest of the bloc.

In the second place, if a feature of classical dictatorships is

historical roots of E European totalitarian

their lack of historical roots (frequently they appear to be no more than historical freaks, the fortuitous consequence of fortuitous social processes or of human and mob tendencies), the same cannot be said so facilely about our system. For even though our dictatorship has long since alienated itself completely from the social movements that give birth to it, the authenticity of these movements (and I am thinking of the proletarian and socialist movements of the nineteenth century) gives it undeniable historicity. These origins provided a solid foundation of sorts on which it could build until it became the utterly new social and political reality it is today, which has become so inextricably a part of the structure of the modern world. A feature of those historical origins was the "correct" understanding of social conflicts in the period from which those original movements emerged. The fact that at the very core of this "correct" understanding there was a genetic disposition toward the monstrous alienation characteristic of its subsequent development is not essential here. And in any case, this element also grew organically from the climate of that time and therefore can be said to have its origin there as well.

ideology

One legacy of that original "correct" understanding is a third peculiarity that makes our systems different from other modern dictatorships: it commands an incomparably more precise, logically structured, generally comprehensible and, in essence, extremely flexible ideology that, in its elaborateness and completeness, is almost a secularized religion. It offers a ready answer to any question whatsoever; it can scarcely be accepted only in part, and accepting it has profound implications for human life. In an era when metaphysical and existential certainties are in a state of crisis, when people are being uprooted and alienated and are losing their sense of what this world means, this ideology inevitably has a certain hypnotic charm. To wandering humankind it offers an immediately available home: all one has to do is accept it, and suddenly everything becomes clear once more, life takes on new meaning, and all mysteries, unanswered questions, anxiety, and loneliness vanish. Of course, one pays dearly for this low-rent home: the price is abdication of one's own reason, conscience, and responsibility, for an essential aspect of this ideology is the consignment of reason and conscience to a higher authority. The principle involved here is that the center of power is identical with the center of truth. (In our case, the connection with Byzantine theocracy is direct: the highest secular authority is identical with the highest spiritual authority.) It is true of course that, all this aside, ideology no longer has any great influence on people, at least within our bloc (with the possible exception of Russia, where the serf mentality, with its blind, fatalistic respect for rulers and its automatic acceptance of all their claims, is still dominant and combined with a superpower patriotism which traditionally places the interests of empire higher than the interests of humanity). But this is not important, because ideology plays its role in our system very well (an issue to which I will return) precisely because it is what it is.

Fourth, the technique of exercising power in traditional dictatorships contains a necessary element of improvisation. The mechanisms for wielding power are for the most part not established firmly, and there is considerable room for accident and for the arbitrary and unregulated application of power. Socially, psychologically, and physically, conditions still exist for the expression of some form of opposition. In short, there are many seams on the surface which can split apart before the entire power structure has managed to stabilize. Our system, on the other hand, has been developing in the Soviet Union for over sixty years, and for approximately thirty years in Eastern Europe; moreover, several of its long-established structural features are derived from Czarist absolutism. In terms of the physical aspects of power, this has led to the creation of such intricate and well-developed mechanisms for the direct and indirect manipulation of the entire population that, as a physical power base, it represents something radically new. At the same time, let us not forget that the system is made significantly more effective by state ownership and central direction of all the means of production. This gives the power structure an unprecedented and uncontrollable capacity to invest in itself (in the areas of the bureaucracy and the police, for example) and makes it easier for that structure, as the sole employer, to manipulate the day-to-day existence of all citizens.

Finally, if an atmosphere of revolutionary excitement, heroism, dedication, and boisterous violence on all sides characterizes classical dictatorships, then the last traces of such an atmosphere have vanished from the Soviet bloc. For some time now this bloc has ceased to be a kind of enclave, isolated from the rest of the developed world and immune to processes occurring in it. To the contrary, the Soviet bloc is an integral part of that larger world, and it shares and shapes the world's destiny. This means in concrete terms that the hierarchy of values existing in the developed countries of the West has, in essence, appeared in our society (the long period of co-existence with the West has only hastened this process). In other words, what we have here is simply another form of the consumer and industrial society, with all its concomitant social, intellectual, and psychological consequences. It is impossible to understand the nature of power in our system properly without taking this into account.

The profound difference between our system—in terms of the nature of power—and what we traditionally understand by dictatorship, a difference I hope is clear even from this quite superficial comparison, has caused me to search for some term appropriate for our system, purely for the purposes of this essay. If I refer to it henceforth as a "post-totalitarian" system, I am fully aware that this is perhaps not the most precise term, but I am unable to think of a better one. I do not wish to imply by the prefix "post-" that the system is no longer totalitarian; on the contrary, I mean that it is totalitarian in a way fundamentally different from classical dictatorships, different from totalitarianism as we usually understand it.

The circumstances I have mentioned, however, form only

a circle of conditional factors and a kind of phenomenal framework for the actual composition of power in the post-totalitarian system, several aspects of which I shall now attempt to identify.

III

THE MANAGER of a fruit-and-vegetable shop places in his window, among the onions and carrots, the slogan: "Workers of the world, unite!" Why does he do it? What is he trying to communicate to the world? Is he genuinely enthusiastic about the idea of unity among the workers of the world? Is his enthusiasm so great that he feels an irrepressible impulse to acquaint the public with his ideals? Has he really given more than a moment's thought to how such a unification might occur and what it would mean?

I think it can safely be assumed that the overwhelming majority of shopkeepers never think about the slogans they put in their windows, nor do they use them to express their real opinions. That poster was delivered to our greengrocer from the enterprise headquarters along with the onions and carrots. He put them all into the window simply because it has been done that way for years, because everyone does it, and because that is the way it has to be. If he were to refuse, there could be trouble. He could be reproached for not having the proper decoration in his window; someone might even accuse him of disloyalty. He does it because these things must be done if one is to get along in life. It is one of the thousands of details that guarantee him a relatively tranquil life "in harmony with society," as they say.

Obviously the greengrocer is indifferent to the semantic content of the slogan on exhibit; he does not put the slogan in his window from any personal desire to acquaint the public with the ideal it expresses. This, of course, does not mean that his action has no motive or significance at all, or that the slogan communicates nothing to anyone. The slogan is really a sign, and as such it contains a subliminal but very definite

the real meaning :

message. Verbally, it might be expressed this way: "I, the greengrocer XY, live here and I know what I must do. I behave in the manner expected of me. I can be depended upon and am beyond reproach. I am obedient and therefore I have the right to be left in peace." This message, of course, has an addressee: it is directed above, to the greengrocer's superior, and at the same time it is a shield that protects the greengrocer from potential informers. The slogan's real meaning, therefore, is rooted firmly in the greengrocer's existence. It reflects his vital interests. But what are those vital interests?

Let us take note: if the greengrocer had been instructed to display the slogan "I am afraid and therefore unquestioningly obedient," he would not be nearly as indifferent to its semantics, even though the statement would reflect the truth. The greengrocer would be embarrassed and ashamed to put such an unequivocal statement of his own degradation in the shop window, and quite naturally so, for he is a human being and thus has a sense of his own dignity. To overcome this complication, his expression of loyalty must take the form of a sign which, at least on its textual surface, indicates a level of disinterested conviction. It must allow the greengrocer to say, "What's wrong with the workers of the world uniting?" Thus the sign helps the greengrocer to conceal from himself the low foundations of his obedience, at the same time concealing the low foundations of power. It hides them behind the facade of something high. And that something is ideology.

Ideology is a specious way of relating to the world. It offers human beings the illusion of an identity, of dignity, and of morality while making it easier for them to part with them. As the repository of something suprapersonal and objective, it enables people to deceive their conscience and conceal their true position and their inglorious *modus vivendi*, both from the world and from themselves. It is a very pragmatic but, at the same time, an apparently dignified way of legitimizing what is above, below, and on either side. It is directed toward people and toward God. It is a veil behind which human beings can hide their own fallen existence, their trivialization, and their adaptation to the status quo. It is an excuse that everyone can use, from the greengrocer, who conceals his fear of losing his job behind an alleged interest in the unification of the workers of the world, to the highest functionary, whose interest in staying in power can be cloaked in phrases about service to the working class. The primary excusatory function of ideology, therefore, is to provide people, both as victims and pillars of the post-totalitarian system, with the illusion that the system is in harmony with the human order and the order of the universe.

The smaller a dictatorship and the less stratified by modernization the society under it, the more directly the will of the dictator can be exercised. In other words, the dictator can employ more or less naked discipline, avoiding the complex processes of relating to the world and of self-justification which ideology involves. But the more complex the mechanisms of power become, the larger and more stratified the society they embrace, and the longer they have operated historically, the more individuals must be connected to them from outside, and the greater the importance attached to the ideological excuse. It acts as a kind of bridge between the regime and the people, across which the regime approaches the people and the people approach the regime. This explains why ideology plays such an important role in the post-totalitarian system: that complex machinery of units, hierarchies, transmission belts, and indirect instruments of manipulation which ensure in countless ways the integrity of the regime, leaving nothing to chance, would be quite simply unthinkable without ideology acting as its all-embracing excuse and as the excuse for each of its parts.

IV

BETWEEN the aims of the post-totalitarian system and the aims of life there is a yawning abyss: while life, in its essence, moves toward plurality, diversity, independent self-constitution, and self-organization, in short, toward the fulfillment of its own

the system perpetuates itself

freedom, the post-totalitarian system demands conformity, uniformity, and discipline. While life ever strives to create new and improbable structures, the post-totalitarian system contrives to force life into its most probable states. The aims of the system reveal its most essential characteristic to be introversion, a movement toward being ever more completely and unreservedly itself, which means that the radius of its influence is continually widening as well. This system serves people only to the extent necessary to ensure that people will serve it. Anything beyond this, that is to say, anything which leads people to overstep their predetermined roles is regarded by the system as an attack upon itself. And in this respect it is correct: every instance of such transgression is a genuine denial of the system. It can be said, therefore, that the inner aim of the post-totalitarian system is not mere preservation of power in the hands of a ruling clique, as appears to be the case at first sight. Rather, the social phenomenon of self-preservation is subordinated to something higher, to a kind of blind automatism which drives the system. No matter what position individuals hold in the hierarchy of power, they are not considered by the system to be worth anything in themselves, but only as things intended to fuel and serve this automatism. For this reason, an individual's desire for power is admissible only in so far as its direction coincides with the direction of the automatism of the system.

Ideology, in creating a bridge of excuses between the system and the individual, spans the abyss between the aims of the system and the aims of life. It pretends that the requirements of the system derive from the requirements of life. It is a world of appearances trying to pass for reality.

The post-totalitarian system touches people at every step, but it does so with its ideological gloves on. This is why life in the system is so thoroughly permeated with hypocrisy and lies: government by bureaucracy is called popular government; the working class is enslaved in the name of the working class; the complete degradation of the individual is presented as his ultimate liberation; depriving people of information is called making it available; the use of power to manipulate is called the public control of power, and the arbitrary abuse of power is called observing the legal code; the repression of culture is called its development; the expansion of imperial influence is presented as support for the oppressed; the lack of free expression becomes the highest form of freedom; farcical elections become the highest form of democracy; banning independent thought becomes the most scientific of world views; military occupation becomes fraternal assistance. Because the regime is captive to its own lies, it must falsify everything. It falsifies the past. It falsifies the present, and it falsifies the future. It falsifies statistics. It pretends not to possess an omnipotent and unprincipled police apparatus. It pretends to respect human rights. It pretends to persecute no one. It pretends to fear nothing. It pretends to pretend nothing.

Individuals need not believe all these mystifications, but they must behave as though they did, or they must at least tolerate them in silence, or get along well with those who work with them. For this reason, however, they must live within a lie. They need not accept the lie. It is enough for them to have accepted their life with it and in it. For by this very fact, individuals confirm the system, fulfill the system, make the system, *are* the system.

V

WE HAVE seen that the real meaning of the greengrocer's slogan has nothing to do with what the text of the slogan actually says. Even so, this real meaning is quite clear and generally comprehensible because the code is so familiar: the greengrocer declares his loyalty (and he can do no other if his declaration is to be accepted) in the only way the regime is capable of hearing; that is, by accepting the prescribed ritual, by accepting appearances as reality, by accepting the given rules of the game. In doing so, however, he has himself become a player in the game, thus making it possible for the game to go on, for it to exist in the first place.

If ideology was originally a bridge between the system and the individual as an individual, then the moment he steps on to this bridge it becomes at the same time a bridge between the system and the individual as a component of the system. That is, if ideology originally facilitated (by acting outwardly) the constitution of power by serving as a psychological excuse, then from the moment that excuse is accepted, it constitutes power inwardly, becoming an active component of that power. It begins to function as the principal instrument of ritual communication *within* the system of power.

The whole power structure (and we have already discussed its physical articulation) could not exist at all if there were not a certain metaphysical order binding all its components together, interconnecting them and subordinating them to a uniform method of accountability, supplying the combined operation of all these components with rules of the game, that is, with certain regulations, limitations, and legalities. This metaphysical order is fundamental to, and standard throughout, the entire power structure; it integrates its communication system and makes possible the internal exchange and transfer of information and instructions. It is rather like a collection of traffic signals and directional signs, giving the process shape and structure. This metaphysical order guarantees the inner coherence of the totalitarian power structure. It is the glue holding it together, its binding principle, the instrument of its discipline. Without this glue the structure as a totalitarian structure would vanish; it would disintegrate into individual atoms chaotically colliding with one another in their unregulated particular interests and inclinations. The entire pyramid of totalitarian power, deprived of the element that binds it together, would collapse in upon itself, as it were, in a kind of material implosion.

As the interpretation of reality by the power structure, ideology is always subordinated ultimately to the interests of the structure. Therefore, it has a natural tendency to disengage itself from reality, to create a world of appearances, to become ritual. In societies where there is public competition for power and therefore public control of that power, there *ideology separates from reality*

also exists quite naturally public control of the way that power legitimates itself ideologically. Consequently, in such conditions there are always certain correctives that effectively prevent ideology from abandoning reality altogether. Under totalitarianism, however, these correctives disappear, and thus there is nothing to prevent ideology from becoming more and more removed from reality, gradually turning into what it has already become in the post-totalitarian system: a world of appearances, a mere ritual, a formalized language deprived of semantic contact with reality and transformed into a system of ritual signs that replace reality with pseudo-reality.

Yet, as we have seen, ideology becomes at the same time an increasingly important component of power, a pillar providing it with both excusatory legitimacy and an inner coherence. As this aspect grows in importance, and as it gradually loses touch with reality, it acquires a peculiar but very real strength. It becomes reality itself, albeit a reality altogether self-contained, one that on certain levels (chiefly inside the power structure) may have even greater weight than reality as such. Increasingly, the virtuosity of the ritual becomes more important than the reality hidden behind it. The significance of phenomena no longer derives from the phenomena themselves, but from their locus as concepts in the ideological context. Reality does not shape theory, but rather the reverse. Thus power gradually draws closer to ideology than it does to reality; it draws its strength from theory and becomes entirely dependent on it. This inevitably leads, of course, to a paradoxical result: rather than theory, or rather ideology, serving power, power begins to serve ideology. It is as though ideology had appropriated power from power, as though it had become dictator itself. It then appears that theory itself, ritual itself, ideology itself, makes decisions that affect people, and not the other way around.

If ideology is the principal guarantee of the inner consistency of power, it becomes at the same time an increasingly important guarantee of its continuity. Whereas succession to power in classical dictatorship is always a rather complicated

Ideology becomes its own dictator

affair (the pretenders having nothing to give their claims reasonable legitimacy, thereby forcing them always to resort to confrontations of naked power), in the post-totalitarian system power is passed on from person to person, from clique to clique, and from generation to generation in an essentially more regular fashion. In the selection of pretenders, a new "king-maker" takes part: it is ritual legitimation, the ability to rely on ritual, to fulfill it and use it, to allow oneself, as it were, to be borne aloft by it. Naturally, power struggles exist in the post-totalitarian system as well, and most of them are far more brutal than in an open society, for the struggle is not open, regulated by democratic rules, and subject to public control, but hidden behind the scenes. (It is difficult to recall a single instance in which the First Secretary of a ruling Communist Party has been replaced without the various military and security forces being placed at least on alert.) This struggle, however, can never (as it can in classical dictatorships) threaten the very essence of the system and its continuity. At most it will shake up the power structure, which will recover quickly precisely because the binding substance—ideology—remains undisturbed. No matter who is replaced by whom, succession is only possible against the backdrop and within the framework of a common ritual. It can never take place by denying that ritual.

Because of this dictatorship of the ritual, however, power becomes clearly anonymous. Individuals are almost dissolved in the ritual. They allow themselves to be swept along by it and frequently it seems as though ritual alone carries people from obscurity into the light of power. Is it not characteristic of the post-totalitarian system that, on all levels of the power hierarchy, individuals are increasingly being pushed aside by faceless people, puppets, those uniformed flunkeys of the rituals and routines of power?

The automatic operation of a power structure thus dehumanized and made anonymous is a feature of the fundamental automatism of this system. It would seem that it is precisely the *diktat*s of this automatism which select people lacking individual will for the power structure, that it is precisely the *diktat* of the empty phrase which summons to power people who use empty phrases as the best guarantee that the automatism of the post-totalitarian system will continue.

Western Sovietologists often exaggerate the role of individuals in the post-totalitarian system and overlook the fact that the ruling figures, despite the immense power they possess through the centralized structure of power, are often no more than blind executors of the system's own internal laws—laws they themselves never can, and never do, reflect upon. In any case, experience has taught us again and again that this automatism is far more powerful than the will of any individual; and should someone possess a more independent will, he must conceal it behind a ritually anonymous mask in order to have an opportunity to enter the power hierarchy at all. And when the individual finally gains a place there and tries to make his will felt within it, that automatism, with its enormous inertia, will triumph sooner or later, and either the individual will be ejected by the power structure like a foreign organism, or he will be compelled to resign his individuality gradually, once again blending with the automatism and becoming its servant, almost indistinguishable from those who preceded him and those who will follow. (Let us recall, for instance, the development of Husák or Gomułka.) The necessity of continually hiding behind and relating to ritual means that even the more enlightened members of the power structure are often obsessed with ideology. They are never able to plunge straight to the bottom of naked reality, and they always confuse it, in the final analysis, with ideological pseudo-reality. (In my opinion, one of the reasons the Dubček leadership lost control of the situation in 1968 was precisely because, in extreme situations and in final questions, its members were never capable of extricating themselves completely from the world of appearances.)

It can be said, therefore, that ideology, as that instrument of internal communication which assures the power structure of inner cohesion is, in the post-totalitarian system, something that transcends the physical aspects of power, something that dominates it to a considerable degree and, therefore, tends to assure its continuity as well. It is one of the pillars of the system's external stability. This pillar, however, is built on a very unstable foundation. It is built on lies. It works only as long as people are willing to live within the lie.

VI

WHY IN FACT did our greengrocer have to put his loyalty on display in the shop window? Had he not already displayed it sufficiently in various internal or semipublic ways? At trade union meetings, after all, he had always voted as he should. He had always taken part in various competitions. He voted in elections like a good citizen. He had even signed the "anti-Charter." Why, on top of all that, should he have to declare his loyalty publicly? After all, the people who walk past his window will certainly not stop to read that, in the greengrocer's opinion, the workers of the world ought to unite. The fact of the matter is, they don't read the slogan at all, and it can be fairly assumed they don't even see it. If you were to ask a woman who had stopped in front of his shop what she saw in the window, she could certainly tell whether or not they had tomatoes today, but it is highly unlikely that she noticed the slogan at all, let alone what it said.

It seems senseless to require the greengrocer to declare his loyalty publicly. But it makes sense nevertheless. People ignore his slogan, but they do so because such slogans are also found in other shop windows, on lampposts, bulletin boards, in apartment windows, and on buildings; they are everywhere, in fact. They form part of the panorama of everyday life. Of course, while they ignore the details, people are very aware of that panorama as a whole. And what else is the greengrocer's slogan but a small component in that huge backdrop to daily life?

The greengrocer had to put the slogan in his window, there-

fore, not in the hope that someone might read it or be persuaded by it, but to contribute, along with thousands of other
slogans, to the panorama that everyone is very much aware
of. This panorama, of course, has a subliminal meaning as
well: it reminds people where they are living and what is expected of them. It tells them what everyone else is doing, and
indicates to them what they must do as well, if they don't want
to be excluded, to fall into isolation, alienate themselves from
society, break the rules of the game, and risk the loss of their
peace and tranquility and security.

The woman who ignored the greengrocer's slogan may well
have hung a similar slogan just an hour before in the corridor
of the office where she works. She did it more or less without
thinking, just as our greengrocer did, and she could do so
precisely because she was doing it against the background of
the general panorama and with some awareness of it, that is,
against the background of the panorama of which the greengrocer's shop window forms a part. When the greengrocer
visits her office, he will not notice her slogan either, just as
she failed to notice his. Nevertheless, their slogans are mutually dependent: both were displayed with some awareness of
the general panorama and, we might say, under its *diktat*.
Both, however, assist in the creation of that panorama, and
therefore they assist in the creation of that *diktat* as well. The
greengrocer and the office worker have both adapted to the
conditions in which they live, but in doing so, they help to
create those conditions. They do what is done, what is to be
done, what must be done, but at the same time—by that very
token—they confirm that it must be done in fact. They conform to a particular requirement and in so doing they themselves perpetuate that requirement. Metaphysically speaking,
without the greengrocer's slogan the office worker's slogan
could not exist, and vice versa. Each proposes to the other
that something be repeated and each accepts the other's proposal. Their mutual indifference to each other's slogans is
only an illusion: in reality, by exhibiting their slogans, each
compels the other to accept the rules of the game and to

confirm thereby the power that requires the slogans in the first place. Quite simply, each helps the other to be obedient. Both are objects in a system of control, but at the same time they are its subjects as well. They are both victims of the system and its instruments.

If an entire district town is plastered with slogans that no one reads, it is on the one hand a message from the district secretary to the regional secretary, but it is also something more: a small example of the principle of social auto-totality at work. Part of the essence of the post-totalitarian system is that it draws everyone into its sphere of power, not so they may realize themselves as human beings, but so they may surrender their human identity in favor of the identity of the system, that is, so they may become agents of the system's general automatism and servants of its self-determined goals, so they may participate in the common responsibility for it, so they may be pulled into and ensnared by it, like Faust by Mephistopheles. More than this: so they may create through their involvement a general norm and, thus, bring pressure to bear on their fellow citizens. And further: so they may learn to be comfortable with their involvement, to identify with it as though it were something natural and inevitable and, ultimately, so they may—with no external urging—come to treat any non-involvement as an abnormality, as arrogance, as an attack on themselves, as a form of dropping out of society. By pulling everyone into its power structure, the post-totalitarian system makes everyone an instrument of a mutual totality, the auto-totality of society.

Everyone, however, is in fact involved and enslaved, not only the greengrocers but also the prime ministers. Differing positions in the hierarchy merely establish differing degrees of involvement: the greengrocer is involved only to a minor extent, but he also has very little power. The prime minister, naturally, has greater power, but in return he is far more deeply involved. Both, however, are unfree, each merely in a somewhat different way. The real accomplice in this involvement, therefore, is not another person, but the system itself.

Position in the power hierarchy determines the degree of responsibility and guilt, but it gives no one unlimited responsibility and guilt, nor does it completely absolve anyone. Thus the conflict between the aims of life and the aims of the system is not a conflict between two socially defined and separate communities; and only a very generalized view (and even that only approximative) permits us to divide society into the rulers and the ruled. Here, by the way, is one of the most important differences between the post-totalitarian system and classical dictatorships, in which this line of conflict can still be drawn according to social class. In the post-totalitarian system, this line runs *de facto* through each person, for everyone in his own way is both a victim and a supporter of the system. What we understand by the system is not, therefore, a social order imposed by one group upon another, but rather something which permeates the entire society and is a factor in shaping it, something which may seem impossible to grasp or define (for it is in the nature of a mere principle), but which is expressed by the entire society as an important feature of its life.

The fact that human beings have created, and daily create, this self-directed system through which they divest themselves of their innermost identity is not therefore the result of some incomprehensible misunderstanding of history, nor is it history somehow gone off its rails. Neither is it the product of some diabolical higher will which has decided, for reasons unknown, to torment a portion of humanity in this way. It can happen and did happen only because there is obviously in modern humanity a certain tendency toward the creation, or at least the toleration, of such a system. There is obviously something in human beings which responds to this system, something they reflect and accommodate, something within them which paralyzes every effort of their better selves to revolt. Human beings are compelled to live within a lie, but they can be compelled to do so only because they are in fact capable of living in this way. Therefore not only does the system alienate humanity, but at the same time alienated humanity supports this system as its own involuntary master-plan, as a degenerate image of its own degeneration, as a record of people's own failure as individuals.

The essential aims of life are present naturally in every person. In everyone there is some longing for humanity's rightful dignity, for moral integrity, for free expression of being and a sense of transcendence over the world of existence. Yet, at the same time, each person is capable, to a greater or lesser degree, of coming to terms with living within the lie. Each person somehow succumbs to a profane trivialization of his inherent humanity, and to utilitarianism. In everyone there is some willingness to merge with the anonymous crowd and to flow comfortably along with it down the river of pseudo-life. This is much more than a simple conflict between two identities. It is something far worse: it is a challenge to the very notion of identity itself.

In highly simplified terms, it could be said that the post-totalitarian system has been built on foundations laid by the historical encounter between dictatorship and the consumer society. Is it not true that the far-reaching adaptability to living a lie and the effortless spread of social auto-totality have some connection with the general unwillingness of consumption-oriented people to sacrifice some material certainties for the sake of their own spiritual and moral integrity? With their willingness to surrender higher values when faced with the trivializing temptations of modern civilization? With their vulnerability to the attractions of mass indifference? And in the end, is not the grayness and the emptiness of life in the post-totalitarian system only an inflated caricature of modern life in general? And do we not in fact stand (although in the external measures of civilization, we are far behind) as a kind of warning to the West, revealing to its own latent tendencies?

VII

LET US now imagine that one day something in our greengrocer snaps and he stops putting up the slogans merely to ingratiate himself. He stops voting in elections he knows are a farce. He begins to say what he really thinks at political meetings. And he even finds the strength in himself to express solidarity with those whom his conscience commands him to support. In this revolt the greengrocer steps out of living within the lie. He rejects the ritual and breaks the rules of the game. He discovers once more his suppressed identity and dignity. He gives his freedom a concrete significance. His revolt is an attempt to live within the truth.

The bill is not long in coming. He will be relieved of his post as manager of the shop and transferred to the warehouse. His pay will be reduced. His hopes for a holiday in Bulgaria will evaporate. His children's access to higher education will be threatened. His superiors will harass him and his fellow workers will wonder about him. Most of those who apply these sanctions, however, will not do so from any authentic inner conviction but simply under pressure from conditions, the same conditions that once pressured the greengrocer to display the official slogans. They will persecute the greengrocer either because it is expected of them, or to demonstrate their loyalty, or simply as part of the general panorama, to which belongs an awareness that this is how situations of this sort are dealt with, that this, in fact, is how things are always done, particularly if one is not to become suspect oneself. The executors, therefore, behave essentially like everyone else, to a greater or lesser degree: as components of the post-totalitarian system, as agents of its automatism, as petty instruments of the social auto-totality.

Thus the power structure, through the agency of those who carry out the sanctions, those anonymous components of the system, will spew the greengrocer from its mouth. The system, through its alienating presence in people, will punish him for his rebellion. It must do so because the logic of its automa-

tism and self-defense dictate it. The greengrocer has not committed a simple, individual offense, isolated in its own
uniqueness, but something incomparably more serious. By
breaking the rules of the game, he has disrupted the game as
such. He has exposed it as a mere game. He has shattered the
world of appearances, the fundamental pillar of the system.
He has upset the power structure by tearing apart what holds
it together. He has demonstrated that living a lie is living a
lie. He has broken through the exalted facade of the system
and exposed the real, base foundations of power. He has said
that the emperor is naked. And because the emperor is in
fact naked, something extremely dangerous has happened: by
his action, the greengrocer has addressed the world. He has
enabled everyone to peer behind the curtain. He has shown
everyone that it *is* possible to live within the truth. Living
within the lie can constitute the system only if it is universal.
The principle must embrace and permeate everything. There
are no terms whatsoever on which it can co-exist with living
within the truth, and therefore everyone who steps out of line
denies it in principle and threatens it in its entirety.

This is understandable: as long as appearance is not confronted with reality, it does not seem to be appearance. As
long as living a lie is not confronted with living the truth, the
perspective needed to expose its mendacity is lacking. As soon
as the alternative appears, however, it threatens the very existence of appearance and living a lie in terms of what they
are, both their essence and their all-inclusiveness. And at the
same time, it is utterly unimportant how large a space this
alternative occupies: its power does not consist in its physical
attributes but in the light it casts on those pillars of the system
and on its unstable foundations. After all, the greengrocer
was a threat to the system not because of any physical or
actual power he had, but because his action went beyond itself, because it illuminated its surroundings and, of course,
because of the incalculable consequences of that illumination. In the post-totalitarian system, therefore, living within
the truth has more than a mere existential dimension (return-

ing humanity to its inherent nature), or a noetic dimension (revealing reality as it is), or a moral dimension (setting an example for others). It also has an unambiguous political dimension. If the main pillar of the system is living a lie, then it is not surprising that the fundamental threat to it is living the truth. This is why it must be suppressed more severely than anything else.

In the post-totalitarian system, truth in the widest sense of the word has a very special import, one unknown in other contexts. In this system, truth plays a far greater (and, above all, a far different) role as a factor of power, or as an outright political force. How does the power of truth operate? How does truth as a factor of power work? How can its power—as power—be realized?

VIII

INDIVIDUALS can be alienated from themselves only because there is something in them to alienate. The terrain of this violation is their authentic existence. Living the truth is thus woven directly into the texture of living a lie. It is the repressed alternative, the authentic aim to which living a lie is an inauthentic response. Only against this background does living a lie make any sense: it exists *because* of that background. In its excusatory, chimerical rootedness in the human order, it is a response to nothing other than the human predisposition to truth. Under the orderly surface of the life of lies, therefore, there slumbers the hidden sphere of life in its real aims, of its hidden openness to truth.

The singular, explosive, incalculable political power of living within the truth resides in the fact that living openly within the truth has an ally, invisible to be sure, but omnipresent: this hidden sphere. It is from this sphere that life lived openly in the truth grows; it is to this sphere that it speaks, and in it that it finds understanding. This is where the potential for communication exists. But this place is hidden and therefore, from the perspective of power, very dangerous. The complex ferment that takes place within it goes on in semidarkness, and by the time it finally surfaces into the light of day as an assortment of shocking surprises to the system, it is usually too late to cover them up in the usual fashion. Thus they create a situation in which the regime is confounded, invariably causing panic and driving it to react in inappropriate ways.

It seems that the primary breeding ground for what might, in the widest possible sense of the word, be understood as an opposition in the post-totalitarian system is living within the truth. The confrontation between these opposition forces and the powers that be, of course, will obviously take a form essentially different from that typical of an open society or a classical dictatorship. Initially, this confrontation does not take place on the level of real, institutionalized, quantifiable power which relies on the various instruments of power, but on a different level altogether: the level of human consciousness and conscience, the existential level. The effective range of this special power cannot be measured in terms of disciples, voters, or soldiers, because it lies spread out in the fifth column of social consciousness, in the hidden aims of life, in human beings' repressed longing for dignity and fundamental rights, for the realization of their real social and political interests. Its power, therefore, does not reside in the strength of definable political or social groups, but chiefly in the strength of a potential, which is hidden throughout the whole of society, including the official power structures of that society. Therefore this power does not rely on soldiers of its own, but on the soldiers of the enemy as it were—that is to say, on everyone who is living within the lie and who may be struck at any moment (in theory, at least) by the force of truth (or who, out of an instinctive desire to protect their position, may at least adapt to that force). It is a bacteriological weapon, so to speak, utilized when conditions are ripe by a single civilian to disarm an entire division. This power does not participate in any direct struggle for power; rather, it makes its influence felt in the obscure arena of being itself. The hidden movements it gives rise to there, however, can issue forth (when, where, under what circumstances, and to what extent are difficult to predict) in something visible: a real political act or event, a social movement, a sudden explosion of civil unrest, a sharp conflict inside an apparently monolithic power structure, or simply an irrepressible transformation in the social and intellectual climate. And since all genuine problems and matters of critical importance are hidden beneath a thick crust of lies, it is never quite clear when the proverbial last straw will fall, or what that straw will be. This, too, is why the regime prosecutes, almost as a reflex action preventively, even the most modest attempts to live within the truth.

Why was Solzhenitsyn driven out of his own country? Certainly not because he represented a unit of real power, that is, not because any of the regime's representatives felt he might unseat them and take their place in government. Solzhenitsyn's expulsion was something else: a desperate attempt to plug up the dreadful wellspring of truth, a truth which might cause incalculable transformations in social consciousness, which in turn might one day produce political debacles unpredictable in their consequences. And so the post-totalitarian system behaved in a characteristic way: it defended the integrity of the world of appearances in order to defend itself. For the crust presented by the life of lies is made of strange stuff. As long as it seals off hermetically the entire society, it appears to be made of stone. But the moment someone breaks through in one place, when one person cries out, "The emperor is naked!"—when a single person breaks the rules of the game, thus exposing it as a game—everything suddenly appears in another light and the whole crust seems then to be made of a tissue on the point of tearing and disintegrating uncontrollably.

When I speak of living within the truth, I naturally do not have in mind only products of conceptual thought, such as a protest or a letter written by a group of intellectuals. It can be any means by which a person or a group revolts against manipulation: anything from a letter by intellectuals to a workers' strike, from a rock concert to a student demonstration, from refusing to vote in the farcical elections to making an open speech at some official congress, or even a hunger strike, for instance. If the suppression of the aims of life is a complex process, and if it is based on the multifaceted manipulation of all expressions of life, then, by the same token, every free expression of life indirectly threatens the post-totalitarian system politically, including forms of expression to which, in other social systems, no one would attribute any potential political significance, not to mention explosive power.

The Prague Spring is usually understood as a clash between two groups on the level of real power: those who wanted to maintain the system as it was and those who wanted to reform it. It is frequently forgotten, however, that this encounter was merely the final act and the inevitable consequence of a long drama originally played out chiefly in the theatre of the spirit and the conscience of society. And that somewhere at the beginning of this drama, there were individuals who were willing to live within the truth, even when things were at their worst. These people had no access to real power, nor did they aspire to it. The sphere in which they were living the truth was not necessarily even that of political thought. They could equally have been poets, painters, musicians, or simply ordinary citizens who were able to maintain their human dignity. Today it is naturally difficult to pinpoint when and through which hidden, winding channel a certain action or attitude influenced a given milieu, and to trace the virus of truth as it slowly spread through the tissue of the life of lies, gradually causing it to disintegrate. One thing, however, seems clear: the attempt at political reform was not the cause of society's reawakening, but rather the final outcome of that reawakening.

I think the present also can be better understood in the light of this experience. The confrontation between a thousand Chartists and the post-totalitarian system would appear to be politically hopeless. This is true, of course, if we look at it through the traditional lens of the open political system, in which, quite naturally, every political force is measured chiefly in terms of the positions it holds on the level of real power. Given that perspective, a mini-party like the Charter would certainly not stand a chance. If, however, this confrontation is seen against the background of what we know about power in the post-totalitarian system, it appears in a fundamentally different light. For the time being, it is impossible to say with any precision what impact the appearance of Charter 77, its existence, and its work has had in the hidden sphere, and how the Charter's attempt to rekindle civic self-awareness and confidence is regarded there. Whether, when, and how this investment will eventually produce dividends in the form of specific political changes is even less possible to predict. But that, of course, is all part of living within the truth. As an existential solution, it takes individuals back to the solid ground of their own identity; as politics, it throws them into a game of chance where the stakes are all or nothing. For this reason it is undertaken only by those for whom the former is worth risking the latter, or who have come to the conclusion that there is no other way to conduct real politics in Czechoslovakia today. Which, by the way, is the same thing: this conclusion can be reached only by someone who is unwilling to sacrifice his own human identity to politics, or rather, who does not believe in a politics that requires such a sacrifice.

The more thoroughly the post-totalitarian system frustrates any rival alternative on the level of real power, as well as any form of politics independent of the laws of its own automatism, the more definitively the center of gravity of any potential political threat shifts to the area of the existential and the pre-political; usually without any conscious effort, living within the truth becomes the one natural point of departure for all activities that work against the automatism of the system. And even if such activities ultimately grow beyond the area of living within the truth (which means they are transformed into various parallel structures, movements, institutions, they begin to be regarded as political activity, they bring real pressure to bear on the official structures and begin in fact to have a certain influence on the level of real power), they always carry with them the specific hallmark of their origins. Therefore it seems to me that not even the so-called dissident movements can be properly understood without constantly bearing in mind this special background from which they emerge.

IX

THE PROFOUND crisis of human identity brought on by living within a lie, a crisis which in turn makes such a life possible, certainly possesses a moral dimension as well; it appears, among other things, as a deep moral crisis in society. A person who has been seduced by the consumer value system, whose identity is dissolved in an amalgam of the accouterments of mass civilization, and who has no roots in the order of being, no sense of responsibility for anything higher than his own personal survival, is a demoralized person. The system depends on this demoralization, deepens it, is in fact a projection of it into society.

Living within the truth, as humanity's revolt against an enforced position, is, on the contrary, an attempt to regain control over one's own sense of responsibility. In other words, it is clearly a moral act, not only because one must pay so dearly for it, but principally because it is not self-serving: the risk may bring rewards in the form of a general amelioration in the situation, or it may not. In this regard, as I stated previously, it is an all-or-nothing gamble, and it is difficult to imagine a reasonable person embarking on such a course merely because he reckons that sacrifice today will bring rewards tomorrow, be it only in the form of general gratitude. (By the way, the representatives of power invariably come to terms with those who live within the truth by persistently ascribing utilitarian motivations to them—a lust for power or fame or wealth—and thus they try, at least, to implicate them in their own world, the world of general demoralization.)

If living within the truth in the post-totalitarian system be-comes the chief breeding ground for independent, alternative political ideas, then all considerations about the nature and future prospects of these ideas must necessarily reflect this moral dimension as a political phenomenon. (And if the rev-olutionary Marxist belief about morality as a product of the "superstructure" inhibits any of our friends from realizing the full significance of this dimension and, in one way or another, from including it in their view of the world, it is to their own detriment: an anxious fidelity to the postulates of that world view prevents them from properly understanding the mechanisms of their own political influence, thus para-doxically making them precisely what they, as Marxists, so often suspect others of being—victims of "false conscious-ness.") The very special political significance of morality in the post-totalitarian system is a phenomenon that is at the very least unusual in modern political history, a phenomenon that might well have—as I shall soon attempt to show—far-reaching consequences.

X

UNDENIABLY, the most important political event in Czecho-slovakia after the advent of the Husák leadership in 1969 was the appearance of Charter 77. The spiritual and intellectual climate surrounding its appearance, however, was not the product of any immediate political event. That climate was created by the trial of some young musicians associated with a rock group called "The Plastic People of the Universe." Their trial was not a confrontation of two differing political forces or conceptions, but two differing conceptions of life. On the one hand, there was the sterile puritanism of the post-totalitarian establishment and, on the other hand, unknown young people who wanted no more than to be able to live within the truth, to play the music they enjoyed, to sing songs that were relevant to their lives, and to live freely in dignity and partnership. These people had no past history of political activity. They were not highly motivated members of the opposition with political ambitions, nor were they former politicians expelled from the power structures. They had been given every opportunity to adapt to the status quo, to accept the principles of living within a lie and thus to enjoy life undisturbed by the authorities. Yet they decided on a different course. Despite this, or perhaps precisely because of it, their case had a very special impact on everyone who had not yet given up hope. Moreover, when the trial took place, a new mood had begun to surface after the years of waiting, of apathy and of skepticism toward various forms of resistance. People were "tired of being tired"; they were fed up with the stagnation, the inactivity, barely hanging on in the hope that things might improve after all. In some ways the trial was the final straw. Many groups of differing tendencies which until then had remained isolated from each other, reluctant to cooperate, or which were committed to forms of action that made cooperation difficult, were suddenly struck with the powerful realization that freedom is indivisible. Everyone understood that an attack on the Czech musical underground was an attack on a most elementary and important thing, something that in fact bound everyone together: it was an attack on the very notion of living within the truth, on the real aims of life. The freedom to play rock music was understood as a human freedom and thus as essentially the same as the freedom to engage in philosophical and political reflection, the freedom to write, the freedom to express and defend the various social and political interests of society. People were inspired to feel a genuine sense of solidarity with the young musicians and they came to realize that not standing up for the freedom of others, regardless of how remote their means of creativity or their attitude to life, meant surrendering one's own freedom. (There is no freedom without equality before the law, and there is no equality before the law without freedom; Charter 77 has given this ancient notion a new and characteristic dimension, which has immensely important implications for modern Czech history. What Sládeček, the author of the book *Sixty-eight,* in a brilliant analysis, calls the "principle of exclusion," lies at the root of all our present-day moral and political misery. This principle was born at the end of the Second World War in that strange collusion of democrats and communists and was subsequently developed further and further, right to the bitter end. For the first time in decades this principle has been overcome, by Charter 77: all those united in the Charter have, for the first time, become equal partners. Charter 77 is not merely a coalition of communists and noncommunists—that would be nothing historically new and, from the moral and political point of view, nothing revolutionary—but it is a community that is *a priori* open to anyone, and no one in it is *a priori* assigned an inferior position.) This was the climate, then, in which Charter 77 was created. Who could have foreseen that the prosecution of one or two obscure rock groups would have such far-reaching consequences?

I think that the origins of Charter 77 illustrate very well what I have already suggested above: that in the post-totalitarian system, the real background to the movements that gradually assume political significance does not usually consist of overtly political events or confrontations between different forces or concepts that are openly political. These movements for the most part originate elsewhere, in the far broader area of the "pre-political," where living within a lie confronts living within the truth, that is, where the demands of the post-totalitarian system conflict with the real aims of life. These real aims can naturally assume a great many forms. Sometimes they appear as the basic material or social interests of a group or an individual; at other times, they may appear as certain intellectual and spiritual interests; at still other times, they may be the most fundamental of existential demands, such as the simple longing of people to live their own lives in dignity. Such a conflict acquires a political character, then, not because of the elementary political nature of the aims demanding to be heard but simply because, given the complex system of manipulation on which the post-totalitarian system is founded and on which it is also dependent, every free human act or expression, every attempt to live within the truth, must necessarily appear as a threat to the system and, thus, as something which is political *par excellence.* Any eventual political articulation of the movements that grow out of this "pre-political" hinterland is secondary. It develops and matures as a result of a subsequent confrontation with the system, and not because it started off as a political program, project, or impulse.

Once again, the events of 1968 confirm this. The communist politicians who were trying to reform the system came forward with their program not because they had suddenly experienced a mystical enlightenment, but because they were led to do so by continued and increasing pressure from areas of life that had nothing to do with politics in the traditional sense of the word. In fact, they were trying in political ways to solve the social conflicts (which in fact were confrontations between the aims of the system and the aims of life) that almost every level of society had been experiencing daily, and had been thinking about with increasing openness for years. Backed by this living resonance throughout society, scholars and artists had defined the problem in a wide variety of ways and students were demanding solutions.

The genesis of Charter 77 also illustrates the special political significance of the moral aspect of things that I have mentioned. Charter 77 would have been unimaginable without that powerful sense of solidarity among widely differing groups, and without the sudden realization that it was impossible to go on waiting any longer, and that the truth had to be spoken loudly and collectively, regardless of the virtual certainty of sanctions and the uncertainty of any tangible results in the immediate future. "There are some things worth suffering for," Jan Patočka wrote shortly before his death. I think that Chartists understand this not only as Patočka's legacy, but also as the best explanation of why they do what they do.

Seen from the outside, and chiefly from the vantage point

of the system and its power structure, Charter 77 came as a surprise, as a bolt out of the blue. It was not a bolt out of the blue, of course, but that impression is understandable, since the ferment that led to it took place in the "hidden sphere," in that semidarkness where things are difficult to chart or analyze. The chances of predicting the appearance of the Charter were just as slight as the chances are now of predicting where it will lead. Once again, it was that shock, so typical of moments when something from the hidden sphere suddenly bursts through the moribund surface of living within a lie. The more one is trapped in the world of appearances, the more surprising it is when something like that happens.

XI

IN SOCIETIES under the post-totalitarian system, all political life in the traditional sense has been eliminated. People have no opportunity to express themselves politically in public, let alone to organize politically. The gap that results is filled by ideological ritual. In such a situation, people's interest in political matters naturally dwindles and independent political thought, insofar as it exists at all, is seen by the majority as unrealistic, farfetched, a kind of self-indulgent game, hopelessly distant from their everyday concerns; something admirable, perhaps, but quite pointless, because it is on the one hand entirely utopian and on the other hand extraordinarily dangerous, in view of the unusual vigor with which any move in that direction is persecuted by the regime.

Yet even in such societies, individuals and groups of people exist who do not abandon politics as a vocation and who, in one way or another, strive to think independently, to express themselves and in some cases even to organize politically, because that is a part of their attempt to live within the truth.

The fact that these people exist and work is in itself immensely important and worthwhile. Even in the worst of times, they maintain the continuity of political thought. If some genuine political impulse emerges from this or that "pre-political" confrontation and is properly articulated early enough, thus increasing its chances of relative success, then this is frequently due to these isolated generals without an army who, because they have maintained the continuity of political thought in the face of enormous difficulties, can at the right moment enrich the new impulse with the fruits of their own political thinking. Once again, there is ample evidence for this process in Czechoslovakia. Almost all those who were political prisoners in the early 1970s, who had apparently been made to suffer in vain because of their quixotic efforts to work politically among an utterly apathetic and demoralized society, belong today—inevitably—among the most active Chartists. In Charter 77, the moral legacy of their earlier sacrifices is valued, and they have enriched this movement with their experience and that element of political thinking.

And yet it seems to me that the thought and activity of those friends who have never given up direct political work and who are always ready to assume direct political responsibility very often suffer from one chronic fault: an insufficient understanding of the historical uniqueness of the post-totalitarian system as a social and political reality. They have little understanding of the specific nature of power that is typical for this system and therefore they overestimate the importance of direct political work in the traditional sense. Moreover, they fail to appreciate the political significance of those "pre-political" events and processes that provide the living humus from which genuine political change usually springs. As political actors—or, rather, as people with political ambitions—they frequently try to pick up where natural political life left off. They maintain models of behavior that may have been appropriate in more normal political circumstances and thus, without really being aware of it, they bring an outmoded way of thinking, old habits, conceptions, categories, and notions to bear on circumstances that are quite new and radically different, without first giving adequate thought to the meaning and substance of such things in the new circumstances, to what politics as such means now, to what sort of thing can have political impact and potential, and in what way. Because such people have been excluded from the structures of power and are no longer able to influence those structures directly (and because they remain faithful to traditional notions of politics established in more or less democratic societies or in classical dictatorships) they frequently, in a sense, lose touch with reality. Why make compromises with reality, they say, when none of our proposals will ever be accepted anyway? Thus they find themselves in a world of genuinely utopian thinking.

As I have already tried to indicate, however, genuinely far-reaching political events do not emerge from the same sources and in the same way in the post-totalitarian system as they do in a democracy. And if a large portion of the public is indifferent to, even skeptical of, alternative political models and programs and the private establishment of opposition political parties, this is not merely because there is a general feeling of apathy toward public affairs and a loss of that sense of higher responsibility; in other words, it is not just a consequence of the general demoralization. There is also a bit of healthy social instinct at work in this attitude. It is as if people sensed intuitively that "nothing is what it seems any longer," as the saying goes, and that from now on, therefore, things must be done entirely differently as well.

If some of the most important political impulses in Soviet bloc countries in recent years have come initially—that is, before being felt on the level of actual power—from mathematicians, philosophers, physicians, writers, historians, ordinary workers, and so on, more frequently than from politicians, and if the driving force behind the various dissident movements comes from so many people in nonpolitical professions, this is not because these people are more clever than those who see themselves primarily as politicians. It is because those who are not politicians are also not so bound by traditional political thinking and political habits and therefore, paradoxically, they are more aware of genuine political reality and more sensitive to what can and should be done under the circumstances.

There is no way around it: no matter how beautiful an alternative political model can be, it can no longer speak to the "hidden sphere," inspire people and society, call for real political ferment. The real sphere of potential politics in the post-totalitarian system is elsewhere: in the continuing and cruel tension between the complex demands of that system and the aims of life, that is, the elementary need of human beings to live, to a certain extent at least, in harmony with themselves, that is, to live in a bearable way, not to be humiliated by their superiors and officials, not to be continually watched by the police, to be able to express themselves freely, to find an outlet for their creativity, to enjoy legal security, and so on. Anything that touches this field concretely, anything that relates to this fundamental, omnipresent, and living tension, will inevitably speak to people. Abstract projects for an ideal political or economic order do not interest them to anything like the same extent—and rightly so—not only because everyone knows how little chance they have of succeeding, but also because today people feel that the less political policies are derived from a concrete and human here and now and the more they fix their sights on an abstract "someday," the more easily they can degenerate into new forms of human enslavement. People who live in the post-totalitarian system know only too well that the question of whether one or several political parties are in power, and how these parties define and label themselves, is of far less importance than the question of whether or not it is possible to live like a human being.

To shed the burden of traditional political categories and habits and open oneself up fully to the world of human existence and then to draw political conclusions only after having analyzed it: this is not only politically more realistic but at the same time, from the point of view of an "ideal state of affairs," politically more promising as well. A genuine, profound, and lasting change for the better—as I shall attempt to show—can no longer result from the victory (were such a victory possible) of any particular traditional political conception, which can ultimately be only external, that is, a structural or systemic conception. More than ever before, such a change will have to derive from human existence, from the fundamental reconstitution of the position of people in the world, their relationships to themselves and to each other, and to the universe. If a better economic and political model is to be created, then perhaps more than ever before it must derive from profound existential and moral changes in society. This is not something that can be designed and introduced like a new car. If it is to be more than just a new variation of the old degeneration, it must above all be an expression of life in the process of transforming itself. A better system will not automatically ensure a better life. In fact, the opposite is true: only by creating a better life can a better system be developed.

Once more I repeat that I am not underestimating the importance of political thought and conceptual political work. On the contrary, I think that genuine political thought and genuinely political work is precisely what we continually fail to achieve. If I say "genuine," however, I have in mind the kind of thought and conceptual work that has freed itself of all the traditional political schemata that have been imported into our circumstances from a world that will never return (and whose return, even were it possible, would provide no permanent solution to the most important problems).

The Second and Fourth Internationals, like many other political powers and organizations, may naturally provide significant political support for various efforts of ours, but neither of them can solve our problems for us. They operate in a different world and are a product of different circumstances. Their theoretical concepts can be interesting and instructive to us, but one thing is certain: we cannot solve our problems simply by identifying with these organizations. And the attempt in our country to place what we do in the context of some of the discussions that dominate political life in democratic societies often seems like sheer folly. For example, is it possible to talk seriously about whether we want to change the system or merely reform it? In the circumstances under which we live, this is a pseudo-problem, since for the time being there is simply no way we can accomplish either goal. We are not even clear about where reform ends and change begins. We know from a number of harsh experiences that neither reform nor change is in itself a guarantee of anything. We know that ultimately it is all the same to us whether or not the system in which we live, in the light of a particular doctrine, appears changed or reformed. Our concern is whether we can live with dignity in such a system, whether it serves people rather than people serving it. We are struggling to achieve this with the means available to us, and the means it makes sense to employ. Western journalists, submerged in the political banalities in which they live, may label our approach as overly legalistic, as too risky, revisionist, counter-revolutionary, bourgeois, communist, or as too right-wing or left-wing. But this is the very last thing that interests us.

XII

ONE CONCEPT that is a constant source of confusion chiefly because it has been imported into our circumstances from circumstances that are entirely different is the concept of an opposition. What exactly is an opposition in the post-totalitarian system?

In democratic societies with a traditional parliamentary system of government, political opposition is understood as a political force on the level of actual power (most frequently a party or coalition of parties) which is not a part of the government. It offers an alternative political program, it has ambitions to govern, and it is recognized and respected by the government in power as a natural element in the political life of the country. It seeks to spread its influence by political means, and competes for power on the basis of agreed-upon legal regulations.

In addition to this form of opposition, there exists the phenomenon of the "extra-parliamentary opposition," which again consists of forces organized more or less on the level of actual power, but which operate outside the rules created by the system, and which employ different means than are usual within that framework.

In classical dictatorships, the term "opposition" is understood to mean the political forces which have also come out with an alternative political program. They operate either legally or on the outer limits of legality, but in any case they cannot compete for power within the limits of some agreed-upon regulations. Or the term "opposition" may be applied to forces preparing for a violent confrontation with the ruling power, or who feel themselves to be in this state of confrontation already, such as various guerrilla groups or liberation movements.

An opposition in the post-totalitarian system does not exist in any of these senses. In what way, then, can the term be used?

1. Occasionally the term "opposition" is applied, mainly by Western journalists, to persons or groups inside the power structure who find themselves in a state of hidden conflict with the highest authorities. The reasons for this conflict may be certain differences (not very sharp differences, naturally) of a conceptual nature, but more frequently it is quite simply a longing for power or a personal antipathy to others who represent that power.

2. Opposition here can also be understood as everything that does or can have an indirect political effect in the sense already mentioned, that is, everything the post-totalitarian system feels threatened by, which in fact means everything it *is* threatened by. In this sense, the opposition is every attempt to live within the truth, from the greengrocer's refusal to put the slogan in his window to a freely written poem; in other words, everything in which the genuine aims of life go beyond the limits placed on them by the aims of the system.

3. More frequently, however, the opposition is usually understood (again, largely by Western journalists) as groups of people who make public their nonconformist stances and critical opinions, who make no secret of their independent thinking and who, to a greater or lesser degree, consider themselves a political force. In this sense, the notion of an opposition more or less overlaps with the notion of dissent, although, of course, there are great differences in the degree to which that label is accepted or rejected. It depends not only on the extent to which these people understand their power as a directly political force, and on whether they have ambitions to participate in actual power, but also on how each of them understands the notion of an opposition.

Again, here is an example: in its original declaration, Charter 77 emphasized that it was not an opposition because it had no intention of presenting an alternative political program. It sees its mission as something quite different, for it has not presented such programs. In fact, if the presenting of an alternative program defines the nature of an opposition in post-totalitarian states, then the Charter cannot be considered an opposition. *by put one*

The Czechoslovak government, however, has considered Charter 77 as an expressly oppositional association from the very beginning, and has treated it accordingly. This means that the government—and this is only natural—understands the term "opposition" more or less as I defined it in point 2, that is, as everything that manages to avoid total manipulation and which therefore denies the principle that the system has an absolute claim on the individual.

If we accept this definition of opposition, then of course we must, along with the government, consider the Charter a genuine opposition, because it represents a serious challenge to the integrity of post-totalitarian power, founded as it is on the universality of living with a lie.

It is a different matter, however, when we look at the extent to which individual signatories of Charter 77 think of themselves as an opposition. My impression is that most base their understanding of the term "opposition" on the traditional meaning of the word as it became established in democratic societies (or in classical dictatorships); therefore, they understand opposition, even in Czechoslovakia, as a politically defined force which, although it does not operate on the level of actual power, and even less within the framework of certain rules respected by the government, would still not reject the opportunity to participate in actual power because it has, in a sense, an alternative political program whose proponents are prepared to accept direct political responsibility for it. Given this notion of an opposition, some Chartists—the great majority—do not see themselves in this way. Others—a minority—do, even though they fully respect the fact that there is no room within Charter 77 for "oppositional" activity in this sense. At the same time, however, perhaps every Chartist is familiar enough with the specific nature of conditions in the post-totalitarian system to realize that it is not only the struggle for human rights that has its own peculiar political power, but incomparably more "innocent" activities as well, and therefore they can be understood as an aspect of opposition. No Chartist can really object to being considered an opposition in this sense.

There is another circumstance, however, that considerably complicates matters. For many decades, the power ruling society in the Soviet bloc has used the label "opposition" as the blackest of indictments, as synonymous with the word "enemy." To brand someone "a member of the opposition" is tantamount to saying he is trying to overthrow the government and put an end to socialism (naturally in the pay of the imperialists). There have been times when this label led straight to the gallows, and of course this does not encourage people to apply the same label to themselves. Moreover, it is only a word, and what is actually done is more important than how it is labeled.

The final reason why many reject such a term is because there is something negative about the notion of an "opposition." People who so define themselves do so in relation to a prior "position." In other words, they relate themselves specifically to the power that rules society and through it, define themselves, deriving their own position from the position of the regime. For people who have simply decided to live within the truth, to say aloud what they think, to express their solidarity with their fellow citizens, to create as they want and simply to live in harmony with their better self, it is naturally disagreeable to feel required to define their own original and positive position negatively, in terms of something else, and to think of themselves primarily as people who are against something, not simply as people who *are* what they are.

Obviously, the only way to avoid misunderstanding is to say clearly—before one starts using them—in what sense the terms "opposition" and "member of the opposition" are being used and how they are in fact to be understood in our circumstances.

XIII

IF THE term "opposition" has been imported from democratic societies into the post-totalitarian system without general agreement on what the word means in conditions that are so different, then the term "dissident" was, on the contrary, chosen by Western journalists and is now generally accepted as the label for a phenomenon peculiar to the post-totalitarian system and almost never occurring—at least not in that form—in democratic societies.

Who are these "dissidents"?

It seems that the term is applied primarily to citizens of the Soviet bloc who have decided to live within the truth and who, in addition, meet the following criteria:

1. They express their nonconformist positions and critical opinions publicly and systematically, within the very strict limits available to them, and because of this, they are known in the West.

167

2. Despite being unable to publish at home and despite every possible form of persecution by their governments, they have, by virtue of their attitudes, managed to win a certain esteem, both from the public and from their government, and thus they actually enjoy a very limited and very strange degree of indirect, actual power in their own milieu as well. This either protects them from the worst forms of persecution, or at least it ensures that if they are persecuted, it will mean certain political complications for their governments.

3. The horizon of their critical attention and their commitment reaches beyond the narrow context of their immediate surroundings or special interests to embrace more general causes and, thus, their work becomes political in nature, although the degree to which they think of themselves as a directly political force may vary a great deal.

4. They are people who lean toward intellectual pursuits, that is, they are "writing" people, people for whom the written word is the primary—and often the only—political medium they command, and that can gain them attention, particularly from abroad. Other ways in which they seek to live within the truth are either lost to the foreign observer in the elusive local milieu or—if they reach beyond this local framework—they appear to be only somewhat less visible complements to what they have written.

5. Regardless of their actual vocations, these people are talked about in the West more frequently in terms of their activities as committed citizens, or in terms of the critical, political aspects of their work, than in terms of the real work they do in their own fields. From personal experience, I know that there is an invisible line you cross—without even wanting to or becoming aware of it—beyond which they cease to treat you as a writer who happens to be a concerned citizen and begin talking of you as a "dissident" who almost incidentally (in his spare time, perhaps?) happens to write plays as well.

Unquestionably, there are people who meet all of these criteria. What is debatable is whether we should be using a special term for a group defined in such an essentially accidental way, and specifically, whether they should be called "dissidents." It does happen, however, and there is clearly nothing we can do about it. Sometimes, to facilitate communication, we even use the label ourselves, although it is done with distaste, rather ironically, and almost always in quotation marks.

Perhaps it is now appropriate to outline some of the reasons why "dissidents" themselves are not very happy to be referred to in this way. In the first place, the word is problematic from an etymological point of view. A "dissident," we are told in our press, means something like "renegade" or "backslider." But dissidents do not consider themselves renegades for the simple reason that they are not primarily denying or rejecting anything. On the contrary, they have tried to affirm their own human identity, and if they reject anything at all, then it is merely what was false and alienating in their lives, that aspect of living within a lie.

But that is not the most important thing. The term "dissident" frequently implies a special profession, as if, along with the more normal vocations, there were another special one—grumbling about the state of things. In fact, a "dissident" is simply a physicist, a sociologist, a worker, a poet, individuals who are doing what they feel they must and, consequently, who find themselves in open conflict with the regime. This conflict has not come about through any conscious intention on their part, but simply through the inner logic of their thinking, behavior, or work (often confronted with external circumstances more or less beyond their control). They have not, in other words, consciously decided to be professional malcontents, rather as one decides to be a tailor or a blacksmith.

In fact, of course, they do not usually discover they are "dissidents" until long after they have actually become one. "Dissent" springs from motivations far different from the desire for titles or fame. In short, they do not decide to become "dissidents," and even if they were to devote twenty-four hours a day to it, it would still not be a profession, but primarily an existential attitude. Moreover, it is an attitude that is in no

way the exclusive property of those who have earned themselves the title of "dissident" just because they happen to fulfill those accidental external conditions already mentioned.
There are thousands of nameless people who try to live within
the truth and millions who want to but cannot, perhaps only
because to do so in the circumstances in which they live, they
would need ten times the courage of those who have already
taken the first step. If several dozen are randomly chosen
from among all these people and put into a special category,
this can utterly distort the general picture. It does so in two
different ways. Either it suggests that "dissidents" are a group
of prominent people, a protected species who are permitted
to do things others are not and whom the government may
even be cultivating as living proof of its generosity; or it lends
support to the illusion that since there is no more than a
handful of malcontents to whom not very much is really being done, all the rest are therefore content, for were they not
so, they would be "dissidents" too.

But that is not all. This categorization also unintentionally
supports the impression that the primary concern of these
"dissidents" is some vested interest that they share as a group,
as though their entire argument with the government were
no more than a rather abstruse conflict between two opposed
groups, a conflict that leaves society out of it altogether. But
such an impression profoundly contradicts the real importance of the "dissident" attitude, which stands or falls on its
interest in others, in what ails society as a whole, in other
words, on an interest in all those who do not speak up. If
"dissidents" have any kind of authority at all, and if they have
not been exterminated long ago like exotic insects that have
appeared where they have no business being, then this is not
because the government holds this exclusive group and their
exclusive ideas in such awe, but because it is perfectly aware
of the potential political power of living within the truth
rooted in the hidden sphere, and well aware too of the kind
of world "dissent" grows out of and the world it addresses:
the everyday human world, the world of daily tension be-

tween the aims of life and the aims of the system. (Can there be any better evidence of this than the government's action after Charter 77 appeared, when it launched a campaign to compel the entire nation to declare that Charter 77 was wrong? Those millions of signatures proved, among other things, that just the opposite was true.) The political organs and the police do not lavish such enormous attention on "dissidents"—which may give the impression that the government fears them as they might fear an alternative power clique—because they actually are such a power clique, but because they are ordinary people with ordinary cares, differing from the rest only in that they say aloud what the rest cannot say or are afraid to say. I have already mentioned Solzhenitsyn's political influence: it does not reside in some exclusive political power he possesses as an individual, but in the experience of those millions of Gulag victims which he simply amplified and communicated to millions of other people of good will.

To institutionalize a select category of well-known or prominent "dissidents" means in fact to deny the most intrinsic moral aspect of their activity. As we have seen, the "dissident" movement grows out of the principle of equality, founded on the notion that human rights and freedoms are indivisible. After all, did no well-known "dissidents" unite in KOR to defend unknown workers? And was it not precisely for this reason that they became "well-known dissidents"? And did not the well-known "dissidents" unite in Charter 77 after they had been brought together in defense of those unknown musicians, and did they not unite in the Charter precisely with them, and did they not become "well-known dissidents" precisely because of that? It is truly a cruel paradox that the more some citizens stand up in defense of other citizens, the more they are labeled with a word that in effect separates them from those "other citizens."

This explanation, I hope, will make clear the significance of the quotation marks I have put around the word "dissident" throughout this essay.

XIV

AT THE time when the Czech lands and Slovakia were an integral part of the Austro-Hungarian Empire, and when there existed neither the historical nor the political, psychological, nor social conditions that would have enabled the Czechs and Slovaks to seek their identity outside the framework of this empire, Tomáš Garrigue Masaryk established a Czechoslovak national program based on the notion of "small-scale work" (*drobná práce*). By that he meant honest and responsible work in widely different areas of life but within the existing social order, work that would stimulate national creativity and national self-confidence. Naturally he placed particular emphasis on intelligent and enlightened upbringing and education, and on the moral and humanitarian aspects of life. Masaryk believed that the only possible starting point for a more dignified national destiny was humanity itself. Humanity's first task was to create the conditions for a more human life; and in Masaryk's view, the task of transforming the stature of the nation began with the transformation of human beings.

This notion of "working for the good of the nation" took root in Czechoslovak society and in many ways it was successful and is still alive today. Along with those who exploit the notion as a sophisticated excuse for collaborating with the regime, there are still many, even today, who genuinely uphold the ideal and, in some areas at least, can point to indisputable achievements. It is hard to say how much worse things would be if there were not many hard-working people who simply refuse to give up and try constantly to do the best they can, paying an unavoidable minimum to living within a lie so that they might give their utmost to the authentic needs of society. These people assume, correctly, that every piece of good work is an indirect criticism of bad politics, and that there are situations where it is worthwhile going this route, even though it means surrendering one's natural right to make direct criticisms.

Today, however, there are very clear limitations to this attitude, even compared to the situation in the 1960s. More and more frequently, those who attempt to practice the principle of "small-scale work" come up against the post-totalitarian system and find themselves facing a dilemma: either one retreats from that position, dilutes the honesty, responsibility, and consistency on which it is based, and simply adapts to circumstances (the approach taken by the majority), or one continues on the way begun and inevitably comes into conflict with the regime (the approach taken by a minority).

If the notion of small-scale work was never intended as an imperative to survive in the existing social and political structure *at any cost* (in which case individuals who allowed themselves to be excluded from that structure would necessarily appear to have given up "working for the nation"), then today it is even less significant. There is no general model of behavior, that is, no neat, universally valid way of determining the point at which small-scale work ceases to be for the good of the nation and becomes detrimental to the nation. It is more than clear, however, that the danger of such a reversal is becoming more and more acute and that small-scale work, with increasing frequency, is coming up against that limit beyond which avoiding conflict means compromising its very essence.

In 1974, when I was employed in a brewery, my immediate superior was a certain Š, a person well versed in the art of making beer. He was proud of his profession and he wanted our brewery to brew good beer. He spent almost all his time at work, continually thinking up improvements, and he frequently made the rest of us feel uncomfortable because he assumed that we loved brewing as much as he did. In the midst of the slovenly indifference to work that socialism encourages, a more constructive worker would be difficult to imagine.

The brewery itself was managed by people who understood their work less and were less fond of it, but who were politically more influential. They were bringing the brewery to ruin and not only did they fail to react to any of Š's suggestions, but they actually became increasingly hostile toward him and tried in every way to thwart his efforts to do a good job. Eventually the situation became so bad that Š felt compelled to write a lengthy letter to the manager's superior, in which he attempted to analyze the brewery's difficulties. He explained why it was the worst in the district and pointed to those responsible.

His voice might have been heard. The manager, who was politically powerful but otherwise ignorant of beer, a man who loathed workers and was given to intrigue, might have been replaced and conditions in the brewery might have been improved on the basis of Š's suggestions. Had this happened, it would have been a perfect example of small-scale work in action. Unfortunately, the precise opposite occurred: the manager of the brewery, who was a member of the Communist Party's district committee, had friends in higher places and he saw to it that the situation was resolved in his favor. Š's analysis was described as a "defamatory document" and Š himself was labeled a "political saboteur." He was thrown out of the brewery and shifted to another one where he was given a job requiring no skill. Here the notion of small-scale work had come up against the wall of the post-totalitarian system. By speaking the truth, Š had stepped out of line, broken the rules, cast himself out, and he ended up as a subcitizen, stigmatized as an enemy. He could now say anything he wanted, but he could never, as a matter of principle, expect to be heard. He had become the "dissident" of the Eastern Bohemian Brewery.

I think this is a model case which, from another point of view, illustrates what I have already said in the preceding section: you do not become a "dissident" just because you decide one day to take up this most unusual career. You are thrown into it by your personal sense of responsibility, combined with a complex set of external circumstances. You are cast out of the existing structures and placed in a position of conflict with them. It begins as an attempt to do your work well, and ends with being branded an enemy of society. This is why our situation is not comparable to the Austro-Hungarian Empire, when the Czech nation, in the worst period of Bach's absolutism, had only one real "dissident," Karel Havlíček, who was imprisoned in Brixen. Today, if we are not to be snobbish about it, we must admit that "dissidents" can be found on every street corner.

To rebuke "dissidents" for having abandoned "small-scale work" is simply absurd. "Dissent" is not an alternative to Masaryk's notion, it is frequently its one possible outcome. I say "frequently" in order to emphasize that this is not always the case. I am far from believing that the only decent and responsible people are those who find themselves at odds with the existing social and political structures. After all, the brewmaster Š might have won his battle. To condemn those who have kept their positions simply because they have kept them, in other words, for not being "dissidents," would be just as absurd as to hold them up as an example to the "dissidents." In any case, it contradicts the whole "dissident" attitude— seen as an attempt to live within the truth—if one judges human behavior not according to what it is and whether it is good or not, but according to the personal circumstances such an attempt has brought one to.

XV

OUR GREENGROCER'S attempt to live within the truth may be confined to not doing certain things. He decides not to put flags in his window when his only motive for putting them there in the first place would have been to avoid being reported by the house warden; he does not vote in elections that he considers false; he does not hide his opinions from his superiors. In other words, he may go no further than "merely" refusing to comply with certain demands made on him by the system (which of course is not an insignificant step to take). This may, however, grow into something more. The greengrocer may begin to do something concrete, something that goes beyond an immediately personal self-defensive reaction against manipulation, something that will manifest his newfound sense of higher responsibility. He may, for example, organize his fellow greengrocers to act together in defense of their interests. He may write letters to various institutions, drawing their attention to instances of disorder and injustice around him. He may seek out unofficial literature, copy it, and lend it to his friends.

If what I have called living within the truth is a basic existential (and of course potentially political) starting point for all those "independent citizens' initiatives" and "dissident" or "opposition" movements this does not mean that every attempt to live within the truth automatically belongs in this category. On the contrary, in its most original and broadest sense, living within the truth covers a vast territory whose outer limits are vague and difficult to map, a territory full of modest expressions of human volition, the vast majority of which will remain anonymous and whose political impact will probably never be felt or described any more concretely than simply as a part of a social climate or mood. Most of these expressions remain elementary revolts against manipulation: you simply straighten your backbone and live in greater dignity as an individual.

Here and there—thanks to the nature, the assumptions, and the professions of some people, but also thanks to a number of accidental circumstances such as the specific nature of the local milieu, friends, and so on—a more coherent and visible initiative may emerge from this wide and anonymous hinterland, an initiative that transcends "merely" individual revolt and is transformed into more conscious, structured, and purposeful work. The point where living within the truth ceases to be a mere negation of living with a lie and becomes articulate in a particular way is the point at which something is born that might be called the "independent spiritual, social, and political life of society." This independent life is not separated from the rest of life ("dependent life") by some sharply defined line. Both types frequently co-exist in the same people. Nevertheless, its most important focus is marked by a relatively high degree of inner emancipation. It sails upon the vast ocean of the manipulated life like little boats, tossed by the waves but always bobbing back as visible messengers of living within the truth, articulating the suppressed aims of life.

What is this independent life of society? The spectrum of its expressions and activities is naturally very wide. It includes everything from self-education and thinking about the world, through free creative activity and its communication to others, to the most varied free, civic attitudes, including instances of independent social self-organization. In short, it is an area in which living within the truth becomes articulate and materializes in a visible way.

Thus what will later be referred to as "citizens' initiatives," "dissident movements," or even "oppositions," emerge, like the proverbial one tenth of the iceberg visible above the water, from that area, from the independent life of society. In other words, just as the independent life of society develops out of living within the truth in the widest sense of the word, as the distinct, articulated expression of that life, so "dissent" gradually emerges from the independent life of society. Yet there is a marked difference: if the independent life of society, externally at least, can be understood as a higher form of living within the truth, it is far less certain that "dissident" movements are necessarily a higher form of the independent life of society. They are simply one manifestation of it and, though they may be the most visible and, at first glance, the most political (and most clearly articulated) expression of it, they are far from necessarily being the most mature or even the most important, not only in the general social sense but even in terms of direct political influence. After all, "dissent" has been artificially removed from its place of birth by having been given a special name. In fact, however, it is not possible to think of it separated from the whole background out of which it develops, of which it is an integral part, and from which it draws all its vital strength. In any case, it follows from what has already been said about the peculiarities of the post-totalitarian system that what appears to be the most political of forces in a given moment, and what thinks of itself in such terms, need not necessarily in fact be such a force. The extent to which it is a real political force is due exclusively to its pre-political context.

What follows from this description? Nothing more and nothing less than this: it is impossible to talk about what in fact "dissidents" do and the effect of their work without first talking about the work of all those who, in one way or another, take part in the independent life of society and who are not necessarily "dissidents" at all. They may be writers who write as they wish without regard for censorship or official demands and who issue their work—when official publishers refuse to print it—as *samizdat*. They may be philosophers, historians, sociologists, and all those who practice independent scholarship and, if it is impossible through official or semi-official channels, who also circulate their work in *samizdat* or who organize private discussions, lectures, and seminars. They may be teachers who privately teach young people things that are kept from them in the state schools; clergymen who either in office or, if they are deprived of their charges, outside it, try to carry on a free religious life; painters, musicians, and singers who practice their work regardless of how it is looked upon by official institutions; everyone who shares this independent culture and helps to spread it; people who, using the means available to them, try to express and defend the actual social interests of workers, to put real meaning back into trade unions or to form independent ones; people who are not afraid to call the attention of officials to cases of injustice and who strive to see that the laws are observed; and the different groups of young people who try to extricate themselves from manipulation and live in their own way, in the spirit of their own hierarchy of values. The list could go on.

Very few would think of calling all these people "dissidents." And yet are not the well-known "dissidents" simply people like them? Are not all these activities in fact what "dissidents" do as well? Do they not produce scholarly work and publish it in *samizdat*? Do they not write plays and novels and poems? Do they not lecture to students in private "universities"? Do they not struggle against various forms of injustice and attempt to ascertain and express the genuine social interests of various sectors of the population?

After having tried to indicate the sources, the inner structure, and some aspects of the "dissident" attitude as such, I have clearly shifted my viewpoint from outside, as it were, to an investigation of what these "dissidents" actually do, how their initiatives are manifested, and where they lead.

The first conclusion to be drawn, then, is that the original and most important sphere of activity, one that predetermines all the others, is simply an attempt to create and support the independent life of society as an articulated expression of living within the truth. In other words, serving truth consistently, purposefully, and articulately, and organizing this service. This is only natural, after all: if living within the truth is an elementary starting point for every attempt made by people to oppose the alienating pressure of the system, if it is the only meaningful basis of any independent act of political import, and if, ultimately, it is also the most intrinsic existential source of the "dissident" attitude, then it is difficult to imagine that even manifest "dissent" could have any other basis than the service of truth, the truthful life, and the attempt to make room for the genuine aims of life.

XVI

"defensive" politics: weakness vs. strength

THE POST-TOTALITARIAN system is mounting a total assault on humans and humans stand against it alone, abandoned and isolated. It is therefore entirely natural that all the "dissident" movements are explicitly defensive movements: they exist to defend human beings and the genuine aims of life against the aims of the system.

Today the Polish group KOR is called the "Committee for Social Self-Defense." The word "defense" appears in the names of other similar groups in Poland, but even the Soviet Helsinki monitoring group and our own Charter 77 are clearly defensive in nature.

In terms of traditional politics, this program of defense is understandable, even though it may appear minimal, provisional, and ultimately negative. It offers no new conception, model, or ideology, and therefore it is not politics in the proper sense of the word, since politics always assumes a positive program and can scarcely limit itself to defending someone against something.

b/c Such a view, I think, reveals the limitations of the traditionally political way of looking at things. The post-totalitarian system, after all, is not the manifestation of a particular political line followed by a particular government. It is something radically different: it is a complex, profound, and long-term violation of society, or rather the self-violation of society. To oppose it merely by establishing a different political line and then striving for a change in government would not only be unrealistic, it would be utterly inadequate, for it would never come near to touching the root of the matter. For some time now, the problem has no longer resided in a political line or program: it is a problem of life itself.

Thus, defending the aims of life, defending humanity, is not only a more realistic approach, since it can begin right now and is potentially more popular because it concerns people's everyday lives; at the same time (and perhaps precisely because of this) it is also an incomparably more consistent approach because it aims at the very essence of things.

There are times when we must sink to the bottom of our misery to understand truth, just as we must descend to the bottom of a well to see the stars in broad daylight. It seems to me that today, this "provisional," "minimal," and "negative" program—the "simple" defense of people—is in a particular sense (and not merely in the circumstances in which we live) an optimal and most positive program because it forces politics to return to its only proper starting point, proper that is, if all the old mistakes are to be avoided: individual people. In the democratic societies, where the violence done to human beings is not nearly so obvious and cruel, this fundamental revolution in politics has yet to happen, and some things will probably have to get worse there before the urgent need for that revolution is reflected in politics. In our world, precisely because of the misery in which we find ourselves, it would seem that politics has already undergone that transformation: the central concern of political thought is no longer abstract visions of a self-redeeming, "positive" model (and of course the opportunistic political practices that are the reverse of the same coin), but rather the people who have so far merely been enslaved by those models and their practices.

Every society, of course, requires some degree of organization. Yet if that organization is to serve people, and not the other way around, then people will have to be liberated and space created so that they may organize themselves in meaningful ways. The depravity of the opposite approach, in which people are first organized in one way or another (by someone who always knows best "what the people need") so they may then allegedly be liberated, is something we have known on our own skins only too well.

To sum up: most people who are too bound to the traditional political way of thinking see the weaknesses of the "dissident" movements in their purely defensive character. In contrast, I see that as their greatest strength. I believe that this is precisely where these movements supersede the kind of politics from whose point of view their program can seem so inadequate.

XVII

IN THE "dissident" movements of the Soviet bloc, the defense of human beings usually takes the form of a defense of human and civil rights as they are entrenched in various official documents such as the Universal Declaration of Human Rights, the International Covenants on Human Rights, the

Concluding Act of the Helsinki Agreement, and the constitutions of individual states. These movements set out to defend anyone who is being prosecuted for acting in the spirit of those rights, and they in turn act in the same spirit in their work, by insisting over and over again that the regime recognize and respect human and civil rights, and by drawing attention to the areas of life where this is not the case.

Their work, therefore, is based on the principle of legality: they operate publicly and openly, insisting not only that their activity is in line with the law, but that achieving respect for the law is one of their main aims. This principle of legality, which provides both the point of departure and the framework for their activities, is common to all "dissident" groups in the Soviet bloc, even though individual groups have never worked out any formal agreement on that point. This circumstance raises an important question: Why, in conditions where a widespread and arbitrary abuse of power is the rule, is there such a general and spontaneous acceptance of the principle of legality?

On the primary level, this stress on legality is a natural expression of specific conditions that exist in the post-totalitarian system, and the consequence of an elementary understanding of that specificity. If there are in essence only two ways to struggle for a free society—that is, through legal means and through (armed or unarmed) revolt—then it should be obvious at once how inappropriate the latter alternative is in the post-totalitarian system. Revolt is appropriate when conditions are clearly and openly in motion, during a war, for example, or in situations where social or political conflicts are coming to a head. It is appropriate in a classical dictatorship that is either just setting itself up or is in a state of collapse. In other words, it is appropriate where social forces of comparable strength (for example, a government of occupation versus a nation fighting for its freedom) are confronting each other on the level of actual power, or where there is a clear distinction between the usurpers of power and the subjugated population, or when society finds itself in a state of open crisis. Conditions in the post-totalitarian system—except in extremely explosive situations like the one in Hungary in 1956—are, of course, precisely the opposite. They are static and stable, and social crises, for the most part, exist only latently (though they run much deeper). Society is not sharply polarized on the level of actual political power, but, as we have seen, the fundamental lines of conflict run right through each person. In this situation, no attempt at revolt could ever hope to set up even a minimum of resonance in the rest of society, because that society is soporific, submerged in a consumer rat race and wholly involved in the post-totalitarian system (that is, participating in it and acting as agents of its automatism), and it would simply find anything like revolt unacceptable. It would interpret the revolt as an attack upon itself and, rather than supporting the revolt, it would very probably react by intensifying its bias toward the system, since, in its view, the system can at least guarantee a certain quasi-legality. Add to this the fact that the post-totalitarian system has at its disposal a complex mechanism of direct and indirect surveillance that has no equal in *Surveill* history and it is clear that not only would any attempt to revolt come to a dead end politically, but it would also be almost technically impossible to carry off. Most probably it would be liquidated before it had a chance to translate its intentions into action. Even if revolt were possible, however, it would remain the solitary gesture of a few isolated individuals and they would be opposed not only by a gigantic apparatus of national (and supranational) power, but also by the very society in whose name they were mounting their revolt in the first place. (This, by the way, is another reason why the regime and its propaganda have been ascribing terroristic aims to the "dissident" movements and accusing them of illegal and conspiratorial methods.)

All of this, however, is not the main reason why the "dissident" movements support the principle of legality. That reason lies deeper, in the innermost structure of the "dissident" attitude. This attitude is and must be fundamentally hostile toward the notion of violent change—simply because it places its faith in violence. (Generally, the "dissident" attitude can only accept violence as a necessary evil in extreme situations, when direct violence can only be met by violence and where remaining passive would in effect mean supporting violence: let us recall, for example, that the blindness of European pacifism was one of the factors that prepared the ground for the Second World War.) As I have already mentioned, "dissidents" tend to be skeptical about political thought based on the faith that profound social changes can only be achieved by bringing about (regardless of the method) changes in the system or in the government, and the belief that such changes—because they are considered "fundamental"—justify the sacrifice of "less fundamental" things, in other words, human lives. Respect for a theoretical concept here outweighs respect for human life. Yet this is precisely what threatens to enslave humanity all over again.

"Dissident" movements, as I have tried to indicate, share exactly the opposite view. They understand systemic change as something superficial, something secondary, something that in itself can guarantee nothing. Thus an attitude that turns away from abstract political visions of the future toward concrete human beings and ways of defending them effectively in the here and now is quite naturally accompanied by an intensified antipathy to all forms of violence carried out in the name of a better future, and by a profound belief that a future secured by violence might actually be worse than what exists now; in other words, the future would be fatally stigmatized by the very means used to secure it. At the same time, this attitude is not to be mistaken for political conservatism or political moderation. The "dissident" movements do not shy away from the idea of violent political overthrow because the idea seems too radical, but on the contrary, because it does not seem radical enough. For them, the problem lies far too deep to be settled through mere systemic changes, either governmental or technological. Some people, faithful to the classical Marxist doctrines of the nineteenth century, understand our system as the hegemony of an exploiting class over an exploited class and, operating from the postulate that exploiters never surrender their power voluntarily, they see the only solution in a revolution to sweep away the exploiters. Naturally, they regard such things as the struggle for human rights as something hopelessly legalistic, illusory, opportunistic, and ultimately misleading because it makes the doubtful assumption that you can negotiate in good faith with your exploiters on the basis of a false legality. The problem is that they are unable to find anyone determined enough to carry out this revolution, with the result that they become bitter, skeptical, passive, and ultimately apathetic—in other words, they end up precisely where the system wants them to be. This is one example of how far one can be misled by mechanically applying, in post-totalitarian circumstances, ideological models from another world and another time.

Of course, one need not be an advocate of violent revolution to ask whether an appeal to legality makes any sense at all when the laws—and particularly the general laws concerning human rights—are no more than a facade, an aspect of the world of appearances, a mere game behind which lies total manipulation. "They can ratify anything because they will still go ahead and do whatever they want anyway"—this is an opinion we often encounter. Is it not true that constantly to take them at their word, to appeal to laws every child knows are binding only as long as the government wishes, is in the end just a kind of hypocrisy, a Švejkian obstructionism and, finally, just another way of playing the game, another form of self-delusion? In other words, is the legalistic approach at all compatible with the principle of living within the truth?

This question can only be answered by first looking at the wider implications of how the legal code functions in the post-totalitarian system.

In a classical dictatorship, to a far greater extent than in the post-totalitarian system, the will of the ruler is carried out directly, in an unregulated fashion. A dictatorship has no reason to hide its foundations, nor to conceal the real workings of power, and therefore it need not encumber itself to any great extent with a legal code. The post-totalitarian system, on the other hand, is utterly obsessed with the need to bind everything in a single order: life in such a state is thoroughly permeated by a dense network of regulations, proclamations, directives, norms, orders, and rules. (It is not called a bureaucratic system without good reason.) A large proportion of those norms function as direct instruments of the complex manipulation of life that is intrinsic to the post-totalitarian system. Individuals are reduced to little more than tiny cogs in an enormous mechanism and their significance is limited to their function in this mechanism. Their job, housing accommodation, movements, social and cultural expressions, everything, in short, must be cosseted together as firmly as possible, predetermined, regulated, and controlled. Every aberration from the prescribed course of life is treated as error, license, and anarchy. From the cook in the restaurant who, without hard-to-get permission from the bureaucratic apparatus, cannot cook something special for his customers, to the singer who cannot perform his new song at a concert without bureaucratic approval, everyone, in all aspects of their life, is caught in this regulatory tangle of red tape, the inevitable product of the post-totalitarian system. With ever-increasing consistency, it binds all the expressions and aims of life to the spirit of its own aims: the vested interests of its own smooth, automatic operation.

In a narrower sense the legal code serves the post-totalitarian system in this direct way as well, that is, it too forms a part of the world of regulations and prohibitions. At the same time, however, it performs the same service in another indirect way, one that brings it remarkably closer—depending on which level of the law is involved—to ideology and in some cases makes it a direct component of that ideology.

1. Like ideology, the legal code functions as an excuse. It wraps the base exercise of power in the noble apparel of the

letter of the law; it creates the pleasing illusion that justice is done, society protected, and the exercise of power objectively regulated. All this is done to conceal the real essence of post-totalitarian legal practice: the total manipulation of society. If an outside observer who knew nothing at all about life in Czechoslovakia were to study only its laws, he would be utterly incapable of understanding what we were complaining about. The hidden political manipulation of the courts and of public prosecutors, the limitations placed on lawyers' ability to defend their clients, the closed nature, *de facto,* of trials, the arbitrary actions of the security forces, their position of authority over the judiciary, the absurdly broad application of several deliberately vague sections of that code, and of course the state's utter disregard for the positive sections of that code (the rights of citizens): all of this would remain hidden from our outside observer. The only thing he would take away would be the impression that our legal code is not much worse than the legal code of other civilized countries, and not much different either, except perhaps for certain curiosities, such as the entrenchment in the constitution of a single political party's eternal rule and the state's love for a neighboring superpower.

But that is not all: if our observer had the opportunity to study the formal side of the policing and judicial procedures and practices, how they look "on paper," he would discover that for the most part the common rules of criminal procedure are observed: charges are laid within the prescribed period following arrest, and it is the same with detention orders. Indictments are properly delivered, the accused has a lawyer, and so on. In other words, everyone has an excuse: they have all observed the law. In reality, however, they have cruelly and pointlessly ruined a young person's life, perhaps for no other reason than because he made *samizdat* copies of a novel written by a banned writer, or because the police deliberately falsified their testimony (as everyone knows, from the judge on down to the defendant). Yet all of this somehow remains in the background. The falsified testimony is not necessarily obvious from the trial documents and the section of the Criminal Code dealing with incitement does not formally exclude the application of that charge to the copying of a banned novel. In other words, the legal code—at least in several areas—is no more than a facade, an aspect of the world of appearances. Then why is it there at all? For exactly the same reason as ideology is there: it provides a bridge of excuses between the system and individuals, making it easier for them to enter the power structure and serve the arbitrary demands of power. The excuse lets individuals fool themselves into thinking they are merely upholding the law and protecting society from criminals. (Without this excuse, how much more difficult it would be to recruit new generations of judges, prosecutors, and interrogators!) As an aspect of the world of appearances, however, the legal code deceives not only the conscience of prosecutors, it deceives the public, it deceives foreign observers, and it even deceives history itself.

2. Like ideology, the legal code is an essential instrument of ritual communication outside the power structure. It is the legal code that gives the exercise of power a form, a framework, a set of rules. It is the legal code that enables all components of the system to communicate, to put themselves in a good light, to establish their own legitimacy. It provides their whole game with its rules and engineers with their technology. Can the exercise of post-totalitarian power be imagined at all without this universal ritual making it all possible, serving as a common language to bind the relevant sectors of the power structure together? The more important the position occupied by the repressive apparatus in the power structure, the more important that it function according to some kind of formal code. How, otherwise, could people be so easily and inconspicuously locked up for copying banned books if there were no judges, prosecutors, interrogators, defense lawyers, court stenographers, and thick files, and if all this were not held together by some firm order? And above all, without that innocent-looking Section 100 on incitement? This could all be done, of course, without a legal code and its

accessories, but only in some ephemeral dictatorship run by a Ugandan bandit, not in a system that embraces such a huge portion of civilized humankind and represents an integral, stable, and respected part of the modern world. That would not only be unthinkable, it would quite simply be technically impossible. Without the legal code functioning as a ritually cohesive force, the post-totalitarian system could not exist.

The entire role of ritual, facades, and excuses appears most eloquently, of course, not in the proscriptive section of the legal code, which sets out what a citizen may not do and what the grounds for prosecution are, but in the section declaring what he may do and what his or her rights are. Here there is truly nothing but "words, words, words." Yet even that part of the code is of immense importance to the system, for it is here that the system establishes its legitimacy as a whole, before its own citizens, before schoolchildren, before the international public, and before history. The system cannot afford to disregard this because it cannot permit itself to cast doubt upon the fundamental postulates of its ideology, which are so essential to its very existence. (We have already seen how the power structure is enslaved by its own ideology and its ideological prestige.) To do this would be to deny everything it tries to present itself as and, thus, one of the main pillars on which the system rests would be undermined: the integrity of the world of appearances.

If the exercise of power circulates through the whole power structure as blood flows through veins, then the legal code can be understood as something that reinforces the walls of those veins. Without it, the blood of power could not circulate in an organized way and the body of society would hemorrhage at random. Order would collapse.

A persistent and never-ending appeal to the laws—not just to the laws concerning human rights, but to all laws—does not mean at all that those who do so have succumbed to the illusion that in our system the law is anything other than what it is. They are well aware of the role it plays. But precisely because they know how desperately the system depends on it—on the "noble" version of the law, that is—they also know how enormously significant such appeals are. Because the system cannot do without the law, because it is hopelessly tied down by the necessity of pretending the laws are observed, it is compelled to react in some way to such appeals. Demanding that the laws be upheld is thus an act of living within the truth that threatens the whole mendacious structure at its point of maximum mendacity. Over and over again, such appeals make the purely ritualistic nature of the law clear to society and to those who inhabit its power structures. They draw attention to its real material substance and thus, indirectly, compel all those who take refuge behind the law to affirm and make credible this agency of excuses, this means of communication, this reinforcement of the social arteries outside of which their will could not be made to circulate through society. They are compelled to do so for the sake of their own consciences, for the impression they make on outsiders, to maintain themselves in power (as part of the system's own mechanism of self-preservation and its principles of cohesion), or simply out of fear that they will be reproached for being clumsy in handling the ritual. They have no other choice: because they cannot discard the rules of their own game, they can only attend more carefully to those rules. Not to react to challenges means to undermine their own excuse and lose control of their mutual communications system. To assume that the laws are a mere facade, that they have no validity, and that therefore it is pointless to appeal to them would mean to go on reinforcing those aspects of the law that create the facade and the ritual. It would mean confirming the law as an aspect of the world of appearances and enabling those who exploit it to rest easy with the cheapest (and therefore the most mendacious) form of their excuse.

I have frequently witnessed policemen, prosecutors, or judges—if they were dealing with an experienced Chartist or a courageous lawyer, and if they were exposed to public attention (as individuals with a name, no longer protected by the anonymity of the apparatus)—suddenly and anxiously begin to take particular care that no cracks appear in the ritual. This does not alter the fact that a despotic power is hiding behind that ritual, but the very existence of the officials' anxiety necessarily regulates, limits, and slows down the operation of that despotism.

This, of course, is not enough. But an essential part of the "dissident" attitude is that it comes out of the reality of the human here and now. It places more importance on often repeated and consistent concrete action—even though it may be inadequate and though it may ease only insignificantly the suffering of a single insignificant citizen—than it does in some abstract fundamental solution in an uncertain future. In any case, is not this in fact just another form of "small-scale work" in the Masarykian sense, with which the "dissident" attitude seemed at first to be in such sharp contradiction?

This section would be incomplete without stressing certain internal limitations to the policy of taking them at their own word. The point is this: even in the most ideal of cases, the law is only one of several imperfect and more or less external ways of defending what is better in life against what is worse. By itself, the law can never create anything better. Its purpose is to render a service and its meaning does not lie in the law itself. Establishing respect for the law does not automatically ensure a better life for that, after all, is a job for people and not for laws and institutions. It is possible to imagine a society with good laws that are fully respected but in which it is impossible to live. Conversely, one can imagine life being quite bearable even where the laws are imperfect and imperfectly applied. The most important thing is always the quality of that life and whether or not the laws enhance life or repress it, not merely whether they are upheld or not. (Often strict observance of the law could have a disastrous impact on human dignity.) The key to a humane, dignified, rich, and happy life does not lie either in the constitution or in the Criminal Code. These merely establish what may or may not be done and, thus, they can make life easier or more difficult. They limit or permit, they punish, tolerate, or defend, but they can never give life substance or meaning. The struggle for what is called "legality" must constantly keep this legality in perspective against the background of life as it really is. Without keeping one's eyes open to the real dimensions of life's beauty and misery, and without a moral relationship to life, this struggle will sooner or later come to grief on the rocks of some self-justifying system of scholastics. Without really wanting to, one would thus become more and more like the observer who comes to conclusions about our system only on the basis of trial documents and is satisfied if all the appropriate regulations have been observed.

XVIII

IF THE basic job of the "dissident" movements is to serve truth, that is, to serve the real aims of life, and if that necessarily develops into a defense of individuals and their right to a free and truthful life (that is, a defense of human rights and a struggle to see the laws respected), then another stage of this approach, perhaps the most mature stage so far, is what Václav Benda called the development of "parallel structures."

When those who have decided to live within the truth have been denied any direct influence on the existing social structures, not to mention the opportunity to participate in them, and when these people begin to create what I have called the independent life of society, this independent life begins, of itself, to become structured in a certain way. Sometimes there are only very embryonic indications of this process of structuring; at other times, the structures are already quite well developed. Their genesis and evolution are inseparable from the phenomenon of "dissent," even though they reach far beyond the arbitrarily defined area of activity usually indicated by that term.

What are these structures? Ivan Jirous was the first in Czechoslovakia to formulate and apply in practice the concept of a "second culture." Although at first he was thinking chiefly of nonconformist rock music and only certain literary, artistic, or performance events close to the sensibilities of those nonconformist musical groups, the term second culture very rapidly came to be used for the whole area of independent and repressed culture, that is, not only for art and its various currents but also for the humanities, the social sciences, and philosophical thought. This second culture, quite naturally, has created elementary organizational forms: *samizdat* editions of books and magazines, private performances and concerts, seminars, exhibitions, and so on. (In Poland all of this is vastly more developed: there are independent publishing houses and many more periodicals, even political periodicals; they have means of proliferation other than carbon copies, and so on. In the Soviet Union, *samizdat* has a longer tradition and clearly its forms are quite different.) Culture, therefore, is a sphere in which the parallel structures can be observed in their most highly developed form. Benda, of course, gives thought to potential or embryonic forms of such structures in other spheres as well: from a parallel information network to parallel forms of education (private universities), parallel trade unions, parallel foreign contacts, to a kind of hypothesis on a parallel economy. On the basis of these parallel structures, he then develops the notion of a "parallel *polis*" or state or, rather, he sees the rudiments of such a *polis* in these structures.

At a certain stage in its development, the independent life of society and the "dissident" movements cannot avoid a certain amount of organization and institutionalization. This is a natural development, and unless this independent life of society is somehow radically suppressed and eliminated, the tendency will grow. Along with it, a parallel political life will also necessarily evolve, and to a certain extent it exists already in Czechoslovakia. Various groupings of a more or less political nature will continue to define themselves politically, to act and confront each other.

These parallel structures, it may be said, represent the most articulated expressions so far of living within the truth. One of the most important tasks the "dissident" movements have set themselves is to support and develop them. Once again, it confirms the fact that all attempts by society to resist the pressure of the system have their essential beginnings in the "pre-political" area. For what else are parallel structures than an area where a different life can be lived, a life that is in harmony with its own aims and which in turn structures itself in harmony with those aims? What else are those initial attempts at social self-organization than the efforts of a certain part of society to live—as a society—within the truth, to rid itself of the self-sustaining aspects of totalitarianism and, thus, to extricate itself radically from its involvement in the post-totalitarian system? What else is it but a nonviolent attempt by people to negate the system within themselves and to establish their lives on a new basis, that of their own proper identity? And does this tendency not confirm once more the principle of returning the focus to actual individuals? After all, the parallel structures do not grow *a priori* out of a theoretical vision of systemic changes (there are no political sects involved), but from the aims of life and the authentic needs of real people. In fact, all eventual changes in the system, changes we may observe here in their rudimentary forms, have come about as it were *de facto,* from "below," because life compelled them to, not because they came before life, somehow directing it or forcing some change on it.

Historical experience teaches us that any genuinely meaningful point of departure in an individual's life usually has an element of universality about it. In other words, it is not something partial, accessible only to a restricted community, and not transferable to any other. On the contrary, it must be potentially accessible to everyone; it must foreshadow a general solution and, thus, it is not just the expression of an introverted, self-contained responsibility that individuals have to and for themselves alone, but responsibility to and for the world. Thus it would be quite wrong to understand the parallel structures and the parallel *polis* as a retreat into a ghetto and as an act of isolation, addressing itself only to the welfare of those who had decided on such a course, and who are indifferent to the rest. It would be wrong, in short, to consider it an essentially group solution that has nothing to do with the general situation. Such a concept would, from the start, alienate the notion of living within the truth from its proper point of departure, which is concern for others, transforming it ultimately into just another more sophisticated version of living within a lie. In doing so, of course, it would cease to be a genuine point of departure for individuals and groups and would recall the false notion of "dissidents" as an exclusive group with exclusive interests, carrying on their own exclusive dialogue with the powers that be. In any case, even the most highly developed forms of life in the parallel structures, even that most mature form of the parallel *polis* can only exist—at least in post-totalitarian circumstances—when the individual is at the same time lodged in the "first," official structure by a thousand different relationships, even though it may only be the fact that one buys what one needs in their stores, uses their money, and obeys their laws. Certainly one can imagine life in its baser aspects flourishing in the parallel *polis*, but would not such a life, lived deliberately that way, as a program, be merely another version of the schizophrenic life within a lie which everyone else must live in one way or another? Would it not just be further evidence that a point of departure that is not a model solution, that is not applicable to others, cannot be meaningful for an individual either? Patočka used to say that the most interesting thing about responsibility is that we carry it with us everywhere. That means that responsibility is ours, that we must accept it and grasp it here, now, in this place in time and space where the Lord has set us down, and that we cannot lie our way out of it by moving somewhere else, whether it be to an Indian ashram or to a parallel *polis*. If Western young people so often discover that retreat to an Indian monastery fails them as an individual or group solution, then this is obviously because, and only because, it lacks that element of universality, since not everyone can retire to an ashram. Christianity is an example of an opposite way out: it is a point of departure for me here and now—but only because anyone, anywhere, at any time, may avail themselves of it.

In other words, the parallel *polis* points beyond itself and makes sense only as an act of deepening one's responsibility to and for the whole, as a way of discovering the most appropriate *locus* for this responsibility, not as an escape from it.

XIX

I HAVE already talked about the political potential of living within the truth and of the limitations on predicting whether, how, and when a given expression of that life within the truth can lead to actual changes. I have also mentioned how irrelevant trying to calculate the risks in this regard are, for an essential feature of independent initiatives is that they are always, initially at least, an all-or-nothing gamble.

Nevertheless, this outline of some of the work done by "dissident" movements would be incomplete without considering, if only very generally, some of the different ways this work might actually affect society; in other words, about the ways that responsibility to and for the whole might (without necessarily meaning that it must) be realized in practice.

In the first place, it has to be emphasized that the whole sphere comprising the independent life of society, and even more so the "dissident" movement as such, is naturally far from being the only potential factor that might influence the history of countries living under the post-totalitarian system. The latent social crisis in such societies can at any time, independently of these movements, provoke a wide variety of political changes. It may unsettle the power structure and induce or accelerate various hidden confrontations, resulting in personnel, conceptual, or at least "climactic" changes. It may significantly influence the general atmosphere of life, evoke unexpected and unforeseen social unrest and explosions of discontent. Power shifts at the center of the bloc can influence conditions in the different countries in various ways. Economic factors naturally have an important influence, as do broader trends of global civilization. An extremely important area, which could be a source of radical changes and political upsets, is represented by international politics, the policies adopted by the other superpower and all the other countries, the changing structure of international interests and the positions taken by our bloc. Even the people who end up in the highest positions are not without significance, although as I have already said, one ought not overestimate the importance of leading personalities in the post-totalitarian system. There are many such influences and combinations of influence, and the eventual political impact of the "dissident" movement is thinkable only against this general background and in the context that this background provides. That impact is only one of the many factors (and far from the most important one) that affect political developments, and it differs from the other factors perhaps only in that its essential focus is reflecting upon that political development from the point of view of a defense of people and seeking an immediate application of that reflection.

The primary purpose of the outward direction of these movements is always, as we have seen, to have an impact on society, not to affect the power structure, at least not directly and immediately. Independent initiatives address the hidden sphere; they demonstrate that living within the truth is a human and social alternative and they struggle to expand the space available for that life; they help—even though it is, of course, indirect help—to raise the confidence of citizens; they shatter the world of appearances and unmask the real nature of power. They do not assume a messianic role; they are not a social avant-garde or elite that alone knows best, and whose task it is to "raise the consciousness" of the "unconscious" masses (that arrogant self-projection is, once again, intrinsic to an essentially different way of thinking, the kind that feels it has a patent on some ideal project and therefore that it has the right to impose it on society). Nor do they want to lead anyone. They leave it up to each individual to decide what he will or will not take from their experience and work. (If official Czechoslovak propaganda described the Chartists as "self-appointees," it was not in order to emphasize any real avant-garde ambitions on their part, but rather a natural expression of how the regime thinks, its tendency to judge others according to itself, since behind any expression of criticism it automatically sees the desire to cast the mighty from their seats and rule in their places "in the name of the people," the same pretext the regime itself has used for years.)

These movements, therefore, always affect the power structure as such indirectly, as a part of society as a whole, for they are primarily addressing the hidden spheres of society, since it is not a matter of confronting the regime on the level of actual power.

I have already indicated one of the ways this can work: an awareness of the laws and the responsibility for seeing that they are upheld is indirectly strengthened. That, of course, is only a specific instance of a far broader influence, the indirect pressure felt from living within the truth: the pressure created by free thought, alternative values and alternative behavior, and by independent social self-realization. The power structure, whether it wants to or not, must always react to this pressure to a certain extent. Its response, however, is always limited to two dimensions: repression and adaptation. Sometimes one dominates, sometimes the other. For example, the Polish "flying university" came under increased persecution and the "flying teachers" were detained by the police. At the same time, however, professors in existing official universities tried to enrich their own curricula with several subjects hitherto considered taboo and this was a result of indirect pressure exerted by the "flying university." The motives for this adaptation may vary from the ideal (the hidden sphere has received the message and conscience and the will to truth are awakened) to the purely utilitarian: the regime's instinct for survival compels it to notice the changing ideas and the changing mental and social climate and to react flexibly to them. Which of these motives happens to predominate in a given moment is not essential in terms of the final effect.

Adaptation is the positive dimension of the regime's response, and it can, and usually does, have a wide spectrum of forms and phases. Some circles may try to integrate values of people from the "parallel world" into the official structures, to appropriate them, to become a little like them while trying to make them a little like themselves, and thus to adjust an obvious and untenable imbalance. In the 1960s, progressive communists began to "discover" certain unacknowledged cultural values and phenomena. This was a positive step, although not without its dangers, since the "integrated" or "appropriated" values lost something of their independence and originality, and having been given a cloak of officiality and conformity, their credibility was somewhat weakened. In a further phase, this adaptation can lead to various attempts on the part of the official structures to reform, both in terms of their ultimate goals and structurally. Such reforms are usually halfway measures; they are attempts to combine and realistically coordinate serving life and serving the post-totalitarian automatism. But they cannot be otherwise. They muddy what was originally a clear demarcation line between living within the truth and living with a lie. They cast a smoke-screen over the situation, mystify society, and make it difficult for people to keep their bearings. This, of course, does not alter the fact that it is always essentially good when it happens because it opens out new spaces. But it does make it more difficult to distinguish between "admissible" and "inadmissible" compromises.

Another—and higher—phase of adaptation is a process of internal differentiation that takes place in the official structures. These structures open themselves to more or less institutionalized forms of plurality because the real aims of life demand it. (One example: without changing the centralized and institutional basis of cultural life, new publishing houses, group periodicals, artists' groups, parallel research institutes and workplaces, and so on, may appear under pressure from below. Or another example: the single, monolithic youth organization run by the state as a typical post-totalitarian "transmission belt" disintegrates under the pressure of real needs into a number of more or less independent organizations such as the Union of University Students, the Union of Secondary School Students, the Organization of Working Youth, and so on.) There is a direct relationship between this kind of differentiation, which allows initiatives from below to be felt, and the appearance and constitution of new structures which are already parallel, or rather independent, but which at the same time are respected, or at least tolerated in varying degrees, by official institutions. These new institutions are more than just liberalized official structures adapted to the authentic needs of life; they are a direct expression of those needs, demanding a position in the context of what is already here. In other words, they are genuine expressions of the tendency of society to organize itself. (In Czechoslovakia in 1968 the best-known organizations of this type were KAN, the Club of Committed Non-Communists, and K231, an organization of former political prisoners.)

The ultimate phase of this process is the situation in which the official structures—as agencies of the post-totalitarian system, existing only to serve its automatism and constructed in the spirit of that role—simply begin withering away and dying off, to be replaced by new structures that have evolved from below and are put together in a fundamentally different way.

Certainly many other ways may be imagined in which the aims of life can bring about political transformations in the general organization of things and weaken on all levels the hold that techniques of manipulation have on society. Here I have mentioned only the way in which the general organization of things was in fact changed as we experienced it ourselves in Czechoslovakia around 1968. It must be added that all these concrete instances were part of a specific historical process which ought not be thought of as the only alternative, nor as necessarily repeatable (particularly not in our country), a fact which, of course, takes nothing away from the importance of the general lessons which are still sought and found in it to this day.

While on the subject of 1968 in Czechoslovakia, it may be appropriate to point to some of the characteristic aspects of developments at that time. All the transformations, first in the general mood, then conceptually, and finally structurally, did not occur under pressure from the kind of parallel structures that are taking shape today. Such structures—which are sharply defined antitheses of the official structures—quite simply did not exist at the time, nor were there any "dissidents" in the present sense of the word. The changes that took place were simply a consequence of pressures of the most varied sort, some thoroughgoing, some partial. There were spontaneous attempts at freer forms of thinking, independent creation, and political articulation. There were long-term, spontaneous, and inconspicuous efforts to bring about the interpenetration of the independent life of society with the existing structures, usually beginning with the quiet institutionalization of this life on and around the periphery of the official structures. In other words, it was a gradual process of social awakening, a kind of creeping process in which the hidden spheres gradually opened out. (There is some truth in the official propaganda which talks about a "creeping counterrevolution" in Czechoslovakia, referring to how the aims of life proceed.) The motive force behind this awakening did not have to come exclusively from the independent life of society, considered as a definable social milieu (although of course it did come from there, a fact that has yet to be fully appreciated). It could also simply have come from the fact that people in the official structures who more or less identified with the official ideology came up against reality as it really was and as it gradually became clear to them through latent social crises and their own bitter experiences with the true nature and operations of power. (I am thinking here mainly of the many antidogmatic reform communists who grew to become, over the years, a force inside the official structures.) Neither the proper conditions nor the *raison d'être* existed for those limited, "self-structuring" independent initiatives familiar from the present era of "dissident" movements that stand so sharply outside the official structures and are unrecognized by them *en bloc*. At that time, the post-totalitarian system in Czechoslovakia had not yet petrified into the static, sterile, and stable forms that exist today, forms that compel people to fall back on their own organizing capabilities. For many historical and social reasons, the regime in 1968 was more open. The power structure, exhausted by Stalinist despotism and helplessly groping about for painless reform, was inevitably rotting from within, quite incapable of offering any intelligent opposition to changes in the mood, to the way its younger members regarded things and to the thousands of authentic expressions of life on the "pre-political" level that sprang up in that vast political terrain between the official and the unofficial.

From the more general point of view, yet another typical circumstance appears to be important: the social ferment that came to a head in 1968 never—in terms of actual structural changes—went any further than the reform, the differentiation, or the replacement of structures that were really only of secondary importance. It did not affect the very essence of the power structure in the post-totalitarian system, which is to say its political model, the fundamental principles of social organization, not even the economic model in which all economic power is subordinated to political power. Nor were any essential structural changes made in the direct instruments of power (the army, the police, the judiciary, etc.). On that level, the issue was never more than a change in the mood, the personnel, the political line and, above all changes in how that power was exercised. Everything else remained at the stage of discussion and planning. The two officially accepted programs that went furthest in this regard were the April 1968 Action Program of the Communist Party of Czechoslovakia and the proposal for economic reforms. The Action Program—it could not have been otherwise—was full of contradictions and halfway measures that left the physical aspects of power untouched. And the economic proposals, while they went a long way to accommodate the aims of life in the economic sphere (they accepted such notions as a plurality of interests and initiatives, dynamic incentives, restrictions upon the economic command system), left untouched the basic pillar of economic power, that is, the principle of state, rather than genuine social ownership of the means of production. So there is a gap here which no social movement in the post-totalitarian system has ever been able to bridge, with the possible exception of those few days during the Hungarian uprising.

What other developmental alternative might emerge in the future? Replying to that question would mean entering the realm of pure speculation. For the time being, it can be said that the latent social crisis in the system has always (and there is no reason to believe it will not continue to do so) resulted in a variety of political and social disturbances. (Germany in 1953, Hungary, the U.S.S.R. and Poland in 1956, Czechoslovakia and Poland in 1968, and Poland in 1970 and 1976), all of them very different in their backgrounds, the course of their evolution, and their final consequences. If we look at the enormous complex of different factors that led to such disturbances, and at the impossibility of predicting what accidental accumulation of events will cause that fermentation in the hidden sphere to break through to the light of day (the problem of the "final straw"); and if we consider how impossible it is to guess what the future holds, given such opposing trends as, on the one hand, the increasingly profound integration of the "bloc" and the expansion of power within it, and on the other hand the prospects of the U.S.S.R. disintegrating under pressure from awakening national consciousness in the non-Russian areas (in this regard the Soviet Union cannot expect to remain forever free of the worldwide struggle for national liberation), then we must see the hopelessness of trying to make long-range predictions.

In any case, I do not believe that this type of speculation

has any immediate significance for the "dissident" movements since these movements, after all, do not develop from
speculative thinking, and so to establish themselves on that
basis would mean alienating themselves from the very source
of their identity.

As far as prospects for the "dissident" movements as such
go, there seems to be very little likelihood that future developments will lead to a lasting co-existence of two isolated,
mutually noninteracting and mutually indifferent bodies—
the main *polis* and the parallel *polis*. As long as it remains
what it is, the practice of living within the truth cannot fail
to be a threat to the system. It is quite impossible to imagine
it continuing to co-exist with the practice of living within a
lie without dramatic tension. The relationship of the post-
totalitarian system—as long as it remains what it is—and the
independent life of society—as long as it remains the *locus* of
a renewed responsibility for the whole and to the whole—will
always be one of either latent or open conflict.

In this situation there are only two possibilities: either the
post-totalitarian system will go on developing (that is, will be
able to go on developing), thus inevitably coming closer to
some dreadful Orwellian vision of a world of absolute manipulation, while all the more articulate expressions of living
within the truth are definitely snuffed out; or the independent life of society (the parallel *polis*), including the "dissident" movements, will slowly but surely become a social
phenomenon of growing importance, taking a real part in the
life of society with increasing clarity and influencing the general situation. Of course this will always be only one of many
factors influencing the situation and it will operate rather in
the background, in concert with the other factors and in a
way appropriate to the background.

Whether it ought to focus on reforming the official structures or on encouraging differentiation, or on replacing them
with new structures, whether the intent is to ameliorate the
system or, on the contrary, to tear it down: these and similar
questions, insofar as they are not pseudo-problems, can be

posed by the "dissident" movement only within the context
of a particular situation, when the movement is faced with a
concrete task. In other words, it must pose questions, as it
were, ad hoc, out of a concrete consideration of the authentic
needs of life. To reply to such questions abstractly and to
formulate a political program in terms of some hypothetical
future would mean, I believe, a return to the spirit and methods of traditional politics, and this would limit and alienate
the work of "dissent" where it is most intrinsically itself and
has the most genuine prospects for the future. I have already
emphasized several times that these "dissident" movements
do not have their point of departure in the invention of systemic changes but in a real, everyday struggle for a better life
here and now. The political and structural systems that life
discovers for itself will clearly always be—for some time to
come, at least—limited, halfway, unsatisfying, and polluted by
debilitating tactics. It cannot be otherwise, and we must expect
this and not be demoralized by it. It is of great importance
that the main thing—the everyday, thankless, and never-
ending struggle of human beings to live more freely, truthfully, and in quiet dignity—never impose any limits on itself,
never be halfhearted, inconsistent, never trap itself in political tactics, speculating on the outcome of its actions or entertaining fantasies about the future. The purity of this struggle
is the best guarantee of optimum results when it comes to
actual interaction with the post-totalitarian structures.

XX

THE SPECIFIC nature of post-totalitarian conditions—with their
absence of a normal political life and the fact that any far-
reaching political change is utterly unforeseeable—has one
positive aspect: it compels us to examine our situation in
terms of its deeper coherences and to consider our future in
the context of global, long-range prospects of the world of
which we are a part. The fact that the most intrinsic and fundamental confrontation between human beings and the sys-

tem takes place at a level incomparably more profound than that of traditional politics would seem, at the same time, to determine as well the direction such considerations will take.

Our attention, therefore, inevitably turns to the most essential matter: the crisis of contemporary technological society as a whole, the crisis that Heidegger describes as the ineptitude of humanity face to face with the planetary power of technology. Technology—that child of modern science, which in turn is a child of modern metaphysics—is out of humanity's control, has ceased to serve us, has enslaved us and compelled us to participate in the preparation of our own destruction. And humanity can find no way out: we have no idea and no faith, and even less do we have a political conception to help us bring things back under human control. We look on helplessly as that coldly functioning machine we have created inevitably engulfs us, tearing us away from our natural affiliations (for instance, from our habitat in the widest sense of that word, including our habitat in the biosphere) just as it removes us from the experience of Being and casts us into the world of "existences." This situation has already been described from many different angles and many individuals and social groups have sought, often painfully, to find ways out of it (for instance, through oriental thought or by forming communes). The only social, or rather political, attempt to do something about it that contains the necessary element of universality (responsibility to and for the whole) is the desperate and, given the turmoil the world is in, fading voice of the ecological movement, and even there the attempt is limited to a particular notion of how to use technology to oppose the dictatorship of technology.

"Only a God can save us now," Heidegger says, and he emphasizes the necessity of "a different way of thinking," that is, of a departure from what philosophy has been for centuries, and a radical change in the way in which humanity understands itself, the world, and its position in it. He knows no way out and all he can recommend is "preparing expectations."

Various thinkers and movements feel that this as yet unknown way out might be most generally characterized as a broad "existential revolution." I share this view, and I also share the opinion that a solution cannot be sought in some technological sleight of hand, that is, in some external proposal for change, or in a revolution that is merely philosophical, merely social, merely technological, or even merely political. These are all areas where the consequences of an existential revolution can and must be felt; but their most intrinsic *locus* can only be human existence in the profoundest sense of the word. It is only from that basis that it can become a generally ethical—and, of course, ultimately a political—reconstitution of society.

What we call the consumer and industrial (or postindustrial) society, and Ortega y Gasset once understood as "the revolt of the masses," as well as the intellectual, moral, political, and social misery in the world today: all of this is perhaps merely an aspect of the deep crisis in which humanity, dragged helplessly along by the automatism of global technological civilization, finds itself.

The post-totalitarian system is only one aspect—a particularly drastic aspect and thus all the more revealing of its real origins—of this general inability of modern humanity to be the master of its own situation. The automatism of the post-totalitarian system is merely an extreme version of the global automatism of technological civilization. The human failure that it mirrors is only one variant of the general failure of modern humanity.

This planetary challenge to the position of human beings in the world is, of course, also taking place in the Western world, the only difference being the social and political forms it takes. Heidegger refers expressly to a crisis of democracy. There is no real evidence that Western democracy, that is, democracy of the traditional parliamentary type, can offer solutions that are any more profound. It may even be said that the more room there is in the Western democracies (compared to our world) for the genuine aims of life, the better the crisis is hidden from people and the more deeply do they become immersed in it.

It would appear that the traditional parliamentary democracies can offer no fundamental opposition to the automatism of technological civilization and the industrial-consumer society, for they, too, are being dragged helplessly along by it. People are manipulated in ways that are infinitely more subtle and refined than the brutal methods used in the post-totalitarian societies. But this static complex of rigid, conceptually sloppy, and politically pragmatic mass political parties run by professional apparatuses and releasing the citizen from all forms of concrete and personal responsibility; and those complex focuses of capital accumulation engaged in secret manipulations and expansion; the omnipresent dictatorship of consumption, production, advertising, commerce, consumer culture, and all that flood of information: all of it, so often analyzed and described, can only with great difficulty be imagined as the source of humanity's rediscovery of itself. In his June 1978 Harvard lecture, Solzhenitsyn describes the illusory nature of freedoms not based on personal responsibility and the chronic inability of the traditional democracies, as a result, to oppose violence and totalitarianism. In a democracy, human beings may enjoy many personal freedoms and securities that are unknown to us, but in the end they do them no good, for they too are ultimately victims of the same automatism, and are incapable of defending their concerns about their own identity or preventing their superficialization or transcending concerns about their own personal survival to become proud and responsible members of the *polis,* making a genuine contribution to the creation of its destiny.

Because all our prospects for a significant change for the better are very long range indeed, we are obliged to take note of this deep crisis of traditional democracy. Certainly, if conditions were to be created for democracy in some countries in the Soviet bloc (although this is becoming increasingly improbable), it might be an appropriate transitional solution that would help to restore the devastated sense of civic aware-

ness, to renew democratic discussion, to allow for the crystallization of an elementary political plurality, an essential
expression of the aims of life. But to cling to the notion of
traditional parliamentary democracy as one's political ideal
and to succumb to the illusion that only this tried and true
form is capable of guaranteeing human beings enduring
dignity and an independent role in society would, in my
opinion, be at the very least shortsighted.

I see a renewed focus of politics on real people as something far more profound than merely returning to the everyday mechanisms of Western (or, if you like, bourgeois)
democracy. In 1968, I felt that our problem could be solved
by forming an opposition party that would compete publicly
for power with the Communist Party. I have long since come
to realize, however, that it is just not that simple and that no
opposition party in and of itself, just as no new electoral laws
in and of themselves, could make society proof against some
new form of violence. No "dry" organizational measures in
themselves can provide that guarantee, and we would be hard-
pressed to find in them that God who alone can save us.

XXI

AND NOW I may properly be asked the question: What then is
to be done?

My skepticism toward alternative political models and the
ability of systemic reforms or changes to redeem us does not,
of course, mean that I am skeptical of political thought altogether. Nor does my emphasis on the importance of focusing
concern on real human beings disqualify me from considering the possible structural consequences flowing from it. On
the contrary, if A was said, then B should be said as well.
Nevertheless, I will offer only a few very general remarks.

Above all, any existential revolution should provide hope
of a moral reconstitution of society, which means a radical
renewal of the relationship of human beings to what I have
called the "human order," which no political order can re-

place. A new experience of being, a renewed rootedness in the universe, a newly grasped sense of higher responsibility, a newfound inner relationship to other people and to the human community—these factors clearly indicate the direction in which we must go.

And the political consequences? Most probably they could be reflected in the constitution of structures that will derive from this new spirit, from human factors rather than from a particular formalization of political relationships and guarantees. In other words, the issue is the rehabilitation of values like trust, openness, responsibility, solidarity, love. I believe in structures that are not aimed at the technical aspect of the execution of power, but at the significance of that execution in structures held together more by a commonly shared feeling of the importance of certain communities than by commonly shared expansionist ambitions directed outward. There can and must be structures that are open, dynamic, and small; beyond a certain point, human ties like personal trust and personal responsibility cannot work. There must be structures that in principle place no limits on the genesis of different structures. Any accumulation of power whatsoever (one of the characteristics of automatism) should be profoundly alien to it. They would be structures not in the sense of organizations or institutions, but like a community. Their authority certainly cannot be based on long-empty traditions, like the tradition of mass political parties, but rather on how, in concrete terms, they enter into a given situation. Rather than a strategic agglomeration of formalized organizations, it is better to have organizations springing up ad hoc, infused with enthusiasm for a particular purpose and disappearing when that purpose has been achieved. The leaders' authority ought to derive from their personalities and be personally tested in their particular surroundings, and not from their position in any *nomenklatura*. They should enjoy great personal confidence and even great lawmaking powers based on that confidence. This would appear to be the only way out of the classic impotence of traditional democratic organizations, which frequently seem founded more on mistrust than mutual confidence, and more on collective irresponsibility than on responsibility. It is only with the full existential backing of every member of the community that a permanent bulwark against creeping totalitarianism can be established. These structures should naturally arise from below as a consequence of authentic social self-organization; they should derive vital energy from a living dialogue with the genuine needs from which they arise, and when these needs are gone, the structures should also disappear. The principles of their internal organization should be very diverse, with a minimum of external regulation. The decisive criterion of this self-constitution should be the structure's actual significance, and not just a mere abstract norm.

Both political and economic life ought to be founded on the varied and versatile cooperation of such dynamically appearing and disappearing organizations. As far as the economic life of society goes, I believe in the principle of self-management, which is probably the only way of achieving what all the theorists of socialism have dreamed about, that is, the genuine (i.e., informal) participation of workers in economic decision making, leading to a feeling of genuine responsibility for their collective work. The principles of control and discipline ought to be abandoned in favor of self-control and self-discipline.

As is perhaps clear from even so general an outline, the systemic consequences of an existential revolution of this type go significantly beyond the framework of classical parliamentary democracy. Having introduced the term "posttotalitarian" for the purposes of this discussion, perhaps I should refer to the notion I have just outlined—purely for the moment—as the prospects for a "post-democratic" system.

Undoubtedly this notion could be developed further, but I think it would be a foolish undertaking, to say the least, because slowly but surely the whole idea would become alienated, separated from itself. After all, the essence of such a "post-democracy" is also that it can only develop *via facti,* as a process deriving directly from life, from a new atmosphere and a new spirit (political thought, of course, would play a role here, though not as a director, merely as a guide). It would be presumptuous, however, to try to foresee the structural expressions of this new spirit without that spirit actually being present and without knowing its concrete physiognomy.

XXII

I WOULD probably have omitted the entire preceding section as a more suitable subject for private meditation were it not for a certain recurring sensation. It may seem rather presumptuous, and therefore I will present it as a question: Does not this vision of "post-democratic" structures in some ways remind one of the "dissident" groups or some of the independent citizens' initiatives as we already know them from our own surroundings? Do not these small communities, bound together by thousands of shared tribulations, give rise to some of those special humanly meaningful political relationships and ties that we have been talking about? Are not these communities (and they *are* communities more than organizations)—motivated mainly by a common belief in the profound significance of what they are doing since they have no chance of direct, external success—joined together by precisely the kind of atmosphere in which the formalized and ritualized ties common in the official structures are supplanted by a living sense of solidarity and fraternity? Do not these "post-democratic" relationships of immediate personal trust and the informal rights of individuals based on them come out of the background of all those commonly shared difficulties? Do not these groups emerge, live, and disappear under pressure from concrete and authentic needs, unburdened by the ballast of hollow traditions? Is not their attempt to create an articulate form of living within the truth and to renew the feeling of higher responsibility in an apathetic society really a sign of some kind of rudimentary moral reconstitution?

In other words, are not these informed, nonbureaucratic, dynamic, and open communities that comprise the "parallel *polis*" a kind of rudimentary prefiguration, a symbolic model of those more meaningful "post-democratic" political structures that might become the foundation of a better society?

I know from thousands of personal experiences how the mere circumstance of having signed Charter 77 has immediately created a deeper and more open relationship and evoked sudden and powerful feelings of genuine community among people who were all but strangers before. This kind of thing happens only rarely, if at all, even among people who have worked together for long periods in some apathetic official structure. It is as though the mere awareness and acceptance of a common task and a shared experience were enough to transform people and the climate of their lives, as though it gave their public work a more human dimension than is seldom found elsewhere.

Perhaps all this is only the consequence of a common threat. Perhaps the moment the threat ends or eases, the mood it helped create will begin to dissipate as well. (The aim of those who threaten us, however, is precisely the opposite. Again and again, one is shocked by the energy they devote to contaminating, in various despicable ways, all the human relationships inside the threatened community.)

Yet even if that were so, it would change nothing in the question I have posed.

We do not know the way out of the marasmus of the world, and it would be an expression of unforgivable pride were we to see the little we do as a fundamental solution, or were we to present ourselves, our community, and our solutions to vital problems as the only thing worth doing.

Even so, I think that given all these preceding thoughts on post-totalitarian conditions, and given the circumstances and the inner constitution of the developing efforts to defend human beings and their identity in such conditions, the questions I have posed are appropriate. If nothing else, they are an invitation to reflect concretely on our own experience and to give some thought to whether certain elements of that experience do not—without our really being aware of it—point somewhere further, beyond their apparent limits, and whether right here, in our everyday lives, certain challenges are not already encoded, quietly waiting for the moment when they will be read and grasped.

For the real question is whether the brighter future is really always so distant. What if, on the contrary, it has been here for a long time already, and only our own blindness and weakness has prevented us from seeing it around us and within us, and kept us from developing it?

October 1978

Reports on
My House Arrest

"Reports on My House Arrest" are two related texts
dated January 6, 1979 and March 23, 1979. The
events described in them anticipate Havel's arrest
later that year, in May. An abridged and adapted
version of the reports appeared in *Encounter* (September 1979), under the title "The Age of Chica-
nery: Technical Notes on My House-Arrest." This
translation, slightly abridged, is by Paul Wilson.

I

SINCE August 5, 1978, I have been under constant observation by the police. There have been different forms of
surveillance at different times, but essentially these changes
indicate that the surveillance is intensifying.

PHASE ONE: From August 5 to the end of the month, a police
car occupied by a pair of uniformed policemen (who change
shifts every eight hours) has been parked constantly at the
end of the driveway to my home in Hrádeček near Vlčice,
where I now spend most of my time. Moreover, the road running past our house has been blocked from one side by a
barricade of gravel, and from the other side by a sign saying
"No Entry." At the end of August, both the barricade and the
sign suddenly disappeared.

The police engaged in the following activities:

a. They stopped cars that drove past (given the measures
mentioned above, there weren't many of those); they fined

the drivers, occasionally confiscating operating permits and even driver's licenses.

b. Any car coming to our place was subjected to stricter controls, and my guests were always told to proceed "at their own risk." At least twice I asked what the danger was (if there was any, surely I had a right to know), only to be told that members of the police force were not authorized to specify the danger. Visitors on foot also had their IDs checked, and were warned.

c. When I went anywhere by car, a police car followed; when I went around the shops and on other errands, a policeman with a walkie-talkie walked directly behind me or beside me, trying to hear what I was saying, and checking the identity papers of anyone with whom I had a conversation. He would look over my shoulder when I sent off letters, listen at the telephone booth when I made my calls, and so on. If I called on someone, the police would not try to enter their house, nor would they prevent me from making the visit.

d. When I left my house on foot, for instance, to take the dog for a walk, a policeman always went with me.

PHASE TWO: In September and October, this surveillance was relaxed. During the week, they watched the house only during the daylight hours; round-the-clock surveillance tended to be only on weekends, and some days, I was not under observation at all.

PHASE THREE: On the evening of November 6, I became one of the official spokesmen for Charter 77. I stayed over in Prague and the very next morning, on November 7, I discovered that I was under surveillance by what they called an "operative." This phenomenon is familiar enough, so I'll limit myself to the basic facts: it consists of three men in plain clothes in a Tatra 603. When I'm home, they sit in the car and watch the door of our apartment building. If I go somewhere by car, they follow me and usually stop in front of the building I enter (disregarding the traffic signs) and keep an eye on the building (sometimes they walk up and down the sidewalk in front of it). If I go anywhere by foot or by subway, two of them are always behind me, while the third creeps along nearby in the Tatra 603. They are in constant touch with each other by walkie-talkie. They go into pubs, bars, and restaurants with me (though they sit at a separate table), and they have even taken a sauna with me. They do not, however, follow me into private flats. They check the identity of everyone I talk to (if the person doesn't tell them himself to avoid being checked in public), and sometimes they photograph me and the people I'm talking to.

PHASE FOUR: This began exactly a month later, that is, on December 7, when I was in Prague. It differed from the earlier surveillance in that, in addition to the regular "operative," two uniformed policemen with a small table and a walkie-talkie appeared outside the door of our Prague flat, or more precisely, on the landing half a flight below, where they kept a round-the-clock watch. This, too, is a familiar enough technique, but in my case, it differed in that these policemen let no one into our flat, though they checked the identity of everyone who tried to visit us, nor was I allowed to leave. At first they didn't even let my wife out, but then that changed. Once they did let me go—whether deliberately or by accident, I don't know—only to arrest me shortly afterward in my father's flat, where I had gone to visit, and return me home and intern me once more. One peculiarity of this phase was that one of the policemen was extremely abusive to us. For example, he would suddenly ring our doorbell and say, "Today, you son-of-a-bitch, we're going to beat the shit out of you." After that I didn't open the door or let my wife out unless we could ensure that a third party was present as witness. The abusive policeman would never threaten us in the presence of a civilian.

PHASE FIVE: After three days, that is on December 9, my wife
and I decided to go back to Hrádeček. On the surface, the
phase that followed is similar to the first and second phases:
a police car with two uniformed policemen was constantly
parked at the head of our driveway. But on December 28, a
new element was added: directly across from our house a peculiar guardhouse on spindly legs, bearing a distant resem-
blance to the Soviet *Lunochod,* was erected. The police car
remains in its usual place, but the police sit in this monstrous
structure, where they keep an eye on the two main entrances
to my home. Sometimes they have round-the-clock shifts (during the holidays, for instance); sometimes they work only during the day, that is, from eight to five. When surveillance is
stepped up, there are more of them, though it's hard to say
how many, since some of them, it seems, keep to the woods
around the house.

a. No one is allowed to see us.

b. I am let out only to go shopping, or to the post office. I
cannot go on trips or visits. Sometimes I'm allowed to go for
walks, sometimes I'm not (in each case they have to radio to
the operations officer in Trutnov, who in turn has to phone
the regional headquarters of the Secret Police in Hradec Králové). Sometimes I am only allowed to walk around the house,
and sometimes they tell me I can go on a hike anywhere
within a ten-kilometer radius.

c. All my movements outside the house are observed, as I
have already described in phase one. On hikes, they either
follow me on foot or—if I walk on the road—they send a car
to crawl along close behind me.

d. Sometimes—especially when they have reinforcements—
they come onto our property and walk around outside the
house, peering in the windows or taking up positions around
the house so that nothing will escape them. (They did this
earlier too, especially when the weather was good.)

· · ·

POLICEMEN from the whole district are obviously taking part in my surveillance, because I keep seeing new faces. With the exception of a few who take their work extremely seriously, most behave on the whole correctly toward me, given their absurd mission; that is, they don't speak abusively to me, they are not deliberately mean, they don't try to humiliate me, and so on. They are conscientious about their duty, but they try to get along with me, and when they follow me around Trutnov on shopping expeditions, they usually walk beside me and try to engage in friendly conversation, so that if you didn't know what was really going on, you might think two acquaintances were walking along—one in uniform and the other not. Of course, something that would go unnoticed in the big city has become a notorious regional curiosity around Trutnov; everyone knows what's going on, because it's obviously never happened around here before. And I know from a thousand personal experiences, and from what I hear from others, that the local people sharply disapprove of the police for doing this; they consider it ridiculous and undignified, a waste of public money, and so on. I could tell many stories confirming this, but I won't so as not to bring harm to anyone. As far as I know, even the police themselves find this duty unpleasant; it does not fit with their notion of a policeman's job, and they take it badly when people criticize them for it, or when their friends laugh at them for doing it.

THESE actions against me appear to be directed from the district headquarters of the Secret Police in Hradec Králové. The many things they've directed against me in the past few years could provide material for a relatively thick book. One of the more recent ones was a coaxial cable laid ten centimeters under the ground and leading from a trailer about two kilometers away to a building on a nearby hillside with a good view of our house. The cable can transmit both audio and video signals. Some workers found it as they were digging in the woods; on police orders they were immediately transferred to a job at the other end of the district, and all work in the woods around our house was stopped, from which I conclude that the cable was neither the work of an eccentric individual, nor of foreign intelligence agencies.

Another operation, far worse, was a series of interrogations in which people living nearby were forced to break off all contact with us, including the giving or receiving of any help in an emergency, should one arise. In the mountains, as we know, there is a stronger ethic of mutual assistance than elsewhere. People here give each other help, and indeed, cannot do without it. They have it in their blood, as it were, and if they are forbidden to act and, what is worse, told that if they do, their children will not be allowed to go to school and so on, they understand this as an incomprehensible, brutal, and insulting attack on their elementary moral values. This operation is especially disgusting, not because of us—we shall survive this blockade—but because of those people. It is terrible to see them suffering such humiliation.

Along with the increasing attention paid to me by the police, the attentions of Unknown Perpetrators increased as well. When I was under house arrest in Prague (phase four), Unknown Perpetrators thoroughly slashed all the tires of my car, and smashed my windshield. (Experts at the repair shop said it didn't look like ordinary vandalism or the work of drunks; this was the result of concentrated, unhurried work.) Another Unknown Perpetrator disconnected our telephone line in the junction box in our basement, but even I knew how to repair that.

The Unknown Perpetrators, however, displayed far more concentration and skill in the damages they inflicted on our country house. When we returned to Hrádeček—after a mere three weeks' absence—the central heating, the water, and the drains were all out of order. They had always served us faithfully in the past, regardless of how long we had been away, and my first response was that this was an unfortunate coincidence. The experts told me I was crazy to think so, and they set me right: it was no accident that the boiler's ignition system had been cut, or that the water pump was stuffed with wool, or that all the drainpipes under the sinks and bathtub were filled with tough, impenetrable resin. (The only way to repair it is to dig out the pipes and replace them.) Confronted with this evidence, I had to admit that the Unknown Perpetrators were probably behind this, all the more probably because they had a key to the house, as earlier visits had shown. It made no sense to change the locks, since it was clearly no problem for these Unknown Perpetrators to obtain an impression of the new key, or get hold of a skeleton key. [. . .] I needn't emphasize that it was not at all easy to fix the damage in a situation in which people are afraid to come to our house, and when the winter this year is calamitously harsh.

I'M NOT describing these things because I think they are especially important, or because what I am going through is unbearable or worse than what is done to many of my fellow citizens, either in or out of prison. I have done it only because my friends asked me to, both because they are interested in what is happening to me, and because they believe, quite correctly, that my harassment illustrates the general situation and should therefore not remain a secret.

II

ALMOST three months have gone by since January 6, 1979, when I wrote the first report on my house arrest for my friends. Some new things have been happening, and I have decided to write another report.

THE CONDITIONS of my house arrest at my cottage near Vlčice, where I continue to spend most of my time, have not changed in any essential way. Every day, from eight to five, two uniformed policemen occupy the observation post which I have called *Lunochod*. It is only occasionally occupied in the evening or night, usually when the Prague secret police think I could be expecting a visit, or when they think I might be going somewhere. Whenever I'm away, the officers allow no one to enter the house, and when I'm at home, they let me out only to do the shopping or walk the dog. In both cases, one of them always follows me closely.

Shopping expeditions are often complicated affairs. I always have to wait for approval from on high, and sometimes that approval does not come. I often have to wait as well for a police car to follow me, since now my guards do not usually have a car with them during the day. When I shop, they now stick so close to me that if they were to slip their arm into mine, we'd look like lovers. At the post office, they boldly read my correspondence over my shoulder, and once they snatched the letters out of my hand and recorded the name of my correspondents (not very useful, since most of them only sign with their Christian names).

If I attempt to pick up hitchhikers, they forbid them to get into my car, and once they stopped me from giving a tow to a car with a family in it that had broken down on a dark, seldom traveled road (yet they often check to see that I am carrying the towing rope prescribed by law with me). In shops that I've been going to for years and where the sales staff knows me, my constant chaperones are, with increasing frequency, the occasion of quiet ridicule and expressions of solidarity with me (I am slipped goods in short supply, for instance), and sometimes they elicit sarcastic remarks uttered aloud. Although most of them continue to behave correctly, some of them have tried to provoke me (for instance by fining me if I cross the street except at the badly marked crosswalks).

NOT LONG ago, when some Unknown Perpetrators had again damaged my windshield, this time in a way that made vision difficult, the local police stopped me on my way to the Vlčice post office and withdrew my technical certification on the grounds that the windshield was opaque (though this had never bothered them before). After difficult negotiations, they agreed to let me drive to the service station in Česke Skalice to have the glass replaced. I arrived at the service station (in the company of my warders, of course, who came inside and stayed close to me the whole time), a proper work order was filled out and I was promised that the windshield would be replaced within an hour, since they had plenty of glass in stock. When I returned an hour later, the mechanic, in a state of great embarrassment, took me to the manager, who with equal embarrassment told me they had received orders from above not to replace the windshield. When I asked him if the police had ordered this, he asked me not to ask him questions like that, to understand that he couldn't give me an answer, and that I should realize where I was living. My work order was canceled and it was recommended that I go to Chrudim to buy the windshield, and then, he said, they'd be willing to replace it. I noticed that this encounter caused a great deal of excitement in the service station among the employees and the customers, and as I learned several days later, it had become common knowledge throughout the district of Náchod, where the service station was located.

After waiting an hour, I got permission to drive to Chrudim where, to my astonishment, I got a new windshield (true, I phoned there in advance and asked the manager to give me his word of honor that when I arrived two hours later he would sell me the glass). I brought the windshield home, and a friend of mine from Trutnov installed it for me. (The very next week this friend had both his technical certification and his driver's license confiscated on some pretext; in addition, Unknown Perpetrators had loosened the nuts on his front wheels, which might have caused a serious accident. It's worth remarking that, although the police made no mention of the loose nuts when they confiscated his papers, (and he himself had no idea they were loose since they were discovered later in the repair shop), when the police were recertifying his car, an officer asked him if he'd fixed those nuts on his front wheels. It is also worth remarking that a police officer called Dvořák—as I discovered in a roundabout way—was heard to say in the presence of his friends: "That's what he gets for fixing the windshield.")

After the windshield was replaced, my car was recertified, but I was then asked to requalify for my driver's license. (I passed.) This happened somewhat later, when the snow had melted and it was clear I would be using the car more. Then once, when I was setting off to do the shopping, the police stopped me as soon as I'd pulled out of the garage, and conducted a spot check (which they do frequently, in any case). When, despite great effort, they found nothing wrong, I heard them radio back to headquarters that they had been unable to confiscate my papers. Shortly afterward, they took my driver's license on a ridiculous pretext, claiming that in making a turn I had failed to use the turn signal indicator in time, and had not yielded the right of way to an oncoming car, although this car was creeping along at some distance and had I waited for it to pass, I would have pointlessly held up traffic. (I knew they had orders to confiscate my driver's license at any cost, but I took the trip knowing that if they didn't do it then, they would do it the next time.)

I don't know when I will be invited for yet another retesting (or rather for a "settlement of my case," as the police call it), but it won't be soon. Officers Dvořák and Novotný are particularly keen when it comes to harassment in this sphere. I cannot recall that they ever stopped any of my friends (back when they were still allowed to visit me) without fining them or taking away their technical papers. [. . .] They make a strange couple, those two. When Mr. Dvořák, for instance, found Tomáš Petřivý in the woods near our house and, of course, checked his identity, he was so excited about his coup that later, in Trutnov, he was heard to shout joyously: "That kid will never finish university!" His entire hope was based on the bare fact that Tomáš Petřivý, thanks to his, Dvořák's, vigilance, had been discovered close to my house.

UNKNOWN Perpetrators also managed to introduce a large amount of sugar in my gas tank, which hopelessly gummed up the gas line, the fuel pump, and the carburetor; so far, the repairs have cost me a thousand crowns. (It's worth mentioning that this happened when my car was either locked in the shed or when I was shopping, and hence it was under the watchful eye of the police. I pointed these circumstances out when I reported the incident, expressing the hope that it shouldn't therefore be difficult for the police to track down the guilty party.)

MY VISIT to Prague at the end of February and the beginning of March took a curious turn. I had gone to Prague chiefly because I'd been summoned to an interrogation in Ruzyně by Captain Smolík, who has been prosecuting the case against Jiří Gruša. During this interrogation, as is his wont, Lieutenant Colonel Noga dropped in to tell me what he always tells me: that I'm defending people who aren't worth it (Captain Říha, I believe, put it even more succinctly when he said, "What do you care about some worker from Most?"), that there was no way I could change things and that I should try to behave myself before I end up in Ruzyně again.

After the interrogation, the old secret police "operative" showed up in front of our house—those three familiar gentlemen in the Tatra 603 that follow me everywhere when I'm in Prague. (Usually they have Petr Uhl under surveillance, so he gets a break from them when I come to town.) One day I left our building and returned to it through the back door (not to give my operative the slip, but because it's closer to the nearest streetcar that way), and so I was spared their company. But the next day, as I made my rounds about Prague, they found me: I'd spent fifteen minutes with Václav Benda, and when I left, there they were, waiting for me. The same evening I was taken into custody and driven to the Krakovská Street police station, where two policemen told me the same thing I'd been told on my previous visit to Prague, that if I didn't return to Hrádeček at once, they'd arrest me (the in-dictment, they said, was prepared). Advising people to run away to avoid arrest does not strike me as normal police prac-tice; nevertheless, for various reasons, I did not take this warning lightly. Still, I told the officers that as long as I was a free man, I would freely decide what my own movements would be.

The next day, two uniformed police officers set up their little table outside our flat. They told me that from now on, no one was allowed to visit me, nor was I allowed to leave, not even to buy groceries. They said for all they cared I could starve to death, and they'd be only too happy to arrange a coffin for me.

This total house arrest lasted three days, and was only in-terrupted once, briefly. When the three spokesmen of Char-ter 77 tried to visit me, Zdena Tominová—thanks to her remarkable tenacity and her wonderful feminine audacity—managed to get permission for me to visit the nearest store and buy food. Also during this time, I made two attempts, the second of which was successful, to smuggle out an open letter to the Minister of the Interior protesting against all this. (In the first attempt, I threw the letter in a bag from the rear balcony to Vlasta Třešňák after he threw breakfast up to me; the bag was confiscated.) Then, for two days, I was allowed to go out (visits to me, of course, were still forbidden), always in the company of the operative, whereupon there was another three days of total house arrest, interrupted only once, again by Zdena Tominová, who accompanied me to the nearest store along with the operative and one of the uniformed po-liceman guarding my door.

Apart from the police on the door, our building was also watched by the operative, clearly to stop any contact with the world via the balcony or the window. (Tomáš Petřivý, who by this time had indeed been expelled from university, was even prevented from entering our street.) I was not allowed to leave the house until there was a truly serious reason: a summons, this time to the police headquarters on Bartolomějská Street. Meanwhile, friends were repairing the sugar damage to my car, and later, when it was fixed, I returned to Hrádeček in the company of the Prague operative. (They were sincerely impressed with the *Lunochod* and unabashedly envious of their colleagues from Trutnov; they said that this was precisely what they needed in front of my house, and Petr Uhl's house, in Prague.)

During the period of total house arrest, the police on the door made my life unpleasant in their usual ways: they rang my bell, insulted me, tried to provoke me, constantly turned the electricity off in our flat, and so on. They refused to let my brother visit me, and they even refused Dr. Danisz, my lawyer, access, thus depriving me of rights that a real prison inmate has. [. . .] One attempt by a foreign reporter to see me was piquant: the police allowed me to stand in the open door of the flat while they checked his documents (in other such cases, they push me inside), but only because they were forced to use me as an interpreter—the only foreign word they knew was the international police expression *dokumente*. I was delighted to be able to translate for them, in turn, that the reporter had brought me greetings from the minister of culture of his country. Then I had to translate for him their message, that they would not answer any of his questions, and that he should get lost, in his own interest.

THE COLORFUL experiences I describe here, of course, pale beside other dramatic incidents that took place during my house arrest and about which, unfortunately, I will only be able to write, should anyone still be interested, in a somewhat different time.

. . .

I SUPPOSE the motive behind all this harassment and provo-
cation is none other than to break my nerve, and possibly the
hidden hope that I will eventually decide to emigrate. Several
times, during interrogation, I was told that if I wished I could
have a passport to emigrate within twenty-four hours. This
hypothesis is confirmed by the fact that a rumor was circulated around Prague that I in fact intended to emigrate. I
have no doubts about who started it. I have no intention of
emigrating, and I have never given it any thought. (I also do
not hold it against anyone who has emigrated: what kind of
human rights activists would we be if we were to deny people
the right that every swallow has!)

I ADMIT that all these petty things—the constant presence of
the police outside the window, the constant uncertainty about
what mischief they will dream up for me tomorrow, the hopeless complications surrounding every detail of life, and the
constant need to overcome, within oneself, the desire to respond naturally to all this (at the very least, to say what I think
about them)—have not been good for my nerves. I have not
been able to concentrate on writing, I fell into depressions, I
suffered from insomnia, headaches, stomach trouble, and a
strange bubbling in the blood. In my dreams I was constantly
haunted by the faces of my warders, I heard their steps behind me, and so on. In short, I'm no great hero, even though
some of my friends suspect me of heroic aspirations.

In some regards, this has been harder for me than my first
period in custody, which, unlike the second, I did not take
very well. I even went to see a doctor in Trutnov—of course
in the company of my policeman, though the doctor finally
persuaded him to get out of his office—and he told me I was
suffering from "neuro-vegetative difficulties." All of this, of
course, was true of the first few months of my house arrest,
whereas now I feel, more clearly all the time, that my old
equanimity is returning. I don't want to speak too soon, but
I feel more and more certain all the time; their games don't

affect me—neither in the sense that they would force me to back down, nor in the opposite sense, that I would let them provoke me into doing or saying something extreme.

AGAIN, as I said at the conclusion of my first report, I know there are hundreds of people who are infinitely worse off than I am (above all those who are in prison, are seriously ill and denied medical care). If I write about my own situation (and I will continue to write about such matters in the future), if I speak about it in various interviews and send complaints about it to the relevant authorities, this is certainly not because I think my own tribulations are so important, but because—as Patočka once wrote—we don't just have the right, we have the duty to defend ourselves against arbitrary measures. I understand this duty not just as a duty toward one's own human integrity, but as a duty to one's fellow citizens. Once in my life—without noticing it in time—I became entangled in the web of my own inappropriate politeness, inexperience, credulity, incomprehensible stupidity and even less comprehensible underestimation of my opponent's perfidy. This experience taught me that there is nothing worse than having people you care about begin to lose faith in you. Very few know how much I suffered, and I feel strongly that after such a lesson, it would be very hard indeed to get me to give in over something essential, no matter what "neurovegetative difficulties" I might have.

January 1979
March 1979

Two Letters
from Prison

"Two Letters from Prison": Havel and several other members of VONS (the Committee to Defend the Unjustly Prosecuted) were arrested on May 29, 1979, and charged with subversion. At a trial in October, Havel was sentenced to four and a half years in prison. During that time, he was allowed to correspond only with his wife Olga, to whom he wrote regularly. Although the final letter in the collected edition of *Letters to Olga* is dated September 4, 1982, Havel continued to write her after that. This is a slightly abridged version of two letters written shortly before his release on February 7, 1983. Published here for the first time in English, they were translated by Paul Wilson.

January 22, 1983

From time to time I get wind of someone's catastrophic voice, warning that in our circles everyone is arguing with each other; no one's doing anything useful, they're drinking too much, emigrating (only to cause even greater scandals once they are outside the country), looking out only for themselves, taking money that doesn't belong to them, while the better known merely cultivate their fame and ignore the others, and so on and so forth. I don't know if this is true or not, but I'm taking it with a grain of salt: I know how easy it is to generalize from two or three superficial chance encounters, particularly when the phenomenon we are looking at is so varied, so diffuse, so chaotic, so unknowable in its entirety. I'm not writing about this now because I am giving any particular weight to these and similar reports, or because they worry me, and certainly not because I have any conclusions to draw from them. I will see for myself once I'm released: perhaps things aren't that bad; perhaps they're even worse. Right now, however, I'm concerned about something else.

[. . .]

When a person chooses to take a certain stand, when he breathes some meaning into his life, it gives him perspective, hope, purpose. When he arrives at a certain truth and decides to "live in it," it is his act and his alone; it is an existential, moral, and ultimately a metaphysical act, growing from the depths of his heart and aimed at filling his own being; from a certain point of view, it is a self-sufficient act, essentially independent of the shifts and tides in his surroundings, of the so-called general situation, regardless of how it appears at the moment. If such an orientation is true and deep, no change in external conditions and circumstances can alter his choice in its deepest foundations. (At the very most, it can only change his way of behavior.)

Someone who does not draw strength from himself and who is incapable of finding the meaning of his life within himself will depend on his surroundings, will seek the map to his own orientation somewhere outside himself—in some ideology, organization, or society, and then, however active he may appear to be, he is merely waiting, depending. He waits to see what others will do, or what roles they will assign to him, and he depends on them—and if they don't do anything or if they botch things, he succumbs to disillusion, despair, and ultimately, resignation. The sect he belongs to has disappointed him and he collapses like a punctured balloon.

This is essentially a fanatic approach. Incapable of confronting the alienness of the world alone, the fanatic surrenders his fate to the institution he idolizes and blindly identifies with it. But at the first sign that it is not fulfilling his fantasy about what it should be, he begins to panic. He feels that his

world is falling apart, that life has lost its meaning, and suddenly he becomes willing to do what for years he had so vehemently (he is a fanatic, after all!) condemned: he begins
looking out for himself, he emigrates, he adapts.

Such a person is unhappy: he is always enthusiastic, and at
the same time permanently disappointed; he is ever the naive
optimist, and yet ever in danger of being cast into the abyss
of deepest skepticism by an external accident. He is capable
very easily, very quickly, very emotionally, and without the
slightest inner reserve, of devoting himself to a cause (and of
condemning energetically everyone who does not share that
devotion), but he is just as capable, the moment things begin
to go wrong, of turning away from the same cause and succumbing to the pessimistic view that nothing makes sense,
which he holds until he discovers—or rather, until someone
else discovers—something new that he can identify with again,
something to which he may, once more, delegate all his reason, his conscience, his responsibility.

Genuine constancy is displayed only by someone who depends on himself and not on others, who has the strength to
maintain a sober spirit, his own reason and a healthy self-
control, and an original, that is, unmediated, view of the
world. And of course the opposite is true, too: only someone
who can maintain such a constant overview really believes—
in the sense of belief as a state of the soul, as an "orientation
toward Being," and not belief as blind identification with
something that offers itself from the outside.

In other words, even if everyone emigrated, if everyone gave
up, if they all succumbed to "existence-in-the-world," this is
not the slightest reason for one to do the same: one does not
take a stand out of a need to do what others do, and one
cannot therefore surrender it for the paltry reason that others
have surrendered theirs.

Of course, we are delighted when everything is working
properly, when everyone around us is constantly, bravely, and
tirelessly working for his ideals, when everyone is constantly
charitable and loving to each other; and we are depressed

when the opposite is true. Such delight and sadness, however, must not be allowed—one way or another—to touch the basic core of things, that is, the way we have chosen for ourselves, the way we have chosen to be.

But to return to where we began: it seems to me that those catastrophic reports, or at least some of them, reveal far more about the state of mind of those who bear the news than they do about the objective state of affairs. They reveal the person's inability to depend on himself and his need to seek allies, which leads to that unfortunate dependency on "allies" from whom alone he seeks salvation, to whom he is entirely devoted, and with whose collapse he must automatically collapse himself. At the same time, I suspect that in the cases I have in mind, this inner state—should it arise—will even subtly begin to come first, before all those reports about the outer state, and have an influence on them, until ultimately what determines the view, the choice of facts, and how they are evaluated is in fact this lack of self-reliance, strength, constancy, independence, a cheerful long-range view, tolerance, and a kindly understanding that inevitably leads (by way of painful self-regret) to resignation. What compels one to see demoralization everywhere is thus not so much the general demoralization itself, but rather one's own loss of certainty and a sense of the meaning of life. To quote myself: the world is lost only to the extent that I myself am lost.

This may sound odd, but whenever I hear that a certain cause of ours is in crisis, I accept it joyously, as a confirmation that the cause still exists: if it did not exist, it could not be in a state of crisis. I have, you see, fewer illusions than most, because I need them less than most: because I believe. In what? That's hard to say. In life, perhaps.

February 5, 1983

Part of the catastrophic message that reaches me regularly two or three times a year from somewhere is inevitably a complaint that "nothing is happening," that "nothing is being done." You might expect me to be particularly vulnerable to such news, to be upset or depressed by it, to cry out in despair: Why am I here? What sense does any of this make if nothing is happening?

I don't want to simplify things, but I must admit that for some time now I've been responding to this kind of news in exactly the opposite way you'd expect: I usually retort, with some irritation: And what should be happening? And why should anything be happening, anyway? Why should something always be "done"? And what should be done anyway?

My irritation is not, however, a response to a particular item of news as such, but to a certain rather perverse way of grasping things that this kind of news, rightly or wrongly, always reminds me of. It is an understanding of things based on the illusion that everything stands or falls on "doing," that is, doing as such, on the grounds that when something is "doing" it is, in principle, better than "non-doing." In other words, it's a kind of cult of action for the sake of action, doing for the sake of doing, and the only important thing is that something is happening; it is less important, or entirely insignificant, what the activity is, who is doing it and why, what it means and provokes, and what it has come out of. The meaning of the event begins and ends with the mere fact of its having taken place; and if it is not important what that event is, on the contrary it is very important that there be as many events as possible, as often as possible, because their number and frequency are a measure of life.

The corollary of this is the empty belief that "if nothing is happening, nothing is happening." Life thus becomes, *de facto*, a constant dying, interrupted here and there by some event. The more events there are, the more alive we seem, and the fewer there are, the more inevitable death seems. I do not think—in itself—that it is at all important whether a lot is happening, or not very much, and I certainly don't think that the number of events tells us anything essential in itself. The only important thing to me is whether what is happening has meaning or not. The feeling that "if nothing is happening, nothing is happening" is the prejudice of a superficial, dependent, and hollow spirit, one that has succumbed to the age and can prove its own excellence only by the quantity of pseudo-events it is constantly organizing, like a bee, to that end. How often is silence more eloquent than the most eloquent speech! How often does a single well-chosen, well-placed word clear the air more effectively than a hundred pages of well-intentioned prattle!

There have obviously been heroic periods of wonderful confusion and hectic activity, when everyone did everything, everyone was nice to each other and shared the burdens cheerfully, when everyone helped each other and no one was refused. Every community goes through such a period of youth. Obviously people occasionally get nostalgic about it, and against that background it may indeed seem that "nothing is happening anymore." But it's precisely at that point that we have to mobilize all our vigilance and remind ourselves of that familiar, dangerous roller-coaster ride from enthusiasm to nihilism that has, in its time, swept whole regiments of our fellow citizens, who are not much older than we are, along with it. It is truly sad to think that those who, because they were so strongly against fanaticism and illusion, seemed immune to such attitudes, might end up that way themselves.

In other words, I don't care whether a lot or little is happening. I am interested only in whether what is happening—or not happening—has a meaning, and what that meaning is. I am in favor of things that have authenticity, roots, originality, verve, balance, taste, communicativeness, challenge, relevance to their time—in short, things that make sense. One such event—even once every six months, or once a year—is dearer to me than all the drudgery, however noble its motives may be, if the only reason for it is to have something doing. Such activity usually only cheapens positions taken, exhausts (and endangers) people, and leaves a sense of futility in its wake. [. . .]

To maintain one's position silently and constantly means more than shouting it out and then quickly abandoning it. A silent partner, of whom you can never predict when he will speak and what he will say, though you are certain that when he does speak it will be as clear as the striking of a bell, is far more capable of disquieting the world than someone everyone has figured out, as it were, beforehand.

January 22, 1983
February 5, 1983

"I Take
the Side of Truth"

*An Interview with
Antoine Spire*

" 'I Take the Side of Truth': An Interview with Antoine Spire" is the first interview Havel gave after
his release from prison in February 1983. Havel
wrote his responses to the French journalist's questions in Czech, and the Czech text of the interview—which provided the basis for all subsequent
versions—was authorized in Prague and dated
April 3, 1983. It was first published in *Le Monde*
(April 10–11, 1983), with the title "Mon prison, mon
pays . . ." It appeared first in English in the *Help and
Action Newsletter*, Paris, no. 26 (May–June 1983), and
later in *Index on Censorship* (December 1983). The
translation is by George Theiner.

*You have been let out of prison after almost four years "inside."
What exactly is your present legal position?*

I have been granted a so-called judicial suspension of my
sentence (that means without any set time limit) on grounds
of ill-health. In theory, it is possible that as soon as the doctor
pronounces me fit, I may find a summons in my mailbox,
ordering me to report on such-and-such a day to complete

my jail term—I have another ten months to go. In actual fact, I don't believe that the authorities intend me—at least in the near future—to go back to prison. In the long term, as always, it will depend more on the overall political situation than on me. As far as I am concerned, I'm trying to behave cautiously—I certainly have no intention of rushing back to jail—but on the other hand I don't mean to give up my views or my standpoint either.

Czechoslovak officials claim that in their country people do not go to jail for their views.

No, not for their views, only for expressing them. But what kind of a view is it that does not get expressed? Surely it only becomes a view when it finds expression.

You spent almost a month in a civilian hospital, now several more weeks at home. How do the police behave toward you?

At the moment I'd call it an armistice. Apart from run-of-the-mill harassment carried out by other authorities, such as the endeavor to deprive me of my Prague apartment under the pretext that I have furnished my country cottage in such a way that it has become a second home (according to Czechoslovak law, you are not allowed to own two apartments), the police are leaving me in peace. Or at least they don't give any visible signs of their presence—but it is highly probable that my place is bugged. I expect they're waiting to see what I'm going to do, and it may also be linked with the relaxation of pressure the police have been exerting on the Charter 77 people. This has to do with the general political situation in our country, which is today one of unease and uncertainty where the authorities are concerned. However, when I speak of a relaxation, this is of course purely relative; witness the recent action against the Franciscans.

*You have no doubt heard of the worldwide response to the 1979
Prague trial of members of VONS (Committee to Defend the Unjustly
Prosecuted)—that is, you and your friends—and so you know how
much sympathy and solidarity came to be expressed.*

Yes, I heard something of this while still in prison, and now
I'm gradually catching up on reading the complete documentation, insofar as it survived several house searches. Again
and again I was surprised and moved by the support we received, not only at the time of the trial itself but throughout
our imprisonment. I find it most gratifying and very important—not just for ourselves but on a more general level—that
our case should have aroused the interest and support of so
many foreign government representatives, parties, and other
organizations. I must admit, though, that what pleased me
most were the innumerable expressions of solidarity by people who cannot be suspected of pursuing their own political
agenda, those spontaneous expressions of support inspired
simply by an interest in the fate of their fellow men and by
an understanding of the indivisible nature of spiritual and
civic freedoms. These people understood that whenever freedom and human dignity are threatened in any one country,
they are under threat everywhere, that this signifies an attack
on humanity itself and on the future of all of us. I know that
many of those who took a public stand on our behalf would
themselves behave much as we did, were they to find themselves in similar circumstances, and I know equally that we
would then take their side just as they took ours. Being aware
of this understanding on the part of so many people the world
over who realized *why* we had gone to jail (many of us were
offered ways of avoiding imprisonment, for example, by emigrating) was naturally a great consolation to me during my
years in prison; it is only a pity that I couldn't know then all
I know now.

I cannot, of course, name here all those who gave us public
support, but I cannot omit mentioning at least one such expression of solidarity—that which was so bravely made by our

friends from the Polish Workers' Defense committee, who are today in a similar position as we were then. I think of them constantly, the more so as I have now discovered at first hand what it means to be imprisoned. Let me, however, add one more important thing: it would hardly have been possible for us to receive so much attention abroad had it not been for the self-sacrifice of our friends here at home, the signatories of Charter 77 and in particular those who, as soon as we were arrested, took our places in the Charter and in VONS, who quickly and at great personal risk informed the outside world about what had happened, and who frequently suffered for it.

What would you like to say about the prison and your time in it?

Well, that would provide material for a whole book, and even a book wouldn't really do justice to it. It's an experience that, deep down, can probably not be communicated to others. And so let me be brief: for several years I was forced to live in an environment where every effort was made to break people, systematically to get them to inform on others and to act selfishly; in an atmosphere of fear and intrigue, of mindless discipline and arbitrary bullying, degradation and deliberate insult, being at the same time deprived of even the simplest positive emotional, sensual, or spiritual experience, such as a pretty picture, a kind word, or a sincere handclasp. Again and again I realized that prison was not intended merely to deprive a man of a few years of his life and make him suffer for that length of time, rather it was intended to mark him for life, destroy his personality, score his heart in such a way that it would never heal completely. Prison thus seems to me something like a futurological laboratory of totalitarianism.

All the concealed, indirect, subtle means by which the system manipulates human beings and gains control over them are present in their naked form, much more clearly to be perceived than outside the prison walls. Moreover, they have been perfected to a degree which, in the "outside world," the powers-that-be can only dream about—at least for the time being. What makes all this particularly dramatic is the fact that what is being experimented with in this "laboratory" isn't the docile, obedient citizen, the like of whom our rulers would dearly like to turn us all into, but quite the opposite: prison is the peculiar meeting place of individually minded people, individuals who, in one way or another, differ from the norm—whether by murdering their wives in a fit of jealous rage or by fighting for human rights. The majority, of course—and these are mostly young people—found themselves in jail because they were unable to conform, because they felt oppressed by the stifling environment they lived in, disgusted by the conformist, hypocritical world around them, and consequently they somewhere, somehow revolted. In some cases they didn't even do that, they merely insisted on being "different."

In a single cell holding perhaps twelve, perhaps twenty-five people, you can come across more interesting, unusual, dramatic, tragic, unique life stories than on a housing estate with several thousand inhabitants. And so we have here a harsh confrontation between the past (i.e., a world of individual fates) and the wished-for future (a world of complete and absolute uniformity). Some time ago I read an article in *Rudé právo* by the Minister of the Interior, Dr. Obzina, in which he stated that crime in a socialist society was the result of insufficient social homogeneity of the population. Cross out the word "social" and you have the key to the riddle—once we all become exactly like one another there will be no more need for courts of law and prisons. The way to get rid of weeds is to abolish fields. Quite right: if you deny life—which after all is founded on differentiation and not homogeneity— you *will* prevent crime, genuine as well as imaginary. But to be fair—all this is hardly a specialty of Czech prisons; Foucault's profound analysis of modern prison systems (*Discipline and Punish*) shows that basically it is the same everywhere: less and less is punishment intended as a spontaneous response to a criminal act, more and more is it a systematic deprivation and destruction of human individuality and identity. The thing is that here, in Czechoslovakia, it is all the more blatant and has numerous aspects that are all our own because of the nature of the system. For instance, from my daily, exhaustive reading of *Rudé právo,* which was my only available source of information in prison, I was able to calculate that there are, per capita, four times as many prisoners in Czechoslovakia as in the United States. To put it very simply, prison today is no longer based on physical suffering—even though people *are* sometimes beaten up and *do* occasionally go hungry—but on something worse: on a systematic, everyday, round-the-clock assault on man's psyche, on his nervous system, and his moral integrity.

What is the position of political prisoners in Czechoslovakia today?

Officially, there *are* no political prisoners in Czechoslovakia. There are only "lawbreakers," and the very term "political prisoner" is taboo—though, of course, in conversation everyone uses it, including the jailers. You would think that, in order to bear out this pretense, political prisoners would be given the same conditions as all the other inmates. In fact, this is not so: they are far worse off than the ordinary criminals, being mostly deprived of a large number of rights and privileges such as extra visits or parcels for good behavior, the possibility of work in the prison administration, the right to be appointed to a post in the so-called self-administration, the modest opportunities for cultural expression, and so on. Political prisoners are surrounded by informers and kept under constant surveillance, punished on the slightest of pretexts, have no hope of conditional release, others are punished if they try to contact them (and this in that most "collective" institution of all!); the prison authorities think up all kinds of ways to make life harder for them, for example, by assigning them work in which they cannot fulfill their norms and thus render themselves liable to yet more punishment; and I have personally had the experience of other prisoners being secretly bribed to harm me, for instance, by stealing my cigarettes or vitamins. Yet, the politicals are held in high esteem by the others, even though people can always be found who, in return for minor privileges, will inform on them or intrigue against them. But the majority of prisoners, whether they lend themselves to this sort of thing or not, regard the politicals as innocent, as people who—in the laconic prison jargon—have been jailed "for the truth."

This, of course, means that they are automatically expected not only to know and understand everything, but also to know the very meaning of life, which they are then thought capable at any time of imparting to all and sundry. I thus had to—and so did my friends—act for years as a lawyer, psychologist, confessor (political prisoners alone can be relied on not to inform)—and all this despite the fact that it is strictly forbidden, being seen as a continuation of the criminal activity for which we were sent to prison in the first place. I had to try and give my fellow prisoners new hope when they were depressed, help them solve their marital problems, write their love letters, prevent their suicides, advise them in a variety of ways. Of course this kind of trust is most gratifying, and we liked doing it, but on the other hand it did not serve to make life in prison any easier. Not only because it incensed the warders, but in particular because it put us in a role which made it impossible for *us* to be depressed, to indulge our own problems and uncertainties, and turn to others for help and advice.

Were you able to write in prison?

No, that was strictly forbidden. I wasn't even allowed to have a notebook or paper, much less to make notes. I was once even punished when they found me in possession of some drafts of letters I had legally sent home. The one thing they did not—and could not—stop me doing was to write the officially permitted, naturally censored, letters to my wife. That was my legal right: one letter a week, four pages of standard writing paper, written in a legible hand and within the prescribed margins. There are some 165 of these letters lying here. Writing them was my greatest joy, it made some sense of my incarceration, and in them I tried—under circumstances so difficult that I can't adequately describe them to you—to develop wider themes, topics which I was often forced to think about in prison, like the problem of man's identity and responsibility, of our horizons, and so on. This, too, they forbade for some time; many of my letters weren't allowed through since they were supposed to concern exclusively "family matters"—but in the end they somehow came to accept it.

Did you ever feel hatred toward your jailers?

No, I don't know how to hate, and that pleases me. If for no other reason, then because hatred clouds the vision and makes it difficult to seek the truth.

You were arrested in the spring of 1979, and now suddenly—as if in one leap—you find yourself in 1983. You must thus be able to compare conditions in your country far more acutely than those who had continuity outside. How does the situation strike you?

I wouldn't dare make any general judgments or assessments as yet. I can only describe my initial and entirely subjective impressions. But let me say right at the outset that these have, in every way, exceeded all my expectations.

Charter 77 has survived six, and VONS five, years of persecution, and they are carrying on their work even though their documents no longer get the same publicity as before.

I was astonished both by the breadth and depth of the various unofficial cultural activities, by the number, durability, and quality of the private philosophy seminars, the quantity of *samizdat* literature—not just fiction but also the even larger number of articles and essays, the typewritten magazines, and so on. Methods of work have changed, and there seems to be less fear on the one hand and more cautiousness on the other. I find the extent of all this activity surprising. I don't know how I'm going to catch up. Most surprising of all is the indefatigable energy which people invest in it. Today, it seems to me, there is a greater hunger than ever for cultural products and truthful words, whether these come—so far only sporadically—from the officially sanctioned culture or—and there is incomparably more of this kind—from the sphere of "unofficial," or to quote Ivan Jirous, the "second" culture. It seems to me that some of these texts, which now exist in only a few typewritten copies, could be published in printings of tens of thousands and sold out straightaway. It is as if many people had got tired of their own weariness, unable any longer to suppress their desire for truthful, free artistic creation. It surprises me that those who move in the "official" sphere often know more about the products of the "unofficial" culture than we know about theirs. The once well-defined and impenetrable dividing line between the two cultures appears to be growing fuzzy, with more interesting things appearing within the boundaries of what is permitted—though usually only on the periphery—many of them inspired in one way or another by the "unofficial" culture, relating to it, competing with it, or in some cases almost indistinguishable from it where inner freedom is concerned.

The pressure exerted by the political apparatus on the official culture, which until recently had been safely in its grasp, would appear to be growing, and that is a sure sign that it is again beginning to mean something: I even get the impression that in some sectors this seemingly "safe" culture is getting out of its control. They have been banning plays, theatres and, in particular, numerous rock and jazz bands which not so long ago they had lavished praise on. Many people today no longer know which culture they form part of—whether the "official" or the "other"—people who are still "all right" appear on the same platforms with banned ones, everything seems to have got mixed up. It also seems to me that even some—of course only a few—official artists have changed their attitude toward us. They don't seem so afraid of us anymore; perhaps they realize that they might at any time find themselves in our ranks and that there is no longer any sense in pretending, since that's unlikely to change their fate. But I repeat, these are just my first and totally personal impressions, so they should not be taken as a considered judgment.

To some extent, all this reminds me of the early sixties, when the process of self-realization and spiritual liberation likewise began somewhere on the borders between official and unofficial culture, in that strange area in which the authorities prohibit one thing, only for another to crop up a little way off, unnoticed by the censors. This process, of course, culminated in 1968, when the powers that be were forced to acknowledge, could no longer ignore, the true condition of our society, of its soul.

As regards political matters, it seems to me that the authorities today are facing all the economic, social, political, and cultural problems more hesitantly than it appeared to me while in prison; as if they were growing weary—and is it surprising, when you realize that it is the same old guard, unchanged, which has been in charge for fourteen years? From time to time they show how desperately scared they are of the slightest breath of fresh air by nonsensically banning this or that; at other times you would think that they themselves are beginning to give some thought to how to ventilate this rotting area—while at the same time of course making sure that the draft does not in any way endanger *them*. To this has probably been added a measure of uncertainty: is the present state of affairs at the center of our bloc only provisional, or does it perhaps presage a new era—and if so, what will that signify?

Finally, when we are talking about the changes I have noticed since coming out of prison, I have to say that there has been a distinct increase in the high living of the corrupt elite. Not that I would compare this to the life style of the Roman aristocracy before the fall of Rome—for that, our Czech conditions are far too petty—but I *would* compare it to the last few years of Gierek's rule in Poland. Here, too, the luxury of the official elite is in sharp contrast to the actual economic situation of the country and the everyday consumer worries of its inhabitants.

You are today considered to be a leading Czech dissident or opposition spokesman; how do you view this?

I am not, have never been, nor have I the slightest intention of becoming a politician, a professional revolutionary or professional "dissident." I am a writer, writing what I want to write and not what others might like me to, and if I get involved in any other way except by my writing, then only because I feel this to be my natural human and civic duty, as well as my duty as a writer. That is, my duty as a public figure on whom it is incumbent, just because he *is* known to the public, to express his views more loudly than those who are not so well known. Not because he is more clever or more important than anyone else but simply because he is, whether he likes it or not, in a different position and possessed of a different responsibility. Even though I naturally do have my own opinions on a variety of issues, I don't hold with any particular ideology, doctrine or, even less, any political party or faction. I serve no one—much less any superpower. If I serve anything, then only my own conscience. I am neither a communist nor an anticommunist, and if I criticize my government, then not because it happens to be a communist government but because it is bad. Were this government a Social Democratic or Christian Socialist one, or any other, if it ruled badly I would criticize it in the same way as I criticize the

Czechoslovak government. I am not on the side of any establishment, nor am I a professional campaigner *against* any establishment—I merely take the side of truth against lies, the side of sense against nonsense, the side of justice against injustice.

What are your plans for the future?

Returning from prison is no joke—some in fact say that it is more difficult than going in. I first have to get my bearings, try and fit in, try to understand the world in which I have arrived. And that means meeting a great many people, reading a large number of important texts, going to various performances and concerts, in short, again learning to breathe the air of my times. Without that, you cannot write. And then I'd like at last to start writing another play—it's about six years since I last wrote one.

Do you think your time in prison will affect your future writing?

Undoubtedly, but at the moment I can't say how.

Is this interview likely to have unpleasant consequences for you?

That I don't know. I really don't.

April 1983

Politics and Conscience

"Politics and Conscience" (February 1984): In an author's note, Havel writes, "This speech was written for the University of Toulouse, where I would have delivered it on receiving an honorary doctorate, had I attended. . . ." Havel, of course, had no passport and could not travel abroad. At the ceremony at the University of Toulouse–Le Mirail on May 14, 1984, he was represented by the English playwright Tom Stoppard.

The essay first appeared in Prague in a *samizdat* collection called *The Natural World as Political Problem: Essays on Modern Man* (Prague: Edice Expedice, Vol. 188, 1984). The first English translation, by Erazim Kohák and Roger Scruton, appeared in the *Salisbury Review,* no. 2 (January 1985). This is the translation used here.

I

As a boy, I lived for some time in the country and I clearly remember an experience from those days: I used to walk to school in a nearby village along a cart track through the fields and, on the way, see on the horizon a huge smokestack of some hurriedly built factory, in all likelihood in the service of war. It spewed dense brown smoke and scattered it across the sky. Each time I saw it, I had an intense sense of something profoundly wrong, of humans soiling the heavens. I have no idea whether there was something like a science of ecology in those days; if there was, I certainly knew nothing

249

of it. Still that "soiling of the heavens" offended me spontaneously. It seemed to me that, in it, humans are guilty of something, that they destroy something important, arbitrarily disrupting the natural order of things, and that such things cannot go unpunished. To be sure, my revulsion was largely aesthetic; I knew nothing then of the noxious emissions which would one day devastate our forests, exterminate game, and endanger the health of people.

If a medieval man were to see something like that suddenly on the horizon—say, while out hunting—he would probably think it the work of the Devil and would fall on his knees and pray that he and his kin be saved.

What is it, actually, that the world of the medieval peasant and that of a small boy have in common? Something substantive, I think. Both the boy and the peasant are far more intensely rooted in what some philosophers call "the natural world," or *Lebenswelt,* than most modern adults. They have not yet grown alienated from the world of their actual personal experience, the world which has its morning and its evening, its *down* (the earth) and its *up* (the heavens), where the sun rises daily in the east, traverses the sky and sets in the west, and where concepts like "at home" and "in foreign parts," good and evil, beauty and ugliness, near and far, duty and rights, still mean something living and definite. They are still rooted in a world which knows the dividing line between all that is intimately familiar and appropriately a subject of our concern, and that which lies beyond its horizon, that before which we should bow down humbly because of the mystery about it. Our "I" primordially attests to that world and personally certifies it; that is the world of our lived experience, a world not yet indifferent since we are personally bound to it in our love, hatred, respect, contempt, tradition, in our interests and in that pre-reflective meaningfulness from which culture is born. That is the realm of our inimitable, inalienable, and nontransferable joy and pain, a world in which, through which, and for which we are somehow answerable, a world of personal responsibility. In this world, categories like justice, honor, treason, friendship, infidelity, courage, or empathy have a wholly tangible content, relating to actual persons and important for actual life. At the basis of this world are values which are simply there, perennially, before we ever speak of them, before we reflect upon them and inquire about them. It owes its internal coherence to something like a "pre-speculative" assumption that the world functions and is generally possible at all only because there is something beyond its horizon, something beyond or above it that might escape our understanding and our grasp but, for just that reason, firmly grounds this world, bestows upon it its order and measure, and is the hidden source of all the rules, customs, commandments, prohibitions, and norms that hold within it. The natural world, in virtue of its very being, bears within it the presupposition of the absolute which grounds, delimits, animates, and directs it, without which it would be unthinkable, absurd, and superfluous, and which we can only quietly respect. Any attempt to spurn it, master it, or replace it with something else, appears, within the framework of the natural world, as an expression of *hubris* for which humans must pay a heavy price, as did Don Juan and Faust.

To me, personally, the smokestack soiling the heavens is not just a regrettable lapse of a technology that failed to in-clude "the ecological factor" in its calculation, one which can be easily corrected with the appropriate filter. To me it is more, the symbol of an age which seeks to transcend the boundaries of the natural world and its norms and to make it into a merely private concern, a matter of subjective pref-erence and private feeling, of the illusions, prejudices, and whims of a "mere" individual. It is a symbol of an epoch which denies the binding importance of personal experience—including the experience of mystery and of the absolute—and displaces the personally experienced absolute as the measure of the world with a new, man-made absolute, devoid of mystery, free of the "whims" of subjectivity and, as such, impersonal and inhuman. It is the absolute of so-called objectivity: the objective, rational cognition of the scientific model of the world.

Modern science, constructing its universally valid image of the world, thus crashes through the bounds of the natural world, which it can understand only as a prison of prejudices from which we must break out into the light of objectively verified truth. The natural world appears to it as no more than an unfortunate leftover from our backward ancestors, a fantasy of their childish immaturity. With that, of course, it abolishes as mere fiction even the innermost foundation of our natural world; it kills God and takes his place on the vacant throne so that henceforth it would be science which would hold the order of being in its hand as its sole legitimate guardian and be the sole legitimate arbiter of all relevant truth. For, after all, it is only science that rises above all individual subjective truths and replaces them with a superior, suprasubjective, suprapersonal truth, which is truly objective and universal.

Modern rationalism and modern science, though the work of people that, as all human works, developed within our natural world, now systematically leave it behind, deny it, degrade and defame it—and, of course, at the same time colonize it. A modern man, whose natural world has been properly conquered by science and technology, objects to the smoke from the smokestack only if the stench penetrates his apartment. In no case, though, does he take offense at it metaphysically since he knows that the factory to which the smokestack belongs manufactures things that he needs. As a man of the technological era, he can conceive of a remedy only within the limits of technology—say, a catalytic scrubber fitted to the chimney.

Lest you misunderstand: I am not proposing that humans abolish smokestacks or prohibit science or generally return to the Middle Ages. Besides, it is not by accident that some of the most profound discoveries of modern science render the myth of objectivity surprisingly problematic and, via a remarkable detour, return us to the human subject and his world. I wish no more than to consider, in a most general and admittedly schematic outline, the spiritual framework of modern civilization and the source of its present crisis. And though the primary focus of these reflections will be the political rather than ecological aspect of this crisis, I might, perhaps, clarify my starting point with one more ecological example.

For centuries, the basic component of European agriculture had been the family farm. In Czech, the older term for it was *grunt*—which itself is not without its etymological interest. The word, taken from the German *Grund*, actually means ground or foundation and, in Czech, acquired a peculiar semantic coloring. As the colloquial synonym for "foundation," it points out the "groundedness" of the ground, its indubitable, traditional and pre-speculatively given authenticity and credibility. Certainly, the family farm was a source of endless and intensifying social conflict of all kinds. Still, we cannot deny it one thing: it was rooted in the nature of its place, appropriate, harmonious, personally tested by generations of farmers and certified by the results of their husbandry. It also displayed a kind of optimal mutual proportionality in extent and kind of all that belonged to it; fields, meadows, boundaries, woods, cattle, domestic animals, water, roads, and so on. For centuries no farmer made it the topic of a scientific study. Nevertheless, it constituted a generally satisfactory economic and ecological system, within which everything was bound together by a thousand threads of mutual and meaningful connection, guaranteeing its stability as well as the stability of the product of the farmer's husbandry. Unlike present-day "agribusiness," the traditional family farm was energetically self-sufficient. Though it was subject to common calamities, it was not guilty of them—unfavorable weather, cattle disease, wars and other catastrophes lay outside the farmer's province.

Certainly, modern agricultural and social science could also improve agriculture in a thousand ways, increasing its productivity, reducing the amount of sheer drudgery, and eliminating the worst social inequities. But this is possible only on the assumption that modernization, too, will be guided by a certain humility and respect for the mysterious order of nature and for the appropriateness which derives from it and which is intrinsic to the natural world of personal experience and responsibility. Modernization must not be simply an arrogant, megalomaniac, and brutal invasion by an impersonally objective science, represented by a newly graduated agronomist or a bureaucrat in the service of the "scientific world view."

That, however, is just what happened to our country: our word for it was "collectivization." Like a tornado, it raged through the Czechoslovak countryside thirty years ago, leaving not a stone in place. Among its consequences were, on the one hand, tens of thousands of lives devastated by prison, sacrificed on the altar of a scientific Utopia offering brighter tomorrows. On the other hand, the level of social conflict and the amount of drudgery in the countryside did in fact decrease while agricultural productivity rose quantitatively. That, though, is not why I mention it. My reason is something else: thirty years after the tornado swept the traditional family farm off the face of the earth, scientists are amazed to discover what even a semiliterate farmer previously knew—that human beings must pay a heavy price for every attempt to abolish, radically, once for all and without trace, that humbly respected boundary of the natural world, with its tradition of scrupulous personal acknowledgment. They must pay for the attempt to seize nature, to leave not a remnant of it in human hands, to ridicule its mystery; they must pay for the attempt to abolish God and to play at being God. This is what in fact happened. With hedges plowed under and woods cut down, wild birds have died out and, with them, a natural, unpaid protector of the crops against harmful insects. Huge unified fields have led to the inevitable annual loss of millions of cubic yards of topsoil that have taken centuries to accumulate; chemical fertilizers and pesticides have catastrophically poisoned all vegetable products, the earth and the waters.

Heavy machinery systematically presses down the soil, making it impenetrable to air and thus infertile; cows in gigantic dairy farms suffer neuroses and lose their milk while agriculture siphons off ever more energy from industry—manufacture of machines, artificial fertilizers, rising transportation costs in an age of growing local specialization, and so on. In short, the prognoses are terrifying and no one knows what surprises coming years and decades may bring.

It is paradoxical: people in the age of science and technology live in the conviction that they can improve their lives because they are able to grasp and exploit the complexity of nature and the general laws of its functioning. Yet it is precisely these laws which, in the end, tragically catch up with them and get the better of them. People thought they could explain and conquer nature—yet the outcome is that they destroyed it and disinherited themselves from it. But what are the prospects for man "outside nature"? It is, after all, precisely the sciences that are most recently discovering that the human body is actually only a particularly busy intersection of billions of organic microbodies, of their complex mutual contacts and influences, together forming that incredible mega-organism we call the "biosphere" in which our planet is blanketed.

The fault is not one of science as such but of the arrogance of man in the age of science. Man simply is not God, and playing God has cruel consequences. Man has abolished the absolute horizon of his relations, denied his personal "preobjective" experience of the lived world, while relegating personal conscience and consciousness to the bathroom, as something so private that it is no one's business. Man rejected his responsibility as a "subjective illusion"—and in place of it installed what is now proving to be the most dangerous illusion of all: the fiction of objectivity stripped of all that is concretely human, of a rational understanding of the cosmos, and of an abstract schema of a putative "historical necessity." As the apex of it all, man has constructed a vision of a scientifically calculable and technologically achievable "universal welfare," that need only be invented by experimental institutes while industrial and bureaucratic factories turn it into reality. That millions of people will be sacrificed to this illusion in scientifically run concentration camps is not something that concerns our modern man unless by chance he himself lands behind barbed wire and is thrown drastically back upon his natural world. The phenomenon of empathy, after all, belongs with that abolished realm of personal prejudice which had to yield to science, objectivity, historical necessity, technology, system, and the apparat—and those, being impersonal, cannot worry. They are abstract and anonymous, ever utilitarian, and thus ever *a priori* innocent.

And as for the future, who, personally, would care about it or even worry about it when the perspective of eternity is one of the things locked away in the bathroom, if not expelled outright into the realm of fairy tales? If a contemporary scientist thinks at all of what will be in two hundred years, he does so solely as a disinterested observer who, basically, could not care less whether he is doing research on the metabolism of the flea, on the radio signals of pulsars, or on the global reserves of natural gas. And a modern politician? He has absolutely no reason to care, especially if it might interfere with his chances in an election, as long as he lives in a country where there are elections.

II

THE CZECH philosopher Václav Bělohradský has persuasively developed the thought that the rationalistic spirit of modern science, founded on abstract reason and on the presumption of impersonal objectivity, has its father not only in the natural sciences—Galileo, but also a father in politics—Machiavelli, who first formulated (albeit with an undertone of malicious irony) a theory of politics as a rational technology of power. We could say that, for all the complex historical detours, the origin of the modern state and of modern political power may be sought precisely here, that is, once again in a moment when human reason begins to "liberate" itself from the human being as such, from his personal experience, personal conscience, and personal responsibility and so also from that to which, within the framework of the natural world, all responsibility is uniquely related, his absolute horizon. Just as the modern scientists set apart the actual human being as the subject of the lived experience of the world, so, ever more evidently, do both the modern state and modern politics.

To be sure, this process by which power becomes anonymous and depersonalized, and reduced to a mere technology of rule and manipulation, has a thousand masks, variants, and expressions. In one case it is covert and inconspicuous, while in another case it is entirely overt; in one case it sneaks up on us along subtle and devious paths, in another case it is brutally direct. Essentially, though, it is the same universal trend. It is the essential trait of all modern civilization, growing directly from its spiritual structure, rooted in it by a thousand tangled tendrils and inseparable even in thought from its technological nature, its mass characteristics, and its consumer orientation.

Rulers and leaders were once personalities in their own right, with particular human faces, still in some sense personally responsible for their deeds, good and ill, whether they had been installed by dynastic tradition, by the will of the people, by a victorious battle, or by intrigue. But they have been replaced in modern times by the manager, the bureaucrat, the apparatchik—a professional ruler, manipulator, and expert in the techniques of management, manipulation, and obfuscation, filling a depersonalized intersection of functional relations, a cog in the machinery of state caught up in a predetermined role. This professional ruler is an "innocent" tool of an "innocent" anonymous power, legitimized by science, cybernetics, ideology, law, abstraction, and objectivity—that is, by everything except personal responsibility to human beings as persons and neighbors. A modern politician is transparent: behind his judicious mask and affected diction there is not a trace of a human being rooted in the order of the natural world by his loves, passions, interests, personal opinions, hatred, courage, or cruelty. All that he, too, locks away in his private bathroom. If we glimpse anything at all behind the mask, it will be only a more or less competent technician of power. System, ideology, and apparat have deprived us—rulers as well as the ruled—of our conscience, of our common sense and natural speech and thereby, of our actual humanity. States grow ever more machinelike; people are transformed into statistical choruses of voters, producers, consumers, patients, tourists, or soldiers. In politics, good and evil, categories of the natural world and therefore obsolete remnants of the past, lose all absolute meaning; the sole method of politics is quantifiable success. Power is *a priori* innocent because it does not grow from a world in which words like "guilt" and "innocence" retain their meaning.

This impersonal power has achieved what is its most complete expression so far in the totalitarian systems. As Bělohradský points out, the depersonalization of power and its conquest of human conscience and human speech have been successfully linked to an extra-European tradition of a "cosmological" conception of the empire (identifying the empire, as the sole true center of the world, with the world as such, and considering the human as its exclusive property). But, as the totalitarian systems clearly illustrate, this does not mean that modern impersonal power is itself an extra-European affair. The truth is the very opposite: it was precisely Europe, and the European West, that provided and frequently forced on the world all that today has become the basis of such power: natural science, rationalism, scientism, the industrial revolution, and also revolution as such, as a fanatical abstraction, through the displacement of the natural world to the bathroom down to the cult of consumption, the atomic bomb, and Marxism. And it is Europe—democratic western Europe—which today stands bewildered in the face of this ambiguous export. The contemporary dilemma, whether to resist this reverse expansionism of its erstwhile export or to yield to it, attests to this. Should rockets, now aimed at Europe thanks to its export of spiritual and technological potential, be countered by similar and better rockets, thereby demonstrating a determination to defend such values as Europe has left, at the cost of entering into an utterly immoral game being forced upon it? Or should Europe retreat, hoping that the responsibility for the fate of the planet demonstrated thereby will infect, by its miraculous power, the rest of the world?

I think that, with respect to the relation of western Europe to the totalitarian systems, no error could be greater than the one looming largest: that of a failure to understand the totalitarian systems for what they ultimately are—a convex mirror of all modern civilization and a harsh, perhaps final call for a global recasting of how that civilization understands itself. If we ignore that, then it does not make any essential difference which form Europe's efforts will take. It might be the form of taking the totalitarian systems, in the spirit of Europe's own rationalistic tradition, for a locally idiosyncratic attempt at achieving general welfare, to which only men of ill-will attribute expansionist tendencies. Or, in the spirit of the same rationalistic tradition, though this time in the Machiavellian conception of politics as the technology of power, one might perceive the totalitarian regimes as a purely external threat by expansionist neighbors who can be driven back within acceptable bounds by an appropriate demonstration of power, without having to be thought about more deeply. The first alternative is that of the person who reconciles himself to the chimney belching smoke, even though that smoke is ugly and smelly, because in the end it serves a good purpose, the production of commonly needed goods. The second alternative is that of the man who thinks that it is simply a matter of a technological flaw, which can be eliminated by technological means, such as a filter or a scrubber.

The reality, I believe, is unfortunately more serious. The chimney "soiling the heavens" is not just a technologically corrigible flaw of design, or a tax paid for a better consumerist tomorrow, but a symbol of a civilization which has renounced the absolute, which ignores the natural world and disdains its imperatives. So, too, the totalitarian systems warn of something far more serious than Western rationalism is willing to admit. They are, most of all, a convex mirror of the inevitable consequences of rationalism, a grotesquely magnified image of its own deep tendencies, an extreme offshoot of its own development and an ominous product of its own expansion. They are a deeply informative reflection of its own crisis. Totalitarian regimes are not merely dangerous neighbors and even less some kind of an avant-garde of world progress. Alas, just the opposite: they are the avant-garde of a global crisis of this civilization, first European, then Euro-American, and ultimately global. They are one of the possible futurological studies of the Western world, not in the sense that one day they will attack and conquer it, but in a far deeper sense— that they illustrate graphically the consequences of what Bělohradský calls the "eschatology of the impersonal."

It is the total rule of a bloated, anonymously bureaucratic power, not yet irresponsible but already operating outside all conscience, a power grounded in an omnipresent ideological fiction which can rationalize anything without ever having to come in contact with the truth. Power as the omnipresent monopoly of control, repression, and fear; power which makes thought, morality, and privacy a state monopoly and so dehumanizes them; power which long since has ceased to be the matter of a group of arbitrary rulers but which, rather, occupies and swallows up everyone so that all should become integrated within it, at least through their silence. No one actually possesses such power, since it is the power itself which possesses everyone; it is a monstrosity which is not guided by humans but which, on the contrary, drags all persons along with its "objective" self-momentum—objective in the sense of being cut off from all human standards, including human reason, and hence entirely irrational—toward a terrifying, unknown future.

Let me repeat: totalitarian power is a great reminder to contemporary civilization. Perhaps somewhere there may be some generals who think it would be best to dispatch such systems from the face of the earth and then all would be well. But that is no different from an ugly woman trying to get rid of her ugliness by smashing the mirror that reminds her of it. Such a "final solution" is one of the typical dreams of impersonal reason—capable, as the term "final solution" graphically reminds us, of transforming its dreams into reality and thereby reality into a nightmare. It would not only fail to resolve the crisis of the present world but, assuming anyone survived at all, would only aggravate it. By burdening the already heavy account of this civilization with further millions of dead, it would not block its essential trend to totalitarianism but would rather accelerate it. It would be a Pyrrhic victory, because the victors would emerge from a conflict inevitably resembling their defeated opponents far more than anyone today is willing to admit or able to imagine. Just a minor example: imagine what a huge Gulag Archipelago would have to be built in the West, in the name of country, democracy, progress, and war discipline, to contain all who refuse to take part in the effort, whether from naivete, principle, fear, or ill will!

No evil has ever been eliminated by suppressing its symptoms. We need to address the cause itself.

III

FROM time to time I have a chance to speak with Western intellectuals who visit our country and decide to include a visit to a dissident in their itinerary—some out of genuine interest, or a willingness to understand and to express solidarity, others simply out of curiosity. Beside the Gothic and Baroque monuments, dissidents are apparently the only thing of interest to a tourist in this uniformly dreary environment. Those conversations are usually instructive: I learn much and come to understand much. The questions most frequently asked are these: Do you think you can really change anything when you are so few and have no influence at all? Are you opposed to socialism or do you merely wish to improve it? Do you condemn or condone the deployment of the Pershing II and the Cruise missiles in western Europe? What can we do for you? What drives you to do what you are doing when all it brings you is persecution, prison—and no visible results? Would you want to see capitalism restored in your country?

Those questions are well intentioned, growing out of a desire to understand and showing that those who ask do care about the world, what it is and what it will be.

Still, precisely these and similar questions reveal to me again and again how deeply many Western intellectuals do not understand—and in some respects, cannot understand— just what is taking place here, what it is that we, the so-called dissidents, are striving for and, most of all, what the overall meaning of it is. Take, for instance, the question: "What can we do for you?" A great deal, to be sure. The more support, interest, and solidarity of free-thinking people in the world we enjoy, the less the danger of being arrested, and the greater the hope that ours will not be a voice crying in the wilderness. And yet, somewhere deep within the question there is built-in misunderstanding. After all, in the last instance the point is not to help us, a handful of "dissidents," to keep out of jail a bit more of the time. It is not even a question of helping these nations, Czechs and Slovaks, to live a bit better, a bit more freely. They need first and foremost to help themselves. They have waited for the help of others far too often, depended on it far too much, and far too many times came to grief: either the promised help was withdrawn at the last moment or it turned into the very opposite of their expectations. In the deepest sense, something else is at stake—the salvation of us all, of myself and my interlocutor equally. Or is it not something that concerns us all equally? Are not my dim prospects or, conversely, my hopes *his* dim prospects and hopes as well? Was not my arrest an attack on him and the deceptions to which he is subjected an attack on me as well? Is not the suppression of human beings in Prague a suppression of all human beings? Is not indifference to what is happening here or even illusions about it a preparation for the kind of misery elsewhere? Does not their misery presuppose ours? The point is not that some Czech dissident, as a person in distress, needs help. I could best help myself out of distress simply by ceasing to be a "dissident." The point is what that dissident's flawed efforts and his fate tell us and mean, what they attest about the condition, the destiny, the opportunities, and the problems of the world, the respects in which they are or could be food for thought for others as well, for the way they see their, and so our, shared destiny, in what ways they are a warning, a challenge, a danger, or a lesson for those who visit us.

Or the question about socialism and capitalism! I have to admit that it gives me a sense of emerging from the depths of the last century. It seems to me that these thoroughly ideological and often semantically confused categories have long since been beside the point. The question is wholly other, deeper and equally relevant to all: whether we shall, by whatever means, succeed in reconstituting the natural world as the true terrain of politics, rehabilitating the personal experience of human beings as the initial measure of things, placing morality above politics and responsibility above our desires, in making human community meaningful, in returning content to human speech, in reconstituting, as the focus of all social action, the autonomous, integral, and dignified human "I," responsible for ourselves because we are bound to something higher, and capable of sacrificing something, in extreme cases even everything, of his banal, prosperous private life—that "rule of everydayness," as Jan Patočka used to say—for the sake of that which gives life meaning. It really is not all that important whether, by accident of domicile, we confront a Western manager or an Eastern bureaucrat in this very modest and yet globally crucial struggle against the momentum of impersonal power. If we can defend our humanity, then perhaps there is a hope of sorts—though even then it is by no means automatic—that we shall also find some more meaningful ways of balancing our natural claims to shared economic decision-making and to dignified social status, with the tried-and-true driving force of all work: human enterprise realized in genuine market relations. As long, however, as our humanity remains defenseless, we will not be saved by any technical or organizational trick designed to produce better economic functioning, just as no filter on a factory smokestack will prevent a general dehumanization. To what purpose a system functions is, after all, more important than how it does so. Might it not function quite smoothly, after all, in the service of total destruction?

I speak of this because, looking at the world from the perspective which fate allotted me, I cannot avoid the impression that many people in the West still understand little of what is actually at stake in our time.

If, for instance, we take a second look at the two basic political alternatives between which Western intellectuals oscillate today, it becomes apparent that they are no more than two different ways of playing the same game, proffered by the anonymity of power. As such, they are no more than two diverse ways of moving toward the same global totalitarianism. One way of playing the game of anonymous reason is to keep on toying with the mystery of matter—"playing God"—inventing and deploying further weapons of mass destruction, all, of course, intended "for the defense of democracy" but in effect further degrading democracy to the "uninhabitable fiction" which socialism has long since become on our side of Europe. The other form of the game is the tempting vortex that draws so many good and sincere people into itself, the so-called struggle for peace. Certainly it need not always be so. Still, often I do have the impression that this vortex has been designed and deployed by that same treacherous, all-pervasive impersonal power as a more poetic means of colonizing human consciousness. Please note, I have in mind impersonal power as a principle, globally, in all its instances, not only Moscow—which, if the truth be told, lacks the capability of organizing something as widespread as the contemporary peace movement. Still, could there be a better way of rendering an honest, free thinking man (the chief threat to all anonymous power) ineffectual in the world of rationalism and ideology than by offering him the simplest thesis possible, with all the apparent characteristics of a noble goal? Could you imagine something that would more effectively fire a just mind—preoccupying it, then occupying it, and ultimately rendering it intellectually harmless—than the possibility of "a struggle against war"? Is there a more clever means of deceiving men than with the illusion that they can prevent war if they interfere with the deployment of weapons (which will be deployed in any case)? It is hard to imagine an easier way to a totalitarianism of the human spirit. The more obvious it becomes that the weapons will indeed be deployed, the more rapidly does the mind of a person who has totally identified with the goal of preventing such deployment become radicalized, fanaticized and, in the end, alienated from itself. So a man sent off on his way by the noblest of intentions finds himself, at the journey's end, precisely where anonymous power needs to see him: in the rut of totalitarian thought, where he is not his own and where he surrenders his own reason and conscience for the sake of another "uninhabitable fiction"! As long as that goal is served, it is not important whether we call that fiction "human well-being," "socialism," or "peace."

Certainly, from the standpoint of the defense and the interests of the Western world, it is not very good when someone says "Better Red than dead." But from the viewpoint of the global, impersonal power, which transcends power blocs and, in its omnipresence, represents a truly diabolical temptation, there could be nothing better. That slogan is an infallible sign that the speaker has given up his humanity. For he has given up the ability personally to guarantee something that transcends him and so to sacrifice, *in extremis,* even life itself to that which makes life meaningful. Patočka once wrote that a life not willing to sacrifice itself to what makes it meaningful is not worth living. It is just in the world of such lives and of such a "peace"—that is, under the "rule of everydayness"— that wars happen most easily. In such a world, there is no moral barrier against them, no barrier guaranteed by the courage of supreme sacrifice. The door stands wide open for the irrational "securing of our interests." The absence of heroes who know what they are dying for is the first step on the way to the mounds of corpses of those who are slaughtered like cattle. The slogan "Better Red than dead" does not irritate me as an expression of surrender to the Soviet Union, but it terrifies me as an expression of the renunciation by Western people of any claim to a meaningful life and of their acceptance of impersonal power as such. For what the slogan really says is that nothing is worth giving one's life for. However, without the horizon of the highest sacrifice, all sacrifice becomes senseless. Then nothing is worth anything. Nothing means anything. The result is a philosophy of sheer negation of our humanity. In the case of Soviet totalitarianism, such a philosophy does no more than offer a little political assistance. With respect to Western totalitarianism, it is what constitutes it, directly and primordially.

In short, I cannot overcome the impression that Western culture is threatened far more by itself than by SS–20 rockets. When a French leftist student told me with a sincere glow in his eyes that the Gulag was a tax paid for the ideals of socialism and that Solzhenitsyn is just a personally embittered man, he cast me into a deep gloom. Is Europe really incapable of learning from its own history? Can't that dear lad ever understand that even the most promising project of "general well-being" convicts itself of inhumanity the moment it demands a single involuntary death—that is, one which is not a conscious sacrifice of a life to its meaning? Is he really incapable of comprehending that until he finds himself incarcerated in some Soviet-style jail near Toulouse? Did the newspeak of our world so penetrate natural human speech that two people can no longer communicate even such a basic experience?

IV

I PRESUME that after all these stringent criticisms, I am expected to say just what I consider to be a meaningful alternative for Western humanity today in the face of political dilemmas of the contemporary world.

As all I have said suggests, it seems to me that all of us, East and West, face one fundamental task from which all else should follow. That task is one of resisting vigilantly, thoughtfully, and attentively, but at the same time with total dedication, at every step and everywhere, the irrational momentum of anonymous, impersonal, and inhuman power—the power of ideologies, systems, apparat, bureaucracy, artificial languages, and political slogans. We must resist its complex and wholly alienating pressure, whether it takes the form of consumption, advertising, repression, technology, or cliché—all of which are the blood brothers of fanaticism and the wellspring of totalitarian thought. We must draw our standards from our natural world, heedless of ridicule, and reaffirm its denied validity. We must honor with the humility of the wise the limits of that natural world and the mystery which lies beyond them, admitting that there is something in the order of being which evidently exceeds all our competence. We must relate to the absolute horizon of our existence which, if we but will, we shall constantly rediscover and experience. We must make values and imperatives the starting point of all our acts, of all our personally attested, openly contemplated, and ideologically uncensored lived experience. We must trust the voice of our conscience more than that of all abstract speculations and not invent responsibilities other than the one to which the voice calls us. We must not be ashamed that we are capable of love, friendship, solidarity, sympathy, and tolerance, but just the opposite: we must set these fundamental dimensions of our humanity free from their "private" exile and accept them as the only genuine starting point of meaningful human community. We must be guided by our own reason and serve the truth under all circumstances as our own essential experience.

I know all that sounds very general, very indefinite, and very unrealistic, but I assure you that these apparently naive words stem from a very particular and not always easy experience with the world and that, if I may say so, I know what I am talking about.

The vanguard of impersonal power, which drags the world along its irrational path, lined with devastated nature and launching pads, is composed of the totalitarian regimes of our time. It is not possible to ignore them, to make excuses for them, to yield to them or to accept their way of playing the game, thereby becoming like them. I am convinced that we can face them best by studying them without prejudice, learning from them, and resisting them by being radically different, with a difference born of a continuous struggle against the evil which they may embody most clearly, but which dwells everywhere and so even within each of us. What is most dangerous to that evil are not the rockets aimed at this or that state but the fundamental negation of this evil in the very structure of contemporary humanity: a return of humans to themselves and to their responsibility for the world; a new understanding of human rights and their persistent reaffirmation, resistance against every manifestation of impersonal power that claims to be beyond good and evil, anywhere and everywhere, no matter how it disguises its tricks and machinations, even if it does so in the name of defense against totalitarian systems.

The best resistance to totalitarianism is simply to drive it out of our own souls, our own circumstances, our own land, to drive it out of contemporary humankind. The best help to all who suffer under totalitarian regimes is to confront the evil which a totalitarian system constitutes, from which it draws its strength and on which its "vanguard" is nourished. If there is no such vanguard, no extremist sprout from which it can grow, the system will have nothing to stand on. A reaffirmed human responsibility is the most natural barrier to all irresponsibility. If, for instance, the spiritual and technological potential of the advanced world is spread truly responsibly, not solely under the pressure of a selfish interest in profits, we can prevent its irresponsible transformation into weapons of destruction. It surely makes much more sense to operate in the sphere of causes than simply to respond to their effects. By then, as a rule, the only possible response is by equally immoral means. To follow that path means to continue spreading the evil of irresponsibility in the world, and so to produce precisely the poison on which totalitarianism feeds.

I favor "antipolitical politics," that is, politics not as the technology of power and manipulation, of cybernetic rule over humans or as the art of the utilitarian, but politics as one of the ways of seeking and achieving meaningful lives, of protecting them and serving them. I favor politics as practical morality, as service to the truth, as essentially human and humanly measured care for our fellow humans. It is, I presume, an approach which, in this world, is extremely impractical and difficult to apply in daily life. Still, I know no better alternative.

V

WHEN I was tried and then serving my sentence, I experienced directly the importance and beneficial force of international solidarity. I shall never cease to be grateful for all its expressions. Still, I do not think that we who seek to proclaim the truth under our conditions find ourselves in an asymmetrical position, or that it should be we alone who ask for help and expect it, without being able to offer help in the direction from which it also comes.

I am convinced that what is called "dissent" in the Soviet bloc is a specific modern experience, the experience of life at the very ramparts of dehumanized power. As such, that "dissent" has the opportunity and even the duty to reflect on this experience, to testify to it and to pass it on to those fortunate enough not to have to undergo it. Thus we too have a certain opportunity to help in some ways those who help us, to help them in our deeply shared interest, in the interest of mankind.

One such fundamental experience, that which I called "antipolitical politics," *is* possible and can be effective, even though by its very nature it cannot calculate its effect beforehand. That effect, to be sure, is of a wholly different nature from what the West considers political success. It is hidden, indirect, long-term, and hard to measure; often it exists only in the invisible realm of social consciousness, conscience, and subconsciousness, and it can be almost impossible to determine what value it assumed therein and to what extent, if any, it contributes to shaping social development. It is, however, becoming evident—and I think that is an experience of an essential and universal importance—that a single, seemingly powerless person who dares to cry out the word of truth and to stand behind it with all his person and all his life, ready to pay a high price, has, surprisingly, greater power, though formally disfranchised, than do thousands of anonymous voters. It is becoming evident that even in today's world, and especially on this exposed rampart where the wind blows most sharply, it is possible to oppose personal experience and the natural world to the "innocent" power and to unmask its guilt, as the author of *The Gulag Archipelago* has done. It is becoming evident that truth and morality can provide a new starting point for politics and can, even today, have an undeniable political power. The warning voice of a single brave scientist, besieged somewhere in the provinces and terrorized by a goaded community, can be heard over continents and addresses the conscience of the mighty of this world more clearly than entire brigades of hired propagandists can, though speaking to themselves. It is becoming evident that wholly personal categories like good and evil still have their unambiguous content and, under certain circumstances, are capable of shaking the seemingly unshakable power with all its army of soldiers, policemen, and bureaucrats. It is becoming evident that politics by no means need remain the affair of professionals and that one simple electrician with his heart in the right place, honoring something that transcends him and free of fear, can influence the history of his nation.

Yes, "antipolitical politics" is possible. Politics "from below." Politics of man, not of the apparatus. Politics growing from the heart, not from a thesis. It is not an accident that this hopeful experience has to be lived just here, on this grim battlement. Under the "rule of everydayness" we have to descend to the very bottom of a well before we can see the stars.

When Jan Patočka wrote about Charter 77, he used the term "solidarity of the shaken." He was thinking of those who dared resist impersonal power and to confront it with the only thing at their disposal, their own humanity. Does not the perspective of a better future depend on something like an international community of the shaken which, ignoring state boundaries, political systems, and power blocs, standing outside the high game of traditional politics, aspiring to no titles and appointments, will seek to make a real political force out of a phenomenon so ridiculed by the technicians of power—the phenomenon of human conscience?

February 1984

Six Asides
About Culture

"Six Asides About Culture" (August 1984) was first published inside Czechoslovakia in a *samizdat* cultural journal, *Jednou nohu (Revolver Review)*, no. 1 (1985). It first appeared in English in *A Besieged Culture: Czechoslovakia Ten Years After Helsinki*, edited by A. Heneka, et al. (Stockholm & Vienna: The Charter 77 Foundation and the International Helsinki Federation for Human Rights, 1985). Subsequently it appeared in *Václav Havel or Living in Truth*, edited by Jan Vladislav (London: Faber & Faber, 1986). Translated by Erazim Kohák.

I

WHILE I consider it highly unlikely, I cannot exclude the theoretical possibility that tomorrow I shall have some fabulous idea and that, within the week, I shall have written my best play yet. It is equally possible that I shall never write anything again.

When even a single author—who is not exactly a beginner and so might be expected to have at least a rough idea of his abilities and limits—cannot foresee his own literary future, how can anyone foresee what the overall development of culture will be?

If there is a sphere whose very nature precludes all prognostication, it is that of culture, and especially of the arts and humanities. (In the natural sciences we can, perhaps, make at least general predictions.)

Culture in our country could go any number of ways. Perhaps the police pressure will intensify, perhaps many more artists and scholars will go into exile, many others will lose all desire to do anything and the last remnants of imagination with it, and the entire so-called second culture will gradually die out while the "first culture" will become entirely sterile. Or again, perhaps that second culture will suddenly, unexpectedly blossom to an unprecedented extent and form, to the amazement of the world and the astonishment of the government. Or again, perhaps the first culture will massively awaken, perhaps wholly improbable "new waves" will arise within it and the second culture will quietly, inconspicuously, and gladly merge into its shadow. Perhaps original creative talents and spiritual initiatives will suddenly emerge on the horizon, expanding somewhere in a wholly new space between the two present cultures so that both will only stare in amazement. Or again, perhaps nothing new will come up at all, perhaps everything will remain as it is: Dietl will go on writing his TV serials and Vaculík his feuilletons. I could continue listing such possibilities as long as I please; there isn't the least reason to consider one of them any more probable than any other.

The secrets of culture's future are a reflection of the very secrets of the human spirit. That is why, having been asked to reflect on the prospects for Czechoslovak culture, I shall not write about those prospects, but will rather limit myself to a few, more or less polemical and marginal comments on its present. If anyone chooses to derive something from them for the future, that will be his business and on his head be it.

II

AT ONE time, the state of culture in Czechoslovakia was described, rather poignantly, as a "Biafra of the spirit." Many authors, myself included, when considering what happened in Czechoslovak culture after 1968, turned to the metaphor of the graveyard. Yet recently, as I came across some such metaphor, something within me rebelled. We should, after all these years, at least specify the field to which the metaphor is supposed to apply.

It is certainly still valid with respect to the comportment of the regime in the area of culture, that is, in its cultural policy. Something is always being banned, now as then; virtually nothing is permitted, suppressed journals remain suppressed, manipulated institutions continue to be manipulated, and so on. The regime genuinely behaves like a gravedigger, while virtually all that is lively and yet has to be permitted lives almost by accident, almost by mistake, almost purely on a word of honor, though always with endless complications and no assurance about tomorrow. .

What is true of the regime, however, is not necessarily true of the real spiritual potential of our community. However suppressed beneath the public surface, however silenced and even however frustrated, in some way that potential is still here. Somewhere, somehow it remains alive. It certainly does not deserve to be pronounced dead. I simply do not believe that we have all lain down and died. I see far more than graves and tombstones around me.

I see evidence of this in far more than the hundreds of *samizdat* volumes, dozens of typewritten magazines, private or semi-official exhibitions, seminars, concerts, and other events: besides, there are theatres crammed full of people grateful for every nuance of meaning, frantically applauding every knowing smile from the stage (had we played to such houses in the early sixties in the theatre where I then worked, I can't imagine how we would have managed to complete any play!); all-night queues at some theatres when the month's tickets were about to go on sale; queues at book stores when one of Hrabal's books, emasculated though it may be, was about to appear; expensive books on astronomy printed in a hundred thousand copies (they would hardly find that many readers in the USA); young people traveling halfway across the country to attend a concert that may not take place at all. Is all that—and more—really a graveyard? Is that really a "Biafra of the spirit"?

I do not know what will happen in the culture of the years to come. I do know, though, that it will depend, if not entirely then to a great extent, on future developments in the confrontation between the graveyard intentions of the powers that be and this irrepressible cultural hunger of the community's living organism, or perhaps of that part of it which has not surrendered to total apathy. Nor would I dare predict what might come to life, given this or that change in our circumstances, and what would happen in that part which today appears to have given up.

III

I HAVE read somewhere that in a totalitarian system martyrdom does better than thought.

I am a realist and as such far from the patriotic illusion that the world, due to its hopeless ignorance, remains deprived of some fabulous intellectual achievement waiting here on every corner. And yet something in me rebels as well against the claim that history has condemned us to the unenviable role of mere unthinking experts in suffering, poor relations of those in the "free world" who do not have to suffer and have time to think.

First of all, it does not seem to me that many people here suffer from some kind of masochistic delight, or for want of better ways to kill time. Besides, what tends to be called "martyrdom"—with a slightly contemptuous undertone, let's admit—in our country seems to me neither a particularly common pastime nor for the most part just a blind rush into an abyss. We live in a land of notorious realism, far removed from, say, the Polish courage for sacrifice. I would therefore be very hesitant about denying the capacity for thought to those among us who might be suspected of martyrdom. On the contrary, it seems to me that thought has been a prominent component of the Czech type of "martyrdom." Think of Jan Patočka: is it not symptomatic that the best-known victim of "the struggle for human rights" in our country was also our most important philosopher? And again, as I follow from a distance various individual actions and social upheavals in the "free world," I am not at all sure that they are inevitably characterized by penetrating thought. I fear that far too often the idea comes limping behind the enthusiasm. And might that just not be because for the most part no great price need be paid for that enthusiasm? Are thought and sacrifice really so mutually exclusive? Might not sacrifice, under some circumstances, be simply the consequence of a thought, its proof or, conversely, its moving force?

In short, I simply would not dare claim that we think less in our country because we also suffer. On the contrary, I believe that with a bit of good will, a great deal that is generally relevant could be derived from our thought, perhaps precisely because it was bought at a price and because it grew out of something difficult. Admittedly, that thought is often tangled, hesitant, and intermittent. Our texts do not display the easy virtuosity of global best-sellers. English elegance or French charm, alas, are really far more traditional to England and France and are not native to our somewhat heavy-handed Central Europe, though I would avoid drawing any far-reaching conclusions from that: it is simply the way it is.

I do not know to what extent the fact that we do (occasionally) think will affect our prospects for the better, but it will surely not harm them. Neither will it harm them if, here and there, someone ignores the danger of being labeled a martyr for his stubbornness.

IV

WHAT exactly is a "parallel culture"? Nothing more and nothing less than a culture which for various reasons will not, cannot, or may not reach out to the public through the media which fall under state control. In a totalitarian state, this includes all publishing houses, presses, exhibition halls, theatres and concert halls, scholarly institutes, and so on. Such a culture, therefore, can make use only of what is left—

typewriters, private studios, apartments, barns, etc. Evidently the "parallel" nature of this culture is defined wholly externally and implies nothing directly about its quality, aesthetics, or eventual ideology.

I think it important to stress this rather trivial fact if only because, in recent times, particularly in the exile press, various critiques of the parallel culture as a whole have appeared, and they were possible only because their authors were not aware of this trivial definition of what it means to be "parallel."

To simplify it a little, such authors followed this common reasoning: the official culture is subservient to some official ideology, naturally bad. The parallel culture is, or should be, a better alternative. To what better ideology is *it* subservient? Does it have any ideology at all? Any program? Any conception? Or any orientation, any philosophy? They reached the disappointing conclusion that it does not.

They could have saved themselves disappointment if they had noted at the very start that, by its very nature, the parallel culture can display none of those features. All those hundreds, perhaps thousands of people of all sorts and conditions— young, old, gifted, untalented, believers, unbelievers— gathered under the umbrella of "parallel culture," were led to it exclusively by the incredible narrow-mindedness of a regime which tolerates practically nothing. They can never agree on a common program because the only real thing they have in common (which is why they found themselves under the common umbrella in the first place) is their diversity and their insistence on being just what they are. And if, in spite of everything, they were to agree a common program, it would be the saddest outcome of all: one uniform confronting another. If there is no great surplus of master works in the parallel culture today, there would be nothing in it at all, were that to come to pass. If there is anything essentially foreign to culture, it is the uniform. The parallel culture was born precisely because the official uniform was too constricting for the spiritual potential of our community, because it would not fit inside it and so spilled over beyond the limits within which a uniform is obligatory. It would be suicide if, having done that, that potential voluntarily sought to fit into another uniform, no matter how much prettier than the one it had escaped.

I recall how, in my youth, I found it amusing that the lead paper at various writers' conferences and congresses would invariably be entitled: "The Tasks of Literature in Such-and-Such a Period," or "... After Such-and-Such a Party Congress," or "... In a Given Five-Year Plan"—and that, in spite of all the tasks that were constantly assigned to it, literature would keep on doing only what it wanted. And if by chance it did not make an effort to carry out its assigned tasks, it was invariably the worse for it. Its only hope, no less so under the conditions of "parallelism" (and especially then—that is why it chose them!) is to ignore the tasks anyone would assign to it, no matter how good his intentions, and go on doing only what it wants to do.

There are no more gifted writers, painters, or musicians in Czechoslovakia today than there were at any time in the past. The disappointment that the parallel culture is no better than it is, to be sure, is quite understandable. The more one is repelled by the official culture, the more one expects from the other, and the more one turns toward it. Still, such disappointment is not objectively relevant. By what odd whim of history would there be more of everything, and better, today in our stifled conditions, than ever before?

A great many people can peck at a typewriter and, fortunately, no one can stop them. But for that reason, even in *samizdat,* there will always be countless bad books or poems for every important book. If anything, there will be more bad ones than in the days of printing because, even in the most liberated times, printing is still a more complicated process than typing. But even if, objectively, there were some possibility of selection, who could claim the right to exercise it? Who among us would dare to say that he can unerringly distinguish something of value—even though it may still be nascent, unfamiliar, as yet only potential—from its counterfeit? Who among us can know whether what may seem today to be marginal graphomania might not one day appear to our descendants as the most substantial thing written in our time? Who among us has the right to deprive them of that pleasure, no matter how incomprehensible it may seem to us? Was not the basic presupposition of editorial selection in freer times that a rejected author could turn to a competitor or publish his manuscript at his own cost? Would any of our great editors and publishers—Firt, Škeřík, Vilímek, Otto, Laichter, and all the others—ever have dared to make up their minds about anything, had it not been for that possibility?

Petlice Editions is by no means the only *samizdat* series; still, for those who measure parallel literature according to *Petlice* and the misery and hopes of the nation according to parallel literature, we should note that *Petlice* is something of an author-run service in which everyone is responsible for himself alone. Should anyone not like something that appears in *Petlice*, let him sing his disappointment to the author and not blame anyone else. Fortunately, there is no editor-in-chief of *Petlice*, or director-in-chief of *Samizdat and Co.* responsible for what had been allowed to be typed.

All this, I know, is obvious. Still it seems that even such obvious matters need to be aired from time to time, especially for our exiles whose perspective, often influenced by the random selection of domestic texts that they happen to come across, might at times be distorted.

V

IN AN essay "Prague 1984" (written for *Art Forum*; Czech version in the *samizdat* journal *Kritický sborník*, 1984, no. 2), Jindřich Chalupecký writes that the artist "either submits to the state power, produces works that propagate socialism and is respected and rewarded, or he protests in the name of freedom and leads the romantic life of a rebellious bohemian. If such official art arouses little interest, we can hardly expect much from the anti-official art. Both are equally conditioned by political perspectives and though certain political goals might be most noble and relevant, it turns out again and again that the world of modern art is not the world of modern politics. Neither politics nor art can profit from such efforts." It is not quite clear whether Chalupecký is speaking for himself here, or whether he is paraphrasing the perspective of Hans-Heinz Holze, whose views he outlines in his preceding paragraph. He is, however, clearly speaking for himself when he writes, later on, in reference to several recent exhibits of Czechoslovak artists in the West: "It was not 'socialist realism.' Neither was it 'anti-official art.' The political context was missing, and there was no way of supplying it."

Such formulations, along with other passages in Chalupecký's essay, might give the impression that there are, in Czechoslovakia, actually three cultures, or rather three kinds of art: official art, adapted to the ruling ideology; "anti-official" art, evidently of the "dissident" variety, produced by the people with a peculiar penchant for the "romantic life of a rebellious bohemian," a culture as feebleminded as the official one and differing from it only in the political ideas it serves; and finally true, modern art, which alone is good because it stands aside from politics and all ideologies.

Chalupecký's text, for the most part informative, does not make it entirely clear whether the author really sees those three divisions in the panorama of contemporary Czech art, and so I do not wish to argue with Chalupecký, but solely with that odd "trinitarian" vision.

If we start with the presupposition that art constitutes a distinctive way of seeking truth—truth in the broadest sense of the word, that is, chiefly the truth of the artist's inner experience—then there is only one art, whose sole criterion is the power, the authenticity, the revelatory insight, the courage and suggestiveness with which it seeks its truth, or perhaps the urgency and profundity of this truth. Thus, from the standpoint of the work and its worth, it is irrelevant to which political ideas ·the artist as a citizen claims allegiance, which ideas he would like to serve with his work, or whether he holds any such ideas at all. And just as the attractiveness or repulsiveness of political ideas guarantees nothing about a work of art and likewise does not disqualify it in advance, so, too, whether or not an artist is interested in politics neither authorizes nor disqualifies him at the start. If so much of the art shown in official exhibits is indeed below average, and better art can be found only on the periphery of public art (in marginal or semi-official exhibition halls) or entirely beyond public view (in studios), then this is so not because the creators of the former involve themselves in politics while those of the latter do not, but simply because the prospect of public recognition and lucrative commissions in our country, today more than at other times and in other places, is incompatible with that stubborn, uncompromising effort to reach out for some personal truth without which, it seems, there can be no real art. The more an artist compromises to oblige power and gain advantages, the less good art we can expect from him; the more freely and independently, by contrast, he pursues his own vision—whether with the expression of a "rebellious bohemian" or without it—the better his chances of creating something good—though it remains only a chance: what is uncompromising need not automatically be good.

Thus, it does not seem to me particularly meaningful to divide art into the official and anti-official on the one hand and the independent (that is, politically neutral) on the other. Surely the measure of artistic power is something other than whether or not the art displays a political concern. If we do speak of "two cultures," one official and one "parallel," it does not mean—at least as I understand it—that the one serves one set of political ideas and the second another set (which would force us to assume, in addition, a "third" culture, subservient to no politics), but refers solely to the external framework of culture. The "first" culture resides in the vaguely defined area of what is permitted, subsidized, or at least tolerated, an area that naturally tends to attract more of those who, for reasons of advantage, are willing to compromise their truth, while the "second" refers to culture in an area constituted through self-help, which is the refuge, voluntary or enforced, of those who refuse all compromise (regardless of how overtly political or nonpolitical their work is).

Any *a priori* division of art into the "anti-official" (necessarily inferior) and the "apolitical" (necessarily better) seems to me rather dangerous. Unwittingly, it applies to art a notorious extra-artistic standard, albeit this time turned inside out: the value of art is no longer judged in terms of its overtly political nature but, conversely in terms of its overtly nonpolitical nature. Surely, if Magda Jetelová constructs somewhere her evocative staircases and Ludvík Vaculík writes a novel about cops and dissidents, the artistic power of each has nothing to do with the fact that a staircase (albeit only on a primitive, thematic basis) is considered nonpolitical while the confrontation of cops and dissidents is eminently political. The "nonpolitical" stairness of staircases and the "political" copness of the cops *of themselves* neither guarantee nor preclude anything. The only thing that matters is the urgency of artistic truth which both artists pursue (and I believe that is indubitable in both cases). The degree to which politics is present or absent has no connection with the power of artistic truth. If anything matters, it is, quite logically, only the degree to which an artist is willing, for external reasons, to compromise the truth.

In any case, it seems that our regime can sniff out far better than many an art theoretician what it should consider really dangerous to itself. Hundreds of examples testify that the regime prosecutes most vigorously not what threatens it overtly but has little artistic power, but whatever is artistically most penetrating, even though it does not seem all that overtly political. The essence of the conflict, in other words, is not a confrontation between two ideologies (for instance, a socialist with a liberal one) but a clash between an anonymous, soulless, immobile, and paralyzing ("entropic") power, and life, humanity, Being and its mystery. The counterpart of power in this conflict is not an alternative political idea but the autonomous, free humanity of man and with it necessarily also art—precisely as art!—as one of the most important expressions of this autonomous humanity.

VI

AT TIMES we encounter something we might call a sectarian view of parallel culture, that is, the view that whatever does not circulate only in typescript or whatever was not recorded only privately is necessarily bad, and that not being printed, publicly performed, or exhibited is in itself an achievement or an honor, while the reverse is always and automatically a mark of moral and spiritual decay, if not of outright treason.

I could name quite a few very worthwhile and important achievements of the most varied kinds which I have encountered in the sphere of the "first" culture and which deny the legitimacy of such a view. I refrain from naming them solely because it might complicate the lives of the authors or call them to the attention of those thanks to whose inattention they were able to do what they did. I never take any pleasure in seeing someone from the "first" culture fall into the "second"; rather, I am always happy whenever I encounter anything in the "first" culture that I would have tended to expect in the "second."

Even though the "second" or "parallel" culture represents an important fertile ground, a catalytic agent, and often even the sole bearer of the spiritual continuity of our cultural life, like it or not, it is the "first" culture that remains the decisive sphere. Only once the suppressed spiritual potential of our community begins more distinctly to win back this culture (and, to be sure, without its "interim" existence in the "parallel" culture it would really have no base of operation) will things begin visibly to improve, not only in culture itself but in a broader and related social sense as well. It will be in the "first" culture that the decision will be made about the future climate of our lives; through it our citizens will have the first genuine, wide-scale chance to stand up straight and liberate themselves. The "second" culture's relation to it will be analogous to that of a match to a glowing stove; without it, the fire might not have started at all, yet by itself it cannot heat the room.

Perhaps such a notion might be suspected of treating culture instrumentally—as if I wished artists to have public opportunity because it increases hope of some overall improvement of our conditions. So let me make it a bit more precise: every meaningful cultural act—wherever it takes place—is unquestionably good in and of itself, simply because it exists and because it offers something to someone. Yet can this value in itself really be separated from the common good? Is one not an integral part of the other from the start? Does not the bare fact that a work of art has meant something to someone—even if only for a moment, perhaps to a single person—already somehow change, however minutely, the overall condition for the better? Is it not itself an inseparable component of that condition, transforming it by its very nature? And does not a change in conditions mediated by a cultural achievement open the door to further cultural achievements? Is not culture itself a common good? Is not some improvement in conditions—in the most general, the deepest and, I would say, the existential sense of the word—precisely what makes culture culture? Being happy if five thousand rather than five people can read a good text or see a good painting is, I think, a wholly legitimate understanding of the meaning of culture—even when that joy comes from our perception that things are beginning to move. Or is not precisely some impulse to move—again in that deeper, existential sense—the primordial intent of everything that really belongs to culture? After all, that is precisely the mark of every good work of culture: it sets our drowsy souls and our lazy hearts moving! And can we separate the awakening human soul from what it always is—an awakening human community?

August 1984

Thriller

"Thriller" (November 1984): Originally written at the request of the Hessischer Rundfunk for their series on mythology in modern life, this essay first appeared in English in *The Idler* magazine, Toronto, no. 6 (June–July 1985). Translated by Paul Wilson.

B EFORE ME lies the famous *Occult Philosophy* of Heinrich Cornelius Agrippa von Nettesheim, where I read that the ingestion of the living (and if possible still beating) heart of a hoopoe, a swallow, a weasel, or a mole will bestow upon one the gift of prophecy. It is nine o'clock in the evening and I turn on the radio. The announcer, a woman, is reading the news in a dry, matter-of-fact voice: Mrs. Indira Gandhi has been shot by two Sikhs in her personal bodyguard. The corpse of Father Popiełuszko, kidnapped by officers of the Polish police, has been fished out of the Vistula River. International aid is being organized for Ethiopia, where a famine is threatening the lives of millions, while the Ethiopian regime is spending almost a quarter of a billion dollars to celebrate its tenth anniversary. American scientists have developed plans for a permanent observatory on the Moon and for a manned expedition to Mars. In California, a little girl has received a heart transplanted from a baboon; various animal welfare societies have protested.

ANCIENT myths are certainly not just a manifestation of archetypal images from man's collective unconsciousness. But they are undoubtedly that as well. Much of the mystery of

285

being and of man, many of his dark visions, obsessions, long-ings, forebodings, much of his murky "pre-scientific" knowl-edge and many important metaphysical certainties are obviously encoded in old myths. Such myths, of course, tran-scend their creators: something higher spoke through them, something beyond their creators, something that not even they were fully able to understand and give a name to. The authority invested in old myths by people of ancient cultures indicates that this higher power, whatever it is, was once gen-erally felt and acknowledged. If we go no further than Jung's interpretation of myths, it is obvious that they introduced a partial or temporary "order" into the complex world of those unconscious forebodings, unprovable certainties, hidden in-stincts, passions, and longings that are an intrinsic part of the human spirit. And they obviously exercised something like a "check" or "supervisory power" over those forces of the hu-man unconscious.

The civilization of the new age has robbed old myths of their authority. It has put its full weight behind cold, des-criptive Cartesian reason and recognizes only thinking in concepts.

I am unwilling to believe that this whole civilization is no more than a blind alley of history and a fatal error of the human spirit. More probably it represents a necessary phase that man and humanity must go through, one that man—if he survives—will ultimately, and on some higher level (un-thinkable, of course, without the present phase), transcend.

Whatever the case may be, it is certain that the whole rationalistic bent of the new age, having given up on the au-thority of myths, has succumbed to a large and dangerous illusion: it believes that no higher and darker powers—which these myths in some ways touched, bore witness to, and whose relative "control" they guaranteed—ever existed, either in the human unconscious or in the mysterious universe. Today, the opinion prevails that everything can be "rationally ex-plained," as they say, by alert reason. Nothing is obscure—and if it is, then we need only cast a ray of scientific light on it and it will cease to be so.

This, of course, is only a grand self-delusion of the modern spirit. For though it make that claim a thousand times, though it deny a thousand times the "averted face" of the world and the human spirit, it can never eliminate that face, but merely push it further into the shadows. At the most, it will drive this entire complex world of hidden things to find surrogate, counterfeit, and increasingly confusing manifestations; it will compel the "order" that myth once brought into this world to vanish along with the myth, and the "forces of the night" to go on acting, chaotically and uncontrollably, shocking man again and again by their, for him, inexplicable presence, which glimmers through the modern shroud that conceals them. But more than that: the good powers—because they were considered irrational as well—were buried along with the dark powers. Olympus was completely abolished, leaving no one to punish evil and drive the evil spirits away. Goodness, being well mannered, has a tendency to treat these grand obsequies seriously and withdraw; evil, on the contrary, senses that its time has come, for people have stopped believing in it altogether.

To this day, we cannot understand how a great, civilized nation—or at least a considerable part of it—could, in the twentieth century, succumb to its fascination for a single, ridiculous, complex-ridden *petit bourgeois*, could fall for his pseudo-scientific theories and in their name exterminate nations, conquer continents, and commit unbelievable cruelties. Positivistic science, Marxism included, offers a variety of scientific explanations for this mysterious phenomenon, but instead of eliminating the mystery, they tend rather to deepen it. For the cold, "objective" reason that speaks to us from these explanations in fact only underlines the disproportion between itself—a power that claims to be the decisive one in this civilization—and the mass insanity that has nothing in common with any form of rationality.

Yes, when traditional myth was laid to rest, a kind of "order" in the dark region of our being was buried along with it. And what modern reason has attempted to substitute for this order has consistently proved erroneous, false, and disastrous, because it is always in some way deceitful, artificial, rootless, lacking in both ontology and morality. It may even border on the ludicrous, like the cult of the "Supreme Being" during the French Revolution, the collectivist folklore of totalitarian systems, or their "realist," self-celebrating art. It seems to me that with the burial of myth, the barn in which the mysterious animals of the human unconscious were housed over thousand of years has been abandoned and the animals turned loose—on the tragically mistaken assumption that they were phantoms—and that now they are devastating the countryside. They devastate it, and at the same time they make themselves at home where we least expect them to—in the secretariats of modern political parties, for example. These sanctuaries of modern reason lend them their tools and their authority so that ultimately the plunder is sanctioned by the most scientific of world views.

Generally, people do not begin to grasp the horror of their situation until too late: that is, until they realize that thousands of their fellow humans have been murdered for reasons that are utterly irrational. Irrationality, hiding behind sober reason and a belief that the inexorable march of history demands the sacrifice of millions to assure a happy future for billions, seems essentially more irrational and dangerous than the kind of irrationality that, in and through myth, admits to its own existence, comes to terms with the "positive powers," and, at most, sacrifices animals. The demons simply do what they want while the gods take diffident refuge in the final asylum to which they have been driven, called "human conscience." And so at last bloodlust, disguised as the most scientific of the world's views (which teaches, by the way, that conscience must submit to historical necessity) throws a twentieth-century John of Nepomuk into the Vistula. And the nation immediately canonizes its martyr in spirit.

IN THE events which chance tossed together in a single newscast, and juxtaposed with Agrippa's *Occult Philosophy,* I begin to see a sophisticated collage that takes on the dimensions of a symbol, an emblem, a code. I do not know what message is hidden in that unintentional artifact, which might be called "Thriller," after Michael Jackson's famous song. I only feel that chance—that great poet—is stammering an indistinct message about the desperate state of the modern world.

First, Marxist demonologists in the Polish papers label Popiełuszko a practitioner of black magic who, with the assistance of the Devil, serves the black mass of anticommunism in the church of St. Stanisław Kostka; then, other scientific Marxists waylay him at night, beat him to death, and throw him into the Vistula; and finally, still other "scientists" on one sixth of the earth's surface claim that the Devil in disguise—the CIA, in other words—is behind it. It is all pure medieval history. Except that the actors are scientists, people shielded by science, possessing an allegedly scientific world view. Of course that makes the whole thing so much more powerful. The demons have been turned loose and go about, grotesquely pretending to be honorable twentieth-century men who do not believe in evil spirits.

The Sikhs do not even need to masquerade as men of science. Confronting this modern world with modern machine guns in their hands, they believe themselves to be instruments of providence: after all, they are merely meting out punishment in accordance with the ancient prophecy about the desecrator of their Golden Temple. The Hindus then turn around and murder Sikhs, burning them alive, as though all Sikhs, to the last man, had taken part in Mrs. Gandhi's murder. How can this happen in the century of science and reason? How can science and reason explain it? How does it relate to colonizing the Moon and making ready an expedition to Mars? How does it relate to an age capable of transplanting the heart of a baboon into a person? Could we be getting ready to go to Mars in the secret hope of leaving our demons behind on the earth and so disposing of them? And who, in fact, has a baboon heart: that little girl in California—or the Marxist government of Ethiopia, building its mausoleums in a time of famine; or the Polish police; or the Sikhs in the personal bodyguard of the Indian prime minister who died—thanks to their belief in ancient prophecies—like an antique emperor at the hands of his own servants?

It seems to me that man has what we call a human heart, but that he also has something of the baboon within him. The modern age treats the heart as a pump and denies the presence of the baboon within us. And so again and again, this officially nonexistent baboon, unobserved, goes on the rampage, either as the personal bodyguard of a politician, or wearing the uniform of the most scientific police force in the world.

Modern man, that methodical civil servant in the great bureaucracy of the world, mildly frustrated by the collapse of his "scientific" world view, finally switches on his video recorder to watch Michael Jackson playing a vampire in "Thriller," the best-selling video cassette in the history of the world, then goes into the kitchen to remove from a thermos flask—behind the backs of all animal welfare societies—the still warm heart of a hoopoe. And he swallows it, hoping to have the gift of prophecy conferred upon him.

November 1984

Anatomy of
a Reticence

"Anatomy of a Reticence" (April 1985) was written, according to a note by the author, "to be delivered at a peace conference in Amsterdam, in my absence; and for an international collection of essays on European identity being prepared by the Suhrkamp publishing house." It first appeared in Czech in *Obsah*, a *samizdat* publication, in April 1985. Its first publication in English was as a Charter 77 Foundation pamphlet (*Voices from Czechoslovakia*, 1), Stockholm, 1985. Subsequently it was published in *Václav Havel or Living in Truth*, edited by Jan Vladislav. The translation is by Erazim Kohák.

I

WESTERN peace groups, it seems, in ever greater numbers are turning for natural allies not to the official, state-sponsored Peace Committees in the eastern part of Europe but to those ordinary citizens who concern themselves with global issues independently of their governments, that is, they are turning to the so-called dissidents. We are invited to peace congresses—the fact that we are unable to attend them is another matter. We receive visitors representing various peace groups; we are called upon for dialogue and cooperation. All this, to be sure, does not mean that this is a spontaneous and universal attitude within the Western peace movement. The opposite appears closer to the truth. When it comes to the "dissidents" in Eastern Europe, the prevailing mood seems to be one of reticence, of caution, if not of out-right distrust and uneasiness.

The reasons for this reticence are not hard to imagine. Our governments resent anyone contacting us, and, after all, it is they, not us, who can most affect the fortunes of the world, and so they need the primary contacts. Besides, to the West-ern peace fighters the dissidents in the eastern half of Europe must seem strangely absorbed in their provincial concerns, exaggerating human rights (as if human survival were not more important!), suspiciously prejudiced against the realities of socialism, if not against socialist ideals themselves, insuffi-ciently critical of Western democracy and perhaps even sym-pathizing, albeit secretly, with those detested Western armaments. In short, for them the dissidents tend to appear as a fifth column of Western establishments east of the Yalta line.

The reticence, to be sure, is mutual. It is not less noticeable in the attitude of Eastern European dissidents toward the West-ern peace movement. When we read Western texts dealing with the issues of peace, we usually find in them shades of opinion that give us reason for a degree of reticence, as well.

I do not know whether I shall succeed in contributing to better mutual understanding—I tend to be skeptical in that respect. Still, I want to try to describe some of the reasons for one of those two cases of reticence, the one on our side.

Seen from the outside, the dissidents appear to be a mi-nuscule and rather singular enclave—singularly radical, that is—within a monolithic society which speaks with an entirely different voice. In a sense, they really are such an enclave: there is but a handful of them and the state does everything in its power to create a chasm between them and society at large. They are in fact different from the majority in one respect: they speak their mind openly, heedless of the conse-quences. That difference, however, is hardly significant. What matters is whether the views they express differ significantly from those of the majority of their fellow citizens. I do not think they do. Quite the contrary, almost every day I come across some piece of heartening evidence that the dissidents are really saying nothing other than what the vast majority of their fellow citizens think privately. Actually, if we were to compare what the dissidents write in their texts with what we can hear their fellow citizens saying—albeit privately or, at most, over beer—we would reach the paradoxical conclusion that the dissidents constitute the less radical, more loyal, and more peaceful segment of the population. I say this because, if we want to consider the particular reticence among the dissidents when it comes to issues of peace, we need first to consider the social context of their actions, that is, the common experiences, perspectives, and feelings they echo, express politically, or follow through in their own distinctive way.

II

PERHAPS the first thing to understand is that, in our part of the world, the word "peace" has been drained of all content. For thirty-seven years every possible and impossible open space in Czechoslovakia has been decorated with slogans such as "Building up our homeland strengthens peace," "The Soviet Union, guarantor of world peace," "For the even greater flowering of the peaceful labor of our people!" and so on and so forth. For thirty-seven years our newspapers and the other media have been saturated with the same weary clichés about peace. For thirty-seven years our citizens have been required to carry the same old peace placards in the mandatory parades. For thirty-seven years a few individuals clever enough to establish themselves as our professional "peace fighters," being particularly adept at repeating the official pronouncements, have engaged in extensive peace-congress tourism at state expense. For thirty-seven years, in other words, "the struggle of peace" has been part and parcel of the ideological facade of the system within which we live.

Yet every citizen knows from a thousand daily, intensely personal experiences that this official facade conceals an utterly different reality that is growing ever more disheartening:

the wasteland of life in a totalitarian state, with its all-powerful center and all-powerless inhabitants. The word "peace"— much like the words "socialism," "homeland," and "the people"—has been reduced to serving both as one rung on the ladder up which clever individuals clamber, and as a stick for beating those who stand aloof. The word has become one of the official incantations which our government keeps muttering while doing whatever it wants (or perhaps whatever it has been ordered) to do, and which its subjects must mutter along with it to purchase at least a modicum of tranquillity.

Can you wonder, under these circumstances, that this word awakens distrust, skepticism, ridicule, and revulsion among our people? This is not distaste for peace as such: it is distaste for the pyramid of lies into which the word has been traditionally integrated.

The extent of that distaste—and so its seriousness as a social phenomenon—can be illustrated by the fact that when our dissidents occasionally attempt to express their views on peace issues publicly, no matter how much they differ from the views of the government, they become mildly suspect to the public simply because they express serious interest in the issues of peace at all. While people listen with interest to other Charter 77 documents in foreign broadcasts, seek them out, and copy them, Charter 77's documents dealing with peace are guaranteed universal lack of interest in advance. The citizens of our country simply start to yawn whenever they hear the word "peace."

The complete devaluation and trivialization of this word by official propaganda is, to be sure, only one reason—and a rather superficial one at that—for the reserve which people here display (including to some extent the dissidents themselves, since they live in a climate not unlike that of others) when they regard the "struggle for peace" and the peace movement.

III

AGAINST whom exactly is this officially sponsored "struggle for peace" in our country directed? Naturally, against Western imperialists and their armaments. Thus the word "peace" in our country means nothing more than unswerving concurrence with the policies of the Soviet bloc, with its uniformly negative attitude toward the West. In our newspeak, the phrase "Western imperialists" does not refer to certain individuals obsessed by a vision of world domination, but rather to the more or less democratically elected Western governments and the more or less democratic Western political system.

Add to this one more circumstance: our media, in reporting world news, have for decades systematically sought to create the impression that virtually the only thing which ever happens in the West is the "peace struggle"—naturally in the sense that word has here. That is to say, the peace movement is used as evidence of the eagerness with which the people of the West await Soviet-style communism.

In such circumstances, what do you expect the average citizen thinks? Simply that those Western peace fighters should get their wish—let them be punished for their naivete and their inability to learn!

Try to imagine what would happen if a young, enthusiastic, and sincere Western peace fighter were to approach not a prominent dissident but an ordinary Czechoslovak citizen and and were to ask him to sign, say, a petition against the completion of NATO's armament plans. In principle I can imagine two possible outcomes. One is that this ordinary citizen would politely show his visitor the door. The other (probably more likely) is that he would take him for an agent of the secret police and would promptly sign the proffered paper just as he signs scores of similar papers presented for his signature at work—without studying it, simply and solely to stay out of trouble. (A more alert citizen, regardless of his attitude toward armament plans, might try to squeeze an invitation to the West out of the whole thing. Ultimately he is accustomed to looking out for "number one": there might be time to visit Paris for the first time in his life before Europe is consumed in an atomic conflagration.)

Let me make it even more emphatic. Imagine that through some unfortunate coincidence our Western visitor happened to hit upon an older citizen who has lived all his life on Letná in Prague—and who, together with hundreds of others, is soon to be forcibly moved to some housing development on the out-skirts of Prague, losing his life-long home and being forced to pay perhaps double the rent (out of what?), simply because Soviet officers have decided that Letná is where they want to live. Soviet officers—the most militant peace fighters of all. Would the Western enthusiast be justified in his surprise over the cold reception he would receive in this household?

I know that some people in the West believe the entire Western peace movement is a Soviet plot. Others perceive it as a collection of naive dreamers whose great enthusiasm and minimal knowledge are cleverly utilized by the Soviets.

I do not share these views. Still, I have the impression that if one could determine what the people of Eastern Europe really think, it would turn out that these views have more supporters here than in the West itself.

I think that a mutual exchange of such hard truths, with no punches pulled, is the first precondition for any meaningful European rapprochement.

IV

THE MORE enlightened among the Western peace fighters de-mand not only the disarmament of their own countries but the simultaneous disarmament of everyone else. For that rea-son they expect the people of Eastern Europe to struggle against the various Soviet rockets rather than against the Pershings. This surely makes sense: let everyone first put his own house in order.

Since my topic today is the reticence toward "peace" in our part of Europe, I need to call attention to something that tends to be overlooked: that any, even the most diffident, expression of disagreement with government policy in an area as sensitive as defense is infinitely more dangerous here than in the West. After all, whereas the Western press publishes maps showing projected or completed rocket bases, the location of any weapons whatever is considered a state secret in our countries. Simply revealing the location of a base would undoubtedly lead to a prison term of many years. And when I try to imagine someone daring to approach a rocket base with an antiwar placard or—perish the thought!—trying to interfere with its construction, I break out in a cold sweat. It would mean not fourteen days in jail, with visits and packages, as in England, but fourteen cruel years in Valdice, our Czech Sing Sing. When I once mentioned this to one of my interrogators during a police interrogation occasioned by an encounter of mine with some Western peace activists, he floored me with his answer. "Different countries, different customs," he said.

Yes, different country, different customs. To my countrymen I have always stressed that we should not lie our way out of our responsibility and blame everything on prevailing conditions, on the superpowers, and on the big, bad world. To readers abroad, though, I would like to point out that we live in a country where the "customs" are indeed different. To speak out against the rockets here means, in effect, to become a dissident. Specifically, it means the complete transformation of one's life. It means accepting a prison term as one of life's natural possibilities. It means giving up at a stroke many of the few openings available to a citizen in our country. It means finding oneself, day after day, in a neurotic world of constant fear of the doorbell. It means becoming a member of that microscopic "suicide-pact" enclave surrounded, to be sure, by the unspoken good wishes of the public but at the same time by unspoken amazement that anyone would choose to risk so much for something as hopeless as seeking to change what cannot be changed.

The peace movement in the West has a real impact on the dealings of parliaments and governments, without risking jail.

Here the risk of prison is real and, at least at this point, the impact on the government's decision making is zero.

I'm not saying that all action here is pointless. I only want to explain why so few people choose to act. I do not believe that, as a nation, we are significantly more cowardly. If the same conditions obtained in the West, I doubt that significantly more people there would choose to act than among us.

All this, I hope, is obvious. Still, it is important to repeat it over and over again—among other reasons, to prevent the gradual growth in European minds of the wholly erroneous impression that the only dangerous weapons are those surrounded by encampments of demonstrators.

V

I WOULD not presume to speak about conditions in the entire Soviet bloc. I believe, however, that I can say at least of the Czechoslovak citizen that his world is characterized by a perennial tension between "their" omnipotence and his impotence.

This citizen, for instance, knows "they" can do anything they want—take away his passport, have him fired from his job, order him to move, send him to collect signatures against the Pershings, bar him from higher education, take away his driver's license, build a factory producing mostly acid fumes right under his windows, pollute his milk with chemicals to a degree beyond belief, arrest him simply because he attended a rock concert, raise prices arbitrarily, any time and for any reason, turn down all his humble petitions without cause, prescribe what he must read before all else, what he must demonstrate for, what he must sign, how many square feet his apartment may have, whom he may meet and whom he must avoid. The citizen picks his way through life in constant fear of "them," knowing full well that even an opportunity to work for the public good is a privilege "they" have bestowed upon him, conditionally. (One of my friends, an expert in a certain area of medicine, was invited to attend a conference in her field in the neighboring German Democratic Republic. Her own scholarly society supported her request to attend, but she was turned down by her superior—who of course was a bureaucrat, not a doctor—simply because, as he made clear, learning about the methods of scientists in other countries is not, in this country, a question of natural interest in scientific development and in patient care, but a favor bestowed upon doctors by their bureaucratic superiors.) The average citizen living in this stifling atmosphere of universal irritability, servility, perpetual defensiveness, backbiting, nervousness, and an ever smoldering compensatory contentiousness, knows perfectly well, without having to read any dissident literature, that "they" can do anything and he can do nothing. (That there is no clear division between those "down below" and those "up above," that no one really knows who "they" are, and that all of us, drawn into the same plot, are in part "they," while "they" are at the same time partly "we," "they" are subordinate citizens dependent on some other "they"—this is a different matter, outside the present context.)

And now try to imagine, my dear Western peace activist, that you confront this half-exhausted citizen with the question of what he is willing to do for world peace. Are you surprised to find him staring at you uncomprehendingly, wondering to himself what kind of trap has been laid for him this time?

You see, for him matters far simpler than questions of peace and war are—or, under our present conditions, appear to be—utterly beyond his competence. Since he can have absolutely nothing to say about the possible conversion of a large tract of his homeland into a desert for the sake of a bit of inferior coal that God knows what industry needs for God knows what purpose, since he cannot protect even his children's teeth from deteriorating due to environmental pollution, since he cannot even obtain a permit to move for the sake of his children's teeth and souls from northern to southern Bohemia, how could he influence something on the order of some sort of "Star Wars" between two superpowers? All that appears so terribly distant to him, as far beyond his influence as the stars above, that it really can exercise only people free of all his "ordinary" concerns and restless from sheer boredom.

Mrs. Thatcher was charmed by Mr. Gorbachev. In a completely rationalized world of computers even capable, I have heard, of launching a nuclear war, the entire civilized world is irrationally fascinated by the fact that Mr. G drinks whiskey and can play golf—thanks to which, we are told, humankind is not utterly bereft of all hope of survival. But how does this appear to our weary little Czech? As yet another proof of what he has known all along: that war and peace are the business of Messrs G and R. What could he add to it? How can he enter into their thoughts? Can he join them for a glass of whiskey and a few holes of golf? He cannot even enter into the thoughts of some petty bureaucrat at the passport office who will decide, with no appeal possible, whether to permit him to have the two-week vacation in Yugoslavia for which he has been saving all year long. Is it surprising that he does not consider some mysterious stellar pact between Messrs R and G as an "important step toward peace," but simply as yet another plot against him?

I am trying to show that the general reserve in questions of war and peace is not—at least in my country—the result of a genetically determined indifference to global problems, but rather a completely understandable consequence of the social atmosphere in which it is our lot to live.

I repeat, I do not claim that there is nothing we can do. I am trying to say only that I can understand why so many people around me think they can do nothing. I would beg our friends—the peace fighters in the West—to try to empathize with the situation of these people. Please try, in our common interest!

VI

FROM time to time there appear in this world people who can no longer bear the spectacle of life's outrageous chaos and mysterious fecundity. They are the people tragically oppressed by the terror of nothingness and fear of their own being, who need to gain inner peace by imposing order ("peace") upon a restless world, placing in a sense their whole unstable existence into that order, ridding themselves of their furies once and for all. The desperate impatience of such people drives them compulsively to construct and impose various projects directed toward a rationally ordered common good; their purpose is to make sure that, at long last, things will be clear and comprehensible, that the world will stride onward toward a goal, finally putting an end to all the infuriating uncertainty of history. No sooner do they set out to achieve this—if the world has had the misfortune to have given them the opportunity—than they encounter difficulties. A great many of their fellow humans would prefer to go on living as they like. Their proposal, for all its perfection, does not attract those people. They treat it spitefully, putting obstacles in its path, whether intentionally or simply by their very nature. The fanatic of the abstract project, that practicing utopian, is incapable of tolerating that sort of thing, not only because it destabilizes his own center of gravity, but because he can no longer perceive the integrity of all that exists, and can see only his own dream of what should be. So he decides to impose his project upon the world—for its own good, to be sure. That is how it begins. Then that strange "arithmetic of the common good" comes into play, demonstrating that it is proper to sacrifice a few thousand recalcitrants for the contentment of millions, or perhaps to sacrifice a few million for the contentment of billions. How it must end is evident—in universal misery.

It is the tragic story of what might be called a "mental short circuit": Why bother with a ceaseless and in fact hopeless search for truth when truth can be had readily, all at once, in the form of an ideology or a doctrine? Suddenly it is all so simple. So many difficult questions are answered in advance! So many laborious existential tasks from which our minds are freed once and for all! The essence of this short circuit is a fatal mistake: the tacit assumption that some ingenious, universally applicable product—and is a doctrine or an ideology ever anything more than a human product?—can lift from our shoulders the burden of the incessant, always unique, and essentially inalienable question, and utterly transform man from a "being in question" into an "existing answer." This is the illusion that the demanding, unending, and unpredictable dialogue with conscience or with God can be replaced by the clarity of a pamphlet, that some human product, like a set of pulleys freeing us from physical effort, can liberate us from the weight of personal responsibility and timeless sorrow.

Extreme examples of this mental short circuit, some quite sad, some rather tragic, and some nothing short of monstrous, are familiar from history—Marat, Robespierre, Lenin, Baader, Pol Pot. (I would not include Hitler and Stalin in this category; if I did, it would have to include every criminal.) However, I am less concerned with these well-known luminaries of fanaticism than I am with the inconspicuous temptation containing the germ of utopianism (and with it of totalitarianism) present in perhaps everyone who is not wholly indifferent. Visions and dreams of a better world are surely a fundamental aspect of authentic humanity; without them, and without that transcendence of the "given" which they represent, human life loses meaning, dignity, its very humanness. Is it any wonder then that this diabolical temptation to take the shortcut is no less omnipresent? An atom of it is hidden in every beautiful dream!

So it is only a "minor detail": to recognize in time that fateful first moment of deterioration, when an idea ceases to express the transcendent dimension of being human and degenerates into a substitute for it, the moment when product, the plan for a better world, ceases to be an expression of man's responsible identity and begins, on the contrary, to expropriate his responsibility and identity, when the abstraction ceases to belong to him and he instead begins to belong to it.

I believe that a distinctive Central European skepticism is inescapably a part of the spiritual, cultural, and intellectual phenomenon that is Central Europe as it has been formed and is being formed by certain specific historical experiences, including those which today seem to lie dormant in our collective unconscious. That skepticism has little in common with, say, English skepticism. It is generally rather stranger, a bit mysterious, a bit nostalgic, often tragic, and at times even heroic, occasionally somewhat incomprehensible in its heavy-handed way, in its gentle cruelty and its ability to turn a provincial way of seeing into a global anticipation of things to come. At times it gives the impression that people here are endowed with some inner radar capable of recognizing an approaching danger long before it becomes visible and recognizable as a danger.

Among the dangers for which our mind has such an exceptionally keen sense is the one of which I have been speaking, utopianism. Or, more precisely, we are keenly sensitive to the danger that a living idea, at once the product and the emblem of meaningful humanity, will petrify into a Utopia, into technical instructions for doing violence to life and intensifying its pain. (This skepticism may also be reinforced by the fact that, in our area, it must co-exist permanently with a great deal that is not far from the utopian mentality. I am thinking for instance of our provincial enthusiasm, our periodic inclination to illusions, our tendency to trust, at times to the point of servility, everything that comes to us from elsewhere, the grand words and short-windedness of our courage, an inclination to sudden euphoria which, predictably, turns to frustration, resignation, and apathy at the first setback, and so on and so forth.)

Once and only once in this country did a number of Czechs and Slovaks fall prey to unambiguous utopianism (and for historically intelligible reasons at that—it was in the atmosphere of the moral collapse of the older orders). That was when they came to believe that the merciless introduction of Leninist-Stalinist socialism (with the help, of course, of its world headquarters) would secure those "glowing tomorrows" for us—and when, heedless of the will of the rest of the populace, they proceeded to carry out that intent. (After many tragic experiences and after what was for some a long process of self-liberation and for others an awakening, we did attempt something like a revision of the misfortune, a "socialism with a human face." But that too, alas, was colored by the utopianism that had survived in many of us as a fundamental habit, more persistent than the individual illusions on which it had focused. The utopian aspect of that effort was not so much the faith that democratic institutions could be erected under Moscow's rule as it was the faith that we might secure approval from above—that the Kremlin, if only we could explain it all properly, must understand and approve. As it turned out, this faith proved a rather insecure foundation for such an undertaking. The response to the plea for understanding was to send in the tanks.

Our country has paid a cruel price for its postwar lapse into utopianism. It helped cast us—and for God knows how long—into a subjugation in which we need not have found ourselves at all.

The result of this story is obvious—a new, far-reaching reinforcement of our Central European skepticism about utopianism of all colors and shadings, about the slightest suggestion of utopianism. Today there is actually more of this skepticism than is good for us, for it has spilled over into the will to resist evil as such. The result is that even a timid, hesitant, tactful appeal to justice—and officially proclaimed justice at that—though it puts no pressure on anyone, is kept in check by both individual reflection and conscience, and is anti-utopian in its entire moral essence, will be suspected of utopianism (which is something the dissidents in particular know well).

I have spoken about all this at length because I suspect that the reserve people here feel toward the Western peace movement is rooted not merely in the banal suspicion that it is all a communist plot but much more in our region's fundamental skepticism about utopianism. Rightly or wrongly—but not surprisingly—our people ask themselves whether the Western peace fighters aren't just offering more of the same. Bogged down in a wearying, exhausting everyday existence, crushed in the name of his putative well-being by bureaucratic might, the Czechoslovak citizen tends to ask who is proposing still more "glowing tomorrows" for us this time? Who is disturbing us again with some Utopia? And what new catastrophes are being prepared for us—with the best of intentions? Why should I get burned in some attempt to save the world when I don't even know what miserable new scheme my boss will come up with at work tomorrow, naturally in the name of a better world? As if I didn't have enough problems already! Should I create more problems with pipe-dreams about a peaceful, disarmed, democratic Europe of free nations, when merely a whisper about such a dream can land me in troubles for the rest of my life—while Mr. G will still go on playing golf just as he pleases? Isn't it better to attempt to live with dignity and modesty even in this morass, so I will not have to be ashamed in front of my children, than to get mixed up in some platonic reorganization of Europe? Western peace fighters will get me mixed up in something and then, without giving it a second thought, they'll be off to a demonstration somewhere in Hanover, while I'll be left here at the mercy of the nearest secret-police department which, for my concern about the future of the world, will arrange to have me fired from a job I find half-decent—and in addition my children will have their very real futures ruined too. (For the sake of accuracy, let us note that this distrust applies to every utopianism, not only to the leftist variety: militant anticommunism, in which reason is crowded out by obsession and reality by a dream, evokes, I think, the same reactions, at least among sensible people.)

Hand in hand with skepticism about all Utopias goes, quite understandably, skepticism about the different types and manifestations of the ideological mentality. I have taken part in enough political debates in my life to be used to quite a bit, at least in this respect, but I must admit that even I am taken aback by the extent to which so many Westerners are addicted to ideology, much more than we who live in a system which is ideological through and through. Those perennial reflections about whom this or that view serves or abets, what political tendency it reinforces or weakens! Which idea can or cannot be misused by someone! That endless, exhausting examination of this or that attitude, opinion, or person to determine whether they are rightist or leftist, left of center or right of center, right of the left or left of the right! As if the proper pigeonhole were more important than the substance of an opinion! I can understand that in a world where political forces interact freely, this might be to some extent unavoidable. Still, I wish it could be understood why for us, against the background of our experiences, in circumstances where ideology has utterly terrorized the truth, this all seems petty, erroneous, and far removed from what is actually at stake.

Perhaps my description is overstated and oversimplified. Still, it seems to me that anyone who is seriously concerned about the future of Europe would do well to familiarize himself as closely as possible, for his own as well as the general good, with the various aspects of the skepticism which people here in the heart of Europe feel with respect to all visions of "glowing tomorrows." Few people would be happier than a Pole, a Czechoslovak, or a Hungarian were Europe soon to become a free community of independent countries in which no great power would have its armies and its rockets. And at the same time, I am sure that no one would be more skeptical about accomplishing this by appeals to anyone's good will, even assuming someone might get around to making such appeals. Let us not forget that few have had such a good opportunity to learn directly about the reason for the presence of superpower armies and rockets in certain European countries. Their purpose is not so much defense against a putative enemy as it is the supervision of conquered territories.

VII

SOME time ago, two appealing young Italian women arrived in Prague with a declaration of women calling for all things good: respect for human rights, disarmament, demilitarization of children's education, respect for all human beings. They were collecting signatures from both parts of our di-

vided Europe. I found them touching: they could easily have
been cruising the Mediterranean on yachts with wealthy hus-
bands (they could surely have found some)—yet here they
were, rattling around Europe, trying to make the world better. I felt all the sorrier for them because virtually none of
the better-known Prague women dissidents wanted to sign
(the petitioners understandably did not even try to approach
nondissidents). The reason was not that Prague women dissidents could not agree with the content of the declaration.
Without conferring in any way about it, they all, individually,
agreed on a different reason: it seemed to them ridiculous
that they should sign something *as women.* Men, who had
nothing to sign, treated this feminine action with gallant at-
tentiveness and a quiet smile, while among the ladies the
prevalent mood was one of vigorous distaste for the whole
matter, a distaste all the more vigorous for the fact that they
were not absolved from deciding whether to sign or not; they
experienced no need to be gallant. (Incidentally, in the end
about five of them did sign.)

I wondered where this sudden, spontaneous distaste for as-
sociating on the basis of gender among my women friends
had come from. It surprised me.

Only some time later did I come up with an explanation.
One of the traditions of the Central European climate of which
I have been speaking is, after all, a deepened sense of irony
and self-irony, together with humor and black humor, and
perhaps most important in this context, an intense fear of
exaggerating our own dignity to an unintentionally comic degree, a fear of pathos and sentimentality, of overstatement,
and of what Kundera calls the lyric relation to the world. Yes,
my women friends were suddenly seized with the fear that, as
participants in an international women's venture, they might
make themselves ridiculous. It was the fear that they would
become "dada," to borrow a term from the Czech theoretician of art, Karel Teige—that, unwittingly, they would become laughable in the earnestness with which they sought to
reinforce their civic opinion by stressing their defenseless

femininity. Apparently they had suddenly remembered how repulsive it was when, in her televised talks, the vice president of Czechoslovak Television, Mrs. Baláš, larded the official "peace" theses with constant references, full of fake sentimentality, to women and children. My women friends among the dissidents undoubtedly know a great deal about the sad position of women in our country. Despite this, they found even the vague suggestion of feminism in the fact that the declaration in question was to be strictly a women's affair intrinsically objectionable. I do not wish to ridicule feminism; I know little about it and am prepared to believe that it is far from being the invention of a few hysterical women, bored housewives, or cast-off mistresses. Still, I have to note that in our country, even though the position of women is incomparably worse than in the West, feminism seems simply "dada."

Feminism, to be sure, is not the issue here. I want only to illustrate that strange, almost mysterious horror of everything overstated, enthusiastic, lyrical, histrionic, or overly serious that is inseparable from our spiritual climate. It is of the same kind, and stems from analogous roots, as our skepticism about utopianism, with which it is often co-extensive: emotional enthusiasm and rationalistic utopianism are often no more than two sides of the same coin.

I can cite another example. It would be obviously inappropriate for Charter 77 to make jokes in its documents. Recently, however, it occurred to me in a particular context that some people might be getting bored with Charter 77 because it may seem to be taking itself much too seriously. Knowing only its documents and not its authors, they might easily gain the impression that Charter 77, forced for years to repeat the same theme over and over, has become stuck in the rut of its own seriousness, its martyrdom, its fame, that it lacks the ability to rise above itself, to look at itself from a distance, to make light of itself—and for that very reason, it might end up looking unintentionally ridiculous. I do not know whether such an impression really exists, and if it exists, how widespread it may be; even less can I judge to what degree it might be justified or unfair to us. In any case, it is something to think about.

It seems that in our Central European context what is most earnest has a way of blending uneasily with what is most comic. It seems that it is precisely the dimension of distance, of rising above oneself and making light of oneself, which lends to our concerns and actions precisely the right amount of shattering seriousness. Is not Franz Kafka, one of the most serious and tragic authors of this century, at the same time a humorist? Anyone who does not laugh when reading his novels (as Kafka himself is supposed to have done when he read them out loud to his friends) does not understand them. Is not a Czech Hašek or an Austrian Musil a master of tragic irony or of ironic tragedy? Is not Vaculík's *Czech Dreambook* (to cite a contemporary dissident writer) oppressive in its humor and merry in its hopelessness?

The life of a dissident in Czechoslovakia is really not particularly jolly, and spending time in Czechoslovak jails is even less so. Our frequent jesting about these matters is not in conflict with their seriousness; rather, it is their inevitable consequence. Perhaps we simply couldn't bear it at all if we were not at once aware of how absurd and so how comic it all is. Many of those who sympathize with us abroad would not understand our joking or would take it for cynicism. (More than once I have noted that, when meeting with foreigners, I do not translate much of what we say, just to be sure.) And when a dissident friend of mine, tasting what, for us, were exotic delights at the American Embassy, hailed them with Patočka's famous remark, "There are things worth suffering for," we all laughed; it never occurred to any of us to consider this unworthy of the dignity of Patočka's heritage, of his tragic death, and of the moral foundations of the dissident stance in general.

In short, perhaps it is part of the plebeian tradition of Czech culture, but here we tend to be more acutely aware of the fact that anyone who takes himself too seriously soon becomes

ridiculous, while anyone who always manages to laugh at himself cannot be truly ridiculous.

People in the West are, for various reasons, more afraid of
war than we are. They are also significantly more free, they
live more freely, and their opposition to armaments has no
unacceptably serious consequences for them. Perhaps all of
this makes the peace fighters on the other side seem, at least
from here, a bit too earnest, perhaps even slightly histrionic.
(There is something else here as well, something which we
are probably insufficiently aware of—that for them, the fight
for peace is probably more than a simple matter of particular
demands for disarmament, it is an opportunity to erect non-
conforming, uncorrupted social structures, an opportunity for
life in a humanly richer community, for self-realization outside the stereotypes of a consumer society and for expressing
their resistance to those stereotypes.)

Our distrust of all overstatement and of any cause incapable of seeing itself in perspective may also affect that reticence which I have sought to analyze here. Since we pay a
somewhat harsher price for our interest in the destiny of the
world, we may also have a stronger need to make light of
ourselves, to desecrate the altar, as Bakhtin so aptly put it.
For this reason alone we have to be a bit more reserved than
we might wish in our reaction to the earnest hyperbole (which,
at the same time, and not accidentally, is not purchased at as
high a risk) with which some Western peace fighters come to
us. It would be absurd to force on them our black humor and
our invincible skepticism or even to demand of them that
they undergo our serious tribulations and learn to see them
in an ironic perspective, as we do. It would, however, be
equally absurd if they expected from us their own brand of
overstatement. To understand each other does not mean
to become like each other, only to understand each other's
identity.

VIII

THERE are, to be sure, still other reasons for the reticence with which I am concerned here. For instance: Czechoslovaks learned only too well, from their own fate, where a policy of appeasement can lead, and they still have not quite got over it. For many years to come, historians are likely to speculate about whether the world could have avoided the Second World War, with its millions of corpses, if the Western democracies had stood up to Hitler forcefully and in time. Is it any wonder that in this country, whose present decline began at Munich, people are especially sensitive to anything even remotely reminiscent of the prewar capitulation to evil? I do not know how much genuine courage there would be in this country in any extreme situation. I do know, however, that one idea is firmly rooted in our common awareness: that the inability to risk, *in extremis,* even life itself to save what gives it meaning and a human dimension leads not only to the loss of meaning but finally and inevitably to the loss of life as well—and not one life only but thousands and millions of lives. Certainly in a world of nuclear arms capable of exterminating all of humankind, many things have changed. Still, the fundamental lesson of experience, that one must not tolerate violence in silence in the hope that it will simply run its course, retains its validity. (To believe the opposite would mean, among other things, to surrender to the inhumanity of technology once and for all.) Should such an attitude by some miracle avert rather than accelerate the coming of war, I cannot imagine to what kind of world, to what kind of humanity, to what kind of life and to what kind of "peace" it would open the door. To be sure, a universal moral imperative and concrete political techniques for implementing it are two different things. I believe there are more effective and more meaningful ways of resisting violence or the threat of violence than blindly imitating it (that is, promptly matching each of your opponent's actions with one of your own). That question, however, would take me too far afield.

So let me cite just one example to complete the picture. How much trust or even admiration for the Western peace movement can we expect from a simple yet sensitive citizen of Eastern Europe when he has noticed that this movement has never, at any of its congresses or at demonstrations involving hundreds of thousands of participants, got around to protesting the fact that five years ago, one important European country attacked a small neutral neighbor and since that time has been conducting on its territory a war of extermination which has already claimed a million dead and three million refugees? Seriously, what are we to think of a peace movement, a European peace movement, which is virtually unaware of the only war being conducted today by a European state? As for the argument that the victims of aggression and their defenders enjoy the sympathies of Western establishments and so are not worthy of support from the left, such incredible ideological opportunism can provoke only one reaction—utter disgust and a sense of limitless hopelessness.

IX

IT SHOULD be evident that the reticence of the inhabitants of the Soviet bloc with respect to peace issues has a variety of causes; some are probably found in all its countries, some are primary in one land, others in another.

Understandably, these elements enter to a greater or lesser degree into the reflections of Eastern European dissidents as well. If we also take into account the fact that the specific social situation differs in each of the Soviet-bloc countries, that each nation has its own historical, social, and cultural traditions, experiences, and models of behavior, and finally, when we consider that the dissidents, though not numerous, still constitute a highly variegated group (in a way the dissent in each of these nations mirrors the whole spectrum of political attitudes, as would become evident if it were ever allowed to emerge), it becomes quite clear that the Western peace movement is unlikely ever to receive a unified and specific peace program from our side.

And yet there is, it seems to me, something like a "common denominator" even here, some basic thoughts upon which we could probably all agree if we ever had the opportunity to do so. At least that is my impression from the texts I have seen: certain motifs recur in them with a surprising regularity. That cannot be a coincidence. Evidently analogous experiences lead to analogous considerations, perspectives, and convictions. And if they indeed represent something like a common denominator of the Eastern European experience and thought, it is surely worth noting.

It is not the aim of this essay to formulate this "common denominator." I shall only try to sum up some of the points that appear to be common to all independent East-Central European thinking about peace and the peace movement and are characteristic of it.

1. Most important, despite the general reticence, there appears to be a certain basic sympathy for the moral ethos of those who, living in a mature consumer society, place their concern for the destiny of the world ahead of a mere concern for personal well-being. Are we not doing something similar here, albeit in different ways and under different conditions? This "pre-rational" consideration guarantees of itself a certain basic weakness for the Western peace movement among our dissidents.

2. A close second, however, may be a clearly polemical conviction: the danger of war is not caused by weapons as such but by political realities (including the policies of political establishments) in a divided Europe and a divided world, realities which make possible or simply require the production and installation of these weapons and which in the end could lead to their utilization as well. No lasting, genuine peace can be achieved simply by opposing a particular weapons system, because this deals only with consequences, not with causes. Opposition to weapons—assuming, of course, that it is an

opposition to all weapons and not only to those suitable for protest encampments—can at best induce governments to accelerate various disarmament negotiations, that being probably the most we can expect.

3. Disarmament negotiations alone cannot resolve the present crisis, even if they are successful (which in the light of our experience thus far seems unlikely). So far, everything an agreement had slowed down soon accelerated again, without any agreement, a short time later. At best, successful negotiations might create a more favorable atmosphere for a real resolution of the crisis. Atmospherics, however, are one thing, the will to resolve the crisis another. Basically, they can achieve nothing more than the perpetuation of an explosive status quo—but with a smaller amount of explosive technology.

4. Thus the sole meaningful way to genuine European peace—and not simply to some armistice or "non-war"—is by fundamentally restructuring the political realities that are at the roots of the current crisis. This would require both sides to abandon radically their defensive policy of maintaining the status quo (that is, the division of Europe into blocs) as well as policies based on power or superpower "interests." They would have to subordinate all their efforts to something quite different—to the ideal of a democratic Europe as a friendly community of free and independent nations. What threatens peace in Europe is not the prospect of change but the existing situation.

5. Without free, self-respecting, and autonomous citizens, there can be no free and independent nations. Without internal peace, that is, peace among citizens and between the citizens and their state, there can be no guarantee of external peace. A state that ignores the will and the rights of its citizens can offer no guarantee that it will respect the will and the rights of other peoples, nations, and states. A state that refuses its citizens their right to public supervision of the exercise of power will not submit to international supervision. A state that denies its citizens their basic rights becomes

a danger to its neighbors as well: internal arbitrary rule will be reflected in arbitrary external relations. The suppression of public opinion, the abolition of public competition for power and its public exercise opens the way for the state power to arm itself in any way it sees fit. A manipulated population can be misused in serving any military adventure whatever. Unreliability in some areas arouses justifiable fear of unreliability in everything. A state that does not hesitate to lie to its own people will not hesitate to lie to other states. All of this leads to the conclusion that respect for human rights is the fundamental condition and the sole, genuine guarantee of true peace. Suppressing the natural rights of citizens and peoples does not secure peace—quite the contrary, it endangers it. A lasting peace and disarmament can only be the work of free people.

THE POSITION I have tried to sketch out here has been articulated in detail and with supporting arguments in innumerable, highly diverse works devoted to this topic by independent writers in our part of Europe. To quote them at length or to repeat what has already been written about it would be superfluous. This is roughly the attitude of various independent civic initiatives and groupings in the countries of the Soviet bloc.

It has become evident that reflection on the bitter daily experiences of the citizen in a totalitarian state always leads quite logically to the same point—a new appreciation of the importance of human rights, human dignity, and civic freedom. This is the focus of my remarks, and the focus, with good reason, of all reflections about peace as well. It may be that this understanding of the fundamental preconditions of peace, purchased at a high price and marked by a new vehemence, is the most important contribution that independently thinking people in our part of the world can make to our common awareness today.

For us it is simply no longer comprehensible how anyone

can still believe in the possibility of a disarmament that would bypass human beings or be purchased at the cost of their enslavement. This appears to us to be the most foolish of all Utopias, comparable perhaps only to a hope that all the weapons in the world will, on their own, deliver themselves to the scrap heap or turn into musical instruments.

The intensity and manner of emphasizing the continuity between peace and human freedom tend naturally to vary at different times and in different places in our part of the world, and they depend, in various ways, on the specific situation and context. Still, when we are confronted with the view that our insistence on introducing human rights into every discussion about peace complicates the situation and interferes with agreement, we all, for evident reasons, fall prey to the hopeless feeling that those who will not hear are beyond help.

X

SINCE the matters I have just discussed appear to us almost banally obvious, it is almost embarrassing to be forced to explain them again and again. It seems, however, that they are anything but obvious to many adherents of the peace movement and that we have no option other than to go on explaining. More than once in conversations with peace activists or while signing shared position papers, I have encountered the notion that our ideas may be remarkable, perhaps even surprising (!), but they are also too abstract, too "philosophical," not sufficiently political, clearly comprehensible, or hard-hitting, and thus difficult to implement. I had the impression that my interlocutors were far more accustomed to the kind of slogans, proclamations, and clear, unambiguous demands that are more suitable for placards and T-shirts than they are for serious, general thinking on the matter. But we can't help it. Our ideas are derived from the world of practical, real politics.

Still, our position remains simple enough as long as we are asked for no more, and no less, than a clarification of our fundamental perspective on the topic of peace. More serious complications arise when, for whatever reason, we are asked to explain how we imagine projecting our global or "philosophical" conception into the real world of political action: what should we actually be demanding, and what political measures, and in what order, would we expect Europe to take in the light of our perspective?

An initial difficulty here is that even when Eastern European dissidents have definite views on this matter, those views differ widely.

There are some, for instance in Poland and Hungary, who believe that the first and perhaps the most important step toward transforming the status quo in Europe and thus toward genuine peace should be the creation of a belt of neutral states in Central Europe in place of the present abrupt frontier between the two blocs. The objection of many to this suggestion is that this is the least realistic of all possible demands—surely the Soviet Union will not be willing to give up several of its European client states and to guarantee their neutrality to boot. Besides, it is said, this would be immoral because it would in fact mean a solution to the detriment of others—as long as we are free, let the rest of Europe manage as best it can! According to the critics of such a solution, that immorality is linked with its hopelessness: a "no-man's-land" between the blocs into which Europe is divided will not bring peace. The danger of conflict would continue, and were it to come, the Central European states would be the first to be blown sky-high (was it ever otherwise in our remembered history?) while the neutrality behind which, Swiss style, they sought to hide from the world's turmoils, would become a scrap of paper overnight.

Others suggest a straightforward dissolution of the two military blocs and withdrawal of American and Soviet armies from the territories of their European allies (which would naturally lead to the liquidation of all nuclear weapons stationed in or aimed at Europe). Speaking personally, this seems simply lovely, although it is not quite clear to me who or what could induce the Soviet Union to dissolve the entire phalanx of its European satellites—especially since it is evident that, with its armies gone from their territories, it would sooner or later have to abandon its political domination over them as well.

Another voice, incidentally a particularly authoritative one, seeks to show that Europe will remain divided as long as Germany remains divided. For that reason (and not simply because of the German right to unification) we should first of all demand a German peace treaty which would confirm the present European frontiers but would at the same time offer the two German states the prospect of gradual confederation. With the German problem resolved, a dissolution of the two pacts might be far more realistic. This perspective is rather persuasive: would a Europe without pacts and without the protection—or rather the "protection"—of the superpowers be imaginable if Berlin were to remain cut in two by a wall and the German problem left unresolved?

This proposal also evokes a series of objections: it is said to be provocative, stirring up all kinds of ghosts and emotions on every side; many judicious people fear the reconstitution of a greater Germany, with its danger of automatic German predominance in Europe, and so on.

Finally, still others believe there is no point in raising any of these bold proposals since no one is prepared to act on them in any case, and the mighty find them needlessly irritating. It makes more sense, they would say, to take the various treaties already on the books at face value (for example, the Concluding Act of the Helsinki Agreement) and to demand that they be observed. Or perhaps it might be better to support without bombastic gestures a variety of small steps which would gradually lead to a healthier climate throughout Europe, to cooler heads and so to a gradual limitation of armaments, and to a relaxation of tensions.

In all likelihood, numerous other proposals and perspectives exist. (For completeness' sake, although this is not directly related to the various perspectives on the restructuring of Europe, I would like to mention one other point that divides the dissidents rather significantly—their attitude toward the United States. On one side of the spectrum, anti-Americanism is nearly as strong as it is among Western leftists; on the other, the viewpoint tends to be Reaganite: the Soviet Union is the evil empire, the United States the land of the good. As for myself—should anyone care to know—I have no great illusions about America, about the American establishment, and about American foreign policy. Still, the degree of internal freedom and consequently of international political credibility characteristic of the two superpowers appears to me so profoundly different that to consider the current situation as symmetrical, in the sense that both colossi are equally dangerous, appears to me a monstrous oversimplification. Yes, both are dangerous, but each in a different way; they definitely are not dangerous in the same way.)

Another difficulty involved in considerations of this kind in our part of Europe is more serious than that deriving from the difference of opinion we have just described. It is rooted in a rather vague, difficult to explain, and yet immensely powerful sense of the futility and senselessness of all such considerations. It may seem strange, however, as I shall try to explain, that ultimately it is quite logical that this feeling came over us not when we confined ourselves to "philosophizing" generally about peace, but only at the point when our reflections had to touch upon concrete politics.

A Central European mind—skeptical, sober, anti-utopian, understated, crushed by daily confrontation with unprincipled power—when suddenly cast in the role of arbiter of Europe's future, cannot avoid the feeling that this is "dada." It is no great problem for a local dissident to concoct this or that vision of European development and of Europe's future. The problem is how to shake off the feeling of the utter hopelessness and pointlessness of such work, how to rid oneself of the fear that any specific, technical, conception of the longed-for transformation of Europe into a continent of peace is every bit as ludicrous nowadays as any other utopian construction, how to rid oneself both of the fear that he will become a target for his sober neighbors' ridicule, and of the feeling that, for the first time, he is actually drifting away from real life and up into the stratospheric realm of fairy tales.

A trace of the heroic dreamer, mad and unrealistic, is hidden in the very genesis of the dissident perspective. The dissident is essentially something of a Don Quixote. He writes his critical analyses and demands freedoms and rights all alone, merely with a pen in his hand, face to face with the gargantuan might of the state and its police. He writes, cries out, screams, requests, appeals to the law—and all the time he knows that, sooner or later, they will lock him up for it. Why, then, such scruples? Amid clouds of folly should he not feel like a fish in water? I will attempt to explain the difference between the "natural folly" of the dissident's world and the type of folly that terrifies him when he is asked to sign a program for the peaceful reordering of Europe.

As I have written more than once, I believe the phenomenon of dissent grows out of an essentially different conception of the meaning of politics than that prevailing in the world today. That is, the dissident does not operate in the realm of genuine power at all. He does not seek power. He has no desire for office and does not woo voters. He does not attempt to charm the public, he offers nothing and promises nothing. He can offer, if anything, only his own skin—and he offers it solely because he has no other way of affirming the truth he stands for. His actions simply articulate his dignity as a citizen, regardless of the cost. The innermost foundation of his "political" undertaking is moral and existential. Everything he does, he does initially for himself: something within has simply revolted and left him incapable of continuing to "live a lie." Only then does there follow (and can there possibly follow) a "political" motive: the hope—vague, indefinite, and difficult to justify—that this course of action is also good for something in general. It is the hope that "politics beyond politics," that "politics outside the sphere of power," does make some sense, that by whatever hidden and complex ways it leads to something, evokes something, produces some effect. That even something as apparently ephemeral as the truth spoken aloud, as an openly expressed concern for the humanity of man, carries a power within itself and that even a word is capable of a certain radiation, of leaving a mark on the "hidden consciousness" of a community. (An intrinsic aspect of this perspective is that the dissident is more likely to describe and analyze the present than to project a future. He is far more a critic of what is wrong here and now than a planner of something better to come. He sees his mission more in defending man against the pressures of the system than in imagining better systems. As for the future, he is more concerned with the moral and political values on which it should rest than with premature speculations about how and by whom these values will be secured for humankind. He knows, after all, that the nature of this future does not depend on his present wishes but on the difficult-to-predict course of things to come.)

This, then, is the "natural folly" of the world of dissent. It is meaningful because, within its limits, it is consistent. It is tactical because it does not let itself be guided by tactical considerations. It is political because it does not play politics. It is concrete, real, effective—not in spite of its folly but because of it. To be sure, it is also this because there is something honest about its folly, it is faithful to itself, it is whole and undivided. This may be a world of dreams and of the ideal, but it is not the world of Utopia.

Why deny it, this world of truth, however uncomfortable to live in, offers at the same time definite advantages: finding himself outside the universe of real power and traditional practical politics, that is, outside the matrix of utility, tactics, success, compromise, and the inevitable manipulations of half-truths and deceptions, the dissident can be himself and can even make fun of himself without danger of becoming ridiculous to everyone.

A dissident runs the risk of becoming ridiculous only when he transgresses the limits of his natural existence and enters into the hypothetical realm of real power, that is, in effect, into the realm of sheer speculation. For only then does he risk becoming a utopian. Here he accepts the perspective of real power without having any genuine power whatever; he enters the world of tactics incapable of tactical maneuver and without being either licensed or compelled to do so by real power; he leaves the world of service to truth and attempts to smuggle his truth into the world of service to power without being able or even willing to serve it himself. He attempts to go on speaking the truth outside the world of truth; standing outside the world of power, he attempts to speculate about power or to organize it. He trades the respectable role of a champion for the somewhat grotesque role of a self-appointed adviser to the mighty. In the role of a dreamer, he was not ludicrous, just as a tactician is not ludicrous in a tactician's role. He becomes ludicrous only when he becomes a dreamer playing at tactics. A dreamer playing at tactics is a minister without a ministry, a general without an army, a president without a republic. Alienated from his role as a witness of history, yet unwelcome in the role of its organizer, he finds himself in a strange vacuum—outside the credibility of power and outside the credibility of truth.

In all of this I do not wish to suggest that Soviet-bloc dissidents should not comment on the political realities and political possibilities where they live, that they should not examine the different limits on their effectiveness and seek to expand them, that they should not reflect on how and where they can or cannot project their truth. History is unpredictable, and we need to be prepared for a whole range of eventualities: recall, for instance, how the dissidents of the Polish Workers' Defense Committee had to become practical politicians overnight.

I have sought only to explain why I believe that Eastern European dissidents are, and in all likelihood will remain, cautious in their own distinctive manner whenever they are called upon to take part in peace activities.

April 1985

Two Notes on
Charter 77

"Two Notes on Charter 77" (March 29, 1986) was written as an essay for *Infoch*, a *samizdat* information bulletin put out by Charter 77. It was intended as part of an internal discussion on Charter 77 sponsored by *Infoch* in late April 1986. This is its first appearance in English. Translation by Paul Wilson.

I

FROM the moment it appeared until today, Charter 77 has been the object of different kinds of suspicions, fears, and attacks, and of hopes. The common denominator of all these attitudes is a single, fundamental misunderstanding: the belief that Charter 77 is a political movement in the traditional sense of the word, a force or organization that is politically defined, that sees itself as an opposition with a program, and that may even desire political power. In most cases, the misunderstanding is just that, and not an expression of ill will. I also think that this error has many more or less understandable causes.

Perhaps the most important of these lies in the peculiarities of the system in which the Charter exists, in which everything inevitably appears political, especially a group of citizens expressing themselves freely. From the beginning we have tried to deal with this misunderstanding (how many texts have already been written on that theme!) and we obviously have no choice but to continue our efforts.

I should mention here briefly another set of causes that has led to this misunderstanding. As we know, Charter 77 is a citizens' initiative in which a wide variety of people have joined together to demand that the laws be observed, that basic human rights be respected. They have also taken action against injustice of all kinds and subjected many social phenomena to the kind of critical examination that is impossible to do officially. Among the active Chartists there are many people with a highly specific political or religious background: socialists, Catholics, Protestants, democrats, and so on.

Two things must be said about this. First: regardless of how many such people there are, and no matter how much is heard about them (for reasons that, again, are quite understandable), they are far from being the majority. Most signatories of Charter 77, on the contrary, do not espouse any specific ideology, political program, or confessional group. Second: even if this were not so and every last signatory were highly political, it would change nothing in the purely civic, nonideological, and nonpolitical base on which the Charter stands and on which its signatories stand united.

The presence of these politically minded people, and chiefly the fact that they naturally tend to express themselves publicly in the spirit of their political convictions, is undoubtedly one of the reasons for the misunderstandings and errors I am talking about. Again and again, we forget that any directly political or ideological expression or activity on the part of such people has nothing whatsoever to do with the Charter. Such work is done by these people or their groups exclusively in their own right and in their own names. To judge the Charter according to the politics of particular Chartists is at least as foolish as judging it according to the kind of plays I write.

It is just as absurd to speculate about its political makeup or the direction the Charter might take on the basis of the political past or political opinions of its spokesmen. Unfortunately, this happens a lot too. I think that the Charter would remain what it is regardless of who the spokesmen were, and personally, I couldn't care less whether they happen to be three former communists, or, on the contrary, three Catholics. All that interests me is the quality of the documents they publish, and, of course, whether the character of those documents does not in some way go beyond the mandate the Charter set for itself.

In this connection, it won't hurt to recall a somewhat different matter that is not always obvious even to us. In the preparation of some of the Charter documents, it has not always been easy for their authors to separate what are legitimate Chartist concerns from what might overstep that legitimacy. [. . .]

In any case, there is no index of words, expressions, or ideas that are "authentically Chartist," so the territory of what is "authentically Chartist" has no precise and determinable borders. Everything is a matter of a freely determined consensus and agreement, which of course can be influenced by a thousand circumstances both internal and external. Because of this, and because of the often rather chaotic conditions in which these documents are prepared, the general consensus may be in some respects trespassed against, which results in stormy debates within the Charter and thousands of frequently rather absurd speculations outside the Charter about the slippery slope down which we are sliding in one direction or the other—which means to the left or to the right. If in such cases there is an obvious "slip," then we must, first, remember that we are living and therefore erring people, with the right occasionally to make a mess of things, and second, admit our mistakes as promptly and sincerely as possible and draw the appropriate conclusions. But is there any point in drawing catastrophic conclusions from those occasional errors the Charter made?

I'd like to remark on one more thing in this connection: if Charter documents are not to become completely depersonalized, shapeless, anonymous, bureaucratic texts, with an official tone as soporific as party speeches and resolutions, then there is nothing wrong with injecting into them a more personal tone, and perhaps even a provocative idea, insight, or formulation, especially when a document has obviously come from a particular pen. [. . .] Wouldn't this too be in harmony with the pluralistic nature of the Charter and with the fact that the Charter is an expression of particular people working to defend other particular people and their rights against the anonymous machinery of a depersonalized and therefore irresponsible power? After all, the Charter is not a new anonymous machine standing against the old ones. In any case, though it's been said long ago and it always seems to be forgotten, the Charter documents do not claim any definitive validity for themselves, but are merely proposals or appeals for a wider discussion on a particular subject. [. . .]

II

A KIND of bi-polar political thinking is becoming more and more common in today's politically polarized world. Everyone is expected to say clearly whether he belongs here, or there; whether he is a friend or an enemy; and then everyone is expected to be unquestionably loyal to the position he belongs to or has been assigned to. People who live in the world of such thinking have constant and understandable problems with Charter 77. If it is right-wing, then why isn't it properly, openly, and consistently right-wing? If it is left-wing, why isn't it properly, openly, and consistently left-wing? We hear such questions—formulated more subtly, of course—all the time.

Such questions also spring from a misunderstanding of what the Charter really is. Charter 77 is neither left-wing nor right-wing, not because it is "somewhere in the middle," but because it has nothing whatever in common with that spectrum, because in essence, it lies outside it. As a civic initiative that is politically undefined and does not seek to implement a political program of its own, it is—if I may say so—"above" it all, or, to put it more modestly, outside it all. It is concerned with the truth, with a truthful description of conditions, and with a free and objective criticism of those conditions. Which means that it is and must be concerned with truth no matter whom that truth favors.

If it were not so constituted, if it were to look to certain "political interests" or limit its veracity by being loyal to certain political forces or tendencies, or even maintaining discipline common to higher political structures—in other words, indulging in tactics—it would have no right to consider itself independent and free, and it would become something quite different from what it was when it came into being. The Charter does not submit to anyone, and just as it is not a secret branch plant of the Husák regime (which some of the more militant warriors for democracy suspect it of being), so it is not a secret Czechoslovak branch of the Reagan administration (which, again, some of the more militant warriors for socialism suspect). If the Charter enjoys a kind of respect among enlightened people, this is only because it is genuinely independent and it accepts the unpleasant but entirely natural fact that it will always bother someone. If one believes that the Devil of communism must be eliminated, that this can only be done under Reagan's leadership, and that every sign of disagreement with this leadership amounts to supporting the Devil, then such a belief is his own private affair, and it is not my business to tell him he can't see past the tip of his democratic nose.

It is obviously worth telling everyone frequently and loudly that the Charter recognizes only a single authority, and that is the authority of truth and the authority of the conscience that demands it speak the truth. And if we are not all-knowing like God, and the information we provide seems limited or distorted to many people, if at times we see some things wrongly, if we believe people we ought not to have believed and have not believed people we ought to have believed, if we are not always able to articulate truth well—all of that is another matter altogether. We have made mistakes and we will not, unfortunately, avoid error in the future either. But, as I've said, these mistakes are the result of our human imperfections; they should not be made an occasion to think that we belong under a particular political flag (positive or negative) which we are attempting to serve or, on the contrary, which we have reprehensibly betrayed.

March 1986

Stories and Totalitarianism

"Stories and Totalitarianism" (April 1987) was written for the underground cultural journal *Jednou nohu (Revolver Review)*, and dedicated to Ladislav Hejdánek on his seventieth birthday. In English, it appeared in *Index on Censorship*, no. 3 (March 1988) and, in a slightly different version, in *The Idler*, Toronto, no. 18 (July–August 1988). Translation by Paul Wilson.

A FRIEND of mine who is heavily asthmatic was sentenced, for political reasons, to several years in prison, where he suffered a great deal because his cellmates smoked and he could scarcely breathe. All his requests to be moved to a cell with nonsmokers were ignored. His health, and perhaps even his life, were threatened. An American woman who learned of this and wanted to help telephoned an acquaintance, an editor on an important American daily. Could he write something about it, she asked. "Call me when the man dies," was the editor's reply.

It's a shocking incident but in some ways understandable. Newspapers need a story. Asthma is not a story. Death could make it one.

IN PRAGUE there is only one Western news agency with long-term accreditation. In Lebanon, a country far smaller than Czechoslovakia, there are reporters by the hundreds. Perhaps this is understandable, for, as they say, "Nothing is happening here." Lebanon, on the other hand, is full of stories. It is also a land of murder, war, death. But as long as humans can remember, death has been the point at which all the lines of every real story converge.

Our condition is like that of my friend: we are unworthy of attention because we have no stories, and no death. We have only asthma. And why should anyone be interested in listening to our cough?

One can't go on writing forever about how hard it is to breathe.

It DOESN'T bother me that terrorists are not on the loose here, or that there are no big scandals over corruption in high places, and no violent demonstrations or strikes.

What bothers me is something else: that this remarkable absence of newsworthy stories is not an expression of social harmony, but the outward consequence of a dangerous and profound process: the destruction of "the story" altogether. Almost every day I am struck by the ambiguity of this social quiescence, which is the visible expression of an invisible war between the totalitarian system and life itself.

It is not true that Czechoslovakia is free of warfare and murder. The war and the killing assume a different form: they have been shifted from the daylight of observable public events, to the twilight of unobservable inner destruction. It would seem that the absolute, "classical" death of which one reads in stories (and which for all the terrors it holds is still mysteriously able to impart meaning to human life) has been replaced here by another kind of death: the slow, secretive, bloodless, never-quite-absolute, yet horrifyingly ever-present death of non-action, non-story, non-life, and non-time; the collectively deadening, or more precisely, anesthetizing, process of social and historical nihilization. This nihilization annuls death as such, and thus annuls life as such: the life of an individual becomes the dull and uniform functioning of a component in a large machine, and his death is merely something that puts him out of commission.

All the evidence suggests that this state of things is the intrinsic expression of an advanced and stabilized totalitarian system, growing directly out of its essence.

VISITORS from the West are often shocked to find that for Czechs, Chernobyl and AIDS are not a source of horror, but rather a subject for jokes.

I must admit this doesn't surprise me. Because totalitarian nihilization is utterly immaterial, it is less visible, more present, and more dangerous than the AIDS virus or radioactivity from Chernobyl. On the other hand, it touches each of us more intimately and more urgently and even, in a sense, more physically, than either AIDS or radiation, since we all know it from everyday, personal experience and not just from newspapers and television. Is it any wonder, then, that the less menacing, less insidious, and less intimate threats are relegated to the background and made light of?

There is another reason for the triumph of invisibility. The destruction of the story means the destruction of a basic instrument of human knowledge and self-knowledge. Totalitarian nihilization denies people the possibility of observing and understanding its processes "from outside." There are only two alternatives: either you experience it directly, or you know nothing about it. This menace permits no public reference to itself.

The foreign tourist can form the legitimate impression that Czechoslovakia is a poorer and duller Switzerland, and that press agencies have a legitimate reason for closing their bureaus here: how can they be expected to report that there is nothing to report?

I will attempt to make a few observations on the origin and nature of our asthma.

I will attempt to show that the disappearance of the story from this corner of the world is a story in itself.

. . .

IN THE fifties there were enormous concentration camps in Czechoslovakia filled with tens of thousands of innocent people. At the same time, building sites were swarming with tens of thousands of young enthusiasts of the new faith singing songs of socialist construction. There were tortures and executions, dramatic flights across borders, conspiracies, and at the same time, panegyrics were being written to the chief dictator. The President of the Republic signed the death warrants for his closest friends, but you could still sometimes meet him on the street.

The songs of idealists and fanatics, political criminals on the rampage, the suffering of heroes—these have always been part of history. The fifties were a bad time in Czechoslovakia, but there have been many such times in human history. It still shared something, or at least bore comparison with those other periods; it still resembled history. No one could have said that nothing was happening, or that the age did not have its stories.

The blueprint for political power in Czechoslovakia after the Soviet invasion in 1968 was a document called "Lessons from the Years of Crisis." It was an appropriate title; the powers that be really did learn a lesson from the Prague Spring. They discovered how far things can go when the door to a plurality of opinions and interests is opened: the totalitarian system itself is jeopardized. Having learned this lesson, political power set itself a single aim: self-preservation. In a process with its own, mindless dynamic, all the mechanisms of direct and indirect manipulation of life began to expand and assume unprecedented forms. Henceforth nothing could be left to chance.

The past twenty years in Czechoslovakia can almost serve as a textbook illustration of how an advanced or late totalitarian system works. Revolutionary ethos and terror have been replaced by dull inertia, pretext-ridden caution, bureaucratic anonymity, and mindless, stereotypical behavior, all of which aim exclusively at becoming more and more what they already are.

The songs of zealots and the cries of the tortured are no longer heard; lawlessness has put on kid gloves and moved from the torture chambers into the upholstered offices of faceless bureaucrats. If the President of the Republic is seen in the street at all, he is behind the bulletproof glass of his limousine as it roars off to the airport, surrounded by a police escort, to meet Colonel Qaddafi.

The advanced totalitarian system depends on manipulatory devices so refined, complex, and powerful that it no longer needs murderers and victims. Even less does it need fiery Utopia builders spreading discontent with dreams of a better future. The epithet "Real Socialism," which this era has coined to describe itself, points a finger at those for whom it has no room: the dreamers.

EVERY story begins with an event. This event—understood as the incursion of one logic into the world of another logic—initiates what every story grows out of and draws nourishment from: situations, relationships, conflict. The story has a logic of its own as well, but it is the logic of a dialogue, an encounter, the interaction of different truths, attitudes, ideas, traditions, passions, people, higher powers, social movements, and so on, that is, of many autonomous, separate forces, which had done nothing beforehand to define each other. Every story presupposes a plurality of truths, of logics, of agents of decisions, and of manners of behavior. The logic of a story resembles the logic of games, a logic of tension between what is known and not known, between rules and chance, between the inevitable and the unforeseeable. We never really know what will emerge from the confrontation, what elements may yet enter into it, and how it will end; it is never clear what potential qualities it will arouse in a protagonist and what action he will be led to perform by the action of his antagonist. For this reason alone, mystery is a dimension of every story. What speaks to us through a story is not a particular agent of truth; instead, the story manifests the human world to us as an exhilarating arena where many such agents come into contact with each other.

The fundamental pillar of the present totalitarian system is the existence of one central agent of all truth and all power, an institutionalized "rationale of history," which becomes, quite naturally, the sole agent of all social activity. Public life ceases to be an arena where different, more or less autonomous agents square off, and becomes no more than the manifestation and fulfillment of the truth and the will of this single agent. In a world governed by this principle, there is no room for mystery; ownership of complete truth means that everything is known ahead of time. Where everything is known ahead of time, the story has nothing to grow out of.

Obviously, the totalitarian system is in essence (and in principle) directed against the story.

WHEN the story is destroyed, the feeling of historicity disappears as well. I remember the early seventies in Czechoslovakia as a time when something like a "cessation of history" took place; public life seemed to lose its structure, its impulse, its direction, its tension, its rhythm, its mystery. I can't remember what happened when, or what made one year different from another, and I don't think it matters much, for when the unforeseeable disappears, the sensation of meaning disappears with it.

History was replaced by pseudo-history, by a calendar of rhythmically recurring anniversaries, congresses, celebrations, and mass gymnastic events; by the kind of artificial activity that is not an open-ended play of agents confronting one another but a one-dimensional, transparent, predictable self-manifestation (and self-celebration) of a single, central agent of truth and power.

And since human time can only be experienced through story and history, the experience of time itself began to disappear: time seemed to stand still or go in circles, to disinte-grate into interchangeable fragments. The march of events out of nowhere and to nowhere lost its storylike character and thus lost any deeper meaning as well. When the horizon of historicity was lost, life became nonsense.

Totalitarian power brought bureaucratic order into the liv-ing disorder of history and thus effectively anesthetized it.

In a sense, the government nationalized time. Thanks to that, time encountered the same sad fate as many other na-tionalized entities: it began to wither away.

As I'VE said, the revolutionary ethos in Czechoslovakia has long since vanished. We are no longer governed by fanatics, revolutionaries, or ideological zealots. The country is admin-istered by faceless bureaucrats who profess adherence to a revolutionary ideology, but look out only for themselves, and no longer believe in anything. The original ideology has be-come a formalized ritual that gives them legitimacy in space and time, and provides them with a language for internal communication.

Oddly enough, it is only recently that this ideology has be-gun to bear its most important fruit, to manifest its deepest consequences.

How are we to explain this?

Simply: by the age and the deeply conservative (in the sense of preserving) nature of the system. The further it gets from its original revolutionary fervor, the more slavishly it clings to all its constitutive principles, which it sees as the only cer-tainty in an uncertain world. Inevitably, through its own mindless, automatic motion, it gradually transforms those principles into a monstrous reality. The ceaseless strength-ening and perfecting of totalitarian structures has long since come to serve only the naked self-preservation of power, but this is the best guarantee that what was genetically encoded in the original ideology will flourish undisturbed. The fanatic whose unpredictable zeal for the "higher cause" might threaten this automatic process has been replaced by the bureaucratic pedant whose reliable lack of ideas makes him an ideal guardian of late totalitarianism's vacuous continuity.

The phenomenon of totalitarian nihilization is one of the late fruits of an ideology that has already gone to seed.

The totalitarian system did not fall from the sky fully developed. Nor is it the work of a pervert who has got his hands on a scalpel designed to remove malignant growths and begun killing healthy people with it.

We need only penetrate the tissue of various dialectical sprouts to discover that the germ of this nihilization lies dormant in the heart of the ideology the system is based upon: in its belief that it has fully understood the world and revealed the truth about it. And if the main territory of that belief is history, is it any wonder that its nihilizing intention radiates most strongly from its approach to history?

It began with an interpretation of history from a single aspect, then made that aspect absolute, and finally reduced all of history to that one aspect. The exciting variety of history was discarded in favor of an orderly, easily understood interplay of "historical laws," "social groups," and "relations of production," so pleasing to the eye of the scientist. But this gradually expelled from history the very thing that gives human life, time, and thus history itself a structure: the story. And the story took with it into the kingdom of unmeaning its two essential ingredients: uniqueness and ambiguity. Since the mystery in a story is the articulated mystery of man, history began to lose its human content. The uniqueness of the human creature became a mere embellishment on the laws of history, and the tension and thrill in real events were dismissed as accidental and therefore unworthy of the attention of scholarship. History became boredom.

The nihilization of the past nihilizes the future as well: when the "laws of history" were projected into the future, what would be and what had to be suddenly became obvious. The bright glare of this certainty burned away the essence of the future: its openness. Plans to make an earthly paradise the final end of history, to rid the world of social conflict, of negative human qualities, and even of misery, climaxed the work of destruction. Society was petrified into a fiction of everlasting harmony, and man into a stone monument representing the permanent proprietor of happiness—these were the silent consummations of the intellectual assassination of history.

Yet by presenting itself as an instrument for history's ultimate return to itself, ideology unwittingly admits to its own destructiveness. The claim is that through ideology, history has finally understood itself, understood where it is going and how it must proceed: that is, under ideology's guidance. Ideology revealed the historical necessity of what ought to happen, and in doing so, confirmed the historical necessity of itself, whose mission it is to fulfill that necessity. In other words, history has at last discovered its final meaning. The question is, however, does history that has discovered its own meaning still have any meaning? And is it history anymore?

Ideology, claiming to base its authority on history, becomes history's greatest enemy.

But the hostility is double-edged: if ideology destroys history by explaining it completely, then history destroys ideology by unfolding in an unpredictable way.

Ideology, of course, can destroy history only ideologically, but the power based on that ideology can suppress history in real ways. In fact, it has no choice: if history, by unfolding unpredictably, were allowed to demonstrate that ideology is wrong, it would deprive power of its legitimacy.

By negating history, power is defending not just its ideological legitimacy, but its identity as totalitarian power. This identity too has a firm ideological anchorage: the principle that there is a single central agent of truth and power could scarcely have come into existence, let alone develop and grow strong, had it not initially drawn strength from an ideology that so smugly disdained any viewpoint but its own, and so proudly declared its historical mission, and all the prerogatives this mission endowed it with. After all, totalitarian power has been fed and weaned and to this day is imbued with the intolerant spirit of this ideology, which sees plurality only as a necessary evil, or as a formality. And its central principle is nothing more than the consistent working-through of the original ideology and the perfect incarnation of its vanity; as its legitimate product, it draws on ideology's nihilizing energy, so that it can put the theories of ideology successfully into practice.

The asthma our society is now suffering from is a natural continuation of the war that intellectual arrogance once declared on the story, on history, and thus on life itself.

Boredom has jumped out of the history textbooks and into real life.

ANY FLEDGLING totalitarian power tries first to limit and ultimately to eliminate other sources of power. The first to go is political plurality. But along with it, or shortly afterwards, intellectual and economic plurality disappear as well, since any power that respects these pluralities would not be total.

First, then, the story is driven out of public life.

By virtue of its own specific gravity—its totalitarian gravity—this power deepens its totality and extends its range. Once the claims of central power have been placed above law and morality, once the exercise of that power is divested of public control, and once the institutional guarantees of political plurality and civil rights have been made a mockery of, or simply abolished, there is no reason to respect any other limitations. The expansion of central power does not stop at the frontier between the public and the private, but instead, arbitrarily pushes back that border until it is shamelessly intervening in areas that once were private. For example, a club of pigeon fanciers that had enjoyed a kind of autonomy now suddenly find themselves scrutinized by the central power. Today, that power walks through my bugged bedroom and distinguishes my breathing, which is my own private matter, from what I say, which the state cannot be indifferent to.

When opposition parties are banned and censorship has been introduced, the attack on the story and thus on life itself is not over; it is just beginning.

Because they are better hidden, indirect interventions are in some ways more dangerous. Public life is not as sharply distinguished from private life as it used to be. Countless phenomena in modern civilization bind the two spheres together, and so they have become two faces, two poles, or two dimensions of a single and indivisible life. Though it sometimes happens in complex and hidden ways, everything that takes place in the public sphere eventually influences and shapes the private sphere. When public life is nihilized, private life is distorted and ultimately nihilized too. Every measure taken to establish more complete control over the former has a pernicious effect on the latter.

The attack on plurality and on the story and on public territory is therefore not an attack on a single side of life; it is an attack on all of life.

The web of direct and indirect manipulation is a straitjacket that binds life and necessarily limits the ways it can appear to itself and structure itself. And so it languishes, declines, wastes away. It is cheapened and leveled. It becomes pseudo-life.

WHILE I was in prison, I realized again and again how much more present, compared with life outside, the story was. Almost every prisoner had a life story that was unique and shocking, or moving. As I listened to those different stories, I suddenly found myself in something like a pre-totalitarian world, or in the world of literature. Whatever else I may have thought of my fellow prisoners' colorful narratives, they were not documents of totalitarian nihilization. On the contrary, they testified to the rebelliousness with which human uniqueness resists its own nihilization, and the stubbornness with which it holds to its own and is willing to ignore this negating pressure. Regardless of whether crime or misfortune was predominant in any given story, the faces in that world were specific and personal. When I got back from prison, I wrote somewhere that in a cell of twenty-four people you can probably encounter more real stories than in a high-rise development housing several thousand. People truly afflicted with asthma—those colorless, servile, obedient, homogenized, herdlike citizens of the totalitarian state—are not found in large numbers in prison. Instead, prison tends to be a gathering place for people who stand out in one way or another, the unclassifiable misfits, real individuals with all sorts of obsessions, people who are unable to conform.

There has probably always been a greater concentration of people in prison who stand out in some way. Nevertheless, I'm convinced that what I observed when I was there myself bears directly on conditions under totalitarianism. The nature of many of the stories confirmed this.

On the whole, it's logical: the wider the scope of the instruments by which the system manipulates, de-individualizes, and circumscribes life, the more powerful its embrace, the more thoroughly everything unique is pushed to the periphery of "normal" life and ultimately beyond it, into prison. The repressive apparatus that sends people to jail is an organic part and, indeed, the culmination of the general pressure totalitarianism exerts against life: without this extreme threat, many other threats would lose their credibility. It is certainly no accident that, proportionally, Czechoslovakia has many times more prisoners than the United States. Criminality—I mean real criminality—cannot be that much greater in Czechoslovakia.

What *is* greater is the demand for uniformity and its consequence: the criminalization of difference and variety.

IF THE agents entering into a story can fully manifest their individuality only as the story unfolds, in other words if individuality requires a story to become what it is, then by the same token a story assumes and requires individuality. Without unique—mutually distinguishable—individuals, the story could never get off the ground. Individuality and story are therefore like Siamese twins that cannot be separated.

They also have a common abode: plurality. Individuality, like the story, cannot exist without plurality, since individuality is only possible alongside another individuality with which it can be compared and contrasted; where there are not many individualities, there are none at all.

An attack on plurality is therefore an attack both on the story and on individuality. Indeed, the world of advanced totalitarianism is outstanding for the remarkable decline of individuality; a veil of vague, expressionless indistinguishability clings to everything, coloring it all gray. Paradoxically, this veil clings to its source as well: in banishing all other comparable individual agents from its own world, the central agent divests itself of its own individuality too. Hence the strange facelessness, transparency, and elusiveness of power, hence the blandness of its language, the anonymity of its decisions. Hence too its irresponsibility, for how can an agent be genuinely responsible when its identity is so blurred and when, moreover—because it is so isolated—there is no one left for it to be responsible to?

This antipathy to individuality is not something planned by the individuals who rule, but an intrinsic expression of late totalitarianism. Its centralism cannot co-exist with individuality. If we mix all the colors together, we get a dirty brown. The intention of totalitarianism is to make everything totally the same. Its fruit is uniformity, *Gleichschaltung,* and the herd mentality.

Standardized life creates standardized citizens with no wills of their own. It begets undifferentiated people with undifferentiated stories. It is a mass-producer of banality.

Anyone who resists too much, or despairs too much, or insists too much on having something of his own that exceeds the norm, or who tries to escape the standardized nothingness—either internally or by going abroad—in other words, anyone who sets himself apart is already on his way to a place where he will no longer disrupt the prescribed forms of social life: to jail.

Once a place where crimes were punished, prison is now a "correctional institute": a wastebasket for peculiar humans and their bizarre stories.

WHENEVER I found myself in a new cell, I was asked where I was from, and when I replied, "Prague," the question always came back: "Whereabouts in Prague?"

It would never have occurred to me to say I was from Dejvice, so at first the question surprised me. But very quickly I understood it: in this old-fashioned world of individual stories a thing as old-fashioned as a city quarter still plays a role. Obviously there are still people for whom Dejvice, Holešovice, or Libeň are not just addresses but a real home. People who have not capitulated to the standardizing and nihilizing pressure of the modern housing estate (where you can no longer tell what city you're in) and who still cling to their streets, the pubs on their corners, the former grocery store across the road—and to the mysterious and secret meaning of the stories connected to these localities.

The most natural of questions—where is your home?—I have heard asked most often in prison.

THE HISTORY of the system I live in has demonstrated persuasively that without a plurality of economic initiatives, and of people who participate in them, without competition, without a marketplace and its institutional guarantees, an economy will stagnate and decline.

Why then does this system so stubbornly resist all attempts to restore these proven instruments of economic life? Why is it that all such efforts have so far either been half-baked or else repressed?

The deepest reason is not the leaders' fear that it will conflict with the ideology, nor their personal conservatism, nor even the fear that if the center gives up its economic power, it will give up its political power as well.

The real reason, in my opinion, lies—again—in the totalitarian essence of the system itself, in its overwhelming inertia. It cannot relinquish its control of such an enormous and vital part of life as the economy. If it were to recognize the institutional guarantees of economic plurality and undertake to respect them, it would be acknowledging the legitimacy of something beyond its own claims to total power. This would deny its own totalitarian nature and it would cease to be itself. So far, overwhelming inertia has always prevented the system from carrying out this ontological self-destruction. (A stronger power may someday arise to oppose this inertia and compel the system genuinely to relinquish its essence, but this has never yet happened, anywhere.)

When he can no longer participate with relative autonomy in economic life, man loses some of his social and human individuality, and part of his hope of creating his own human story.

I mention this now because although the standardizing and therefore nihilizing impact of political and intellectual centralization is clear, the analogous impact of economic centralization—as one of the indirect methods of manipulating life in general—is far from being so obvious. And that is what makes it more dangerous.

WHERE there is no natural plurality of economic initiatives, the interplay of competing producers and their entrepreneurial ideas disappears, along with the interplay of supply and demand, the labor and commodity markets, and voluntary employer-employee relations. Gone too are the stimuli to creativity and its attendant risks, the drama of economic success and failure. Man as a producer ceases to be a participant or a creator in the economic story, and becomes an instrument. Everyone is an employee of the state, which is the one proprietor of economic truth and power. Everyone is buried in the anonymity of the collective economic "non-story."

When economic plurality disappears, the motives for competition in the marketplace of consumer goods disappear with it. The central power may talk all it wants about "satisfying differentiated needs" but the pressures of a nonpluralistic economy compel it to do exactly the opposite: to integrate production, standardize goods, and narrow the range of choice. In this artificial economic world, diversity is merely a complication.

Not only do consumers have to depend (as all who live in modern industrial societies do) almost exclusively on commodities they have not produced themselves; they do not have a choice of different commodities, and cannot express their individuality even in this limited way. All they have is what has been allocated by the monopoly producer: the same things that have been allocated to everyone.

A centralized furniture designer may not be the most typical representative of the totalitarian system, but as one who unconsciously realizes its nihilizing intentions, he may have more impact than five government ministers together. Millions of people have no choice but to spend their lives surrounded by his furniture.

Let me exaggerate deliberately. It would be to the greatest advantage of a centrally directed system of production if only one type of a prefabricated panel were produced, from which one type of apartment building would be constructed; these buildings in turn would be fitted with a single kind of door, doorhandle, window, toilet, washbasin, and so on, and together this would create a single type of housing development constructed according to one standardized urban development plan, with minor adjustments for landscape, given the regrettable irregularity of the earth's surface. (In each apartment, of course, there would be the same kind of television set showing the same program.)

Imperceptibly but irresistibly, not deliberately but inevitably, everything begins to resemble everything else: buildings, clothing, workplaces, public decorations, public transport, the forms of entertainment, the behavior of people in public and in their own homes.

This standardization of public and private spaces has a standardizing effect on life and its rhythms, narrowing the sphere of desires and aversions, of sensual experience and taste. It flattens the world and the people in it.

In such an environment, stories become interchangeable.

Is it any wonder that an ambitious reporter would rather risk his life in Lebanon?

IF A CITIZEN of our country wishes to travel abroad, get a new job, exchange his apartment or his stove, organize an amateur event, he is usually compelled to undertake a long and exhausting march through various offices for the necessary permits, certificates, recommendations, and he must frequently demean himself or bite his tongue. It is tiring, boring, and debilitating. Many people, out of disgust, or for fear it will drag them down, quickly give up on their most personal plans.

In doing so, they renounce something of their own potential story. It may be something of little importance. But the process of surrendering oneself begins with small matters.

Obviously, then, the bureaucratic regulation of the everyday details of people's lives is another indirect instrument of nihilization. It is here that public matters infiltrate private life in a way that is very "ordinary," but extremely persistent. The sheer number of small pressures that we are subjected to every day is more important than it may seem at first, because it encloses the space in which we are condemned to breathe.

There is very little air in that space. But not so little that we might suffocate, and thus create a story.

THESE examples do not exhaust the ways in which the totalitarian system, directly and indirectly, negates life.

The elimination of political plurality deprives society of a means to structure itself, because it prevents a variety of in-

344

terests and opinions and traditions from proclaiming their presence. The drastic curtailment of intellectual plurality makes it hard for a person to choose a way to relate to Being, to the world, and to himself. Culture and information controlled from the center narrow the horizon against which people mature. The demand for unquestioning loyalty forces people to become bit players in empty rituals. People cease to be autonomous and self-confident participants in the life of the community and become instruments with which the central agent fulfills itself. The ever present danger of being punished for any original expression compels one to move cautiously across the quicksand of one's potential, a pointlessly exhausting process. The network of bureaucratic limitations affects everything from one's choice of study or profession to the possibility of travel, the limits of admissible creative initiative, right down to the extent and kind of personal ownership, and all of this shrinks the space one has to act in. The total claim of the central power—respecting only those limits it imposes upon itself for practical reasons at a given moment—creates a state of general nervousness: no one is ever sure of the ground he stands on, or what he may venture to do, and what he may not, or what may happen to him if he does. The sway of this power over the executive authority of the legislature and the judiciary, coupled with the actual omnipotence of the police makes people insecure. The imperious vanity of the administrative apparatus, its anonymity, the extinction of individual responsibility in the faceless pseudo-responsibility of the system (anyone may offer excuses for anything, or be accused of anything, since the will of centralized power recognizes no arbitrator in any dispute with an individual) creates a sensation of helplessness and cripples the will to live one's own life.

All of that together—and much that is more subtle—lies behind our asthma.

On the surface of things, everything goes on just as it does anywhere else: people work, have fun, make love, die. Beneath this surface a destructive disease is gnawing away.

"Call me when the man dies."

345

In this case the patient will not die. Nevertheless, to keep his disease a secret amounts to encouraging its spread.

IN RECENT years, several very good film comedies have been made in Czechoslovakia that were successful at home and abroad. A couple of them were even nominated for Oscars.

However much I may enjoy such films, I can't shake the feeling there's something not right about them. American audiences, who do not have to suffer daily the asthma that prevails here, see nothing wrong with them.

What do these films have in common?

One important thing, I think: the stories they tell lack historical background. No matter how many superficial and ornamental techniques these films employ to suggest a specific locality and moment in time, they seem to exist outside space and time. The stories they tell could have happened anywhere.

There are two ways in which totalitarian pressure removes their historicity: directly, through censorship and self-censorship, both of which have evolved a sophisticated sensitivity to anything that might capture the historical dimension of life; and indirectly, by the destruction of historicity in life itself. It is, of course, extremely difficult to grasp the historic quality of a moment when a global attack on the very notion of history is taking place, because it means trying to tell the story of the loss of story, the story of asthma.

This double pressure forces a creative person to turn his attention to private life. And yet—as I've said—private and public life today (particularly under totalitarianism) are inseparable; they are like two linked vessels, and one cannot be represented truthfully if the other is ignored. Private life without an historical dimension is a facade and a lie.

Indeed, the picture of life that has been artificially reduced to its purely private dimension (or provided with superficial reminders of the public dimension, while skirting around everything essential in that dimension) inevitably becomes a strange anecdote, a *genre* picture, a familiar cliché, a fairy tale, a fiction concocted from thousands of living individualities. In such a presentation, even the most private life is oddly distorted, sometimes to the point where it becomes implausibly bizarre, the paradoxical outcome of a paralyzing desire for verisimilitude. It is obvious what has made this desire so intense: the subconscious need to compensate for the absence of the opposite pole—truth. It is as though life in this case were stripped of its inner tension, its true tragedy and greatness, its questions. The more charmingly all of its superficial features are caricatured, the more seriously the work misses the point. Imitating life, it falsifies it. Calligraphy replaces drawing.

In the films I'm talking about, what I miss is not this or that concrete bit of political detail. Some details from political reality are always there, sometimes more than is good for the work. I miss something else: a free vision of life as a whole. This is not a matter of theme: I can well imagine a film about nothing more than love and jealousy, yet where this freedom would not be lacking.

During the Nazi occupation, several popular film comedies were made in Czechoslovakia. They were remarkable for a similar ahistoricity and the untruths that flowed from it. Here again it wasn't the theme that was at fault: it wasn't images from concentration camps that I found lacking. I missed an inner freedom, and felt that their humor was only a slick way of making a virtue from necessity.

You can always tell in the end.

The domestic success of today's Czech film comedies has a problematic side to it. People find in them an odd consolation: their illusions are confirmed, that the asthma does not really exist and that, to the extent that it does exist, they can live with it; that it's not really important; that their lives have not been as ravaged as they sometimes seem in bad moments. It is pacifying.

These films tell unique stories. But they do not show the nihilizing pressure against which these stories were brought to life. People are thrilled to find that stories still exist. They are elated, and end up kidding themselves: they forget that the story is only on the screen. That it is not their story.

I don't know if there is anywhere to hide from the AIDS virus.

It seems to me, however, that there is no hiding place, no reservation, where one is safe from the virus of nihilization.

THERE is one sphere where the symptoms of our asthma can be observed better by a foreigner than by someone suffering from it. That sphere is the visible face of the daily life of society. We have long since got used to this face. But more than one observant visitor has been shocked by it.

Ride the escalators in the Prague subway and watch the faces of people going in the opposite direction. This journey is a pause in the daily rat race, a sudden stoppage of life, a frozen moment that may reveal more about us than we know. Perhaps it is one of those "moments of truth" when a person suddenly stands outside all relationships; he is in public, but alone with himself. The faces moving past are empty, strained, almost lifeless, without hope, without longing, without desire. The eyes are dull.

Or observe how people behave toward each other in stores, in offices, and on the streetcars: they tend to be surly, selfish, impolite, and disobliging; for the counter staff, customers are often an imposition: they serve while talking among themselves. When asked a question, they reply with distaste (if they know an answer at all). Drivers yell at each other, people in lineups elbow ahead and snap at each other. Bureaucrats don't care how many people are waiting to see them, or how long they wait. They often make appointments and fail to keep them. They get no pleasure from helping people and have no regrets when they can't. They are capable of slamming the door in a supplicant's face, cutting him off in mid-sentence. It would not be so depressing if these officials were not so often the final court of appeal.

Or look at people walking the streets: most of them are

rushed, their faces full of worry, inattentive to things around them. The sense of ease, cheerfulness, and spontaneity has vanished from the streets. In the evening or at night the streets are empty, and if you do happen to see a group of relaxed, happy people, they are usually foreigners.

Warmth, openness, kindness, and unassuming friendliness are vanishing from everyday public contacts. Everyone seems to have one thing on his mind: where to find what he is look-ing for. Indifference and bad manners are spreading; even in restaurants, people seem buttoned up. Mindful of their own behavior, they speak in low voices, checking to make sure no one else is listening. Class-four restaurants are the last oases of natural companionship, and they tend to be in the suburbs rather than in the city; these are the places one remembers in prison. But even in such places, more and more people come there just to get drunk.

At the bottom of all this lies a vague stress: people are either nervous, anxious, irritated, or else they are apath-etic. They look as if they expect to be hit from an un-expected quarter. Calm and certainty have been replaced by aggression.

It is the stress of people living under a constant threat. It is the stress of people compelled, every day, to deal with absurdity and nothingness.

It is the stress of a people living in a city under siege.

The stress of a society that is not permitted to live in history. The stress of people exposed to the radiation of totalitarianism.

LIFE, of course, goes on. It resists manipulation in many ways, adapting to it or finding ways to cope. It has not been de-stroyed, nor is it ever likely to be. Cracks can always be found for it to penetrate, levels where it can go on developing, ways in which, even in this suffocating milieu, it can arrange itself into stories. Somehow we will always manage to write our stories by the way we act.

I am not describing anything like the end of humanity. I

am instead trying to draw attention to the inconspicuous and unspectacular war that life wages every day against nothingness.

I am attempting to say that the struggle of the story and of history to resist nihilization is in itself a story, and belongs to history.

It is our special metastory.

We do not yet know how to talk about it because the traditional forms of storytelling fail us here. We do not yet know the laws that govern our metastory. We do not even know yet exactly who or what is the main villain of the story (it is definitely not a few individuals in the power center: they too are victims of something larger, just as we are).

It is clear: we must tell the story of our asthma, not despite the fact that people are dying from it, but because they are not.

One small detail remains: we have to learn how to do it.

April 1987

Meeting Gorbachev

Havel wrote "Meeting Gorbachev" (July 1987) for a collection of essays on Gorbachev prepared by Rowohlt Verlag, Havel's publisher in Hamburg. In Czech *samizdat,* its first appearance was in *Obsah* (September 1987), and in English, in *Granta,* no. 23 (Spring 1988). Translated by George Theiner.

T HE PROPOSED visit by the Glasnost Czar to the very country that is governed by those opposed to glasnost has evidently aroused many expectations. It has brought an unprecedented number of journalists to Prague. They arrive in good time; it is the Glasnost Czar himself who keeps postponing the trip. And so the waiting newsmen occupy themselves as best they can. Dozens of them call on me; they all want to know what I think of the new Czar. But it is embarrassing to have to keep repeating the same thoughts over and again, especially as none of them seems at all original to me: whatever I say, I am struck by the feeling that I have heard it or read it before somewhere.

Finally he arrives, and I can relax. The journalists now have something more interesting to do than listen to me telling them things they have already written.

I LIVE near the Prague National Theatre; it's half-past nine in the evening, not a reporter in sight, so I take my dog for a walk. And what do we see? Endless rows of parked limousines and a vast number of policemen. Of course: Gorbachev is in the National Theatre watching a gala performance. Unable to resist, I make for the theatre, and thanks to my dog, who clears a path through the crowd, I manage to struggle through to the front. I stand and wait; the show must be over any minute. I look around at the people on the pavement and listen. They're just passers-by, not an organized "rent-a-crowd," nor even people who came to catch a glimpse of Gorbachev—just nosy individuals, on their way to or from the pub or out for an evening stroll and who, like me, noticed something unusual and stopped out of curiosity. Their talk is full of sarcasm, aimed in particular at the long ranks of secret policemen, who remain impassive, obviously under orders not to do anything that might cast a shadow on Gorbachev's visit.

At long last the police suddenly come to life, the limousines' lights are switched on and their engines started, the dignitaries begin to trickle out of the theatre. And, lo and behold, there he is, Raisa at his side, plainclothes cops swarming all around them.

Just then I have my first surprise: all these cynics, all these sarcastic wits, who just a few seconds before were making merciless fun of their rulers and their bodyguards, are suddenly transformed, as if by magic, into an enthusiastic, frenetically cheering crowd, fighting to get as near as possible to the leader-in-chief.

No: this is not about "eternal friendship with the Soviet Union"—this is something more dangerous: these people are cheering a man who, they hope, is bringing them freedom.

I feel sad; this nation of ours never learns. How many times has it put all its faith in some external force which, it believed, would solve its problems? How many times had it ended up bitterly disillusioned, forced to admit that it could not expect help from anyone unless it was prepared, first and foremost, to help itself? And yet here we are again, making exactly the same mistake. They seem to think that Gorbachev has come to liberate them from Husák!

By now the Glasnost Czar has reached the spot where I am standing. He is rather short and stocky, a cuddly ball-like figure hemmed in by his gigantic bodyguards, giving the impression of someone shy and helpless. On his face is what I take to be a sincere smile, and he waves to us in an almost conspiratorial way, as if greeting each and every one of us individually.

And then comes my second surprise: all of a sudden I find myself feeling sorry for him.

I try to imagine the life he must lead, all day long in the company of his hard-faced guardians, no doubt with a full agenda, endless meetings, negotiation sessions, and speeches: having to talk to a great many people; remember who is who; say witty things but at the same time make sure they are the *correct* things to say, things that the sensation-seeking outside world can't get hold of and use against him; needing always to be seen smiling and attending functions such as tonight's, when he would surely have preferred a quiet evening and a rest.

But I quickly suppress this twinge of compassion. After all, I say to myself, he has what he wants. He obviously enjoys this sort of life, or he wouldn't have chosen it in the first place. I refuse to feel sorry for him, rebuking myself for acting like all those idiots in the West who melt like snowmen in the sun as soon as some eastern potentate smiles charmingly in their direction. Be realistic, I admonish myself; stick to what you've been handing out to all these foreign journalists for the last three days.

Gorbachev, the same man who here in Prague praised one of the worst governments our country has had in modern times, is walking just a few yards away from me, waving and smiling his friendly smile—and suddenly he seems to be waving and smiling at *me*.

And so to my third surprise: I realize that my sense of courtesy, compelling me to respond to a friendly greeting, works more quickly than my sense of politics, for here I am, shyly raising my arm and waving back at him.

Suddenly the small, ball-like figure disappears inside his official limousine and is driven off at top speed.

The crowd disperses slowly; people continue their journey home or to the pub, wherever it is they were going before coming across this unexpected excitement.

I walk my dog home and try to analyze my reactions.

And so to my fourth and last surprise: I don't feel the slightest regret at having given Gorbachev that shy little wave. I really don't have any reason not to return the Glasnost Czar's greeting. It is, after all, one thing to respond to his smile, but something else again to try and excuse my own reaction by blaming him for smiling in the first place.

July 1987

Farce, Reformability, and the Future of the World

"Farce, Reformability, and the Future of the World" (October 1987) was written for a Czechoslovak-German collection on the twentieth anniversary of the Prague Spring, and dedicated to Jaroslav Šabata on his sixtieth birthday. This is its first appearance in English, in a translation by A. G. Brain.

I

T IS an amusing coincidence: the twentieth anniversary of the Soviet invasion that suppressed the Prague Spring has come at a time when Gorbachev is trying to institute wide-ranging reforms in the Soviet Union and when even in Czechoslovakia, the satraps who were installed by the Soviets and still follow them blindly find themselves obliged to talk of reforms. Marx's well-known dictum that events in history repeat themselves, first as tragedy and then as farce, is perfectly illustrated by what is happening in Czechoslovakia. So far the "second renewal process" in Czechoslovakia has all the trappings of farce. I will explain why this is so, but only briefly, as I think that this "amusing coincidence" invites us to reflect on a number of more general and crucial issues related to communism as such.

BUT LET me deal first of all with what I call the "Czechoslovak farce." Why "farce"?

355

In the wake of the Soviet intervention, when they were looking around for people to run the country and "normalize" it, there were not a lot to choose from. The team that was finally assembled consisted largely of a motley assortment of leftovers from the distant past—hard-line Stalinists and a few life-long toadies who could have worked for any side. It undoubtedly included a few intelligent individuals who had a clear idea where things stood, but these people had little influence, most likely because they lacked the courage to use what little influence they might have had. This team of normalizers has spent twenty years persecuting anyone associated in any way with the attempted reforms of the Prague Spring, as well as all those who were not one hundred percent loyal to the regime. The country's present leadership, in other words, is thoroughly antireformist, and over the past twenty years it has managed to create one of the most rigid, sterile, and stagnant types of communism in the world. When they now start babbling on about reforms, they make themselves a laughingstock. No one takes them seriously. No one believes them. Everyone knows it is empty talk that hides an unbending determination not to change, and not to let anyone else take control. The people who have spent twenty years ruining this country, and who now begin to criticize the devastation and talk about the need for remedies and changes without any intention of giving up their own power and privilege, must be regarded with derision by all sensible people. That is quite simply the way it is.

The Czechs and Slovaks are not passionate people. They seldom get worked up about anything. In 1968, though, they passionately believed that things could get better and they started getting actively involved. But they got burned, and they have been paying for their enthusiasm for twenty years now. Only a fool would expect that after such a bitter experience they could be worked up again and persuaded to risk an analogous fate for their involvement, especially since they are being asked to get involved by the very people who have for so long been systematically punishing them for their past enthusiasm.

Skepticism is now so general and so deep-seated that I find it impossible to imagine the kind of leader it would take to stand in Husák's place and get this society moving again. Of course, we should always take the government at its word and demand that it practice what it proclaims. Charter 77 has been doing this for years now, and quite a few other people and groups are doing likewise. Society as a whole, though, is doing nothing. True, people follow these efforts with interest and sympathy, but although they know it is the right thing to do, they are extremely cautious. History has taught them not to trust communists in any way. As a result, yet another farcical aspect of the situation in Czechoslovakia today is the government's never-ending calls for nationwide discussions—whether of a new "enterprise law," a new constitution, or whatever it is—while people maintain stony silence at all meetings where such discussions are supposed to take place.

A third aspect of the farce comes from ideology. When a regime, after having spent twenty years using ideological means to crush reformist ideas and justify its own opposition to reform, suddenly begins to use its favorite Marxist sophistry to propagate a "new reformism" and portray it as part and parcel of its previous antireformist course, the verbal sleight of hand must inevitably appear comical to those on the receiving end. Some of the speeches by Messrs. Biľak and Fojtík are best-sellers by now and fetch a high price on the alternative book market: not for their boldness but for their crass stupidity.

DON'T get me wrong: I am not advocating skepticism—I simply note its existence.

I have two more general points to make about what has become a regular recurrence of "revivals," "reforms," and "perestroikas," and their repeated suppression.

First, the Kronstadt Mutiny, the Hungarian Revolution, the Prague Spring, the Solidarity era, Khrushchev's thaw, and now Gorbachev's version of it, and so on—all these attempts at "doing something about it"—despite thousands of individual differences, are variations of a single historical trend: society's desire to limit, moderate, or eliminate the totalitarian nature of the communist system. It is no coincidence that, sooner or later, all these events give rise, in one form or another, to the same basic demands: greater intellectual freedom, less centralism, political plurality, a workers' voice in industry, the independence of firms, economic competition, small private enterprise, authentic trade union rights, limits to the omnipotence of the ruling party or of its apparat, curbing the omnipotence of the police, the eliminating of historical and other taboos, the rehabilitation of all victims of tyrannical cruelty, greater respect for national independence and minority rights, and so on.

The communist system is—or, more precisely, has always been so up to now—a totalitarian system, whether it had the "human face" of Dubček's time (when it was even possible to live well) or the gangsterism of Pol Pot's regime (under which death seems to have been the only option). The system's totalitarian character conflicts with life's own intrinsic tendency toward heterogeneity, diversity, uniqueness, autonomy—in a word, toward plurality. This is why life inevitably obstructs and resists a totalitarian system. And it does so in a whole range of ways: on one occasion it might take the form of a bloody uprising, on another the nonviolent creation of parallel structures, while on a third occasion, life's natural demands can infiltrate the very brains and organs of the regime. A fourth kind of resistance is the extraordinary capacity of some people to ignore the regime and its ideology. In all instances, however, it is basically the same resistance to the same phenomenon: it is life versus totalitarianism.

There are some who respect the Kronstadt Mutiny and the Hungarian Revolution and regard all the rest—and most of all Gorbachev's perestroika—as downright fraud, because in their view it should be all or nothing, and because a gun is the only thing communists understand. Then there are those who respect the Prague Spring and rave over Gorbachev but regard everything else, including the Polish Solidarity movement, as indefensible anticommunist, bourgeois-reactionary,

extremist nonsense. Both attitudes come from unhappy individuals locked inside their own political and ideological
paradigms, dogmas, and clichés, or alternatively, in their
pragmatism (which is meant to display their extraordinary
political perspicacity). To the latter, the former are pitiful
slaves of anticommunist ideological fanaticism, who see only
one possible solution: the extermination of the communists.
To the former, the latter are equally pitiful slaves of Marxist
Utopias, and their natural counterparts; they walk a dialectical tightrope, skillfully "differentiating" between what it is
advisable and possible to say, and what is inadvisable to say
if one does not want to risk losing one's left-wing credentials.
But it's hard to persuade history to run according to somebody's ideological dreams. It takes every possible twist and
turn, usually quite different from the course prescribed by
ideological prophets of all hues. This is why life's resistance
to totalitarianism takes so many different forms. [. . .]

Naturally these historical events could all be described and
analyzed in a calm, objective, and qualified fashion. But it is
unacceptable to reject some and accept others solely on the
basis of political or ideological prejudice, because someone
somewhere took a shortcut and identified with one particular
doctrine. Such an approach is unacceptable because in all
cases the outcome would be identical: the meaning of the
events would remain obscured, because their common basis
would remain concealed.

SECOND, in recent years, the Czech and Slovak press—by which
I mean that published both abroad by exiles and at home in
samizdat—has frequently got worked up over a controversy
which I find rather quaint and have never been able to understand. In fact, I find it almost as comical as the present
Czechoslovak "Revival Process II." I refer to the controversy
over communism's "reformability." One side tries to prove
that it is reformable, the other that it is not. Geysers of pas-
sion are released on both sides.

In my opinion, the issue is entirely academic. The only peo-

ple it might interest are those who, for whatever reason, prefer to remain with their heads in the ideological clouds.
Besides, an ideologist is also a prophet, in the sense that his
concern is with the future of the world, and he knows what
can and cannot happen to a particular system. This controversy is comical because it is a quarrel between two groups
of prophets, one of which is convinced that communism—
being unreformable—cannot be reformed, while the other is
convinced that communism—being reformable—is open to
reform.

In the first place, much depends on what meaning is attached to the word "reform." Where does reform begin and
where does it end? What fits the category and what falls outside it? For instance, if we say that communism of a more
bearable kind—one in which we can breathe more freely and
lead a happier existence, one in which there is greater freedom and rational behavior, one in which the police cannot
do whatever they like—is "reformed," "reformist," or "reforming," then the answer is so obvious it makes no sense to
waste any more time on it. We all know, for instance, that it
makes a difference whether we live under Stalin's communism, Dubček's communism, Kádár's communism, Mao's communism, Pol Pot's communism, or Novotný's communism.
Clearly, some of these are more bearable than others, and if
the degree of bearableness is an indicator of reform, then
communism is certainly reformable, otherwise all forms of
communism would be equally unbearable. [. . .]

If, however, we are debating about the totalitarian basis of
communism, that is quite a different matter. Totalitarianism
is intrinsic to communism, a tendency it has always had, ir-
respective of whether a local variant is bearable or totally
unbearable. The external manifestation of this totalitarian basis is the familiar principle of the "leading role of the Communist Party." In more bearable communisms, this principle
is easier to put up with. In fact, it might be said that such
communisms are less totalitarian than others. But nowhere is
there such a thing as nontotalitarian communism, nor has

there ever been. Thus, if the notion that communism is non-reformable is asserted by someone who understands reform to mean communism's abandoning its totalitarian basis, then I have to admit that I fully sympathize with them. So far, no communist state has ever opened itself up to full political pluralism. The totalitarian essence of communism has an enormous inertia and such complex mechanisms of manipulation that any attempt so far to challenge it has always been severely suppressed. But the fact that such protagonists of nonreformability have my sympathy does not mean I share their view. They are probably right about how things have happened so far. But I deny them their claim to certainty that the communist system will never ever abandon its totalitarian nature. How can they possibly tell? What if powerful forces (a deepening economic and social crisis, international pressures, autonomous self-organization of society, a change of heart on the part of political leaders, and so on) should one day combine into one mighty force, so powerful that it overcomes the totalitarian inertia? It might happen dramatically, in the space of a few days, or it might be a gradual process that lasts several decades. But how can one be so arrogant as to maintain with total assurance that something like that could simply never, ever occur?

Anything can happen.

It is hardly likely that in the foreseeable future a communist state will utterly abandon totalitarianism of its own accord (and possibly then only due to the enlightenment of its leaders!). That is more or less obvious. But it seems equally obvious that history is unlikely to remain static, either.

Of course, there could be a world war (though I don't think it very likely). That could lead to communism everywhere— or alternatively, nowhere at all. The most probable result, though, would be neither communism nor democracy, because there would be quite simply nothing left.

But are these really the only alternatives: that history either stands still or comes to an end? Surely this is nonsense. Equally nonsensical, it seems to me, is the assertion that it is entirely out of the question that some bearable form of communism should go on getting more bearable until one day—though God knows when, how, and under what influence—it finally loses its totalitarian essence.

WHERE does that leave us?

The way I see it, the only possible alternative for us is not to worry about ideological nonissues, but instead to make practical efforts—here and now, whatever we are doing, and wherever we are—to change things for the better, to try to win more freedom, more respect for human dignity, to work for an economy that functions better, less destruction of the earth, government by more sensible politicians, the right to speak the truth—and finally, to ensure that people do not lose hope when confronted with the truth, but instead try to draw the practical lessons from it.

October 1987

Thinking About František K.

"Thinking About František K." (January 23, 1988). Havel wrote this on the occasion of what would have been František Kriegel's eightieth birthday. Kriegel, a medical doctor and reform-minded communist, was the only man in Dubček's praesidium who refused to sign the Moscow protocols that essentially legitimized the Soviet invasion of Czechoslovakia in August 1968. He became an "outcast" overnight and joined forces with the dissidents in the 1970s, eventually signing Charter 77. He was placed under constant police surveillance, and died in 1979.

A version of this translation, by A. G. Brain, first appeared in an English edition of *Listy, the Journal of the Czechoslovak Socialist Opposition,* no. 1 (1988).

I HAVE spent the whole day in the company of František Kriegel, sifting through all sorts of documents about him, and reading his personal jottings, his speeches, and his letters. All the while I have been reliving our own meetings, and pondering on him.

As I did so, a strange question crept into my thoughts: Wasn't this man actually a tragic figure, one of the great tragic figures of our recent history?

IT SEEMS that nowadays we are endowed with a dual way of being. As in the past, we are real people living in a familiar, everyday world. At the same time, however, we constitute the building blocks of a world that I would describe (perhaps too forcefully for some ears) as a world of ideological and political babble. It is a world in which everything is done "in the name of" man and for his "good," one in which man is the "first principle" and "supreme goal," the only real concern. It's as if we all were here in two separate guises: as individual human beings living on this planet, and as the abstract subject matter of theories and speeches. However, the more they rant about "our" interests—whether out of obsession, hypocrisy, routine, or callousness—the more we seem to suffer as real people.

František Kriegel was someone who stood squarely on the side of real people. He loved people as individuals and served them all his days—as a doctor in hospitals and on the battlefield, as a neighbor in everyday life, or as a politician. He did so both by being mindful of them and, when necessary, by acting in terms of their own moral standards, from which he refused to be alienated by politics. (And incidentally, this was how he managed to save the reputation of Czechoslovak politics in August 1968.)

This is confirmed in the countless good deeds he performed for people, so many in fact that no one living has a complete idea because he was reluctant to speak about them. It is also confirmed by the things he did not do. For instance, he never became a professional politician—despite the pressures on him to do so—and he systematically refused to accept the privileges that could have been his in the offices he held. He did not wish to alienate himself from the world of real people, and he never confused them with the abstract man so readily invoked by those whose interest in real people goes no further than themselves.

Not only was Kriegel an unassuming, courageous, and magnanimous man, but he was also firmly rooted in a world in which the awareness of what is good and what is evil, what is decent and what is contemptible, what is honor and what is betrayal, has not been reduced and destroyed by ideological juggling, pragmatic political speculation, or Machiavellian

schemes that always manage to show persuasively that something especially nasty has been carried out in the higher interest.

What determined the course of Kriegel's life—as citizen,
doctor, or politician—was an undemonstrative love for real
people and loyalty to his own private human conscience.

I BELIEVE that a basic attitude to life like his cannot be explained solely by psychological makeup. It must derive from
a profound respect (though unconscious, and one to which
a materialist could not admit) for the order of Being that is
hidden beneath the surface of the world of phenomena, and
which is a permanent explanation of its transience. I refer to
that which transcends all individual "minds," in other words,
the only rational source and meaning of true human responsibility: the sort of responsibility that does not need to be
recognized by anyone in the world of phenomena. It is no
coincidence that the only politician who was willing to put
his life on the line in August 1968 for the sake of our national
community was the same man who was later seen on the
streets of Prague paying tribute to one of the victims of the
foreign aggression, believing he went unobserved.

EVERYTHING I have mentioned so far would make him a great
human being, but not necessarily a tragic one. I will try to
explain why I feel there is a tragic dimension to Kriegel's
greatness.

IT IS clearly no easy task to transform one's life into a coherent succession of good deeds that assist specific, individual
people. There are even circumstances in which, for someone
with a sharp intellect and a conscience that cannot be fooled,
such an endeavor can actually become a means of escape and
self-deception. Merely remedying individual ills can be an excuse for not undertaking the more strenuous and important

365

task of seeking their root causes and understanding their wider implications.

As someone who had a personal experience of poverty, injustice, racial hatred, and social inequity, and as an educated person who tried to look beyond private concerns in search of their general significance, Kriegel realized early in his life that he could not confront human suffering solely as a good neighbor and doctor, but, if he was to remain true to his conscience, he had also to try to understand the social context of that suffering and discover a social way to eliminate it. In other words, he had to go into politics.

As he was coming to manhood, he found himself faced with an enticing prospect: a political movement that offered both a consistent explanation of the world's contradictions and a comprehensive program for resolving them. Moreover, the loudly vaunted "scientific" basis of that program appealed to the modern spirit of rationality while at the same time offering, paradoxically, a new variant (and hence one acceptable to someone with such an outlook) of what people from time immemorial have always needed and sought: faith.

František Kriegel became a communist, and remained one throughout his life. As a communist, he fought against fascism in Spain and China. As a communist, he was politically active in postwar Czechoslovakia and participated in the takeover of power by the Communist Party in February 1948. As a communist, he organized the public health service here and in Cuba. As a communist, he worked as a parliamentarian and subsequently in the upper echelons of the Communist Party.

How COULD someone with Kriegel's personal makeup—someone with such a firm attachment to the real world and a distinct preference for real people, someone with such a profound respect for the pre-ideological ethical tenets held by those who truly live in the everyday world—put up with the ideology, beliefs, political methods, and political demands of a movement that had managed to exalt the imaginary—

and hence readily manipulated—world of so-called higher interests and universal ideals above that of ordinary human feelings and common sense (and the discreet way this was done was partly the secret of its success)? How could such a person see eye to eye with a movement that was capable, when the need arose, of dismissing such feelings and common sense as sheer superstition and self-deception? How could a lifelong respect for real people co-exist with a life-long belief in an ideology based—as the years and decades have shown ever more plainly—on an abstract idea of man?

There was nothing of the opportunist, Machiavellian, or cynical pragmatist about František Kriegel. I can't imagine him ever making a cold-blooded, self-interested compromise between the demands of his conscience and those of his ideology and party. Had he been capable of doing so, he would have been neither a great nor a tragic figure, merely someone pitiable and banal.

What lends his fate a tragic dimension—as far as my (necessarily fallible) eyes and senses can tell—is that not only was his conscience true, authentic, and honest, so was his belief. This meant that all the compromises he had to make at one time or another between those two conflicting forces were always intrinsically authentic, sincere, and honest—if that is at all possible. Some of them were undoubtedly good for our country, relatively speaking, at least: his courageous stands in the fifties, his reforming efforts in the sixties, his heroism in 1968, his consistent opposition to Husák's dictatorial regime and his commitment to Charter 77. On the other hand, many of those compromises were undoubtedly destructive and pitiful affairs, such as his part in enforcing the monopoly of the Communist Party under Gottwald. But beneficial or harmful, what makes Kriegel a tragic figure is precisely the fact that these compromises did not emanate from insidious self-interest, they were the work of a human being who was genuine in all his dealings and always intrinsically true to himself.

· · ·

LET US try to put ourselves in his shoes.

Here was an honorable man, one who could never tolerate unfairness and injustice—but who was also a communist and therefore loyal to a party that was responsible for so much unfairness and injustice. How was he to retain his belief and not abet evil?

Here was a man who wanted to help people in practical ways here and now—while at the same time identifying with an ideology capable of justifying any momentary evil by pointing to a utopian vision of radiant tomorrows somewhere in the distant future.

Here was a man who believed heart and soul in the equality of all people, but who was also a member of a party that claimed for its members a higher status than anyone else.

It could not have been easy for such a person—either within his own conscience or within his party. And indeed, in common with many other honest communists, he did find it a constant source of difficulty. The party slandered him for his courageous struggle in Spain, it persecuted him in the fifties, it expelled him in 1969, and mercilessly hounded him to death, before finally displaying the full depth of its depravity when it denied him a dignified funeral.

Yet despite everything, he never renounced his socialist convictions.

He confronted the tragic discrepancy between his convictions and his natural humanity by striving over the years to humanize the communist system where possible and subsequently by identifying with the concept of democratic socialism. But even that compromise was to remain a tragic contradiction: after all, how can genuine democracy be reconciled with the principle of the leading role of a single ideology and a single party whose power is guaranteed for all time? Or, conversely: how, in conditions of a truly democratic contest for power, is it possible to guarantee, once and for all, that the economy will be organized in a single, predetermined manner?

· · ·

As I READ Kriegel's speeches to the National Assembly from all those years ago, I am overcome with sadness at how many good intentions they contain—all of them hopelessly wrapped up in the political prejudices and jargon of those days and all of them relying, incredibly, on a belief in the capacity for democratic improvement in the different institutional constants, factors whose intrinsic purpose is to eliminate the possibility of any such amelioration.

All that wide-ranging, inconspicuous activity, involving such risk and never particularly successful, could not have been the product of opportunism or self-seeking ambition.

For years, František Kriegel sincerely believed that it was possible, from the inside, to breathe more humanity into an inhuman system.

AT LENGTH, of course, tough historical lessons and countless deep disappointments effectively transformed and narrowed the range of issues to which his political convictions drew him. Gradually he was compelled to renounce many of the timeworn dogmas of his belief and acknowledge the malevolence and insidiousness of much of what was formerly sacrosanct. The fabric of the ideology he had once found so robust and inviolable gradually disintegrated in the light of the knowledge revealed to him by his sense of justice and his spiritual integrity.

What a tragic process that must also have been! How cruel it must have been to repudiate things which one has asserted for so long and with such enthusiasm, and to which one has sacrificed so much!

To my knowledge, Kriegel never displayed anguish, disappointment, misgivings, or despair. He kept his bitterness to himself, like a man. He was always a source of encouragement to his companions and never required any consolation in return; he was too proud for that.

And that probably made what was happening inside him all the harder to bear.

. . .

OF COURSE he never gave up his belief entirely: he dedicated his entire life to socialism and died believing in it. He, who knew far better than anyone else what the socialist ideal had become in practice and what—in its Leninist variant, at least— it must inevitably become: total domination by the state as the universal employer and exploiter of all working people, the central manipulator of all areas of life, and the most inept capitalist conceivable. An ideology that originally declared that it would gradually abolish the state had given rise to the mightiest state ever known: the totalitarian state. And the "liberated" working people had ended up casting envious glances at the rights enjoyed by their counterparts in the capitalist countries.

What kind of socialism did the man who realized all that believe in at the end of his days? After all those bitter experiences, what did that word conjure up for him? A pluralist system of autonomous economic entities? Enterprises owned by their employees? Economic self-management? Market relations? Cooperatives and small-scale private enterprise? He must have realized that genuine economic pluralism is impossible without unlimited political pluralism. But what, in his eyes, did such a concept have in common with socialism? After all, as far as the communists were concerned, "socialism" was never anything but a codeword for their monopoly of power (any threats to which were—and still are!—always designated as the "dismantling of socialism by antisocialist forces"). Did he abandon that traditional communist concept of socialism in favor of some other, such as the social democratic one?

I don't know. I had always looked forward to having a frank and detailed discussion of all these matters with him. Even when I was in Ruzyně Prison in 1979 (not long after the morning when they woke me to take me to my father's funeral), I was still planning, as soon as I got out, to invite him and his wife, Riva, for a long discussion. It was not to be: during a recess in our appeal hearing, my co-defendant Otka Bednařová whispered to me the news of his recent death.

All I can do now is speculate. I have the feeling that in the final years of his life, František Kriegel held ideas about the best way of organizing society that were like mine and those of many others who have long since abandoned the word "socialism" because of its semantic ambiguity.

He never gave up using the word, though. Why, I wonder? Had he, toward the end of his days, gone back to where he started—to socialism as an idea—but somehow conceived it afresh? Or was it that the word "socialism," like that other word, "comrade," was the last remaining magic symbol of a long-dissolved community of co-believers, one from which he found it impossible to part? Did he cling to it as a symbol of the ethical continuity of his life? Or was it a reminder of his former ideals and enthusiasm and his bygone struggles, of his historical credentials, so to speak? Was it perhaps a bond with his Eurocommunist friends in the West, those fortunate innocents who had not had the experience and inevitable disillusionment of building socialism, but for whom the word still retained the sweet fragrance of the future? Or was it for him just another name for a better world?

THE TRAGIC paradoxes that I sense in the personality, achievement, and fate of František Kriegel are not exclusive to him, nor even to communists. They epitomize or even symbolize much deeper paradoxes, possibly even the fundamental paradoxes of modern times.

I will try to allude to them by posing a number of questions:

Is it possible in today's complex world for people who are guided by their consciences or the basic ethical categories of the everyday world to take an active part in politics? Or must they always, albeit only within part of themselves, belong also to the world of ideologies, doctrines, political religions, and commonly accepted dogmas and clichés? Is it enough for them to believe in life, in the good, and in their own reason? Or must they also believe in something not quite so pure and simple, such as their own political party? Can people who are truly pure in heart, people of independent spirit determined to be guided by it alone, attain the summit of real power in a world of sectional interests, irrational passions, "political realities," power-seeking ideologies, and blind revolt, in short, in the chaotic world of modern civilization? Can such people be successful in these spheres? Or have they no alternative but to get involved—either for reasons of realistic compromise or idealistic belief—in something else, something that the world finds more credible, something that may be in accord with their consciences in the immediate term but can turn against them at any time?

YOUNG people in Czechoslovakia today are quite unaware that we used to have politicians in this country—even communist ones—who were normal, honorable, and stalwart people, despite their often tragic fates. It is hard for the younger generation to imagine anything of the kind nowadays, since the only national leaders they know are faceless bureaucrats with corpselike expressions, who are driven at breakneck speed through the traffic in their limousines, or are occasionally seen on TV reading tedious platitudes that have scarcely any bearing on real life. If only for the benefit of these young people, František Kriegel deserves to have a true and compelling book written about him; not just to preserve the memory of that remarkable man, but so that the younger generation might gain a better understanding of the complex world they live in, so that they might better understand why their forebears did what they did, and learn more about their problems, ideals, illusions, successes, and defeats. It might also help them to realize that even in today's world it is possible to work for something meaningful so long as they do not fear obstacles and sacrifice. And lastly, it might bring home to them that politics and politicians are not necessarily objects of mockery, but can also be objects of respect.

January 1988

Testing Ground

"Testing Ground" (July 3, 1989) was written for the London daily *The Independent,* where it appeared on July 10, 1989, under the headline "A Society at the End of Its Patience." It comments on the appearance, on June 29, 1989, of a petition called "A Few Sentences," which Havel helped to initiate, and enjoyed enormous support among citizens who had hitherto remained passive. By this time, Charter 77 was by no means the only human rights group in Czechoslovakia, and "A Few Sentences," signed by tens of thousands, was a sign that the barriers between "dissidents" and "ordinary people" had begun to topple. "Testing Ground" was translated by A. G. Brain.

WHILE in their various ways (and with many understandable difficulties) Poland, Hungary, and the U.S.S.R. are trying to transform a communist-style totalitarian system into something more democratic, the Czechoslovak leadership is resisting tooth and nail. Admittedly it, too, vehemently endorses "perestroika" and "democratization." The fact is, however, that it is changing nothing, or countenancing only minor changes—forced on it, moreover, by pressure "from below."

As a policy it quite understandable, to say the least. This leadership was installed by Brezhnev's tanks. Antireformism became its ideological justification and the buttressing of the totalitarian system its daily practice. Naturally they have no wish to change this all of a sudden for fear that they might saw through the branch they are sitting on.

Though long decimated, silenced, and fragmented, society is slowly beginning to lose patience. Aroused by what is happening in the neighboring countries and disgusted at the government's inability to solve the mounting problems, it is beginning to awaken. People are showing increasing interest in public affairs, seeking out truthful information, and losing their fear of speaking their minds. As a result, even the "dissidents"—i.e., people involved in the independent initiatives (of which the oldest and best known is Charter 77), who are prepared to express themselves freely regardless of the personal consequences—are no longer an isolated handful of suicidal maniacs who might enjoy the tacit admiration of the public but could not expect any visible help from it, as was the case for years. As fear of the state police dwindles, so does fear of dissidents.

The spontaneous independent demonstrations in August, October, and December of 1988, and the subsequent January demonstrations in 1989 and everything that has ensued since, provide clear evidence of this movement. When I heard huge crowds shouting "Long live the Charter!" or "The Charter will win!", and when later, after my return from four months in prison, I saw a video of throngs of young people shouting "Release Havel!", I felt the most extraordinary mixture of emotions: as well as being moved and astonished, I also felt a kind of satisfaction. I suddenly realized that the years of onerous efforts by the "suicidal maniacs" in question, efforts which had cost them many dozens of years in prison, were at last beginning to pay off. It was not solely as a sign of respect for the Charter's years of efforts that the slogan "Long live the Charter!" pleased me. It was above all because it expressed an ever deeper yearning for freedom that uses the Charter as a symbol that makes a good slogan, one that leaves no one in any doubt about the attachment to freedom of those who shout it. Another big change is the fact that for the first time in twenty years thousands of well-known artists, performers, and academics employed in the official structures and therefore having every reason to be cautious have found the courage to speak out publicly. Not only did they protest against the actions of the police in January, they actually signed their protests jointly with those feared "dissidents" who for years had been slandered by the state.

For the time being, this social awakening has culminated in the statement entitled "A Few Sentences." This is no longer a mere defense of society against a specific case of tyranny, but instead a positive political statement. Its signatories warn the government that the only way out of the blind alley in which Czechoslovakia finds itself today—and indeed the precondition for any changes toward democracy in the system—is to effect a fundamental alteration of the social climate. In the words of the statement, "the spirit of freedom, trust, tolerance, and plurality" must be restored. The statement puts forward a number of simple demands that are easily fulfilled but which would foster such a climate. The statement is based on the entirely logical argument that if changes in the system are not to be temporary, piecemeal, inconsequential, or half-baked, they must first of all be discussed in a businesslike manner, and conditions must be created to enable such a businesslike discussion to take place.

"A Few Sentences" has already been signed by thousands of people, from well-known actors to unknown workers, from representatives of independent initiatives to rank-and-file communists, from Catholics to former communist leaders. The collection of signatures is continuing throughout the republic in spite of an extremely hasty and violent rebuff on the part of the regime which, according to its twisted Stalinist logic, has dubbed this peaceable call to dialogue "an attempt at confrontation."

For the moment, no one knows what will happen next. The regime has decided on confrontation, and perhaps it will unleash a fresh wave of repression in an attempt to intimidate society once more (which, however, it will have increasing trouble in doing). Maybe this is just its initial terror-stricken emotive reaction, and common sense will eventually prevail within its ranks, bringing hopes at last that Czechoslovakia too will engage in a free, society-wide debate leading to reform. Anything is possible at this particular moment. Never in the past twenty years has the situation been as wide open as now.

I am not writing this as a juicy tidbit about some small, insignificant country, but as someone who is aware that—whether we like it or not—for many different reasons (including geopolitical considerations) what happens in this country invariably involves more than just ourselves. Many European—and most recently global—conflagrations have originated (but also ended!) right here in this country. From time immemorial, we have been a crossroads for every imaginable spiritual and political current; European history is both "raveled" and "unraveled" here. We are a country where on more than one occasion the fate of many other countries was sealed or where their destiny was unwittingly foreshadowed.

Perhaps this is still true. Perhaps Czechoslovakia—without any real wish to do so—will once more hold the key to and determine the fate of the enormous movement we are witnessing in the Soviet bloc, and with it the whole of Europe's hopes for a better future. Maybe this small—and, to some eyes, uninteresting—country will once more become a "testing ground" where we shall find out what is really going on: whether the communist world sincerely wants to change its spots and give humanitarian imperatives priority over questions of power and prestige, as Gorbachev promises—or whether, at this historical crossroads, the aspiration for freedom and human dignity will have to give way at the last minute to the dubious ideal of a monolithic empire with its system of all-powerful satraps.

And it is not inconceivable that the fate of "A Few Sentences" will provide the first convincing clue as to how this test is proceeding.

Summer 1989

A Word About Words

"A Word About Words" (July 25, 1989): In 1989, Havel was awarded the Peace Prize of the German Booksellers Association. It was presented to him, in absentia, at the Frankfurt Book Fair on October 15, 1989. This is his acceptance speech, which was read in Havel's absence by Maximilian Schell. It was translated by A. G. Brain and reprinted in full in *The New York Review of Books,* January 18, 1990.

THE PRIZE which it is my honor to receive today is called a peace prize and has been awarded to me by booksellers, in other words, people whose business is the dissemination of words. It is therefore appropriate, perhaps, that I should reflect here today on the mysterious link between words and peace, and in general on the mysterious power of words in human history.

In the beginning was the Word; so it states on the first page of one of the most important books known to us. What is meant in that book is that the Word of God is the source of all creation. But surely the same could be said, figuratively speaking, of every human action? And indeed, words can be said to be the very source of our being, and in fact the very substance of the cosmic life form we call man. Spirit, the human soul, our self-awareness, our ability to generalize and think in concepts, to perceive the world as the world (and not just as our locality), and lastly, our capacity for knowing that we will die—and living in spite of that knowledge: surely all these are mediated or actually created by words?

If the Word of God is the source of God's entire creation, then that part of God's creation which is the human race exists as such only thanks to another of God's miracles—the miracle of human speech. And if this miracle is the key to the history of mankind, then it is also the key to the history of society. Indeed, it might well be the former just because it is the latter. For the fact is that if they were not a means of communication between two or more human "I"s, then words would probably not exist at all.

All these things have been known to us—or people have at least suspected them—since time immemorial. There has never been a time when a sense of the importance of words was not present in human consciousness.

· But that is not all: thanks to the miracle of speech, we know, probably better than the other animals, that we actually know very little, in other words, we are conscious of the existence of mystery. Confronted by mystery—and at the same time aware of the virtually constitutive power of words for us—we have tried incessantly to address that which is concealed by mystery, and influence it with our words. As believers, we pray to God, as magicians we summon up or ward off spirits, using words to intervene in natural or human events. As people who belong to modern civilization—whether believers or not—we use words to construct scientific theories and political ideologies with which to tackle or redirect the mysterious course of history—successfully or otherwise.

In other words, whether we are aware of it or not, and however we explain it, one thing would seem to be obvious: we have always believed in the power of words to change history—and rightly so, in a sense.

WHY "RIGHTLY SO"?

Is the human word truly powerful enough to change the world and influence history? And even if there were epochs when it did exert such a power, does it still do so today?

You live in a country with considerable freedom of speech.

All citizens without exception can avail themselves of that freedom for whatever purpose, and no one is obliged to pay the least attention, let alone worry their heads over it. You might, therefore, easily get the impression that I overrate the importance of words quite simply because I live in a country where words can still land people in prison.

Yes, I do live in a country where the authority and radio-active effect of words are demonstrated every day by the sanctions which free speech attracts. Just recently the entire world commemorated the bicentenary of the great French Revolution. Inevitably we recalled the famous Declaration of the Rights of Man and the Citizen, which states that every citizen has the right to own a printing press. During the same period, i.e., exactly two hundred years after that declaration, my friend František Stárek was sent to prison for two and a half years for producing the independent cultural journal *Vokno*— not on some private printing press but with a squeaky, ante-diluvian duplicator. Not long before, my friend Ivan Jirous was sentenced to sixteen months' imprisonment for berating, on a typewriter, something that is common knowledge: that our country has seen many judicial murders and that even now it is possible for a person unjustly convicted to die from ill-treatment in prison. My friend Petr Cibulka is in prison for distributing *samizdat* texts and recordings of nonconformist singers and bands.

Yes, all that is true. I do live in a country where a writers' congress, or a speech delivered at it, is capable of shaking the system. Could you conceive of something of the kind in the Federal Republic of Germany? Yes, I live in a country which, twenty-one years ago, was shaken by a text from the pen of my friend Ludvík Vaculík. And as if to confirm my conclusions about the power of words, he entitled his statement: "Two Thousand Words." Among other things, that manifesto served as one of the pretexts for the invasion of our country one night by five foreign armies. And it is by no means fortuitous that as I write these words, the present regime in my country is being shaken by a single page of text entitled—

again as if to illustrate what I am saying—"A Few Sentences."
Yes, I do inhabit a system in which words are capable of shaking the entire structure of government, where words can prove mightier than ten military divisions, where Solzhenitsyn's words of truth were regarded as something so dangerous that their author had to be bundled into an airplane and shipped out. Yes, in the part of the world I inhabit, the word "Solidarity" was capable of shaking an entire power bloc.

All that is true. Reams have been written about it, and my distinguished predecessor in this place, Lev Kopelev, spoke about it also.

BUT IT is a slightly different matter that concerns me here. It is not my intention to speak solely about the incredible importance that unfettered words assume in totalitarian conditions. Nor do I wish to demonstrate the mysterious power of words by pointing exclusively to those countries where a few words can count for more than a whole trainload of dynamite somewhere else.

I want to talk in more general terms and consider the wider and more controversial aspects of my topic.

We live in a world in which it is possible for a citizen of Great Britain to find himself the target of a lethal arrow aimed at him—publicly and unashamedly—by a powerful individual in another country merely because he had written a particular book. That powerful man apparently did it in the name of millions of his fellow believers. And moreover, it is possible in this world that some portion of those millions—one hopes only a small portion—will agree with that death sentence.

What's going on? What does it mean? Is it no more than an icy blast of fanaticism, oddly finding a new lease on life in the era of Helsinki agreements, and oddly resuscitated by the rather destructive consequences of the rather destructive expansion of European civilization into worlds that initially had no interest in the import of foreign civilization, and which, because of that ambivalent import, ended up saddled with astronomical debts they can never repay?

It certainly is all that.

But it is something else as well. It is a symbol.

It is a symbol of the mysteriously ambiguous power of words.

In truth, the power of words is neither unambiguous nor clear-cut. It is not merely the liberating power of Walesa's words or the warning power of Sakharov's. It is not just the power of Rushdie's clearly misconstrued book.

The point is that alongside Rushdie's words, we have Khomeini's. Alongside words that electrify society with their freedom and truthfulness, we have words that mesmerize, deceive, inflame, madden, beguile, words that are harmful—lethal, even. The word as arrow.

I don't think I need to go on at any length to explain to you, of all people, the diabolic power of certain words: you have fairly recent firsthand experience of what indescribable historical horrors can flow, under certain political and social circumstances, from the hypnotically spellbinding, though totally demented, words of a single, average *petit bourgeois*. Admittedly I fail to understand what it was that transfixed a large number of your fathers and mothers, but at the same time I realize that it must have been something extremely compelling as well as extremely insidious if it was capable of beguiling, even if only briefly, that great genius who lent such modern and penetrating meaning to words like *"Sein," "Dasein,"* and *"Existenz."*

The point I am trying to make is that words are a mysterious, ambiguous, ambivalent, and perfidious phenomenon. They can be rays of light in a realm of darkness, as Belinsky once described Ostrovsky's *Storm.* They can equally be lethal arrows. Worst of all, at times they can be one or the other. They can even be both at once!

. . .

THE WORDS of Lenin—what were they? Liberating or, on the contrary, deceptive, dangerous, and ultimately enslaving? This still causes passionate disagreement among aficionados of the history of communism and the controversy is likely to rage on for a good while yet. My own impression of these words is that they were invariably frenzied.

And what about Marx's words? Did they serve to illuminate an entire hidden plane of social mechanisms, or were they just the inconspicuous germ of all those appalling Gulags of the future. I don't know: most likely they were both at once.

And what about Freud's words? Did they disclose the secret cosmos of the human soul, or were they no more than the fountainhead of the illusion, now benumbing half of America, that it is possible to shed one's torments and guilt by having them interpreted away by a well-paid specialist?

But I'd go further and ask an even more provocative question: What was the true nature of Christ's words? Were they the beginning of an era of salvation and among the most powerful cultural impulses in the history of the world—or were they the spiritual source of the crusades, inquisitions, the cultural extermination of the American Indians, and, later, the entire expansion of the white race that was fraught with so many contradictions and had so many tragic consequences, including the fact that most of the human world has been consigned to that wretched category known as the "Third World"? I still tend to think that His words belonged to the former category, but at the same time I cannot ignore the mountain of books which demonstrate that, even in its purest and earliest form, there was something unconsciously encoded in Christianity which, when combined with a thousand other circumstances, including the relative permanence of human nature, could in some way pave the way spiritually, even for the sort of horrors I mentioned.

WORDS can have histories too.

There was a time, for instance, when, for whole generations of the downtrodden and oppressed, the word "socialism" was a mesmerizing synonym for a just world, a time when, for the ideal expressed in that word, people were capable of sacrificing years and years of their lives, and even those very lives. I don't know about your country, but in mine, that particular word—"socialism"—was transformed long ago into an ordinary truncheon used by certain cynical, monied bureaucrats to bludgeon their liberal-minded fellow citizens from morning until night, labeling them "enemies of socialism" and "antisocialist forces." It's a fact: in my country, for ages now, that word has been no more than an incantation to be avoided if one does not wish to appear suspect. I was recently at a spontaneous demonstration, not dissident-organized, protesting the sell-off of one of the most beautiful parts of Prague to an Australian millionaire. When one of the speakers there sought to bolster his stormy denunciation of the project by declaring that he was fighting for his home in the name of socialism, the crowd started to laugh. Not because they had anything against a just social order, but simply because they heard a word which has been used for years and years as an incantation in every possible and impossible context by a regime that only knows how to manipulate and humiliate people.

What a weird fate can befall certain words! At one moment in history, courageous, liberal-minded people can be thrown into prison because a particular word means something to them, and at another moment, the same kind of people can be thrown into prison because that same word has ceased to mean anything to them, because it has changed from the symbol of a better world into the mumbo jumbo of a doltish dictator.

No word—at least not in the rather metaphorical sense I am employing the word "word" here—comprises only the meaning assigned to it by an etymological dictionary. Every word also reflects the person who utters it, the situation in which it is uttered, and the reason for its utterance. The same word can, at one moment, radiate great hope; at another, it can emit lethal rays. The same word can be true at one moment and false the next, at one moment illuminating, at another, deceptive. On one occasion it can open up glorious horizons, on another, it can lay down the tracks to an entire archipelago of concentration camps. The same word can at one time be the cornerstone of peace, while at another, machine-gun fire resounds in its every syllable.

Gorbachev wants to save socialism through the market economy and free speech, while Li Peng protects socialism by massacring students, and Ceausescu by bulldozing his nation. What does that word actually mean on the lips of the one and the lips of the other two? What is this mysterious thing that is being rescued in such disparate ways?

I referred to the French Revolution and the splendid declaration that accompanied it. That declaration was signed by a gentleman who was later among the first to be executed in the name of that superbly humane text. Hundreds and possibly thousands followed him. *Liberté, Egalité, Fraternité*—what wonderful words! And how terrifying their meaning can be. Freedom in the shirt unbuttoned before execution. Equality in the constant speed of the guillotine's fall on different necks. Fraternity in some dubious paradise ruled by a Supreme Being!

The world now echoes to the wonderfully promising word "perestroika." We all believe that it harbors hopes for Europe and the whole world.

I am bound to admit, though, that I sometimes shudder at the thought that this word might become just another incantation, and in the end turn into yet another truncheon for someone to beat us with. It is not my own country I am thinking of: when our rulers utter that word, it means about the same as the words "our monarch" in the mouth of the Good Soldier Švejk. No, what I have in mind is the fact that even the brave man who now sits in the Kremlin occasionally, and possibly only from despair, accuses striking workers, rebellious nations, or national minorities, or holders of rather too unusual minority opinions, of "jeopardizing perestroika." I can understand his feelings. It is terribly difficult to carry out the enormous task he has undertaken. It all hangs by the finest of threads and almost anything could break that thread.

Then we would all fall into the abyss. Even so, I cannot help wondering whether all this "new thinking" does not contain some disturbing relics of the old. Does it not contain some echoes of former stereotyped thinking and the *ancien régime*'s verbal rituals? Isn't the word "perestroika" starting to resemble the word "socialism," particularly on the odd occasion when it is discreetly hurled at the very people who, for so long, were unjustly bludgeoned with the word "socialism"?

YOUR country has made an enormous contribution to modern European history. I refer to the first wave of détente: the celebrated *"Ostpolitik."*

But even that word managed at times to be truly ambivalent. It signified, of course, the first glimmer of hope for a Europe without cold wars or iron curtains. At the same time—unhappily—there were also occasions when it signified the abandonment of freedom: the basic precondition for all real peace. I still vividly recall how, in the early seventies, a number of my West German colleagues and friends avoided me for fear that contact with me—someone out of favor with his government—might needlessly provoke that government and thereby jeopardize the fragile foundations of nascent détente. Naturally I am not mentioning this on my own account, and certainly not out of any self-pity. After all, even in those days it was I who pitied them, since it was not I but they who were voluntarily renouncing their freedom. I mention it only to demonstrate yet again, from another angle, how easy it is for a well-meant cause to betray its own good intentions—and yet again because of a word whose meaning does not seem to have been kept under adequate observation. Something like that can happen so easily that it almost takes you unawares: it happens inconspicuously, quietly, by stealth—and when at last you realize it, there is only one option left to you: belated astonishment.

However, that is precisely the fiendish way that words are

capable of betraying us—unless we are constantly circumspect about their use. And frequently—alas—even a fairly minor and momentary lapse in this respect can have tragic and
irreparable consequences, consequences far transcending the
nonmaterial world of mere words and penetrating deep into
a world that is all too material.

I'M FINALLY getting around to that beautiful word "peace."

FOR FORTY years now I've been reading the front of every
building and in every shop window in my country. For forty
years, an allergy to that beautiful word has been engendered
in me, as it has in every one of my fellow citizens, because I
know what the word has meant here for all those forty years:
ever mightier armies ostensibly to defend peace.

In spite of that lengthy process of systematically divesting
the word "peace" of all meaning—worse than that, investing
it instead with quite the opposite meaning to that given in
the dictionary—a number of Don Quixotes in Charter 77 and
several of their younger colleagues in the Independent Peace
Association have managed to rehabilitate the word and restore its original meaning. Naturally, though, they had to pay
a price for their "semantic perestroika," that is, standing the
word "peace" back on its feet again: almost all the youngsters
who led the Independent Peace Association were obliged to
spend a few months in jail for their pains. It was worth it,
though. One important word has been rescued from total de-
basement. And it is not just a question of saving a word, as I
have been trying to explain. Something far more important
has been saved.

The point is that all important events in the real world—
whether admirable or monstrous—always have their prologue
in the realm of words.

.   .   .

As I'VE already said, my intention here today is not to convey to you the experience of one who has learned that words still count for something when you can go to prison for them. My intention is to tell you about another lesson that we in this corner of the world have learned about the importance of words, a lesson which I believe has universal application: namely, that it always pays to be suspicious of words and to be wary of them, and that we can never be too careful in this respect.

There can be no doubt that distrust of words is less harmful than unwarranted trust in them.

Besides, to be wary of words and of the horrors that might slumber inconspicuously within them—isn't this, after all, the true vocation of the intellectual? I recall that André Glucksmann, the dear colleague who preceded me here today, once spoke in Prague about the need for intellectuals to emulate Cassandra: to listen carefully to the words of the powerful, to be watchful of them, to forewarn of their danger, and to proclaim their dire implications or the evil they might invoke.

THERE is something here that should not escape our attention, and it concerns the fact that for centuries we—the Germans and the Czechs—had all sorts of problems living together in Central Europe. I cannot speak for you, but I think I can rightly say that as far as we Czechs are concerned, the age-old animosities, prejudices, and passions, fueled and fanned in so many ways over the centuries, have evaporated in recent decades. And it is no coincidence that this has happened when we have been saddled with a totalitarian regime. This regime has cultivated in us such a profound distrust of all generalizations, ideological platitudes, clichés, slogans, intellectual stereotypes, and insidious appeals to various levels of our emotions, from the baser to the loftier, that we are now largely immune to all hypnotic enticements, even of the traditionally persuasive national or nationalistic variety. The stifling pall of hollow words that has smothered us for so long has cultivated in us such a deep mistrust of the world of deceptive words that we are now better equipped than ever before to see the human world as it really is: a complex community of thousands and millions of unique, individual human beings in whom hundreds of wonderful qualities are matched by hundreds of faults and negative tendencies. They must never be lumped together into homogeneous masses beneath a welter of hollow clichés and sterile words and then *en bloc*—as "classes," "nations," or "political forces"—extolled or denounced, loved or hated, maligned or glorified.

This is just one small example of the good that can come from treating words with caution. I have chosen the example to suit the occasion, that is, for the moment when a Czech has the honor to address an audience that is overwhelmingly German.

AT THE beginning of everything is the word.

It is a miracle to which we owe the fact that we are human.

But at the same time it is a pitfall and a test, a snare and a trial.

More so, perhaps, than it appears to you who have enormous freedom of speech, and might therefore assume that words are not so important.

They are.

They are important everywhere.

The same word can be humble at one moment and arrogant the next. And a humble word can be transformed easily and imperceptibly into an arrogant one, whereas it is a difficult and protracted process to transform an arrogant word into one that is humble. I tried to demonstrate this by referring to the tribulations of the word "peace" in my country.

As we approach the end of the second millennium, the world, and particularly Europe, finds itself at a peculiar crossroads. It has been a long time since there were so many grounds for hoping that everything will turn out well. At the same time, there have never been so many reasons to fear that if everything went wrong the catastrophe would be final.

It is not hard to demonstrate that all the main threats confronting the world today, from atomic war and ecological disaster to a catastrophic collapse of society and civilization—by which I mean the widening gulf between rich and poor individuals and nations—have hidden deep within them a single root cause: the imperceptible transformation of what was originally a humble message into an arrogant one.

Arrogantly, man began to believe that, as the pinnacle and lord of creation, he understood nature completely and could do what he liked with it.

Arrogantly, he began to think that as the possessor of reason, he could completely understand his own history and could therefore plan a life of happiness for all, and that this even gave him the right, in the name of an ostensibly better future for all—to which he had found the one and only key—to sweep from his path all those who did not fall for his plan.

Arrogantly, he began to think that since he was capable of splitting the atom, he was now so perfect that there was no longer any danger of nuclear arms rivalry, let alone nuclear war.

In all those cases he was fatally mistaken. That is bad. But in each case he is already beginning to realize his mistake. And that is good.

Having learned from all this, we should all fight together against arrogant words and keep a weather eye out for any insidious germs of arrogance in words that are seemingly humble.

Obviously this is not just a linguistic task. Responsibility for and toward words is a task which is intrinsically ethical.

As such, however, it is situated beyond the horizon of the visible world, in that realm wherein dwells the Word that was in the beginning and is not the word of man.

I won't explain why this is so. It has been explained far better than I ever could by your great forebear Immanuel Kant.

July 1989

New Year's Address

"New Year's Address" (January 1990) was Havel's first major public address as president of Czechoslovakia. It was delivered on New Year's Day and broadcast on Czech and Slovak Radio and Television. It was widely published abroad. This translation appeared in *The Spectator*, January 27, 1990. The translator is not identified.

M Y DEAR fellow citizens,
For forty years you heard from my predecessors on this day different variations of the same theme: how our country flourished, how many million tons of steel we produced, how happy we all were, how we trusted our government, and what bright perspectives were unfolding in front of us.

I assume you did not propose me for this office so that I, too, would lie to you.

Our country is not flourishing. The enormous creative and spiritual potential of our nations is not being used sensibly. Entire branches of industry are producing goods which are of no interest to anyone, while we are lacking the things we need. A state which calls itself a workers' state humiliates and exploits workers. Our obsolete economy is wasting the little energy we have available. A country that once could be proud of the educational level of its citizens spends so little on education that it ranks today as seventy-second in the world. We have polluted our soil, our rivers and forests, bequeathed to us by our ancestors, and we have today the most contaminated environment in Europe. Adult people in our country die earlier than in most other European countries.

Allow me a little personal observation: when I flew recently to Bratislava, I found time during various discussions to look out of the plane window. I saw the industrial complex of Slovnaft chemical factory and the giant Petržalka housing estate right behind it. The view was enough for me to understand that for decades our statesmen and political leaders did not look or did not want to look out of the windows of their airplanes. No study of statistics available to me would enable me to understand faster and better the situation into which we had gotten ourselves.

But all this is still not the main problem. The worst thing is that we live in a contaminated moral environment. We fell morally ill because we became used to saying something different from what we thought. We learned not to believe in anything, to ignore each other, to care only about ourselves. Concepts such as love, friendship, compassion, humility, or forgiveness lost their depth and dimensions, and for many of us they represented only psychological pecularities, or they resembled gone-astray greetings from ancient times, a little ridiculous in the era of computers and spaceships. Only a few of us were able to cry out loud that the powers that be should not be all-powerful, and that special farms, which produce ecologically pure and top-quality food just for them, should send their produce to schools, children's homes, and hospitals if our agriculture was unable to offer them to all. The previous regime—armed with its arrogant and intolerant ideology—reduced man to a force of production and nature to a tool of production. In this it attacked both their very substance and their mutual relationship. It reduced gifted and autonomous people, skillfully working in their own country, to nuts and bolts of some monstrously huge, noisy, and stinking machine, whose real meaning is not clear to anyone. It cannot do more than slowly but inexorably wear down itself and all its nuts and bolts.

When I talk about contaminated moral atmosphere, I am not talking just about the gentlemen who eat organic vegetables and do not look out of the plane windows. I am talking about all of us. We had all become used to the totalitarian system and accepted it as an unchangeable fact and thus helped to perpetuate it. In other words, we are all—though naturally to differing extents—responsible for the operation of the totalitarian machinery; none of us is just its victim: we are all also its co-creators.

Why do I say this? It would be very unreasonable to understand the sad legacy of the last forty years as something alien, which some distant relative bequeathed us. On the contrary, we have to accept this legacy as a sin we committed against ourselves. If we accept it as such, we will understand that it is up to us all, and up to us only, to do something about it. We cannot blame the previous rulers for everything, not only because it would be untrue but also because it could blunt the duty that each of us faces today, namely, the obligation to act independently, freely, reasonably, and quickly. Let us not be mistaken: the best government in the world, the best parliament and the best president, cannot achieve much on their own. And it would also be wrong to expect a general remedy from them only. Freedom and democracy include participation and therefore responsibility from us all.

If we realize this, then all the horrors that the new Czecho-slovak democracy inherited will cease to appear so terrible. If we realize this, hope will return to our hearts.

In the effort to rectify matters of common concern, we have something to lean on. The recent period—and in particular, the last six weeks of our peaceful revolution—has shown the enormous human, moral, and spiritual potential and civic culture that slumbered in our society under the enforced mask of apathy. Whenever someone categorically claimed that we were this or that, I always objected that society is a very mysterious creature and that it is not wise to trust only the face it presents to you. I am happy that I was not mistaken. Everywhere in the world people wonder where those meek, humiliated, skeptical, and seemingly cynical citizens of Czecho-slovakia found the marvelous strength to shake from their shoulders in several weeks and in a decent and peaceful way the totalitarian yoke. And let us ask: from where did the young people who never knew another system take their desire for truth, their love of free thought, their political ideas, their civic courage and civic prudence? How did it happen that their parents—the very generation that had been considered as lost—joined them? How is it possible that so many people immediately knew what to do and none of them needed any advice or instruction?

I think that there are two main reasons for this hopeful face of our present situation: first of all, people are never just a product of the external world, but are also always able to relate themselves to something superior, however systematically the external world tries to kill that ability in them; second, the humanistic and democratic traditions, about which there had been so much idle talk, did after all slumber in the unconsciousness of our nations and ethnic minorities, and were inconspicuously passed from one generation to another so that each of us could discover them at the right time and transform them into deeds.

We had to pay, however, for our present freedom. Many citizens perished in jails in the fifties, many were executed, thousands of human lives were destroyed, hundreds of thousands of talented people were forced to leave the country. Those who defended the honor of our nations during the Second World War, those who rebelled against totalitarian rule, and those who simply managed to remain themselves and think freely, were all persecuted. We should not forget any of those who paid for our present freedom in one way or another. Independent courts should impartially consider the possible guilt of those who were responsible for the persecutions, so that the truth about our recent past is fully revealed.

We must also bear in mind that other nations have paid even more dearly for their present freedom and that indirectly they have also paid for ours. The rivers of blood which flowed in Hungary, Poland, Germany, and not long ago in such a horrific manner in Romania, as well as the sea of blood shed by the nations of the Soviet Union, must not be forgotten. First of all because every human suffering concerns every other human being; but more than this: they must also not be forgotten because it is those great sacrifices which form the tragic background of today's freedom, and of the gradual emancipation of the nations of the Soviet bloc. They also form the background of our own newfound freedom: without the changes in the Soviet Union, Poland, Hungary, and the German Democratic Republic, what has happened in our country could scarcely have happened. In any event, it would not have followed such a peaceful course.

The fact that we enjoyed optimal international conditions does not mean that anyone else has directly helped us during the recent weeks. In fact, after hundreds of years, both our nations have raised their heads high of their own initiative without relying on the help of stronger nations or powers. It seems to me that this constitutes the great moral asset of the present moment. This moment holds within itself the hope that in the future we will no longer suffer from the complex of those who must always be expressing their gratitude to somebody. It now depends only on us whether this hope will be realized, and whether our civic, national, and political self-confidence will be awakened in an historically new way.

Self-confidence is not pride. Just the contrary: only a person or a nation that is self-confident in the best sense of the word is capable of listening to others, accepting them as equals, forgiving its enemies, and regretting its own guilt. Let us try to introduce this kind of self-confidence into the life of our community and, as nations, into our behavior on the international stage. Only thus can we restore our self-respect and our respect for one another as well as the respect of other nations.

Our state should never again be an appendage or a poor relation of anyone else. It is true we must accept and learn many things from others, but we must do this again as their equal partners who also have something to offer.

Our first president wrote: "Jesus, not Caesar." In this he followed our philosophers Chelčický and Comenius. I dare to say that we may even have an opportunity to spread this idea further and introduce a new element into European and global politics. Our country, if that is what we want, can now permanently radiate love, understanding, the power of spirit and ideas. It is precisely this glow that we can offer as our specific contribution to international politics.

Masaryk based his politics on morality. Let us try in a new time and in a new way to restore this concept of politics. Let us teach ourselves and others that politics should be an expression of a desire to contribute to the happiness of the community rather than of a need to cheat or rape the community. Let us teach ourselves and others that politics can be not only the art of the possible, especially if this means the art of speculation, calculation, intrigue, secret deals, and pragmatic maneuvering, but that it can even be the art of the impossible, namely, the art of improving ourselves and the world.

We are a small country, yet at one time we were the spiritual crossroads of Europe. Is there any reason why we could not again become one? Would not it be another asset with which to repay the help of others that we are going to need?

Our home-grown mafia of those who do not look out of plane windows and who eat specially fed pigs may still be around and at times may muddy the waters, but they are no longer our main enemy. Even less so is our main enemy the international Mafia. Our main enemy today is our own bad traits: indifference to the common good; vanity; personal ambition; selfishness; and rivalry. The main struggle will have to be fought on this field.

There are free elections and an election campaign ahead of us. Let us not allow this struggle to dirty the so far clean face of our gentle revolution. Let us not allow the sympathies of the world which we have won so fast to be equally rapidly lost through our becoming entangled in the jungle of skirmishes for power. Let us not allow the desire to serve oneself to bloom once again under the fair mask of the desire to serve the common good. It is not really important now which party, club, or group will prevail in the elections. The important thing is that the winners will be the best of us, in the moral, civic, political, and professional sense, regardless of their political affiliations. The future policies and prestige of our state will depend on the personalities we select and later elect to our representative bodies.

[. . .]

In conclusion, I would like to say that I want to be a president who will speak less and work more. To be a president who will not only look out of the windows of his airplane but who, first and foremost, will always be present among his fellow citizens and listen to them well.

You may ask what kind of a republic I dream of. Let me reply: I dream of a republic independent, free, and democratic, of a republic economically prosperous and yet socially just, in short, of a humane republic which serves the individual and which therefore holds the hope that the individual will serve it in turn. Of a republic of well-rounded people, because without such it is impossible to solve any of our problems, human, economic, ecological, social, or political.

The most distinguished of my predecessors opened his first speech with a quotation from the great Czech educator Comenius. Allow me to round off my first speech with my own paraphrase of the same statement:

People, your government has returned to you!

January 1990

Notes

4   "the famous revelations." A reference to Nikita Khrushchev's denunciations of Stalin to the 20th Congress of the Communist Party of the Soviet Union in 1956. Khrushchev's speech signaled the beginning of a political thaw throughout Eastern Europe.

7   Jan Grossman (b. 1925). Literary critic, theatre director. From 1962 to 1968 he was the artistic director of the Theatre on the Balustrade, where Havel was also employed.

9   "Asiatic." Havel is referring to the reimposition by the Soviet Union of a form of absolute rule that many in Eastern Europe associate with oriental despotisms.

"Jan Palach's recent deed." In January 1969, a student called Jan Palach set himself on fire on Wenceslas Square in Prague, in protest against the Soviet occupation of Czechoslovakia. He died a few days later, and his sacrifice evoked widespread sympathy among the population. His massively attended public funeral was the last nationwide public demonstration against the new normalization policies.

17   Josef Florian (1872–1941). A private Czech publisher and a leading figure in the Czech Catholic revival in the early years of this century. He published many important works, both by Czech writers and by modern European authors in translation.

Tomáš Garrigue Masaryk (1850–1937). The first president of Czechoslovakia, who won independence from the Austro-Hungarian empire in 1918. From 1948 until the mid-sixties, Masaryk's name was anathema to the communist regime, and could not appear in print in a positive context. Havel's suggestion that *Tvář* might publish a study on Masaryk is therefore more daring than it appears.

19   Vladimír Holan (1905–1980). One of the great Czech modern lyric poets and translators. Like many writers of his generation, Holan was suppressed in the 1950s. Later, in 1968, he was declared a "National Artist." He translated Rilke, Mallarmé,

p. 19 Baudelaire, and others into Czech. In English: *Selected Poems* (Harmondsworth: Penguin, 1971) and *A Night With Hamlet* (London: Oasis, 1980).

Bohumil Hrabal (b. 1914). Popular Czech poet and novelist. A film based on his novella *Closely Watched Trains* won an Oscar in 1968 for the best foreign film. Recent translations in English are *I Served the King of England* (New York: Harcourt Brace Jovanovich, 1989) and *Too Loud a Solitude* (New York: Harcourt Brace Jovanovich, 1990).

21 Jiří Kolář (b. 1914). A poet and later a visual artist who worked experimentally in the field of visual poetry and ultimately, of three-dimensional collage. He now lives in Paris, France. Kolář was the subject of a major exhibition in the Guggenheim Museum in New York in 1975.

Josef Hiršal (b. 1920). Poet, writes visual and concrete poetry; translator and author of children's books.

Jan Vladislav (b. 1923). Poet, essayist, translator, children's author. Editor-in-chief of *Světová Literatura* (World Literature) 1969–79. Vladislav emigrated to France in 1980. Edited *Václav Havel or Living in Truth*, London: Faber & Faber, 1986.

22 *Plamen, Host do domu.* Two literary magazines that flourished in Czechoslovakia during the 1960s.

Nový Život (New Life). A Stalinist literary magazine put out by the Union of Writers. It ceased publication in the early 1960s.

Jindřich Chalupecký (1910–1990). Art and literary critic, founding member of Group 42, an association of artists established in Prague under the Nazi occupation. Chalupecký edited or worked on many of the most important Czech literary and art journals of his time. From 1971 on, he could publish only abroad, but he continued to write about avant-garde Czech art, especially the work of the younger generations.

Václav Černý (1905–1987). Literary critic and historian, editor and translator. Strong exponent of the Czech liberal, non-communist cultural tradition. In English: *Dostoevski's Devils* (Ann Arbor: Arvidis, 1975).

23   Josef Škvorecký (b. 1924). Novelist, essayist, screenwriter, translator. Škvorecký's first novel, *The Cowards*, was first published in 1958 and subsequently banned. Deputy Editor of *Světová Literatura* (World Literature) from 1956 to 1958. Translated works by Dashiell Hammett, Raymond Chandler, Ernest Hemingway, William Faulkner, William Styron, and others into Czech. Many of his novels are available in English, including *The Cowards, The Miracle Game, The Engineer of Human Souls,* and *Dvořák in Love.*

23   Richard Weiner (1884–1937). Czech poet, essayist, prose writer. Like so many other "difficult" writers of the period between the wars, Weiner's work was not republished under the communists until the mid-1960s.

     Ladislav Klíma (1878–1928). Philosopher and novelist. An eccentric Czech writer who evolved, through works of philosophy and fiction, a view of the world as pure thought and imagination. During the past several decades, much of Klíma's work has been reissued, but mostly as *samizdat.*

24   Jakub Deml (1878–1961). Poet, diarist, essayist and translator. A Catholic priest, Deml was closely associated with Josef Florian and the modern Czech Catholic revival (see note for page 17). His writing did not fit at all into the narrow canon of acceptable literature after 1948, but he enjoyed a strong underground following and a large number of his works circulated in *samizdat.*

40   Edvard Beneš (1884–1948). Czech statesman. Beneš succeeded Masaryk as President of Czechoslovakia in 1935, and was head of the Czechoslovak government in exile in England during the Second World War. He returned after the war, and continued as president until the communist takeover in 1948, when he abdicated.

42   "Švejk-like." A reference to the hero of *The Good Soldier Švejk,* by Jaroslav Hašek. This classic, comic figure in Czech literature survives by obeying all orders to the letter, no matter how absurd.

43   Dr. František Kriegel (1908–1979). For details of Kriegel's life, see the essay "Thinking About František K." on pages 363–372.

p. 43   "the annulment of the 14th Congress." In August 1968, under the Soviet guns, the Czechoslovak Communist Party clandestinely held its 14th Congress, which had been scheduled for the autumn and was expected to endorse the reform process set in motion earlier that year by Alexander Dubček. The Congress did in fact endorse those reforms and condemn the invasion; thus obtaining the annulment of this congress was one of the first Soviet objectives after the invasions.

54   "the ubiquitous, omnipotent state police." Here, and throughout the book, the expression "state police" refers to the security police, commonly called the secret police, a large unit under the Ministry of the Interior that was responsible for monitoring and controlling all forms of dissent in the country.

67   "our national revival." Havel is referring to the period in the nineteenth century when Czech writers, historians, artists, composers, journalists, politicians, and scholars, through their works, attempted to revive and strengthen the Czech language, culture, and political life, which had been curtailed for two hundred years by Hapsburg domination.

80   "We experienced one such explosion not long ago." A reference to the ferment of grassroots political activity during the Prague Spring of 1968.

93   "the play I'm working on at the moment." Havel is probably referring to *The Mountain Hotel*, which he completed in 1976.

96   Ludvík Vaculík (b. 1926). Novelist, essayist, and political commentator. Vaculík, formerly a liberal communist, was active in the 1960s and especially during the Prague Spring in 1968. He was editor of *Literární noviny*, the official Writers' Union weekly, and its subsequent manifestations, until 1969. In the 1970s he established the first major *samizdat* publishing venture, *Edice Petlice*, sometimes translated as "Padlock Editions." Books available in English include *The Guinea-pigs* (London: London Magazine Editions, 1974), and *A Cup of Coffee with My Interrogator*: Prague Chronicles (London: Readers International, 1987).

98   *"zoon politikon."* Greek for "political animal" or "being."

Karel Havlíček (1821–1856). Czech patriot, journalist, editor, satirist. He is generally considered to be the founder of modern Czech political journalism, and supported a limited supranational Slavism based on a realistic view of Czarist Russia. He was active during the revolution of 1848, and was subsequently persecuted by the Austrian authorities. He died of ill health after spending four years (1851–55) in prison in Brixen, Austria.

Masaryk. See note for page 17.

99   "Beneš's position on the Munich crisis." When Hitler threatened to annex the Sudetenland in September 1938, Czechoslovakia's chiefs of staff tried to persuade President Edvard Beneš to fight, arguing that the British and French would ultimately have to join them in the struggle against Hitler. Beneš did not believe they would; he felt that resistance would be catastrophic for the country. Consequently, Czechoslovakia did not oppose Hitler; Beneš abdicated and left for England in October.

"the Second Republic." The period from September 1938, when the Sudetenland region was severed from Czechoslovakia, until the country was occupied by the Germans and dismembered in March 1939, to form two separate entities, the Protectorate of Bohemia and Moravia, and Slovakia.

Emil Hácha (1872–1945). The president of Czechoslovakia after Beneš abdicated in 1938, and then of the Protectorate of Bohemia and Moravia, until his death in 1945.

Klement Gottwald (1896–1953). First Secretary of the Czechoslovak Communist Party when they took power in 1948. After President Beneš abdicated (for a second time), he became president as well. The communists referred to him as "The First Worker's President" in an effort to erase the legacy of Masaryk.

104   Georgi Dimitrov (1882–1949). Bulgarian statesman. In 1933, he was accused by the Germans of setting the Reichstag in Berlin on fire. At his trial, he defended himself with great eloquence. He later went to the Soviet Union, where he became head of the Communist International in 1935. He was prime minister of Bulgaria from 1946 until his death.

p. 104 Ivan Jirous (b. 1944). Art critic, poet, cultural journalist. Artistic director of the rock group *The Plastic People of the Universe* until it disbanded in 1988. Jirous, an outspoken critic of the regime, spent many years in prison. He is now artistic director of *Pulnoc*, a rock band that has carried on the tradition of the Plastic People.

111 Ladislav Hejdánek (b. 1927). Essayist, philosopher. A prominent Protestant layman, Hejdánek was twice a spokesman for Charter 77. He is now a professor of philosophy in the faculty of theology at the Charles University in Prague.

"the Tomin children." A reference to the children of Julius and Zdena Tomin (two prominent dissidents) who were hurt by the secret police in an effort to intimidate the parents.

"the Uhls." Anna Šabata and Petr Uhl, both activists in Charter 77 and VONS. The Uhls also produced a regular *samizdat* information bulletin called *Infoch* (short for "Information on the Charter"), and were the subject of continuous police surveillance and harassment. See "Reports on My House Arrest," on pages 215–229.

114 Martinovský. A secret-police investigator in charge of Havel's case.

125 Jan Patočka (1907–1977). Philosopher, a student of Husserl and Heidegger. He was one of the first three spokesmen for Charter 77. In essays and lectures, Patočka provided the philosophical underpinning for the kind of civic activism represented by Charter 77. He died in March 1977 as a consequence of a police interrogation, shortly after the formation of Charter 77.

155 "Sladeček" is a pseudonym for Petr Pithart (b. 1941). He was active in reform communist circles in 1968, and in Charter 77 as an essayist and author. His *Sixty-eight* is one of the most complete studies of the Prague Spring. Pithart is now prime minister of the Czech Republic.

171 KOR. Polish acronym for the Workers' Defense Committee, a dissident organization established in Poland in the mid-1970s and a precursor of Solidarity.

185 "Švejkian." See note for page 42.

192 Václav Benda (b. 1946). Philosopher, mathematician and essay-ist, and prominent Catholic layman. Havel is here referring to Benda's best-known essay, "The Parallel Polis," in which he dis-cusses the possibility of establishing independent institutions within the totalitarian regime. Benda is a founder of the Chris-tian Democratic Party and a member of the Federal Assembly.

198 "the Polish 'flying university'." An underground university set up in Poland in the 1970s and '80s to teach subjects forbidden in the state universities to students who frequently were not allowed to enroll officially. This "university" was in no fixed place, hence the name. The tradition and the technique go back to the nineteenth century in Poland, when the first "flying uni-versity" was established in 1886 as part of the Polish struggle for independence.

216 Tatra 603. These are black limousines of Czech manufacture used mainly by party officials and bureaucrats.

218 *Lunochod.* The Russian name for an automated module that the Soviets landed on the Moon. The name means "Moon-walker."

220 "in the mountains." The Havels' cottage is in the foothills of the Krkonoše Mountains, northeast of Prague.

225 Ruzyně. The Prague prison where detainees are kept during a criminal investigation, pending trial.

Jiří Gruša (b. 1938). Poet, novelist, literary critic, editor and translator. In 1953, Gruša was a founding editor of *Tvář* maga-zine. In 1978, he spent two months in custody for writing and circulating his novel *The Questionnaire* (New York: Farrar, Straus and Giroux, 1982). This is the case Havel is referring to here. Gruša is now the Czechoslovak ambassador to Germany.

Smolík, Noga, and Říha. All officers in the secret police.

226 Zdena Tominová (b. 1941). Poet, novelist, journalist. Spokesman for Charter 77 in 1979. Since 1980 has lived in London, England. Author of two novels, *Stalin's Shoe* (London: Hutchinson, 1986), and *Coast of Bohemia* (London: Dent, 1988).

p. 228   "some of my friends suspect me of heroic aspirations." A while before writing this account, Havel had engaged in a polemic with Ludvík Vaculík and others, answering Vaculík's implicit criticism of him and other Chartists for risking prison and taking upon themselves more than the average person can bear and thus isolating themselves from the people. Havel responded to this in an open letter to Vaculík dated January 25, 1979.

229   "I became entangled in the web of my own inappropriate politeness . . ." During Havel's first stint in custody over Charter 77, he had written what he thought was a routine letter asking to be released. The authorities misused the letter, deliberately misquoting it in the media to make it appear that Havel had backed down from his commitment to Charter 77 in exchange for his freedom. Although it had been an honest miscalculation, Havel felt humiliated by his "failure," and determined never to make the same mistake again. See *Letters to Olga*, no. 138, and *Disturbing the Peace*, pages 66–67 and pages 142ff. for more detailed accounts of what this incident meant to Havel.

238   "the recent action against the Franciscans." Havel is referring to the arrest of several Catholic priests by the secret police.

240   KOR. See note for page 171.

279   *"Petlice Editions."* One of the first major *samizdat* ventures in post-invasion Czechoslovakia, started by Ludvík Vaculík (see note for page 96) in 1973.

Jindřich Chalupecký. See note for page 22.

307   Milan Kundera (b. 1929). Poet, essayist, playwright, novelist. Kundera left Czechoslovkia in 1975, and since then has lived in France. Most of his novels are available in English, including *The Joke, Life is Elsewhere, The Farewell Party, The Book of Laughter and Forgetting*, and *The Unbearable Lightness of Being*.

309   Jaroslav Hašek (1883–1923). Writer and author of the classic Czech comic novel, *The Good Soldier Švejk* (see note for page 42).

Jan Patočka. See note for page 125.

312   "one important European country attacked a small neutral neighbor." A reference to the Soviet invasion of Afghanistan in 1979.

349   "Class-four restaurants." In the socialist economy, all restaurants were divided into four categories with regard to levels of service and prices. Class-four restaurants were the most rudimentary and the cheapest. At the time Havel is writing, they were being phased out of the center of Prague, much to the dismay of connoisseurs of Czech pub life.

357   "Messrs. Bilák and Fojtík." Vasil Bilák (b. 1917) and Jan Fojtík (b. 1928), both members of Husák's politburo and associated with his "normalization" policies.

364   "how he managed to save the reputation of Czechoslovak politics in August 1968." Kriegel was the only member of Dubček's politburo who, having been arrested by the Soviets during the invasion and taken to Moscow, refused to sign the Moscow agreements. See the introduction to "Thinking about František K." on page 363.

375   "hopes at last that Czechoslovakia too will engage in a free, society-wide debate." Havel is referring indirectly to the Polish roundtable discussions in early 1989, in which, for the first time in history, a Communist Party sat down with an unofficial opposition to work out a way of sharing power.

380   Lev Kopelev (b. 1912). A Russian dissident writer, now living in Germany, and recipient of the German Booksellers' Peace Prize in 1981.

381   " *'Sein,' 'Dasein,'* and *'Existenz.'* " These are basic categories in the work of the German philosopher Martin Heidegger. Havel uses these categories freely in his *Letters to Olga,* where they are translated as "Being," "being-in-the-world," and "existence." (In translations of Heidegger's work into English, *Dasein* is frequently left in German.)

Index

Index

About the Translator

PAUL WILSON lived in Czechoslovakia for ten years, working as a translator and English teacher and playing with an underground rock band, The Plastic People of the Universe. He was expelled in 1977. He has translated several Czech writers, including Josef Škvorecký and Bohumil Hrabal. His most recent translation of Václav Havel's work is the book-length interview *Disturbing the Peace* (1990). He is the co-author of a series of radio documentaries on Eastern Europe for the Canadian Broadcasting Corporation. He is an associate editor of *The Idler* magazine in Toronto, where he lives.